EASTERN EUROPE IN TRANSITION

PUBLISHED IN CO-OPERATION WITH THE
INSTITUTE FOR SINO-SOVIET STUDIES,
THE GEORGE WASHINGTON UNIVERSITY

EASTERN EUROPE IN TRANSITION

edited by
Kurt London

THE JOHNS HOPKINS PRESS
Baltimore

To Vice-Admiral H. Bos
Royal Netherlands Navy (ret.)
in gratitude
for his support
of the Fifth International
Conference on World Politics
Noordwijk, The Netherlands
September, 1965

Contents

Editor's Introduction

I

The Fifth International Conference on World Politics took place from September 13 to 19, 1965, in Noordwijk, The Netherlands. Its hosts were the Netherlands Institute of Foreign Affairs and the Institute of Social Studies, both in The Hague. On its agenda was Eastern Europe, the countries of Central, Eastern, and Southeastern Europe, which until recently were called the satellites. The factors underlying the transformation of this erstwhile monolith—the growth of polycentrism under the impact of the Sino-Soviet conflict, the post-1957 interbloc organizations, and the changing ideological, political, and social attitudes of Eastern Europe—formed the central topic.

The story of this series of international conferences has been outlined in the Introduction to the symposium based on the Fourth International Conference on World Politics, held in Athens in 1962.* As in prior conferences in the series, the papers contributed by participants at Noordwijk were not read but discussed during ten scheduled plenary meetings. In line with the customary practice, the conference was closed to the public but open to a group of observers consisting of diplomats, government officials, academicians, and selected specialists. These observers, barred from active participation in the discussion at previous conferences, were for the first time invited to present their views toward the end of each of the sessions. There were thirty-three participants from ten countries of North America, Europe, and Asia. Unfortunately, several invited African scholars were unable to attend. The thirty-three observers came from the United States, Canada, The Netherlands, Germany, Sweden, Norway, Argentina, Israel, Indonesia, India, and France.

* See Kurt London (ed.), *New Nations in a Divided World: The International Relations of Afro-Asian States* (New York: Frederick A. Praeger, Inc., 1963).

No participants from countries under communist party rule were invited. As before, the Steering Committee and most delegates felt that such participation would radically change the character of these conferences. It is true that private confrontations might have yielded interesting results. However, in the plenary sessions which were the mainstay of the conference, visitors from the "socialist camp" could only have dispensed their party lines, which would have had no value for the conferees and might indeed have inhibited or even stymied the discussions. Conferences with communists are useful and should be held, but primarily for purposes of information and personal contact. They are without value in meetings where free and uninhibited exchange of views among scholars is essential.

II

The proceedings were opened by Professor Dr. I. A. Diepenhorst, Minister of Education and Science of The Netherlands. Present also were the Minister of Foreign Affairs of The Netherlands, Mr. J. M. A. H. Luns; the Ambassador of the United States, Mr. William R. Tyler; the Chargé d'Affaires of Canada, Mr. V. C. Moore; and other diplomatic and academic luminarries.

Different from the Fourth International Conference in Athens, where emotions sometimes overshadowed academic considerations as a result mainly of controversies between African and British scholars, the discussions in Noordwijk remained on an even keel throughout, despite the fact that two distinct schools of thought became apparent early in the meeting. Perhaps the best way to delineate the positions of the majority and minority groups of the East European experts may be to summarize briefly some of the more important disputed areas of the discussions as outlined informally during the final session by Professor R. V. Burks and considered by the plenum to be a fair reflection of the general trend of the conference.

Nationalism

Majority view: Nationalism is on the upsurge in East Central Europe. Although this nationalism takes distinctive forms in accordance with the divergent traditions in the individual countries, it is generally characterized by the conversion of the ruling party to a communist patriotism which in some aspects coincides with the traditional patriotism of the masses. This convergence is leading to a passive acceptance of the regimes by the population and encourages the regimes to seek greater independence from the Soviet Union, since they can now count on some domestic support.

Minority view: The notion of a communist nationalism must be rejected. The concept of class remains fundamental to communist regimes. While it is true that the national groups now have a little more freedom, it would be more accurate to speak of the development since 1956 of ideological fatigue than to cite the emergence of a communist nationalism.

The Effect of the Sino-Soviet Conflict

Majority view: The Sino-Soviet conflict has been a major, but by no means the only, factor in the current loosening of the Soviet bloc. The conflict increased the freedom of maneuver of the East Central European regimes long before 1960, when it came out into the open, though prior to 1958 it was more a controversy than a quarrel. The conflict, together with the other erosive forces at work in the area, is gradually transforming the totalitarian bloc into a traditional military alliance in which one power predominates because of its immense size and military strength, but in which the smaller members act more and more in accordance with their individual national and security interests. The Warsaw Pact continues, however, to operate as a principal cohesive force, and the predominance of the U.S.S.R. in the area has reduced the disruptive effects of the Sino-Soviet dispute to less devastating proportions than in other parts of the world. The regimes of East Central Europe can probably make no further significant gains as a consequence of the dispute.

Minority view: Sino-Soviet differences acquired a conflict character as early as 1954, when the Chinese demanded Outer Mongolia. These differences played a major disruptive role in the politics of East Central Europe as early as the mid-fifties. The disappearance of joint companies in Rumania in 1954 is connected with their dissolution in China that same year, and the withdrawal of Soviet troops from Rumania in 1958 was related to Sino-Soviet negotiations on military matters.

Soviet Aims in Eastern Europe

Majority view: The long-range aims of the Soviet Union probably continue to include the creation of a single federal structure incorporating both the U.S.S.R. and East Central Europe in the Soviet Union—deferred in 1945 possibly because Stalin was awaiting the withdrawal of American troops from Europe, and possibly also because he wished to exact reparations from some of these peoples. Both the Cominform and Council for Economic Mutual Assistance (CEMA) were conceived as interim preparatory arrangements. In the current period of polycentrism the Soviet effort at preparatory integration takes the form of cementing special bilateral relationships with each regime.

Minority view: It may be true that the Soviet Union still aims at the ultimate incorporation of East Central Europe, but it is now increasingly doubtful that Moscow will ever possess either the military strength or the political authority to accomplish this. Currently, Moscow cannot even enforce economic co-operation among the regimes of East Central Europe, let alone establish an effective central planning organ. Communism as a world movement has lost its centralized organization and will probably never recover it. To use a historical analogy, communism has probably already entered the post-Reformation period of its history.

Relations among Eastern European Peoples

Majority view: Despite their common ideologies and comparable social systems, and despite some signs of greater cultural contact, such as an important increase in intracommunist tourism, relations among the peoples of East Central Europe continue in general to be marked by attitudes ranging from indifference or contempt to tension or even hatred. Even if the states of East Central Europe were freed of Soviet domination, they probably could not by themselves develop federal arrangements or a common market.

Minority view: This interpretation ignores certain new elements in the situation of East Central Europe. For one thing, there has been some progress in ethnic relations. The Czechs and Slovaks, for example, appear to be learning to accept each other as equal partners within a common state organization. For another, the peoples of East Central Europe have now endured totalitarian tyranny for nearly thirty years, and this experience has undoubtedly brought about basic changes in their values. An individual and collective search for new values is, in fact, apparent. In 1945 it would have been reasonable to assert that the peoples of Western Europe would never be able to overcome their traditional antagonisms and form a closer union.

The discussions produced more or less a consensus on the following topics, with little dissent.

Areas of Unrest

The return of Gomulka to power in October, 1956, was accomplished without a popular uprising, whereas the return of Nagy to power set off a revolution in Hungary for a number of interrelated reasons: (1) The Poles had experienced the consequences of the failure of the Warsaw uprising of 1944; (2) the Polish Catholic Church was identified with national independence and could use its great influence as a force for peaceful change; (3) the Polish Communist Party having been liquidated by Moscow in 1938, the Polish communists took a more positive attitude toward the policy of de-Stalinization than did their Hungarian counterparts; (4) in Poland the reform faction within the communist party got control of the Central Committee substantially before October, whereas in Hungary the Stalinists remained dominant until the outbreak of violence. On the other hand, the longer-range effect of the revolution in Hungary has been to produce the present Kádár regime, which, in respect of individual liberties, is probably the most advanced in East Central Europe, except for Yugoslavia, whereas in Poland there has been a slow but steady retreat from the gains of October. The East German uprising of 1953 is comparable to the Polish and Hungarian events of 1956 in that it occurred under a divided leadership during a period of material betterment and was spontaneous in character.

Centralized Management of National Economies

Some progress is being made toward the reduction of centralized management of the national economies and toward greater reliance on market forces. But the obstacles to further progress are great; these include, above all, the unwillingness of the party and state apparatuses to surrender their direct control over the economy. Another significant economic development is the growing dependence of the regimes of Eastern Europe, and especially of the Soviet Union, on the import of grain from the West, which may affect the ability of the regimes to import machinery.

Yugoslavia's Role

Yugoslavia has lost much of its political importance in East Central Europe, but its role as a model in the development of semimarket economies is growing. Internally, the regime is subject to increasing strain. There are recurrent economic crises, a resurgence of national and factional conflict, and a decline in the prestige of the leadership. At the same time, the emergence of an extreme revisionism creates the possibility of an eventual return to the multiparty system.*

The West and Eastern Europe

The proper Western policy toward East Central Europe at the present juncture is that of peaceful engagement, i.e. the coordinated use of cultural exchange, financial credit, and diplomatic maneuver to promote the erosive forces already at work in the area. In the immediate sense, the factor most favorable to continuing erosion would be the extension and stabilization of the *détente* in U.S.-Soviet relations, especially since the United States has only a peripheral and not a vital interest in the area.

Whether the states of East Central Europe can acquire greater independence than they now have depends not only on the state of East-West relations, however, but also on the longer-range

---

* Tito's purge of June–July, 1966, eliminating Aleksandr Rankovic as his possible successor, seems to indicate that neither radicalism of the "right" nor of the "left" will be allowed. Since Titoism appears to continue as a nonorthodox type of communism, "extreme" revisionism is unlikely to be permitted and a multiparty system, therefore, can hardly be expected at least while Tito is alive.—Editor.

prospects for basic evolution within the Soviet Union. Another outer limit to erosion is created by the "German Democratic Republic" (G.D.R.), whose existence is the ultimate lever of Soviet domination over East Central Europe. But the reunification of Germany can only come about if the U.S.S.R., Poland, and Czechoslovakia agree to it, and they will do so only if they are given adequate substitutes for the economic, military, and territorial guarantees which the G.D.R. now affords them. Poland's attitude toward the West so far remains highly immobile.

III

As in the previous conferences of this series, no formal conclusions were expected, nor policy recommendations made. At the request of the conference's host organizations and the Dutch newspapers, a press communiqué was issued on the last day of the conference, drafted by a committee of participants and reflecting the general trend of the discussions. It read as follows:

1. Nationalism is reviving in Eastern Europe as the consequence of the gradual conversion of the ruling parties to this point of view. As a consequence there is increasing passive acceptance of the regimes by the population, and the regimes themselves are encouraged to seek greater independence from the Soviet Union.

2. The Sino-Soviet conflict, together with other erosive forces at work in Eastern Europe, such as de-Stalinization, is gradually transforming the totalitarian bloc into a military alliance, in which the Soviet Union predominates because of its great size and military strength, but in which the weaker members act more and more in accordance with their national interests.

3. Despite their common ideologies and comparable social systems, the states of Eastern Europe will probably remain incapable of developing cohesive cooperation among themselves, other than that which the Soviet Union is able to impose upon them. Whether these states can acquire greater independence with the passage of time depends primarily upon the development of East-West relations, on the one hand, and the internal evolution of the Soviet Union, on the other.

4. In Eastern Europe and the Soviet Union some progress is being made toward the reduction of centralized management of the national economies and toward greater reliance on the play of market forces. But the obstacles to further progress are great; these include the unwillingness of the party apparatus to surrender its direct control over the economy and the shortage of managerial talent capable of operating enterprises under semimarket conditions.

5. The efforts of both Moscow and Peking to include within their respective spheres of influence the new one-party states of Africa and Asia continue to meet with severe setbacks. Yugoslav influence in the developing world is declining, and it would be easy to over-estimate the material and ideological interest of the East European regimes generally in the third world.

6. The proper policy of the West toward the evolving situation in Eastern Europe is that of "peaceful engagement," that is, the promotion of further evolution of the regimes and specifically of the erosion of communist power through cultural exchange, increased trade, and diplomatic maneuver. As for the longer run, it must be recognized that the ultimate basis of Soviet domination in Eastern Europe is the existence of the "German Democratic Republic" and the continuing division of Germany. The West should treat the GDR differently from its East European neighbors while recognizing that ultimately reunification, and the dismantling of Soviet domination in Eastern Europe, can only be achieved by giving adequate recognition to Russian security interests in the heart of Europe and by finding an equitable solution to the problem of the frontiers.

Taking note of the fact that a minority did not necessarily agree with these theses, the communiqué concluded:

> While the above points represent the general drift of the discussion, it should be emphasized that on many of the issues there existed a sizeable and vigorous minority opposition. The minority felt, for example, that the general trend of the discussion was overly optimistic as

to the pace and prospect of the decline of organized communist strength and influence. The minority also felt that the parties of Eastern Europe were perhaps adapting themselves to the national sentiments of these populations, without losing their own internationalist character. The minority emphasized that despite temporary difficulties and setbacks, the long-range aims of world communism remained unchanged, and that the danger of the ultimate realization of these aims continued great.

IV

The selection of the papers for this symposium was determined primarily by the need for a sharp focus on the main topics of the agenda. The value of an anthology depends not only on the merit of its individual contributions, but on the manner in which these contributions "hang together." As a result, some meritorious and interesting essays unfortunately could not be incorporated in this volume. It was considered imperative to present to the reader a compact, informative outline of the most important issues of postwar Eastern Europe and thereby contribute to a far too limited literature on this increasingly important area. All authors were given an opportunity to revise their drafts and bring them up to date. The cut-off date for revisions was December 31, 1965.

The Fifth International Conference on World Politics could not have taken place without the vigorous backing of His Excellency Vice Admiral H. Bos of the Cabinet of the Prime Minister of The Netherlands; Dr. D. J. von Balluseck, Director of The Netherlands Institute of International Affairs; Major General Dr. M. W. J. M. Broekmeijer, Director of the National Defense College of The Netherlands; Dr. L. G. M. Jaquet, Secretary General of The Netherlands Institute of International Affairs; and Professor E. de Vries, Rector of the Institute of Social Studies, The Hague. These officials gave freely of their time to set the organizational wheels in motion and to persuade governmental and private agencies to contribute funds to the conference. Among these benefactors were: The Netherlands Minister of Foreign Affairs; The Netherlands Minister of Defense; The Netherlands Minister of Education and Science; the President of Shell Netherlands, Ltd., Rotterdam; the President of Unilever, Rotterdam; the President of Philips, Ltd., Eindhoven; and the President of the AKU (Algemene Kunstzijde Union), Arnhem.

The Conference Steering Committee, consisting of Professor Klaus Mehnert, Professor de Vries, Dr. Jaquet, Major General Broekmeijer, and this writer, speaking for the participants and observers, most gratefully acknowledge the contributions of these organizations. They are particularly obliged to the Organizing Committee under the extraordinarily efficient direction of Mr. C. A. Chorus.

As the editor of this volume, I am deeply indebted to Mrs. Tybel Litwin, whose editorial advice and assistance is greatly responsible for the shape of this book and for the speed with which the manuscript could be transmitted to the publisher.

My thanks also go to Miss Sally Jansen and Mrs. Nancy Hallsted for their dedicated help in preparing a fair copy from a hieroglyphic manuscript.

Kurt London

Institute for Sino-Soviet Studies
The George Washington University
Washington, D.C.

Notes on the Contributors

Dr. Adam Bromke is Associate Professor of Political Science and Chairman of the Soviet and East European Studies Program, Carleton University, Ottawa, Canada.

Dr. R. V. Burks is Professor of History, Wayne State University, Detroit, Michigan.

Dr. Stephen Fischer-Galati is Professor of History, University of Colorado, Boulder, Colorado, and Associate, Russian Research Center, Harvard University, Cambridge, Massachusetts.

Dr. Andrew Gyorgy is Professor of International Affairs, Institute for Sino-Soviet Studies, The George Washington University, Washington, D.C.

Pierre Hassner, Agrégé de Philosophie, is a Research Associate, Centre d'Étude des Relations Internationales, Fondation Nationale des Sciences Politiques, Paris, France, and Visiting Professor in Politics, The Johns Hopkins University European Center, Bologna, Italy.

Dr. Wolfgang H. Kraus is Professor of Political Science and Chairman of the Department of Political Science, The George Washington University, Washington, D.C.

Dr. Ernst Kux is Lecturer in Communist Affairs at the Hochschule für Wirtschafts- und Sozialwissenschaften of St. Gallen, Switzerland, and an editorial writer on Sino-Soviet questions for the *Neue Zürcher Zeitung,* Zürich, Switzerland.

Dr. Kurt London is Professor of International Affairs and Director, Institute for Sino-Soviet Studies, The George Washington University, Washington, D.C.

Dr. Klaus Mehnert is Professor of Political Science and Director, Institute of Political Science, Institute of Technology, Aachen, Germany, and editor of *Osteuropa.*

Dr. Boris Meissner, a member of the Directorate of the Federal Institute for Research in East European and International Studies, Cologne, is also Director of the Institute of East European Law and Professor of Law at the University of Cologne, Germany.

Dr. John Michael Montias is Professor of Economics, Yale University, New Haven, Connecticut.

George A. Schöpflin is a Research Assistant of the Royal Institute of International Affairs, London, England.

Professor Dr. Karl C. Thalheim is Head of the Department for East European Economics of the East European Institute, Free University, West Berlin, Germany.

Dr. Thomas W. Wolfe is a Senior Staff Member of the RAND Corporation, Santa Monica, California.

EASTERN EUROPE IN TRANSITION

Nationalism or Polycentrism: Two Views

Chapter I.

1. The Role of Nationalism in Eastern
Europe: from Monolith to Polycentrism
ANDREW GYORGY

2. Communism in Eastern Europe:
Polycentrism, Splittism, and After
KURT LONDON

1. The Role of Nationalism in Eastern Europe: From Monolith to Polycentrism

Andrew Gyorgy

Nationalism in Eastern Europe has been inextricably interwoven with the twin phenomena of *power* and *revolution*. Clearly, the enormous growth in the power of the modern nation-state has been largely responsible for the violence and political vigor of contemporary nationalism. An array of violent nationalistic outbursts has been engendered in Eastern Europe by the more recent forms of totalitarian state organization, ranging in prototypes from Hitler and Mussolini to Stalin and Khrushchev, with subcategories and subvariations including the Iron Guard in Rumania, Alexander's royal dictatorship in prewar Yugoslavia, and Horthy's semitotalitarian Hungary. The prevailing feature of twentieth-century nationalism has been its power orientation, with a direct and close correlation between the totalitarian characteristics of the government and the relative virulence of the people's nationalistic feelings.

Power-oriented nationalism has expressed itself on the political landscape of Eastern Europe in essentially two forms: violent and non-violent. While the two patterns are basically self-defining, the key question of the transition point between them is a more tenuous proposition: When, under what provocation, and how does a political and paramilitary eruption occur which qualitatively transforms a non-violent underground movement into an abrupt, violent, and totally aboveground act of mass violence? The 1956 experience of the Polish and Hungarian revolutions affords at least an approach to this important theoretical question. We may ask what specific factors were responsible for the crystallization, on the one hand, of Poland's remarkably successful "silent revolution" as against the dreadful bloodbath which drowned the ill-fated nationalist uprising in Hungary. A comprehensive answer is perhaps, at this juncture, impossible. But from the events of June 17, 1953, in Berlin and October 23, 1956, in Hungary, we can generalize with certainty that overt and violent patterns of nationalism have characterized the exploited satellite areas of Eastern Europe almost to the extent (though with less frequency) that countermovements have rent the newly developing, former colonial regions of Africa, the Middle East, and Southeast Asia. Clearly, such extreme pressures as communism, Pan-Arabism, and anti-Westernism, alternating with such internal counteragents as national anticommunism, anti-Arabism, and pro-Western Xenophilia, add to the fuel of local nationalism and contribute to the fires, on occasion producing conflagrations of open, violent mass nationalism. The external impact of these ideologies is thus frequently responsible for transforming dormant local situations into national riots and civil wars.

In its revolutionary aspect, nationalism is based on and reflects the twin dimensions of individual and collective aspirations for freedom. The former stresses the freedom of the individual to belong to the nation of his choice and to assert himself under its aegis; the latter insists on freedom or self-determination for a group, with a view toward its development into a national unit. The revolutionary implications of such a dually based, collectively patterned nationalism have been profound and obvious on the Eastern European political scene. The nineteenth- and early twentieth-century revolutionary struggles aimed against the Ottoman and Hapsburg empires are not only excellent illustrations of this complex phenomenon but gain added perspective when viewed in retrospect along the parallel dimensions of the subjected individual's personal struggle for self-assertion and the nationalist group struggle for attainment of a truly collective freedom. These two dimensions are then intricately combined with each other: the individual's heroics offer the necessary political leadership, while the group is called upon to supply the strongly motivated mass following. One without the other would fail dismally. Both the 1953 East Berlin and the 1956 Hungarian revolts collapsed because they lacked one of the *sine qua non*'s or essential revolutionary preconditions, of nationalist success: inspired and individualized political leadership. Unhappily, without this guidance, mass action has proved to be an insufficient instrument against the complex edifice of contemporary tyrannies.

In his classic essay "Qu'est-ce qu'une nation?" (Paris, 1887), Ernest Renan suggested that modern nationalism combined, in a

more or less harmonious composite, four principal characteristics: a commonly shared territory, a cultural community, a
common history, and—last but not least—a jointly developed
and organized governmental system. The present paper relies on
a minimally valid definition of the nation concept which implies
at least a unit of territory, a people with a common past and
common cultural characteristics, and existing organizational
bases of government.

A CHRONOLOGICAL AND TOPICAL FRAMEWORK

In the thirteen years which have elapsed since Stalin's death,
three successive patterns have evolved in the context of the
intricate interrelationships between communism and nationalism. Only the first two have reasonably distinct and clearcut
terminal points. Inevitably, as we approach the present period,
the outlines become blurred and the prevailing trends become
uncertain. Nevertheless, it is the function of the social scientist to
attempt to superimpose order on political turmoil and ideological chaos. To this end, granting the intangibles and risking the
oversimplification that is built into any such effort to rationalize
the irrational and systematize the unsystematic, we may develop
a framework in which each of the three main patterns is assigned
a time period and identified by a central theme or *leitmotiv*.

The transitional era which followed Stalin's death on March 5,
1953, totally collapsed in the thunder and ashes of the Battle of
Budapest. The cataclysmic events of 1956 saw the end of the post-
Stalinist New Course and ushered in a new phase of recriminations, vindications, and regionwide ideological tightening.
The dominant theme of the 1953–56 period can only be described as the last significant gasp of Moscow-centered communist
internationalism, already a projection of the inevitable end of
the monolith.

The second phase was short-lived and even more markedly
transitional: this phase encompassed the exciting revolutionary
months of 1956–57, starting with the Poznań revolt in Poland in
June, 1956, and ending sometime in mid-1957 with the resolute
liquidation in such countries as Poland, Hungary, and East Germany of the last fleeting vestiges—both tangible and intangible—
of their respective popular revolutions from below. This convul-

sive phase may be spotlighted as one of *heroic transition* marked by more or less violent forms of anticommunist nationalism.

Finally, beginning approximately in the 1958–59 period, we witness the emergence of an increasingly *pluralistic communism* throughout Eastern Europe, reflecting both the weakened power position of the U.S.S.R. and the ominously lengthening shadow of the Sino-Soviet dispute. Nikita Khrushchev's abrupt dismissal in October, 1964, significantly contributed to the breakup of earlier colonial patterns and accentuated—in sharp perspective for communists and non-communists alike—the complexities and expectations of the current era. This paper focuses on post-1958 developments marked by post-heroic pluralism and linked primarily to an anticolonial rather than an anticommunist nationalism.

END OF THE MONOLITH (1953–56)

As Kurt London suggested in *The Permanent Crisis*,[1] the peculiar combination of doctrinal factors and political organization has produced in countries of the communist bloc a set of foreign policy concepts totally different from those of the non-communist and non-revolutionary governments. This characterization bears stark and vigorous application to Eastern Europe under Stalin and in the immediate post-Stalin era. In terms of three parallel factors—doctrinal forces, political-administrative organization, and general policy objectives—Stalin's post-World War II European empire can be portrayed as wholly non-traditional, supra- and antinationalistic in character, as well as both monolithic and revolutionary in behavior. The Stalinist pattern was based on three overlapping notions of undisputed, monopolistic primacy positions. These were: one-man control and leadership by Joseph Stalin over foreign communist parties and states; one-party primacy over all other communist parties, which meant unchallenged CPSU leadership in Eastern Europe; and the full-blown emergence of one city, Moscow, as the capital of world—and particularly of European—communism.

The impact of this triple ring of power and authority could have been foreseeable: The Stalinist pattern was one of a widely smothered nationalism, silencing almost all pre-World War II crisis areas and stirrings of local nationalism, and of a *Lokal-*

patriotismus always so characteristic of the Balkan-Danubian area. Under heavy-handed Stalinism, with Molotov as chief regional supervisor and colonels general of the Red Army as country-by-country executors, the perennial Transylvanian dispute was as efficiently smothered as the Ruthenian, Bessarabian, or Silesian questions. It may be noted in passing that while the economic network of the U.S.S.R. and Eastern Europe, CEMA or COMECON, was born in 1949, mistakenly labeled the Molotov Plan, there was no real need for it in the postwar decade since the institutions of Stalinism provided more than sufficient leverage in exercising economic dictation. Nor was there an immediate need for the Warsaw Treaty Organization; Soviet military satraps, or district governors, continued to perform Stalin's assignments with great agility. Witness Poland's Rokossovsky complex born of the marshal's reimportation to Poland as army chief of staff in 1949.[2]

From the Eastern European satellites' perspective, the most distressing by-product of Stalinism was not its transformation of the basic political organization of the area, but its almost complete breakdown of the individual nation's sense of internal legitimacy. As defined by Karl Deutsch and Carl Friedrich, this important concept implies the population's belief in, and support of, its own government, a government aimed at "mutual political cooperation and *membership in the nation* . . . so that [popular] support for the nation, even in times of adversity, is likely and thus ensures its endurance."[3] Instead of fostering internal legitimacy, the oppressive years of Stalinism produced massive ideological alienation from Warsaw to Tirana.

Stalin's death in 1953 effectively broke the triple monopoly position wielded by Soviet leadership. Even in the elderly dictator's lifetime certain fissures and semiperceptible areas of weakness and challenge began to emerge. Each crack in the monolith contributed to the erosion of a centrally organized and directed, wholly artificial system of communist internationalism. Two such early points of peril are worthy of mention here: the Tito-Stalin dispute of 1948–49, and the gradual reappearance (or reintroduction) of certain native, national communist leaders in the political life of individual satellite countries. Both situations heralded the emergence of what might be described as *peripheral nationalism* in Eastern Europe.

From the historical perspective of almost two decades, the Soviet-Yugoslav dispute looms as a tremendously significant milestone and as a warning signal to externally imposed, alien political systems. Its ideological importance pales, in retrospect, compared with its intensive power struggle characteristics. The real issue was not the angry dialogue between the two leaders or the arguments over who had the paramount claim to the proper interpretation of Marx and Lenin. As a naked power clash, the "Tito and Goliath" dispute involved divergent analyses of the nature of national versus international trends of communism. As Hugh Seton-Watson observed: "The 'Tito clique' did not capitulate, nor did the Yugoslav state break down. . . . The danger from the Cominform did not cause Tito to modify the dictatorship of the Communist Party inside Yugoslavia. . . . He insisted on his determination to base *his* policy on the science of Marxism-Leninism."[4]

The incalculably serious consequence of Yugoslavia's secession from the Soviet-led bloc was not so much the weakening of ideology but, as Ferenc A. Váli has noted, the driving of a "large and dangerous wedge into the otherwise compact satellite area."[5] Thus a fiercely nationalistic foreign body was thrust into the previously closed off, socially and politically quarantined Balkan-Danubian region, to the ultimate chagrin of Stalin's successors.

The other crisis area involved the Stalinist purges of East European leadership elites, purges which set off certain nationalistic repercussions that in the long run adversely affected the Soviet's over-all power position. The last few years of Stalin's rule were characterized by two major and conflicting processes of political tightening and ideological unification in the ranks of communist party personnel. First, the 1948–49 period brought about the purges of certain Tito-type, nationalist, home-grown communists who had had only superficial contacts with Moscow. Rajk, Gomulka, Kostov and others were sacrificed in order to strengthen the Stalin-imposed rule of the so-called Muscovites, a group of Sovietized leaders who had lived in Russia for many years. Thus "the Paukers, Rákosis, Gerös, Slanskys, Bermans, and Bieruts were the personae gratae of this brief era."[6]

The second great wave of purges operated in the 1952–54 period, and—with a dramatic return swing of the pendulum—singled out and closed in on the internationally oriented team of

the Muscovite East European leaders. The members of this cos-
mopolitan faction were soon decimated (the Slansky group in
Czechoslovakia was brutally liquidated, while the "alien" Ana
Pauker and Vasile Luca were removed from Rumania's public
life) and forced to yield to those indigenous leaders who had
escaped the first wave of nationalist purges. In this manner the
years 1953–55 ushered in a gradual return to selected power
positions of such peripheral national communists as Imre Nagy
of Hungary and Gheorghiu-Dej of Rumania. Nikita Khrushchev's dramatic reconciliation with Tito in May, 1955, had the
effect of considerably strengthening the nationalist line in Eastern Europe, serving as a retroactive recognition of the merits and
prestige of the Titoist posture not only in Yugoslavia but
throughout the once monolithic Soviet bloc. Even the Kádárs
and Gomulkas, slowly resuming the careers interrupted by Stalin's 1948–49 purges, were forced to appear as fully home-grown,
national communists in their respective countries, although both
types of leaders proved to be totally acceptable to the Khrushchev regime.

During the fascinating transitional era of the post-Stalinist
New Course, East European nationalism benefitted both from
external and internal relaxation of tensions. While the political
import of the intriguing Belgrade reconciliation between Tito
and Khrushchev was not lost on satellite leadership, Khrushchev's newly initiated foreign policy of "limited concessions" was
of almost equal significance to them. The Austrian State Treaty
of May, 1955, the return of naval bases to Finland, the Geneva
Summit Conference of 1955, and subsequently the dissolution of
the Cominform (yet another Stalinist edifice stifling diversity
and aiming at unification), as well as the dismissal of Foreign
Minister Molotov, played major roles in ushering in a new period of rapprochement. From Khrushchev's perspective the hope
was that remaining major areas of tension in Soviet-satellite
relations would gradually disappear and a true thaw would
characterize both the ideological and power relationships of the
dominant country and its involuntary smaller partners. Instead
of peace, relaxation, and the smooth adoption of these new lines
of Soviet policy, the stage by mid-1956 was set for the first of
several spontaneous nationalist explosions on the Eastern European scene. Khrushchev's ebullient optimism contributed to the

misreading of satellite signals: Relaxation led to revolt, not to mass obedience. Once again the late Albert Einstein's prophetic remark was vindicated: "Politics is harder than physics."

HEROIC TRANSITION (1956–57)

The revolutionary excitement of Eastern Europeans exploded in three major civil war type situations in the course of 1956. An analysis of Eastern European nationalism must take note of certain linkages—and contradictions—among the forces of nationalism, communism, internationalism, and Soviet colonialism.

A brief chronology of revolutionary escalation may be established at the outset. Credit must be given to the frustrated, angry workers of East Berlin's Stalin Allee for expressing, in a fairly violent manner, their pent-up emotions against the Ulbricht leadership as early as June, 1953, a mere three months after Stalin's death. The angry suppression of this revolt by the Soviet military contributed to a three-year hiatus. In June, 1956, passive co-operation turned into active, popular non-co-operation in Poznań, Poland, where transportation workers and students unleashed their ire against the hated Polish secret police. Next came Warsaw's relatively peaceful, moderate, and politically successful revolt beginning on October 15. Finally, the events of October 23–November 4 in Budapest brought to a climax, with a Soviet-staged bloodbath, the year of heroics and transition for all of Eastern Europe. Thus popular bitterness and violence escalated from East Berlin to Budapest, to be nipped in the bud by Red Army suppression in the Hungarian capital.

While the chronological pattern may be partly fortuitous, common threads running through these events seem far from haphazard. Four essential characteristics emerge:

1. National popular revolts of this type do not occur in the midst of deep misery and a concentration-camp atmosphere. On the contrary, each can be linked to a period of psychological and physical improvement—the New Course, the post-Stalin thaw and related relaxation. Heydays of terror are seldom conducive to the outbreak of national revolts, which seem rather to be a curious combination of popular reaction to economic and politi-

cal improvements coupled with short-term irritants. Such irritants are usually incidents which may prove to be immediately explosive, such as in East Berlin or Budapest. At any rate, the truly inflammable revolutionary ideas "spring into insurgent action only . . . when terror relents or when circumstances prevent its full use."[7]

2. Eastern Europe's popular revolts were principally national and anticommunist in nature and only secondarily anti-Soviet in orientation. Their mainspring was a violent pattern of localized political nationalism aimed at their own communist elites and sub-elite groups. Thus they provided case studies neither of national communism, as some American writers have claimed, nor of the growth of an anti-Soviet, anti-Russian form of communism.[8] The prime target of hatred in Poznań was the *Polish* Communist Party secret policeman, and the prime target in Budapest was the fellow *Hungarian* Communist Party secret policeman. The source was nationalism and the target indigenous communism. The fact that the Red Army was called in (or rushed in) to quell the revolt should not muddy or obscure the revolutionaries' original intent: to eliminate their own communist regime, not that of Nikita Khrushchev.

However, the profile of these national anticommunist uprisings would be incomplete if Khrushchev's own inimitable contributions to their outbreak were omitted. The former Soviet leader's massive de-Stalinization campaign must immediately be placed in the ideological context of these revolts. Khrushchev initiated the dramatic repudiation of Stalin as the great leader and of thirty years of Stalinism as a successful political system. In the months following the Twentieth Party Congress of February, 1956, the content of Khrushchev's "secret speech" percolated through the now semicaptive societies of Eastern Europe, triggering feelings of revulsion and a mass rejection of Stalinism and its institutions. Yet when the satellite peoples struck, they struck against their own Stalins—pocket Stalins and Stalinoid types—against their own brand of communism, not against the more distant and less immediately relevant Soviet version which was, moreover, presided over by a seemingly more relaxed and less ominous leadership.

3. Another important feature could be characterized as the art

of probing. The popular revolts implied national probings into the more vulnerable recesses of modern communism. Since the highest degree of vulnerability has existed in the political-ideological and not in the economic sphere, we may regard the order of precedence in the demands for freedom and bread on the banners of the insurgent workers in Poznań as not in the least accidental. Economic demands, in the cases of all three major Eastern European revolts, were subordinated to the much more fundamental yearning for political liberty. We witness here the prototype of what Professor Alexander Rüstow has accurately described as the *"freiheitliche* revolution," or "freedom-aspiring revolt." Such an uprising is intent on probing deeply into the ideological shortcomings of its government or ruling party, motivated primarily by the objective of sweeping aside the impact of a highly oppressive regime.

4. In the short run, the heroic efforts of the Eastern European revolutionaries failed, most conspicuously in East Berlin and Budapest. Yet from the middle-run vantage point of a decade, some of the principal goals seem to have been accomplished. Leaving aside economic factors (living standards, consumer goods, etc.), it is clear already that these superhuman, and frequently suicidal, efforts of anticommunist nationalism have achieved the twin results of: (*a*) shaking up the communist regimes and substituting more acceptable, nationally oriented communist leaders for the extreme and uncompromising Stalinists (witness the post-revolutionary collapse of the Hungarian Communist Party and the emergence of the Kádárs and Gomulkas, replacing the Rákosis and Bieruts), and (*b*) fatally weakening the Stalinist monolith in terms of demanding and receiving differentiated treatment on a country-by-country basis, in effect also terminating (in most cases) a satellite dependency on the U.S.S.R. The popular revolts produced these results even in nations untouched by revolt, such as Rumania and Czechoslovakia, although the humiliating satellite status continued for Bulgaria and East Germany.

Thus, the tactical losses of the revolts have undeniably produced considerable strategic gains: They wrecked the monolithic pattern imposed upon the region by Stalin and thereby helped to set the stage for the current phase of Eastern Europe's communist pluralism and anticolonialism.

COMMUNIST PLURALISM (1958—)

The most recent phase in the political development of Eastern Europe has been marked by the all-pervasive impact of two factors: the steadily deteriorating power position of the Soviet Union, on the one hand, and the lengthening shadow of the Sino-Soviet dispute on the other. Since 1958 the political emotions of most Balkan-Danubian peoples have been tied, with increasing intensity, to anti-Soviet sentiments—to a more or less concealed resentment against the *colonial* power which used to exploit them so mercilessly. Hence the stress in this analysis is on the major theme of the last few years' developments, anticolonialism, not so much now an anticommunist, but a distinctly anti-Soviet, pattern of nationalism.

This exciting phenomenon asserts itself through two principal instruments which have served such notable forms of nationalism as Serbian, Croatian, Polish, and Hungarian patriotism. These are religion and language, as parts of a broader sense of national culture and civilization. The same two factors have contributed significantly to the "three D's" process currently characterizing the Eastern European scene: de-Russification, desatellization, and —last but not least—decolonization. In effect, the two media, in cross-combination, may yet realize the substantial transformation of the *ex pluribus unum* (or monolithic) phase into the more up-to-date *ex uno plures* stage of current polycentrism.

The Impact of Religion. Contemporary European communism, in the opinion of one of its distinguished West German students, can succeed in humanizing and liberalizing itself only through the introduction of "moral values, of a personal mellowing and an intellectual emancipation."[9] All of these revisionist symptoms are imbedded in, and reflected by, the variegated relationships of the Eastern European communist state apparati and the diverse forms of organized churches. National churches have been particularly important in this context as media of political nationalism wherever submerged national groups have vigorous and different beliefs from those of the ruling group. In Stalin's day this was the problem of Catholic Poles versus an Orthodox Russian ruling clique in Warsaw. On an unhappily persistent basis, this is one of the crisis areas today in Ulbricht's East Germany, with a Lutheran and Calvinist majority of Germans facing a disaffected, wholly Sovietized, and thus atheistic ruling clique. The Transylvanian problem has, of course, been immensely complicated by the quixotic and complex arrangements which, at various times in history, saw Orthodox Rumanians over and/or under Hungarian Catholics.

Of all the truly strategic (i. e., long-term) factors which have molded the phenomenally varied national identities of Eastern European countries, organized religion may well rank first in the ultimate judgment of history. Thus, if its ideological fervor is pitted against the secular forces of the state and its dominant party or movement, who can readily and accurately forecast the clear-cut victory of one major antagonist over the other embattled opponent? The challenges are manifold and sharp. Polish Cardinal Wyszinski, enjoying more freedom than his Hungarian or Czech counterparts, stated in a memorable address in March, 1961, that he was the leader of a church militant which wanted not only a taste of freedom, but civic and social freedoms as well. The Polish Catholic church would defend itself against the charges that it was a rebel in its struggle for civic and individual freedom as well as in its religious rights.[10] Cardinal Wyszinski reiterated, time and again, that despite the suppression of religious instruction (schools, seminaries, etc.), the churches remained—as they were before the imposition of communism—truly national institutions.

The Impact of Language and Culture. Historians have noted that by the time of the Balkan Wars of 1912–13 the linguistic factor in this explosive area had become as significant as the force of religion since many Russians, Greeks, Serbs, and Bulgars were fighting each other on an essentially linguistic basis. Today again, the Danubian-Balkan peoples differentiate themselves on the basis of language. The Polish language stresses a Polish national identity, and the Rumanian and Hungarian languages again assume the anticolonial significance they possessed in the dying days of the doomed Turkish, Austro-Hungarian, and Russian empires. The linguistic counterthrusts in Eastern Europe are numerous and their impact on gradual de-Russification is immense. It is worth noting that non-Slavic (and basically anti-Russian) cultures, such as those of Hungary and Rumania, are particularly anxious to decolonize today. Their current models seem to be the border countries of Finland and Austria, where a far greater latitude of freedom and movement exists.

As the Iron Curtain borders have grown more relaxed and Western visitors have increasingly flooded these once quarantined countries, the cultural brand of nationalism has presented an even more direct and ominous threat to Soviet hegemony than its more innocuous political counterpart. Budapest, as a Radio Free Europe research bulletin pointed out, has reacted warmly to Italian suggestions of literary and artistic independence. Indeed, in the cultural sphere the new and semantically fascinating phrase "permissive revisionism" has made its semi-official debut in Warsaw and Budapest, following the advice of Togliatti's 1964 testament that "communists must become the champions of liberty of intellectual life, of free artistic creation, and of scientific progress."

Widely quoted also is the Italian Communist Party's cultural magazine *Il Contemporaneo,* which in a December, 1964, issue explained that the party's policy was to encourage the free interplay of divergent cultural positions: "Today, the development of the national society calls vigorously for a confrontation of cultures . . . no longer . . . popular or mass culture as it was understood ten years ago, but the free interaction of different cultures . . . each of which has its own autonomy and validity."[11]

What does a "confrontation of cultures" actually imply? It has been suggested that it might promote unity in diversity within communism's Eastern European camp, but more significantly it would increase revisionist trends in the body cultural and politic of the region. And the sum total of such civilizational influences must inevitably lead to a further weakening of the once monolithic center. Western revisionist (and thus nationalist) cultural pressures, as a Hungarian Communist plaintively remarked, pour "[in] to us through a sieve which has too coarse a mesh to filter properly these trends . . . which are not always forged in Marxist workshops."[12]

EASTERN EUROPEAN NATIONALISM: AN AUTONOMIST FORMULA

Three major points may be stressed, in conclusion, regarding the role and significance of Eastern European nationalism.

First, we must observe that Eastern European communism is suddenly faced with a novel challenge, one which may never be properly resolved on its small and essentially constricted stage: a desperate search for popular acceptance and for a minimum degree of internal and external respectability. Consequently, the brash loudness of Marxist-Leninist propaganda has been considerably muted in recent years, and a peculiar pattern of ideological neutrality has emerged among people who are sick and tired of playing the usual communist games. Ideology has been supplanted in many areas of daily life by a more potent and motivating popular force: a vigorous but basically old-fashioned form of nationalism. After a twenty-five- to thirty-year silence, a traditional Balkan-Danubian pattern of politico-economic nationalism is beginning to re-emerge. This nationalistic force is neither pro-Western nor always and inevitably anti-Soviet; instead it emphatically echoes the familiar line of bygone eras: "Rumania for the Rumanians!" "Hungary for the Hungarians!" Today's battle cry is modified and qualified as "Communist Rumania for the Rumanians!" "Marxist Hungary for the Hungarians!" But the naked and elemental force of this Balkan-Danubian nationalism must be stressed at all times, distinguishing in its broad context between a *political* and an *economic* pattern of nationalism and viewing with fascination the interaction of these two equally important operational forces.

Secondly, we note that the phenomenon of national communism has been one of the major instruments in causing the end of the monolithic era and in setting the stage for today's pluralism. As a *sui generis* belief system, national communism is the peculiar combination of two distinct forces: a social protest against international communism (its negative feature, as it were) coupled with a strong assertion of national unity and political independence (the positive ingredient). The heart of national communism lies in its autonomist formula, implying the Eastern European peoples' fundamentally "let's go it alone!" attitude in the face of centuries of foreign control and domination. Today the long-term historic perspective is reinforced by a short-term component: a refusal to accept the Kremlin's supremacy and infallibility. The particulars of a Soviet-Yugoslav dispute or of a Soviet-Rumanian disagreement are immaterial. What matters is the existence of a dispute as such. The monolith truly cracked at the moment when the absolute infallibility of the Soviet system was first successfully challenged. The crux of this deviationist pattern was that Tito, Gomulka, Gheorghiu-Dej, and others have seriously questioned the essence of the doctrinal and practical infallibility of the U.S.S.R.

Given this assertion of national unity, the current pattern suggests that the Yugoslav, Polish, Rumanian, and Albanian elite groups (and potential national communist regimes anywhere else) are fully aware of the continuing problem of reconciling the following delicate and perilous tasks: (*a*) the historically proven sturdy nationalism of their people with (*b*) the unpleasant and practical realities of Marxism-Leninism, especially in such areas as collectivization and industrialization, with (*c*) the unpalatable overtones and colonial pressure tactics of a neighboring great power which may once again attempt to force a subservient relationship, a satellite mold, on smaller and weaker countries.

This last feature reflects the essential difference between internationally and nationally oriented communism: The objection to subservience penetrates every aspect of the deviationist nation's ideological posture and domestic political life.

Finally, we may stress the all-important norm of "historical relativity." As Professor Eugen Lemberg recently noted in an excellent essay, "what is revisionism today may easily become tomorrow's generally accepted doctrine."[13] Thus bourgeois nationalism, just as much a sin to orthodox Marxist-Leninists as bourgeois cosmopolitanism, may suddenly be promoted and recognized as part of a formal class ideology. Conversely, internationalism may be tomorrow's revisionist sin. And nationalism, even in its aggressive Eastern European version, may become the basic tenet of communism's next official encyclical.

NOTES

1. See Chapter II, *Foreign Affairs in a Divided World* (New York, 1962), pp. 31–54.

2. The Rokossovsky issue was not resolved until this World War II hero was re-exported to the U.S.S.R. in October, 1956.

3. Karl W. Deutsch and William J. Foltz, *Nation-Building* (New York,

1963) , especially Deutsch's "Nation-Building and National Development," pp. 11–13. (Italics added.)

4. See his *The East European Revolution* (New York, 1961), esp. pp. 225–26.

5. See his *Rift and Revolt in Hungary: Nationalism versus Communism* (Cambridge, Mass., 1961), esp. pp. 503–4.

6. Andrew Gyorgy, "The Internal Political Order," in *Eastern Europe in the Sixties,* ed. Stephen Fischer-Galati (New York, 1963), esp. pp. 174–76.

7. See Erich Goldhagen's excellent article on "The Glorious Future—Realities and Chimeras," *Problems of Communism,* November/December, 1960, pp. 10–18.

8. The author disagrees emphatically, therefore, with Adam Bromke's value judgment that in 1956 "[in] Poland and Hungary, popular discontent with Soviet suzerainty erupted into open revolt." This assumption is certainly not applicable to the Hungarian eruption of 1956. See Adam Bromke, *Eastern Europe in a Depolarized World* (Toronto, 1965), esp. pp. 6–7.

9. Johannes Maass, "Die Schlacht um die hungernden Völker," *Die Politische Meinung,* July, 1961, pp. 39–51, esp. p. 41.

10. See Dr. Lucjan Blit, "Church, Party and State in Poland," a seminar lecture delivered at the Russian Research Center of Harvard University, May 6, 1965, esp. pp. 3–4 of the transcript.

11. William McLaughlin, "Budapest Welcome for Italian Revisionism," February 12, 1965, pp. 1–4. (Published by Free Europe Committee, N.Y.) (Italics added.)

12. Simon I. Sz, "Letters to the Comrades (Part II) ," *Délmagyarország,* November 28, 1964.

13. See his: "Innermarxistische Marxismuskritik in Ostmitteleuropa," *Zeitschrift für Ostforschung,* XIII, No. 4 (December, 1964), 687–708; esp. pp. 689–90.

2. Communism in Eastern Europe: Polycentrism, Splittism—and After

Kurt London

I

Lenin's formulation of the twenty-one conditions for admission to the Comintern, announced in 1920, set the stage for a "democratic centralism" of international communism. The choice of Moscow as the seat of the Comintern almost certainly was prompted more by practical considerations than by Russian nationalism. As a genuine internationalist, Lenin presumably thought in terms of parties rather than countries. Furthermore, there did not exist, prior to World War II, another country ruled by a communist party or by a reasonable facsimile of a Bolshevik regime.

Whether Lenin actually dreamed of a Soviet hegemony over non-Soviet communist-ruled states is a matter of conjecture. His writings mention no such ambitions. His concern was focused on the international movement, not on domination of nation-states. In any event, between the second Comintern Congress of 1920 and his death in 1924, he had little time to think through the consequences of Soviet domination of all communist parties and the Soviet position toward countries in which successful proletarian revolutions might have occurred. Nevertheless, his overwhelming influence over the Comintern prepared the way for Stalin's absolute subjection of world communism to Moscow, which was to mold the pattern of the parties in the image of their Soviet masters for roughly three decades.

Stalin, once he had usurped Lenin's power, against the latter's testamentary wishes, needed only to accentuate Soviet control and to radicalize what Lenin had initiated. His rule over the Comintern presaged his control over the East European states after World War II. These countries, stretching from the Baltic to the Black Sea, became a political vacuum after Hitler's collapse. Churchill foresaw such a possibility when he warned that

Europe's "soft underbelly" needed protection. He did not prevail in Western councils.

Attempts at filling political vacua are standard communist operating procedure. In the case of Central, Eastern, and South-eastern Europe, additional factors came into play—factors akin to those which had been in the minds of the czarist rulers who coveted parts of this area. One concerned physical security aspects: the Soviet Union, after the experience of the German invasion, wanted to create a *cordon sanitaire* on its Western borders and make this belt of states an untouchable Soviet sphere of interest. Another was the need for reliable governments in these countries: Since the Moscow-appointed heads of these governments were communist party members subject to party discipline, they were automatically subject to Soviet party control. The leadership in Moscow and the vanguard of the communist movement, the Communist Party of the Soviet Union, expected unquestioning obedience. Thus, geopolitical, ideological, and organizational interests dovetailed and were cemented by the economic dependence of these states upon the U.S.S.R.

The dissolution of the Comintern in 1943 was not an abandonment of its principles. It was a matter of expedience. After twenty-three years of iron rule, the Kremlin probably considered the component parties of the Comintern to be well indoctrinated and relatively safe. Stalin presumably expected considerable changes in the world situation after the end of the war which might dilute or destroy the effectiveness of the Comintern as an instrument of world communist control. Moreover, during the war, communications between the parties were difficult and the Soviets had to be content with exercising their control through "diplomatic" missions and various overt and covert delegations. Stalin's desire to assuage his temporary allies' fear of communism may also have influenced the decision to abolish the Comintern, but only to a limited extent.

Moscow began to create shadow governments in the form of "national committees" representing various Eastern European countries. Many members of these committees came from Comintern circles. There was little or no contact between them and the Western-supported governments-in-exile which Moscow did not recognize. In this connection, it is worth noting that the consequences of a possible defeat almost certainly were never seriously discussed by communist leaders. The success of Soviet arms was regarded as absolutely essential for the continuation of world communism under Soviet leadership; victory would propagandize the doctrine and sustain the morale of the movement. It would also help to establish communist-controlled governments in the countries of the *cordon sanitaire.*

Stalin's ambitions in Eastern Europe were made abundantly clear at the Yalta conference. Unfortunately, he had his way: American and Allied forces stopped far short of their potential goals, and once the Soviet armies had invaded a territory, conditions for a communist take-over were immediately prepared. Governments-in-exile were outmaneuvered or defeated themselves through internal quarrels. Czechoslovakia was the only country which by electoral processes and socialist betrayal slipped into the Soviet orbit on its own volition, albeit with some prodding by communist action groups.

Thus, after World War II the Stalin regime imposed an alien system upon what became its satellites. For a while it appeared that the establishment of indigenous governments, puppets of the Kremlin, was a measure preparatory to the eventual incorporation of these states into the Soviet Union as Union Republics. But this never came to pass. Indeed, there must have been second thoughts in the minds of the Kremlin leaders regarding the future of these satellites. The Western world, although weary of war, might have resisted outright annexation of these states. This probably became clear to Moscow when Western resistance to Stalin's cold war, which broke out in full force during the year of 1947, began to harden. Certainly Stalin was rational enough not to risk another war with his former allies, whose power he had learned to recognize. Whether he fully understood the meaning of the new nuclear weapons is open to doubt. But he must have realized that another war with the more powerful and far more resourceful West could mean the end of the Soviet regime. Thus Stalin refrained from outright annexation of the East European states, keeping them instead under tight political and economic control.

It is interesting to speculate whether, in the early 1950's, Stalin and his lieutenants may have asked themselves whether Moscow could hope to continue indefinitely its domination of the satellites. Even though the old dictator was about to launch another bloody purge, and terror inside the U.S.S.R. was mounting unbearably, it is conceivable that some doubts had entered his mind regarding the practicability of ruling non-Soviet states ad infinitum.

In the first place, the unimpeded blatant domination of every aspect of satellite life—political, economic, social, psychological, and cultural—was poor propaganda in foreign communist circles. Elements of nationalism still existed among party members and impaired loyalty to the Soviet state and a Soviet-controlled "government." In the second place, political oppression and economic exploitation of the satellites handed the "imperialists" an effective psychological warfare weapon. Furthermore, the unpunished defection of Yugoslavia had aroused a sense of opposition among the satellites: While Yugoslavia was not contiguous to the Soviet Union, she was still a socialist state, though she had freed herself from Soviet rule to create her own national road to socialism. Finally, the Chinese Communists had conquered the mainland and taken over control. They had done so without much Soviet help, and while they loudly protested their devotion to Soviet leadership, they proceeded almost immediately to announce their own rules and to live by them regardless of whether or not the Kremlin approved.

There is some legitimate doubt that Stalin's talents as a communist leader could be matched by his willingness to adapt to changing conditions. But the simple logic of the points just mentioned may well have prompted him to have Malenkov make this statement at the Nineteenth Congress of the Soviet Communist Party:

> In pursuing its peaceful policy, the Soviet Union is in full accord with the other democratic peace-loving states —the Chinese People's Republic, Rumania, Czechoslovakia, Hungary, Bulgaria, Albania, the German Democratic Republic, the Korean People's Democratic Republic, and the Mongolian People's Republic. The USSR's relations with these countries set an example of entirely new relations among states, relations never yet encountered in history. They are based on the prin-

ciples of equality, economic cooperation and respect for
national independence. . . .[1]

We are reminded of Andrei Zhdanov's statement, at the inau-
guration of the Cominform in Belgrade, that "the Soviet Union
unswervingly holds the position that political and economic relations between states must be built on the basis of equality of the
parties and mutual respect of their sovereign rights."[2] This
Machiavellian promise of a fanatical Stalinist clearly was made
in bad faith. In 1947 Stalin did not have to make any concessions
toward any of the satellite states which he dominated absolutely.
But it is interesting to compare Zhdanov's emphasis on parties as
the bases of equality of states with Malenkov's alluring pledge of
national independence within the framework of the socialist
camp. Obviously these words could not be accepted at face value,
but neither could they be altogether discounted. Times had
changed; Yugoslavia had left the Soviet bloc, still unharmed by
the wrath of the aging dictator in the Kremlin. The very fact that
a creature of Stalin used the term "equality" seemed to imply
that, even assuming bad faith, a "promise" of some national
"independence" had become necessary. It would not be too ex-
pensive for the Kremlin, for if there was to be more national
independence, it was conceivable that the satellite leaders would
simply continue in their role as Soviet puppets in the national
garb of their respective countries.

It is possible that Khrushchev's concept of "different roads to
socialism" took Malenkov's declaration as a point of departure.
Three years after Stalin's death, at the Twentieth CPSU Congress in 1956, it became a matter of official policy rather than a
promise of questionable value. Khrushchev seemed to mean what
he said.

Khrushchev's destruction of the myth of infallibility of Soviet
communist leadership at the Twentieth Congress, and the ensuing events, evoked a picture of an Eastern European "hundred
flowers." The outbreak in Poland and the revolution in Hungary
would have been unthinkable without the prior removal of the
Stalinist lid from the boiling satellite kettle. But if there was any
doubt that the Soviet leaders still regarded their safety belt of
states as essential, regardless of nuclear weapons and interconti-
nental missiles, the Soviet action in Hungary removed it. Togli-

atti got his wrist slapped for theorizing on polycentrism;[3] many Hungarians were slaughtered for wanting to live it. Nevertheless, the trend, once permitted to start, became irresistible. Polycentrism had come to stay.

Following the events in Poland and Hungary in 1956, the Kremlin made extraordinary efforts, seemingly successful, to recement the broken pieces which the uprisings had left throughout Eastern Europe and in the communist parties outside the satellites. This was primarily a diplomatic exercise, lasting for approximately one year until the fortieth anniversary gathering in Moscow in 1957. Representatives of communist parties and governments met multilaterally and bilaterally in literally hundreds of conferences to restore a semblance of Soviet hegemony over the U.S.S.R.'s sphere of interest and the parties abroad. It was, on the whole, an astonishing feat of communist diplomacy which achieved the stabilization that was imperative for the 1957 meeting. Even the Chinese Communists tried to help: Chou Enlai traveled to Poland and Hungary in a manifestation of Chinese concern for the unity of the communist movement; and Peking continued to endorse the concept of the Soviet party as the vanguard of world communism.

The 1957 statements sounded self-assured and tough. They indicated give-and-take between Moscow and Peking. They also demonstrated the effect of stabilization. It is all very well, with hindsight, to claim that the statements at that time evinced signs of deteriorating relations between the Soviets and the Chinese Communists. In 1957 one could not be sure at all, and while it was possible to point to some Sino-Soviet differences, the salient fact was that a workable compromise seemed to have been achieved. It was of short duration, however. In subsequent meetings of the parties, beginning in 1960, the cleavage between the Soviets and the Sino-Albanian bloc became wider. The public exchanges between Peking and Moscow, which began in earnest with the Chinese publication of "Long Live Leninism" in 1960 and the communist party congress in Bucharest in June, 1960, clearly indicated to the Eastern European satellites that the time was coming when they might be able to modify their vassal status and become at least semisovereign states again. However, it must be stated emphatically that they did not mean to discard Marxism-Leninism. All they desired was to pursue the goals of Marxian socialism in their own way, suited to their countries' own conditions rather than to those prevailing in the U.S.S.R. They also realized that in matters of foreign policy and military strategy they would have to remain within the Soviet orbit for some time to come. Thus they remained members of the Warsaw Pact organization; the consequences of Nagy's attempt to take Hungary out of it were still vividly remembered. They stayed in the Council for Economic Mutual Assistance (CEMA or COME-CON), although some of them began to take exception to what one might call Soviet neocolonialism.

II

Organization is the foundation on which the communist body politic was built. Marxism provided the building material but lacked the steel girders which Lenin supplied. Thus the Comintern was fashioned. It became Stalin's own organization and was so imbued with his concepts that, for a while, it did not seem to matter when he dissolved it in 1943. While he was alive and in power, the spirit of the Comintern remained by and large intact.[4] Only after he died did this spirit begin to become shaky, and three years later the denigration of Stalin wrecked it. The question then was whether another international organization was required to hold the communist movement together under Moscow's leadership. If world communism was still unitary, a solution was not out of reach. The concept of a "socialist commonwealth" was a non-terroristic, voluntaristic, sophisticated solution—provided the components of the movement adhered to the same beliefs and, even more important, agreed to accept identical interpretations of the gospel.[5]

This was not the case, however. With the end of the monolith which had been fashioned by terror and oppression, communist ideology per se could no longer hold down the human reaction against total regimentation. Moreover, the peoples of Eastern Europe, in particular, regarded communist rule as Soviet rule.

There is perhaps a tendency to overestimate the strength of nationalism and to misread its character under a communist party regime in these countries. Nationalism, in the traditional Western sense of the word, is different from nationalism in a country dominated by a communist party. This difference expresses itself in form, content, and goals. In any event, there was in Eastern Europe no particular desire to return to the "good old days." But neither were the communist party leaders popular. They were regarded as Soviet tools—which they were.

The end of centralized international organization and the double death of Stalin in 1953 and 1956, as well as the new Khrushchev thesis of "different roads to socialism," heightened the awareness of an impending new era. Close co-operation with the U.S.S.R. was taken for granted, but abject thralldom was not.

The situation varied in the different Eastern European states. It was (and still is) an often committed mistake of the West to regard the entire area of Central, Eastern, and Southeastern Europe as a more or less integrated complex. The Baltic states could not be regarded as part of it. They had become component parts of the Soviet Union, and a population shift of major proportion brought Great Russian elements into Lithuania, Latvia, and Estonia. Both Soviet state control and communist doctrinal *Gleichschaltung* eliminated Baltic independence and, with the annexed former East Prussia, created a firm strategic anchor of Soviet military and political posture on the Baltic Sea. East Germany, still a Soviet satellite, is not a state properly speaking. As a part of Germany, it is not a national unit but simply a Soviet zone of occupation controlled by puppets of Moscow, who, without Soviet power, would quickly collapse. The assent of these puppets to a new economic treaty with the Soviet Union, heavily exploiting the East German economy, became known in early December, 1965, when the head of the State Planning Commission of the Soviet zone, Erich Apel, who was also a deputy premier and a member of the ruling party's Central Committee, committed suicide rather than sign this treaty by order of Ulbricht.

Of the states comprising the rest of the Soviet East European security zone, Bulgaria is still the most faithful follower of its big brother. Historical bonds have remained strong. Both deviations favoring the Chinese extreme and trying for greater liberalization were unsuccessful. Poland is in a dilemma: its leadership is both nationalist and communist without being Titoist. Fearing Germany, it relies on Soviet backing. The hatred and fear of Germany substantially outweighs the distrust and dislike of the

Russians. Like all other former satellites, Poland is strongly tied to Soviet foreign and military policy, but it has taken different views in domestic affairs. Nevertheless, the Gomulka regime has not permitted the thaw to become a flood and there have been indications of political retrogression particularly in the intellectual area. The period of relative freedom of expression following the October, 1956, unrest and the Hungarian revolution is gradually being phased out. Nevertheless, Poland, for one, made it clear that it has no intention of becoming a member of a new communist organization which may again result in greater Soviet control.

Czechoslovakia, always cautious, has taken a tortuous road toward polycentrism. Novotny, unsure of himself, was almost as slow as Ulbricht to adjust to the new conditions. But he had to accede to pressures, and the tempo of economic and intellectual developments has since accelerated considerably. In contrast, Hungary is one of the two Eastern European states which has adjusted to Khrushchevite reformism and in some respects has even surpassed it. However, its "liberalization" has remained limited to internal affairs, always subject to subtle control by the ruling party. In the other of these two countries, Rumania, the trend toward independence of action has gone to unexpected lengths. Rumania has successfully sustained a posture of nonpartisanship in the Sino-Soviet quarrel. It has refused to accept Soviet CEMA plans for a division of labor among the members of that organization and instead has insisted on Rumania's right to develop its economy in accordance with its own needs. It has started negotiations with the West and sent delegations to France, the United States, and elsewhere. But it never has renounced its alliance with the Soviet Union nor has it abandoned Marxism-Leninism. It is still part of the Soviet defense system even though its economic policy has wrought itself almost as free of Soviet control as that of Tito, with whom it concluded a treaty in December, 1963, concerning Danube navigational problems in the Iron Gate area.

Albania, of course, is a different case. It has rejected polycentrism and allied itself with Red China. Having never abandoned Stalinism in its virulent form, it shares the revolutionary fervor of Peking. It is not contiguous to Soviet borders and it is further protected from Soviet retaliation by the climate of the very system it condemns, polycentric communism. It is particularly violent in attacking Yugoslavia's "national communism," that paradoxical concept, but at the root of these outbursts is fear of Belgrade's designs on Albanian territory. Albania belongs in the "splittist" camp.

At this juncture it is necessary to limit the use of the term "polycentrism" to Eastern Europe. While it is true that this term was coined in Italy and that the policies of many parties outside the orbit coincide with the Soviet view on this matter, the only practical examples of a polycentric, communist-ruled region can be found in Eastern Europe. However, the Sino-Soviet conflict has distorted the character of budding polycentrism elsewhere in the communist world, especially in Asia, to the extent that, to use communist terminology, it should be called "splittist."

The diversity of communist interpretations of Marxism-Leninism and the changes of international communist organization after Stalin have resulted in two different constellations. The first, polycentrism, is based upon the concept of "different roads to socialism" without abolishing Moscow's communist primacy or minimizing the Soviet Union's revolutionary experience. Historically it began with Yugoslavia's expulsion from the Cominform and unquestionably received further impetus in the self-made Chinese Communist takeover. It was accelerated by Stalin's death and was finally made official by Khrushchev in 1956.

The second, splittism, is the direct result of the Sino-Soviet conflict, which has led to fractionalism within the communist parties. The extent of this development is rather far-ranging. A number of important parties in Asia, Latin America, Australia, and Europe have split into pro-Soviet and pro-Chinese wings although the pro-Chinese elements have been weakened by irresponsible actions of the Mao regime both in external and internal respects. There is no polycentrism involved in Sino-Soviet relations; there is a schism that almost certainly cannot be bridged while Mao, Lin, and their aged comrades-in-arms remain in power. The Eastern European states, to be sure, are not in this league; even the most independent of them, Rumania, remains bound to Soviet political and military policy. There is no indication of splittism in the East European parties. The reasons are clear enough; we need only look back at history after 1945.

After World War II the governments-in-exile, regarded by the West as the legitimate successors to pre-Hitler authority, were ignored by Stalin or, through internal dissension, became amorphous splinter groups without genuine popular representation. Exile leaders who hopefully sought to join their countries were either deprived of influence or fled. In many cases they were arrested, tried, and condemned; some committed suicide. At the same time, the Soviet-sponsored "national committees" inherited power under Moscow's protection. Since the members of these groups were either communists or sympathizers, there developed a special type of relationship between the allegedly sovereign governments of the Eastern European states and the Kremlin.

When we speak of international relations, we mean the free intercourse between sovereign nations regardless of their ideological positions. Such relations did not exist between Moscow and its new vassals. In fact, under Stalin there were no "relations" at all, merely lines of command from the Soviet Party to the leaders of the East European parties. Orders given by Moscow were obeyed, regardless of national interests. The affairs of state were conducted by *ukaz* from the *vozhd,* and the satraps carried them out. The Soviet-East European bloc functioned more or less as one unit. National sovereignty was a sham. Only after Stalin was buried the second time were the leaders of the satellites in a position to present themselves to their peoples not only as communists but also as Poles, Rumanians, Hungarians, and so forth.

At the outset, the position of the Soviet Union vis-à-vis polycentrization was ambiguous. As mentioned above, Togliatti's outspoken statement on polycentrism, a word he coined, was not received with approval in the Kremlin. But at the Twenty-first CPSU Congress in 1959, Khrushchev went a step beyond his thesis of the Twentieth Congress when he observed that in Lenin's view relations between the national contingents of the international working class should be "built on the basis of equality and independence . . . on the basis of the principles of proletarian internationalism." And in December, 1960, the Statement of the Conference of Representatives of Communist and Workers' Parties proclaimed the coequality of all bloc parties even though they acknowledged the CPSU as the "vanguard of the world communist movement" because of its greater experience in revolutionary developments. Finally, in his speech to the meeting of Higher Party Schools of the Central Committee of the CPSU of January 9, 1961, Khrushchev emphatically orated:

> From the tribune of the Congress, we declared before the whole world that in the communist movement, just as in the socialist camp, there has existed and exists complete equality of rights and solidarity of all communist and workers' parties and socialist countries. The CPSU in reality does not exercise leadership over other parties. All communist parties are equal and independent. . . . The role of the Soviet Union does not lie in the fact that it was the first to blaze the trail to socialism. . . .[6]

And he continued to point out that since there exists a group of socialist countries each of which is faced with its own tasks, and since eighty-one communist and workers' parties are functioning, *"it is not possible for leadership over socialist countries and communist parties to be exercised from any center at all."*[7] This indeed was a strong commitment and one which could not have sat well with Mao. It created a dilemma, for, while the Chinese Communists theoretically wished to maintain Moscow as a world communist center as late as 1960,[8] the very center which they regarded as the logical one abdicated, in their view, its responsibilities and seemingly wanted no more than to be just a little more equal than the other members of the socialist camp. Yet while Moscow chose to surrender its traditional prerogatives, Peking was not permitted to inherit the "vanguard" position and Mao was not recognized as the senior communist leader, which he almost certainly believed himself to be after Stalin's death.

Instead, the Soviet side of international communism has sacrificed—or was forced to sacrifice—uniformity for greater national party individualism within the "socialist camp." It did not discard but merely modified some basic principles of Marxism-Leninism. These modifications are really attempts at modernization and adjustment to new conditions. Polycentrism permits greater freedom of parties to adjust to the specific conditions in their respective countries. Implicitly it thereby has enhanced the principles of sovereignty. It has defied the commandments inherent in the twenty-one conditions for admission to the Comintern and thereby abandoned centralized control—alien control in fact —in favor of "national," albeit communist, rule. Such a development appears to contradict the Marxist-Leninist concept of internationalism which is a *conditio sine qua non*, both ideologically and organizationally, for worldwide communist prevalence. Yet one is reminded of Khrushchev's pronunciamento in Leipzig in March, 1959, in which he proclaimed that national frontiers eventually will have to be abolished.

Recent events suggest that this insistence upon the freedom of parties to determine their own "road to socialism" is more likely to impede than to facilitate international communist unity of purpose. It is therefore condemned by the Chinese leaders, who do not believe in Khrushchevian voluntarism. In the West it has been likened to old-fashioned nationalism, and many observers seem to regard the struggle within the communist world in terms of national power contests and national interests. While these elements undoubtedly are present, they are not, in this writer's opinion, the chief rationale of either polycentrism or splittism. Too rarely is it pointed out that the states of the "socialist camp" are still Marxist-Leninist in form and content and that, although they have remained nation-states, they are ruled by communist parties. It is submitted that nationalism in the Western sense is quite different from nationalism under a "socialist" (communist party) regime insofar as both external and internal goals are concerned. It is not, as elsewhere, a creed but a manipulating instrument which can be used successfully for psychological warfare purposes at home and abroad. From the communist point of view it is a temporary phenomenon, eventually doomed to extinction. This is what Khrushchev implied in his Leipzig speech.

It might be countered that such reasoning is no longer permissible in post-Stalinist developments when ideology seems to be declining as a secular faith; that economic and ethnic interests are behind the Eastern European drive for more independence; that decisions no longer are made on the basis of doctrinal considerations; and that the "intelligentsia" of these Soviet vassals are promoting, with some success, more liberal policies under the auspices of greater national sovereignty. Again, the presence of such non-ideological factors cannot be denied, but one must see them in proper proportion. The party governments in the

Eastern European states are still communist and as such are acting according to certain principles which are affected by doctrine—directly or indirectly, consciously or subconsciously. The silver cord between them and Moscow may have been cut, but they are still Moscow's children.

In other words: when we deal with the former satellites, we dare not forget that basically they remain under Soviet souzerainty and therefore semidependent areas. Polycentrism in Eastern Europe is not a solution of its problems but, rather, an alleviating factor which may in time, and with good luck, lead to greater freedom of movement. Nevertheless, in the foreseeable future there is little hope for freeing this Soviet security zone from political and military vassalage. The geopolitical position of the Eastern European states appears to rule out a change from polycentrism to splittism. For all its post-Stalinist modification of the "gospel," polycentric parties generally adhere to Moscow's more relaxed doctrinal stance, accepting a concept of organization without organization, but remaining components of the Soviet bloc. Splittism, on the other hand, wants a return to Comintern principles, regards polycentrism as a deviation from the correct course of revolution, and insists on the re-establishment of *one* world center, presumably in Peking.

III

The interpretation of a faith gives it its *Gestalt* and affects its content, liturgy, and ritual. If this observation can be applied to the secular faith of Marxism-Leninism, may we then conclude that the variety of interpretation in a polycentric system seriously affects its *basic* beliefs? Not necessarily. The proliferation of Christian sects has not led to an end of Christianity. Similarly, it would be a mistake to conclude that differences between interpretations of the original communist gospel must automatically lead to a disintegration of communism. There have been changes, especially in matters of organization. But to reason that post-Stalinist communism is at death's door is simply to postulate that any type of communism that is not Stalinist just is not communism.

For example, there is wishful thinking that the introduction of a consumer-directed economy in the Soviet Union is "capitalistic" or that Rumania's economic policies indicate the beginning of the end of its communist party rule. However, under such rule nationalism, or what is often called "the nationalist interest," is at variance with the Western concept of these terms. In the realm of international relations, the traditions of diplomatic practice have changed. International law, that elusive and as yet unenforceable ideal of men of good will, takes on a whole new interpretation under the law of socialism and that of bourgeois class states. Marxism-Leninism has greatly affected the character and thought processes of the "socialist" states; they speak conceptually different languages even if their intellectuals want to know more about the West, and their economists try to take advantage of techniques that have contributed to the West's greater prosperity.

If we expected communism to become genuinely international during a historically very brief period, we surely expected too much. Ideas of world government have been discussed by Western idealists for centuries, and although it is possible to recognize some infinitesimal progress toward that goal, perhaps under pressure of totalitarian onslaught, we still are very far from this ideal. Compulsion by communist governments toward universal socialist brotherhood has accelerated progress toward that aim somewhat more than the lackadaisical movement in the West, but once the Stalinist terror ended, the speed toward internationalism—not to mention the classless society—slowed down. In this sense polycentrism is an indication of regression just as, in the West, the nationalism advocated by General de Gaulle is a throwback toward a political climate that has done endless harm to Europe and the world. Communist and non-communist internationalisms have vastly different goals, but their failures appear to indicate that humanity cannot be forced to break out of established patterns without long and well-planned preparation. Even then the going will be heavy, and it remains to be seen to what extent, if any, human nature can be changed. The chances for such changes should not be shrugged off; in the fifties we saw how Chinese brainwashing affected its victims. We do not know how long its effects will last. Perhaps there remains an innate sanity which has merely been covered by the debris of ideological holocaust and in the end can be cleaned of its rubble.

Such cataclysmic developments, good or evil, our contemporaries most likely will not live to observe. In the meantime, what may be the alternatives to polycentric or splittist communism? Most of all, within the framework of this essay, how will the Eastern European states be affected by communist retrogression, stagnation, acceleration, or mutation? Any answer to such questions is clearly speculative, but nowadays even scholars must consider alternatives, no matter to what school of thought they belong.

IV

It is conceivable that world communism may officially split into two main branches, one led by Moscow, the other by Peking. Should this happen, each branch probably would seek a tighter organization, resulting in unitary leadership centralized in Moscow and Peking. Each would focus its rivalry on the underdeveloped areas in Africa, Asia, and Latin America and would compete for leadership over as many other regions as possible so as to strengthen its position not only vis-à-vis the opposing communist branch but also the West. Rivalry might even degenerate into local hostilities along thousands of miles of Sino-Soviet border areas.

Such a split between the old and new communist "Romes" might end polycentrism, thus confronting the non-communist world with two tightly knit socialist camps that would be more unitary than the amorphous world movement of the sixties but whose existence would pose a threat to peace. Either Moscow or Peking might strive too hard to show its rival how "imperialism" can be best conquered. It is possible that a split of world communism into two centers would lead to the withdrawal from the United Nations of the countries affiliated with the Peking-led branch. A communist "United Nations" might then be organized by Peking to compete with the existing international organization.

Such a schism, if it remained unbridged, would sharply polarize the communist world and eventually become as established as the schism between Rome and Byzantium. But it must be pointed out that at least Moscow and perhaps not even Peking seems anxious to go that far. If the wait-and-see game continues, the demise of Mao, Lin, and their few remaining comrades-in-arms of the Long March could initiate a more conciliatory attitude toward Moscow—a possibility that allegedly worries Mao. It therefore is suggested that the official establishment of two "Romes" is at best possible, not probable. Even if such a formal split were to take place, presumably during Mao's lifetime, it is questionable whether it would continue after Mao. In communist affairs nothing is certain, everything remains in flux, rendering crystal ball gazing even more hazardous than usual. Those who claim that the Sino-Soviet conflict is "irreversible" are assuming an inflexible attitude which might well confound them in the future. A major *rapprochement* between Moscow and Peking, while scarcely probable at this writing, could occur ten or twenty years hence, if not earlier. It need not but could happen. If it did, one might conjecture that splittism would disappear and polycentrism be extended over the entire communist orbit.

It seems more likely that no official split into two communist branches will occur but that the present messy situation will continue throughout the lifetime of Mao, Lin, *et al.* This means that Soviet-Eastern European polycentrism will continue to develop while Peking pursues its splitting tactics against communist parties throughout the world. To the extent that Peking succeeds, Soviet influence will suffer, except within its Eastern European sphere of influence where party splittism is highly unlikely. The primary bones of contention between Moscow and Peking—Moscow's policy of "peaceful coexistence" vis-à-vis the "imperialists" and the rivalry for the mantle of world communist leadership—would continue to be predominant in the "third world."

Whether, in the course of this struggle, the Eastern European countries could gain further advantages from the Kremlin and manage to make themselves more independent of Soviet foreign policy depends not only upon the Soviet attitude in the conflict but also on these countries themselves. One may assume that their "ruling circles" are not altogether averse to the continuation of the intracommunist conflict since it strengthens their own positions. For the Kremlin has its hands full with problems directly and indirectly pertaining to Red China; the introduction of a neo-Stalinist policy towards Eastern Europe is unlikely; and Moscow is intent on maintaining the loyalty of these states even if it has to pay a price in political and economic currency. But there is a limit to Soviet concessions, and it would be a dangerous error to count on a deterioration of polycentrism into splittism. One might add that the Eastern European parties almost certainly would like to see a definite split into two camps avoided; on the other hand, they are not necessarily sad that Moscow and Peking so far have failed to reach a workable agreement.

A more optimistic contingency, namely, a mellowing of China and the establishment of a less aggressive stance by the communist orbit—possibly connected with a general deterioration of the communist world movement into revisionist reformism—seems unlikely at present. It could occur in a decade or two, provided Mao's policies are radically altered and reasonable solutions of the political, social, and economic problems of the "third world" have been found. This sounds like a vision of a better world which we ardently desire but whose accomplishment we gravely doubt. Certainly, it would be foolhardy to build a policy on the illusion that there could be, in the near future, a restoration of full independence of the Eastern European states, possibly within a framework of regional treaties.

Likewise, the opposite alternative, an outbreak of hostilities between the U.S.S.R. and Red China, can hardly be expected. Too much would be at stake for the communist world and, after all, Marxism-Leninism still is prevalent in both Moscow and Peking, however much its interpretation may differ. Such a war would undoubtedly mean the end of world communism, which, without the strong pillars of its red giants, would founder and become an insignificant element in the political life of nations.

To sum up: The alternatives of the development of polycentric and splittist communism are manifold; those mentioned above are subject to many variations. It would appear that for the time being the former satellites, despite their recent gains in economic self-determination and intellectual development, cannot be regarded as free agents in international affairs but must be considered as part of the Soviet bloc's polycentric socialist camp.

NOTES

1. Leo Gruliow (ed.), *Current Soviet Policies: The Documentary Record of the 19th Communist Party Congress* (New York, 1952), pp. 105–106. (Translated from *Pravda*, October 6, 1952.)

2. *For a Lasting Peace, for a People's Democracy*, No. 1 (November 10, 1947).

3. *Nuovi Argumenti* (Rome), June, 1956.

4. The Cominform was never thought to replace the Comintern and remained a relatively unimportant rump organization of agitprop character.

5. See Kasimierz Grzybowski, *The Socialist Commonwealth of Nations* (New York, 1964), *passim*. See also the author's "The Socialist Commonwealth of Nations," *Orbis*, Winter, 1960.

6. *Pravda*, January 10, 1961. Red China's coequality was acknowledged by Molotov as early as 1955.

7. *Ibid.* (Italics added.)

8. Statement of the eighty-one communist parties, November/December, 1960, Moscow, which was signed by the Chinese delegation.

National Patterns: Three Case Studies

Chapter II.

3. Crisis and Revolt in a Satellite: The East German Case in Retrospect

Wolfgang H. Kraus

Students of the Soviet orbit in Eastern and Central Europe have in the past decade become familiar with the main features of the East German uprising of June 16–17, 1953. A significant body of literature has explored these events in the setting of Ulbricht's "German Democratic Republic," the G.D.R.,[1] and to some extent in the wider framework of the Soviet bloc as a whole. Certain aspects of the revolt, however, notably as it related to the internal affairs of the Socialist Unity Party (SED), have become more clearly understood in recent years.[2] A brief reappraisal may, therefore, be useful.

Certain special characteristics of the G.D.R. distinguish it from its sister "people's democracies" in Eastern and Central Europe. Its very inception was linked with Soviet military conquest and occupation, which eventually resulted in the establishment of a rump state, a political order based on perpetuation of the division of the traditional German system. The steady deepening of the division in a political, socio-economic, and cultural sense, culminating in the erection of the Wall in August, 1961, could not quite erase what has been described as the "geographical and psychological vulnerability of the G.D.R. vis-à-vis West Germany." Even the walling-off "cannot prevent some interflow of ideas: East Germany is forced to keep up the pretense of competing with West German intellectual life."[3] The same applied to the political and economic life of the G.D.R., which in all spheres has felt the tug and pull among segments of a divided nation in an age of nationalism. This condition has been enhanced and continuously sensitized by the division of Berlin, which acts as symbol, thorn, and prod.

At the same time, the people of the G.D.R. belong to the most Western-oriented and certainly one of the most advanced societies within the Soviet orbit. They also have one of the oldest continuous Marxian traditions linked with the deeply rooted labor movements of the German Socialist Party (SPD) and its offshoot, the German Communist Party (KPD). Even the years of Nazi rule had not been able to eradicate this tradition or to liquidate all of its partisans. With the collapse of the Third Reich and the early resumption of political activity, this dormant heritage had reasserted itself, notably in the great industrial and urban areas. How sound a foundation was this going to be for the building of a revolutionary system by a new communist elite? No other satellite society had just emerged in 1945 from a twelve-year experience with a totalitarian rule bent on permeating and harnessing every phase of its life under the cover of Nazi demonology. What lasting effects this experience would have on the mass of the people no one could foretell. Had it magnified the habits of conformity and discipline, which we have come to associate with modern urbanized and industrial ways (and which, according to one school of thought, are sustained by certain German national traits in particular)? Or had the degrading experience of totalitarian coercion tended to develop, on the contrary, a capacity for reactive self-assertion and resistance on the part of individuals and groups? Clearly, alternatives like these are too sweeping. They merely suggest certain complex attitude problems in whose exploration, until quite recently, students of communist affairs professed to take no interest.

In its population, the G.D.R. exhibits the imbalances and dislocations caused by the war and its aftermath. The ratio of men and women among its 18.5 million people was 100 men to 135 women in 1946, 100 to 125 in 1950 (although still 100 to 135 in Berlin). According to the 1964 census, it is still 100 to 119 in a population now approximately 1.5 million smaller than in 1946.[4] The striking over-all decline and the distribution of age groups still show the massive effects of the large-scale flight from the G.D.R. to the West involving 930,000 people between 1945 and 1951, another 182,000 in 1952, and over 330,000 in 1953, with conspicuous increases—ranging from 17,000 to 40,000—in each of the crisis months from November, 1952, to June, 1953. In the early months of 1953 it was determined that workers with their dependents constituted more than half of the defectors entering West Berlin, with government employees and clerks less than half their number (23 per cent) and farmers next (14 per cent). Approximately half of the total, both in 1952 and in 1953, were young people under twenty-five (52 per cent and 49 per cent).[5]

With its initial population imbalances, compounded by the massive drain of economically and socially valuable individuals, East German society appeared in the early 1950's to exhibit symptoms of pressure and malaise to which its rulers might well have attached more than economic importance.[6]

STALINIZATION AND ALIENATION

From the very beginning of the Soviet occupation of the eastern zone of Germany, a group of Russian-trained German communist leaders, headed by Walter Ulbricht, had been engaged in laying the groundwork for a revolutionary order. In a mood of political expansiveness, Ulbricht in 1960 reminisced before a group of associates about their early days, laying much stress on his efforts to obtain the co-operation of non-communists and his restraining influence upon certain impatient German comrades. He conveniently failed to mention his prompt elimination of early antifascist groups in Berlin (Antifa), which had sprung up prior to his arrival, and his cynical instruction to his associates that democratic appearances should be maintained only as long as control rested securely in their hands.[7]

With the forced fusion of the SPD and KPD to form the communist-dominated SED, the harnessing of the other parties into a national front, the formal establishment of the G.D.R. (1949), and the development of an increasingly centralized system of government and administration, the stage was set for accelerated revolutionary changes. The transition to a "people's democratic order" was proclaimed in July, 1952, at the Second Party Conference, apparently held in lieu of the regular party congress which, according to the party statute, should have met that year but did not convene until 1954.

It is unnecessary to review the events of the following months. The steady and unrelenting pressures through which the regime advanced its program of collectivization in agriculture, moved progressively to liquidate private business and industry, and sought to increase the productivity of labor did not attain the massive results projected. The measures taken by the regime succeeded in alienating increasingly large segments of all major social groups, turning them into what Hanna Arendt has called "objective enemies." The simultaneous efforts to mobilize and harness youth and to draw it into police and paramilitary organizations, the intensified disciplining of churches, education, and arts and letters left no doubt about Ulbricht's determination to measure up to the Stalinist model and to keep in step with the revolutionary movement throughout Eastern Europe.[8]

It was during this period that we witnessed the mounting flow of defectors "voting with their feet"—the most remarkable index of the pressure building up in East German society. Nor were signs lacking of significant divisions of opinion in the party elite itself. As early as January, 1952, Rudolf Herrnstadt, an old Soviet hand and since 1949 the editor in chief of *Neues Deutschland*, had published an editorial in the official party paper declaring that the "masses . . . rate each measure here with the anxiety of those beset with doubt, with the bias of the duped and with the longing of the needy. And what do they see? Does the GDR reality match the democratic character of our laws? Does the life of the party match the democratic character of its statute? . . . We are guilty, the party organization is, from the bottom to the top. And the higher up, the more so!"[9] The Prague Slansky trial, whose importance was stressed and exploited in a resolution of the SED Central Committee late in 1952, served as a signal for purges. While Stalin's death in March, 1953, was to avert or delay much of the house-cleaning program in progress, it did not bring about an immediate change in the policies the purges were designed to buttress.

Some years later, addressing his students at the Humboldt University in East Berlin, the physicist and dissident communist Robert Havemann referred in these terms to the dangers involved in "building socialism":

> The revolutionaries of this period [of revolutionary change], the political leadership, must strive to reach the goals as speedily as possible. . . . The leaders . . . are in a difficult situation. The faster they seek to approach the goal the less can they give the people, the more resistance will grow against their policies and the greater the difficulties. It is a kind of vicious circle. Slowing down the development, accumulating less and consuming more will provide greater satisfactions for

the people. As the development is accelerated, their dissatisfaction will grow. To overcome this and permit speedier growth, everything most be done to fill the masses with enthusiasm. We must try to convince them. It is no easy struggle to make people believe in socialism without promptly satisfying their wants. . . .

The fact that accumulation is only possible at the personal sacrifice of millions readily leads to the result that any person who out of personal convictions is insufficiently cooperative is regarded as an enemy of progress. Thus hostility arises against everyone who doubts and raises objections. . . . Whoever does not passionately participate . . . finally becomes suspected of serving a hostile ideology or being an agent of Western capitalism. Such things are, of course, alien to the true nature of socialism. . . . If, beyond all this, a man like Stalin reaches the top, becomes a dictator and thinks himself all-wise and omniscient . . . , his words being constantly proclaimed as gospel, a many-runged hierarchy emerges, with a large bureaucracy exerting a seemless control over each individual, and the rise of careerists and hypocrites becomes inescapable. . . . What is missing and belongs to socialism as an essential condition . . . is democracy. You cannot build socialism without democracy.[10]

Clearly, the general conditions underlying the June revolt were essentially the same as the conditions that were to provide the momentum for the Hungarian and Polish October events of 1956.

THE INGREDIENTS OF REVOLT

A succession of particular factors was to turn the East German situation into a "critical mass." Singly, each ingredient had its counterpart in other satellite societies; in combination they formed a pattern reflecting the G.D.R.'s special situation.

It was both characteristic and ironic that the first ingredient was the result of the relentless drive to increase industrial production. The workers, in whose behalf the SED professed to rule the state and advance the revolution, were continuously prodded to raise their productivity. Unquestionably, shortages of iron and steel, the result of the German partition, together with the large outflow of reparations to the U.S.S.R. in the early postwar period and the loss of important food-producing areas to Poland, had combined to impose severe handicaps on Ulbricht's planners.

Given the nature of the system, it was perhaps inevitable that the growing concern on the part of the leadership over the gap between planning targets and production led to an increasingly harsh and coercive approach. While so-called technically based work norms, adopted in keeping with Soviet doctrine, had been part of collective bargaining procedures prior to 1953, they were increasingly imposed from above by administrative fiat, even though the leadership preferred to acclaim a fictitious voluntary adoption policy. Since the norms characteristically were set on the basis of higher-than-average performance, the workers were in many situations compelled to work much harder in order to maintain their wage level. Without support from their own union organization—the FDGB, itself an instrument of public policy and thus a participant in the productivity drive—and loath to jeopardize their modest living standard, the rank and file found themselves in a squeeze.[11]

Everything points to the fact that this problem, which was widely and bitterly discussed, had become a major cause of growing bitterness and irritation during the spring of 1953. There had already been incidents in industry in various towns in the fall of 1952, as reported by Herrnstadt at the Central Committee's plenary meeting in November, 1952. Other incidents, strike activities, were noted during April and May in Jena, Halle, Eisleben, and East Berlin.

The leadership seemed determined to ignore these danger signals and to persist in its economic policy without the benefit of genuine discussion or consent. This determination was clearly exhibited in an article on cadre policy by Central Committee Secretariat member Hermann Axen published in *Neues Deutschland* on April 30, 1953. Castigating the inadequacies of the party cadres, Axen informed the "new intelligentsia" that it had to be conscious of living in a condition of intensified class struggle. He urged the cadres, young and old, to study the writings of Stalin and Lenin (in that order) for a grasp of German history. Above all, he admonished functionaries to look to the lessons of the purge trials of the traitors Rajk, Kostov, and Slansky for guidance on cadre policy and on establishing appropriate criteria for gauging reliability and selecting cadres. The article contained a particular sideswipe at the unreliability of party members who had been associated with the *émigré* KPD leadership in Paris before the war: This was clearly aimed at Axen's predecessor as SED cadre chief, Franz Dahlem, one of the more eminent critics of Ulbricht's policy in the party elite whom the Central Committee had just dropped from its ranks.[12]

Some two weeks later, a plenary meeting of the SED Central Committee adopted a resolution asking the government to raise work norms at least 10 per cent—a request which, to no one's surprise, the Council of Ministers acknowledged by issuing an order on May 28 for a 10 per cent norm increase to go into effect on June 1. It was a move whose very consistency with the regime's previous course was a measure of its remarkable combination of insensitivity to the workingman's mood and disdain for the serious misgivings expressed by party elements closer and more sympathetic to the problems of the masses.

At approximately this point, a second factor entered the situation which the SED leadership, more especially Ulbricht, had tried in vain to avert. On June 11 it was announced that the SED Politburo had—on June 9—proclaimed the policy of the New Course for the G.D.R. This made East Germany the first among the satellites to adopt the policy departure directed by Moscow. Embarcation on the New Course, coupled as it was with public self-criticism, appeared to constitute a staggering turnabout. It could not help but dismay and bewilder the party echelons and functionaries, while it seemed to hold much promise of relief for those social groups which had been hardest hit until then. The party declaration avowed that "the SED and the Government of the GDR had made a number of mistakes in the past, and these had led to the adoption of certain rules and measures . . . that impaired the interests of . . . the independent farmer, the retailer, the artisan, and the intelligentsia." It promised measures "to remedy these mistakes and to improve the living standards of workers, farmers, the intelligentsia, artisans, and other middle class groups." It even intimated that these mistakes had contributed to the seriousness of the mass flight from the G.D.R.

Within days a number of measures were taken by the Council of Ministers, including the restoration of ration cards to a large segment of the middle class that had recently been deprived of them, a lowering of certain consumer prices, and a number of moves to alleviate the situation of small business, private industry, and farmers. Steps were taken to improve relations with the churches and to remedy certain hardships in social security. There was no mention, however, of the matter of the norms increase. While a policy of moderation and concession was holding out the promise of benefits to a large number of social groups, the most important one of all in the "worker's democracy" found that a vital concern over a policy issue affecting virtually all workers was ignored. Worse than that: On the very day of the New Course announcement, *Neues Deutschland* carried a lead article which, by claiming the workers' enthusiastic support for the norm increases, manifested an almost paranoid disregard for the realities of the situation. On the other hand, the official Soviet paper in Berlin presented to its readers on June 13 an article which suggested that the Soviet authorities were not altogether satisfied with the measures that had been taken.[13]

The ambiguity of the situation was underlined on June 14 by an article in *Neues Deutschland* which severely criticized prevailing practices. It gave an account of harrassment and high-pressure methods used by party officials seeking to impose a change of work norms in the building construction field. The writers urged the party functionaries to abandon their disruptive "blackmailing" methods and see to it that "the decisions of government and party not be carried out in a dictatorial and bureaucratic manner." They urged officials to stop misrepresenting the facts and concern themselves instead "with the human beings in the production process who must above all be won over for the attainment of our political goals: the construction workers and engineers."[14]

Whatever encouragement workers might have derived from this statement by two writers in the official party paper, it was impossible for the ordinary reader to guess whether a change of policy in this area was still under consideration or whether there was possibly a division of opinion over the matter in the party leadership.

This brings us to a third ingredient in the evolving situation. Within the inner circles of the SED leadership, far removed from the prying eyes of the middle or lower echelons, let alone of the non-party masses, a complex struggle over power and policy had in fact been brewing. It involved the relationship between the Kremlin and the SED leadership on the one hand and, on the other, relations within the SED political elite itself. With the death of Stalin on March 5 of that year and the ascendancy of Malenkov and his associates, certain policy changes were in the making, not only within the U.S.S.R. itself, but also with respect to the dependent systems in the orbit. The conception of the New Course, with its shift of emphasis from production goods to consumer goods, was clearly expected to strengthen Malenkov's position vis-à-vis his rivals for the succession at home while enhancing a sense of "decompression" among the peoples in the bloc.

At least since the beginning of the year, the SED leadership had with good reason become deeply disturbed about economic conditions in the G.D.R. An urgent request for help had apparently been presented to Moscow in early April and turned down by mid-April. On this occasion Ulbricht was probably first directed to abandon his hard line in favor of the New Course.[15] Ulbricht manifestly failed to comply. Clearly he was not sufficiently impressed with Malenkov's authority to show him the deference he had always displayed to the old dictator.

Instead, in open defiance of Moscow's directive, Ulbricht proceeded to intensify his tough course by decreeing the 10 per cent norms increase, which he evidently regarded as an economic bootstrap operation. There appears to have been another unsuccessful effort to get Ulbricht to comply. Finally, the pressure from Moscow became irrestible with the arrival on June 5 of Vladimir Semyonov, who had been appointed to the new post of Soviet High Commissioner. Semyonov immediately presented Ulbricht with a memorandum on the New Course policy which was to be adopted forthwith by the SED Politburo. Ulbricht was further humiliated when Semyonov lectured him on the absurdity of a projected birthday celebration promoted by a body called, transparently enough, Commission for the Preparation of Comrade W. Ulbricht's Sixtieth Birthday. Taken together, these were symptoms that Ulbricht's star was on the wane and that the dramatic change in policy, which entailed severe self-criticism for past action and inaction, might well jeopardize his own position.

Yet, even while yielding to the inevitable, Ulbricht managed to fight a rear guard action. First there was delay in the publication of the New Course policy statement. When it was published there was a conspicuous lack of any explanatory comment by government or party, which was sorely needed in view of what was generally understood to be a dramatic reversal of policy. Ulbricht himself, whose name was missing from the announcement, was not to express himself publicly on the new policy changes until June 16.[16]

Becoming at this stage increasingly apprehensive about the widening gap between party and workers, Ulbricht was clearly determined not to risk a meeting of the Central Committee, which was certain to bring up the norms problem under pressure from the cadres below. It has been suggested[17] that he succeeded in getting Semyonov's consent to a postponement and to the maintenance of the work norms policy, since the state of productivity was demonstrably too far below expectations.

The new Moscow leaders' marked concern for the SED's launching on the New Course was strongly affected, we may assume, by their preoccupation with the reduction of tensions with the West. In this framework Malenkov and Beria appear to have had far-reaching plans for a new approach to the problem of German reunification. There are indications that, at one point, they may have given serious consideration to sacrificing the G.D.R. A statement has been ascribed to the chief Polish U.N. delegate, Katz-Suchy, to the effect that Beria had been ready to "write off" the G.D.R. After the Twenty-second Congress of the CPSU had put its seal of approval on Malenkov's political interment, the SED Central Committee at its fourteenth plenum (1961) condemned "the policy of capitulation to imperialism and the surrender of socialism in the GDR represented by Beria and Malenkov with the Zaisser-Herrnstadt faction." Khrushchev himself was to declare in a speech in March, 1963, that Beria and Malenkov had urged the SED "to liquidate the GDR as a socialist state . . . and to repudiate the goal of building socialism."[18] Whether these were merely tactical moves or tied in with broader policy goals, their effective preparation clearly required a broader popular basis and a generally more acceptable political image for the Eastern German dominion.

These interlocking considerations provided the basis for a relationship (whose character and extent are indeterminate) between the new leadership in Moscow and two men who had emerged during this period as leaders of an anti-Ulbricht faction in the SED elite. They were Wilhelm Zaisser, the "General Gomez" of the Spanish Civil War, now Minister of State Security and member of the Politburo, and Rudolf Herrnstadt, chief editor of *Neues Deutschland* and a candidate member of the Politburo. Both men had long and intimate Soviet connections which reached back to the 1920's. Both men, supported by certain influential functionaries, and acting under the guidance or at least with the active approval of Beria (in a sense Zaisser's superior), had early aligned themselves with the advocates of the New Course. Reports indicate that in order to advance the cause of reunification, they roundly condemned the degeneration of the party and demanded that it undergo a drastic renewal in order to become a genuine people's party which would merit the support of the workers and of other classes and sectors. In addition to a variety of reforms in the party and state, it was apparently also proposed to make the trade unions once more genuinely representative of the workers' interests. All this would require a drastic clean-up of the SED leadership and apparatus. Herrnstadt was to take Ulbricht's place, while Zaisser was to serve as Minister of the Interior. Several more members of the Politburo were to be ousted at the same time. By a fluke (Franz Dahlem's "blunder," according to Ulbricht), sufficient information about the project was leaked to Ulbricht, who insisted on a showdown before the Politburo itself. This meeting was scheduled for June 16.

The fourth element in the pattern that formed the backdrop for the uprising was the involvement of people at large, especially of industrial labor, which was to culminate in a dramatic mass strike movement. Ironically enough, about ten months prior to the June days the official SED newspaper, *Neues Deutschland,* had carried an enthusiastic article entitled "The

Political Mass Strike in the National Struggle." The writer, R. Gossweiler, described it "as one of the most decisive weapons of any nation which fights for its liberation from national oppression." He went on to explain that in the mass strike the proletariat "displays its creative abilities, the masses discover and seize new means and methods to make their battle more effective and successful. Political mass strikes also challenge the non-proletarian groups, sweep them into the struggle, and help them to recognize the workers as the true leaders." He then proceeded to cite Lenin's observations about the role of mass strikes in arousing the Russian peasantry in 1905. He even commented on Rosa Luxemburg's essay, "Mass Strike, Party and Unions," countering her belief in the spontaneity of mass strikes with the contention that there never had been a case of workers staging a mass strike without careful propagandistic groundwork by the party. "History also proves," the writer warned, "that a working class which is not prepared to answer attacks on its achievements by a mass strike condemns itself to defeat."[19] That these challenging words were not meant for the workers of the G.D.R. goes without saying—they were directed rather at West German labor, which was urged to rise en masse against the iniquities of Adenauer's foreign policy. Less than a year later this writer's dogmatic rejection of spontaneity (a demonstration of his faithful Leninism) was to be shown up as a fallacy.

It was true, of course, that the strikers had grievously erred. Not only had they taken the G.D.R.'s constitutional right to strike at face value; they had also failed to understand that they were really striking against themselves since their government represented their interests and the means of production were, after all, their own.[20]

THE CLIMAX

We can dispense with a descriptive account of the mass action itself. But it is instructive to point up the main stages of a complex and confusing process whose visible climax was compressed into the span of two days. The *incubation* stage coincides with the impact of the work norms policy which, as we have seen, engendered a growing sense of irritation and frustration among the workers in the spring of 1953. This situation was sharply aggravated by the publication of the May 28 government direc-tive concerning a 10 per cent norms raise. The *crisis* stage was reached with the startling unveiling of the New Course policy, which, instead of extending its concessions to the work force in this crucial matter, was at best noncommittal. On the other hand, Berlin workers could derive a certain amount of encouragement from the *Neues Deutschland* article mentioned earlier, with its sharp attack on the official methods of tough and abusive enforce-ment. It was at this stage, on June 15, that some construction workers at the Friedrichshain building site in East Berlin angrily stopped work because of the norms situation, as did their col-leagues on a Stalin Allee building site (Block 40). The Stalin Allee workers decided to draw up a resolution on grievances, among which the work norms issue ranked high.

The next phase, which might be called the *action release* stage, was set off by the bungling activities of lower echelon officials who, in an uncertain and ambiguous situation, were taking it upon themselves to tell the workers what was really expected of them. Not unnaturally, being accustomed to the zealous imple-mentation of the regime's tough policies, they saw no reason to deviate from the established routine since no one had so far instructed them otherwise. The official organ of the FDGB, *Tribüne*, carried on June 16 an article by a union functionary which informed anyone still in doubt about the work norms declaration in the light of the New Course that the 10 per cent increase was indeed going into effect on June 30 (retroactive to June 1!) and that the work norms policy was still quite sound and correct. This statement became immediately known to the building workers of Block 40. It was reconfirmed by a union representative who, early in the morning of June 16, made an appearance at the building site and fully associated himself with the *Tribüne* article.[21]

These declarations, coming, as it were, from the workers' own officials, acted as a fuse to set in motion the following events. A group of the workers from Stalin Allee, numbering about 80, proceeded to march toward the government center, carrying signs demanding the reduction of norms; eventually their number reached 10,000. Their efforts to obtain access to Ulbricht or Grotewohl at the House of Ministries were unsuccessful. The demonstrators refused to believe that the great men were really unavailable. As we now know, they were elsewhere, engaged in a crucial meeting of the Politburo.

What appeared to the demonstrators as a scornful and contemptuous refusal by the responsible leadership to grant them a hearing was to usher in the next stage of popular action—the transformation of an increasingly sizable social protest movement, with essentially economic and certainly limited objectives, into a *political mass rising* which was to culminate in the countrywide general strike action of June 17.

The shift of mood and direction became increasingly manifest as the demonstrators, mostly workers, changed the character of their slogans and listened to speakers from their midst talking about freedom of a people rising up, demanding free elections, and threatening a general strike unless the leaders made some response. In the absence of such a response from any of the principals, with Ulbricht, Grotewohl, and other ranking leaders ranged in battle over the leadership and far removed from the clamor, the strike call was issued later that afternoon. Not only was it issued by word of mouth in a city which was meanwhile getting more and more carried away by the exhilaration of vigorous, unfettered, and dramatic action, but other channels were also put to use. A delegation had made its way to West Berlin and presented a resolution to RIAS, the American radio station. The resolution called for a strike the next day unless the G.D.R. government adjusted current wages on the basis of the older norms, immediately lowered the cost of living, called free elections with secret balloting, and refrained from punitive action against the strikers. These challenging and far-reaching demands were on the air after 8 P.M.

That afternoon, through the persistence of some party functionaries close to the events, Ulbricht had been made to acknowledge the need for some top-level pronouncement. This had resulted in a Politburo declaration rescinding the norms increase and promising to review the problem with union representatives. It was too little and too late to have any impact. Even after this it appears that at least some participants in the Politburo meeting had not really fully grasped the gravity of the situation. When the regime's planning chief Bruno Leuschner returned to his office that afternoon, he was wholly preoccupied with the immediate convening of a countrywide planning conference which

would bring together the highest political and industrial echelons, presumably for the rapid implementation of the New
Course. This was carried out despite the fact that leading functionaries all over the country, when reached on the telephone by
evening, were quite aware of the crisis and expressed their dismay in no uncertain terms: "You people up there must be completely crazy to call us to Berlin when we are most urgently
needed here. Don't you have any idea how things look here? I
want to say emphatically that I decline any responsibility should
things go wrong, in my absence, which I cannot predict but
fear."[22]

Throughout the evening and night the calls for concerted
popular action went out by word of mouth, by telephone, and,
last but not least, with the aid of continuous news broadcasts by
RIAS.[23] The resulting large-scale strikes, mass marches and demonstrations, which were to culminate in Berlin during the
morning hours of June 17, were actually to affect the entire
country, especially the urban and industrial centers. In the
Halle, Leipzig, and Magdeburg areas alone, 270,000 workers
from 110 industrial enterprises went on strike. An "uprising of
the population" was claimed for 6 district seats, 22 county seats,
and 44 other towns and villages, while a far larger number of
localities experienced "demonstrations."[24]

On June 17 the political character of the movement had become abundantly clear to all observers. Marchers and strikers,
despite their initially good discipline, began in numerous instances to resort to direct action which clearly expressed widespread hostility to the regime. Its targets were often symbolic
institutions[25]—jails from which prisoners would be released,
police quarters, party buildings, and the House of Ministries
itself. There was some incendiarism and physical attack on police
and other functionaries, which accounted for some of the casualties on both sides in this relatively bloodless upheaval.

While there were loud denunciations of Ulbricht, Pieck, and
Grotewohl and demands for free elections and reunification,
there was, throughout, a notable reluctance to express hostility
directly against the Soviet power, which, for its part, seemed
disposed to maintain a careful hands-off policy.

Members of the People's Police, the principal protective
agency of the regime, clearly showed by their behavior that they

were in something of a quandary in this unprecedented situation. In the words of one observer, they had "for years been indoctrinated with the proposition that they were called People's Police because they were, unlike former defenders of the public order, not to proceed against the workers but against the exploiting classes. Now, when they encountered workers in bricklayer's outfits on the square in front of the government buildings [this refers to the events of June 16], they hastily returned to police headquarters to get instructions from the highest level."[26] Not only were the People's Police doubtless hampered by such ambivalence, but they were often—at times successfully—prodded into joining the popular cause. Later they were to be stiffened by a special elite force, the Garrisoned People's Police (KVP). It was much less troubled by any qualms and was eventually to play a crucial role.

According to one source, on the morning of June 17 Zaisser had forbidden his men to use armed force, an order which may have come from Soviet authorities. At that time the party leadership was apparently negotiating with the Soviets, who reportedly wished to avoid bloodshed.[27] That a sense of shock, dismay, and often of disillusionment affected many of the leaders and functionaries, who were confronted with the drama of the mass uprisings and the frequent displays of hatred and contempt for the party and its leadership, can be readily understood. Leuschner, listening to savage and threatening noises outside his office building, is quoted by a former aide as uttering the *cri de coeur*: "And these are the people for whom we have struggled for years and whose interests we claim to represent! Have we done everything wrong?" Bolstering his courage, he quickly adds: "Of course these few thousand people aren't the whole population. And then, we can't take Berlin as a yardstick. The atmosphere here is contaminated from West Berlin. All this surely comes from that damned wasps' nest."[28] His outburst strikingly conveyed the ambivalence on the part of the leaders. For a fleeting moment, one of them, himself a Berlin worker's son and identified with the regime from the beginning, could not help admitting to a sense of guilt, but in order to regain his self-respect (and his authority) he compulsively attributed the glaring failure made public that day to the machinations of "the enemy."

In the absence of an effective or timely counteraction by the leadership, Soviet military intervention to bring the mass action under control was presumably inevitable: it constituted the final phase of the event. Enough of the evidence has been shown to suggest that the explanation for the remarkable ineffectiveness, not to say helplessness, of the regime in the face of acute danger rested mainly on the following factors. Part of the leadership, together with its apparatus, had clearly become overly enmeshed in the taxing routines of its far-flung bureaucratic empire. According to many accounts,[29] the very recent and largely inexplicable shift in the direction of public policy caused disorientation among many of the party and government functionaries. Most important, no doubt, was the intense preoccupation of the top leaders with the imminent threat to their political survival which, by a fluke, had become acute in the midst of a severe policy crisis. Finally, the police and other protective agencies of the regime were hardly adequate for the situation. This was due partly to the genuinely popular character of the mass action, for which most of them were not psychologically or ideologically prepared, and partly to the fact that the G.D.R. at that time did not have any independent military establishment in a formal sense. It is also likely that the Soviet authorities, exercising at least a general policy control over these agencies, had refused to "unleash" them until quite late.

During the night of June 16 Soviet military forces had moved impressive numbers of troops and tanks to the affected areas— 25,000 troops and 300 tanks into Berlin alone. Direct repressive action started in Berlin by noon of June 17. Martial law was imposed in Berlin and in cities and towns throughout the G.D.R. Although on the whole the initial use of Soviet military force was marked by a certain restraint, there was sufficient use of weapons to cause hundreds of casualties.[30]

By nightfall of June 17 an uncertain and uneasy calm was restored to the G.D.R., even though in scattered instances protest actions and other incidents continued in some cases even into July.

As the first shots of the Soviet military action were heard on June 17, one of the public servants of the G.D.R., during a conference, reflected on the meaning of this undertaking: "Marxism-Leninism distinguishes two main classes in modern society which face each other as antagonists, the working and the exploiting class. The socialist camp to which we belong, led by the Soviet Union, represents the interests of the working class. Will somebody tell me whose blood is flowing today? Were those capitalists who crowded the streets today and who are now being shot down?" He expected no answer, and none was forthcoming.[31]

By its intervention the Soviet Union had not only cut short the course of the mass action and thereby secured its G.D.R. base in the heart of Europe; it had also been compelled to become Ulbricht's political savior. It may be reasonably assumed that the internal opposition, encouraged by support in Moscow, had been strong enough on June 16 to overthrow him. However, the outcome of June 17 had made his retention at this point a virtual necessity for Moscow. Having gained time to deal with his enemies and consolidate his power, and having drawn further comfort from Beria's fall on June 26, Ulbricht was now able to deal with his adversaries in the SED. At the fifteenth and sixteenth meetings of the Central Committee plenum, in late July, 1953, and in January, 1954, the fate of the Zaisser and Herrnstadt group was sealed.

CONCLUSIONS

Certain salient conclusions can be drawn from an examination of the uprising and its mass action phase. Complete spontaneity marked its inception and subsequent escalation—a truly "explosive transition from total discipline to total rebellion."[32] In the main it was, as we have seen, a delayed reaction to a policy pressed forward and intensified because of the leadership's compulsive refusal to face social realities inconveniently at odds with ideological goals.

There is no merit in subsequent SED and Soviet contentions that Western subversive activities had been the real culprit. Under the initial shock of the June days, and before recovering their normal posture, Grotewohl and others had found it necessary to make damaging admissions of mismanagement before still aroused working-class audiences. Moreover, the initial silence and the inadequacy of the early responses by Western leaders strongly support the conclusion that they were taken utterly by surprise on June 16.[33]

This quality of spontaneity and the extremely short duration of the rebellion account for the virtual absence of organization and leadership. Everywhere, scattered strike committees were set up by acclamation, but only a very few communitywide central committees had a chance to develop. This accounts for the manifest deficiencies of discipline and an inevitable lack of co-ordinated action. The genesis of the upheaval had determined the leading role of industrial workers as its prime movers. While we cannot in this context go into the problem of the actual social composition of the participants or their area distribution in the mass action, suffice it to say that the scanty evidence does indicate the dominant role of workers and also of the very young, a fairly significant participation of farmers, and a very limited presence of the intelligentsia which was to play such a critical part in the Hungarian case.[34]

This is not the place for a reassessment of the general results of the June events of 1953 for the G.D.R. A few observations seem nonetheless in order. In the short run, the June events impressed the SED leadership with the need to pursue the New Course, including a variety of special conciliatory gestures in order to regain a measure of co-operation and stability. However, this was accompanied by a wave of strong-arm actions and reprisals through which the regime proceeded to deal with its enemies, real and imaginary. In saving Ulbricht at this precarious moment of his career, the uprising had provided him with yet another chance to rebuild his remarkably extended tenure. Conversely, the failure of the Herrnstadt-Zaisser faction to reach its goal while at least one of its Moscow principals was still in power may well have spelled, in the long run, the end of a less dogmatic approach to German reunification. Hence, granting the importance of the time factor, the progressive entrenchment of partition was the likely result.

A number of writers have made highly suggestive observations both on similarities in the patterns of the German, Hungarian, and Polish upheavals and on meaningful dissimilarities.[35] To explore some of these questions in depth would require a separate paper. Hence only a few points will be noted in conclusion, without any claim to originality or finality.

The broad, basic cause for popular discontent was much the same throughout Soviet-dominated Eastern and Eastern Central

Europe during the fifties. It involved the clash of interests between the ruling party and, especially, the urban working class and the peasantry. The workers' frustrations and irritations in particular were rooted in what has been called "the discrepancy between the key symbols defining the party's mission and the available possibilities for practical developmental work."[36] It was Gomulka who, in addressing the Central Committee of the Polish Communist Party on October 20, 1956, was to identify quite concisely the moral issue thus raised: "The loss of the credit of confidence of the working class means the loss of the moral basis of power."[37] This would detract further from popular esteem for the satellite leaders, whose authority was impaired to begin with because of their dependent status.

It is difficult to determine why the Czechs, for example, did not rebel while analogous general causes led to outbreaks elsewhere. One writer has spoken of the importance in this respect of variable "cultural thresholds of aggression,"[38] which he links with such factors as the quality and aims of traditional nationalism, the relative harshness of local Stalinist despotism, and the blunders of the leadership. From this point of view, the strength of the Czechs' pro-Russian sentiments (along with past disillusionments about Western policies) and fear of German revenge would tend to overcome an inclination to stand up to the leaders. While these are significant considerations, any appraisal of their relative weight must raise troublesome questions.

It is easier to identify certain specific factors which appear to underlie, in various combinations, the East German, Polish, and Hungarian uprisings. In all three cases, revolutionary situations developed out of an acute crisis of control and authority. In the German case the immediate aftermath of the Moscow succession crisis, with its policy repercussions in the G.D.R., accentuated internal tensions in the ruling elite which manifested themselves in the contradictory and seemingly inconsistent character of vital political and administrative decisions. In the Hungarian case—which, like the Polish, is part of the aftermath of the Twentieth CPSU Congress—the continuing decline of the party leadership from Rákosi to Gerö became a total collapse of the party when confronted with external events such as the students' rebellion. In the Polish case, too, mounting intraparty divisions were accentuated by "outside" events such as the June uprising of the

Poznań workers and the dramatic activities of dissenting intellectuals.

In the Hungarian case a total collapse of the party was not averted, partly because of Nagy's reluctant and ineffective leadership. In the Polish case, on the other hand, responsible party leaders managed to close ranks and succeeded in recalling in Gomulka, a determined and shrewd leader who, while patching up party problems, could effectively become a national symbol to the non-party masses of the community through his defiance of Moscow. In the German case, while the Stalinist party leadership was jeopardized by the dramatic coincidence of outside insurgency and internal—but non-public—conflict, it managed to ride out the crisis, probably in part because the opposing faction was either irresolute or, at the crucial moment, restrained by Soviet pressure (through Semyonov's personal intercession).

All three cases point to the importance of the complex interaction between internal problems of the Moscow leadership and divisions over power and policy in these countries. In all cases it seems clear enough that the social groups primarily involved in elite or mass actions were not among the totally downtrodden but rather among those on whom their regimes had conferred enough benefit or status to encourage their aggressive rejection of undue curbs or sacrifices, economic, moral or intellectual.

In all three cases the insurrectionary action occurred in a period of anticipated or genuine relaxation, which, while most obvious in the Polish and Hungarian episodes, seems to apply in some measure also to the East German one. The Poznań uprising of June, 1956, also shares with the German and Hungarian cases a quality of manifest spontaneity. While in both the Polish and Hungarian uprisings the ferment of the intellectuals played a significant role, this was hardly true for the G.D.R. It is probable that this was due partly to the destructive experience of prior Nazi totalitarianism and partly to the early defection of many dissenters to the West.[39]

In all three cases the inherent and crucial limitation upon the possibility of success was the strategic interest of the U.S.S.R. which made armed intervention a virtual requirement where these interests appeared threatened. Where, as in the case of Poland, a reintegrated party leadership with strong popular backing was clearly committed to the maintenance of the Moscow bond, there was no need for armed intervention. Both in the East German case and in the first Soviet intervention in Hungary, there were clear indications of Soviet reluctance to resort to armed force.

It is difficult if not impossible to establish an unequivocal connection between the uprisings and subsequent events. Yet the following might be considered. De-Stalinization and liberalization were to make the most rapid headway in the case in which there was no intervention—in Poland, where an impressive solidarity was at least temporarily established between the new party leadership and the community at large. Where, as in Hungary, the collapse of the party was followed by intervention and the crushing of a popular uprising, even the resultant Kádár leadership had eventually to move toward liberalization. A measure of liberalization has occurred most recently (since 1963–64) even in the G.D.R., where military intervention had allowed the political survival of Ulbricht's Stalinoid leadership. An "institutionalized revisionism" has come to acknowledge a new dispensation in intrabloc relations and the need to rejuvenate cadres.[40]

NOTES

1. In using this common abbreviation, the writer is quite aware that its use, especially without the benefit of quotation marks, is frowned upon in some circles, especially in the German Federal Republic. Such political semantics serve little useful purpose.

2. Among the large number of available studies, the following are noted:
Stefan Brant, *The East German Rising* (New York, 1957);

Arnulf Baring, *Der 17. Juni 1953*, in *Bonner Berichte aus Mittel-und Ostdeutschland* series (Bonn, 1957. The revised edition of this study [*Der 17 Juni 1953* (Cologne, 1965)] has become available only since the completion of this essay [hereafter cited as Baring II]);

Karl W. Fricke, *Selbstbehauptung und Widerstand in der Sowjetischen Besatzungszone Deutschlands,* in *Bonner Berichte aus Mittel-und Ostdeutschland* series (Bonn, 1964);

Es Geschah im Juni 1953: Fakten und Daten, in *Bonner Berichte aus Mittel-und Ostdeutschland* series (Bonn, 1963);

Rainer Hildebrandt, *The Explosion: The Uprising behind the Iron Curtain* (New York, 1955);

Fritz Schenk, *Im Vorzimmer der Diktatur. 12 Jahre Pankow* (Cologne, Berlin, 1962);

Arno Scholz, W. Neike, and G. Vetter, *Panzer am Potsdamer Platz* (Berlin [Grunewald], 1954);

George Sherman, *East Germany, The June Days* (St. Antony's Papers on Soviet Affairs) (Oxford, 1955);

Carola Stern's writings, especially *Ulbricht, Eine Politische Biographie* (Cologne, Berlin, 1964) ; despite certain questions raised in a recent review by Ludz, Martin Jaenicke, *Der Dritte Weg. Pt. 1* (Cologne, 1964), is also suggestive.

3. Peter Demetz, "Literature in Ulbricht's Germany," *Problems of Communism,* XI (July/August, 1962), 21.

4. According to the Staatliche Zentral Verwaltung fuer Statistik der Deutschen Demokratischen Republik, as reported in the *Ostspiegel of the SPD Pressedienst* (Bonn), XX, No. 12 (March 23, 1965) (hereafter cited as *OS*).

5. For these figures and their interpretation see, e.g., Regina Bohne, "Die Dritte Welle. Zahlen zur Flucht aus der Ostzone," *Frankfurter Hefte* (Frankfurt), April 8, 1953, pp. 278ff.; B. von Nottbeck, "Gruende und Hintergruende der Zonenflucht," *SBZ Archiv* (Cologne), April 20, 1953, pp. 114ff.; W. Brandt, "Die Bedeutung der Massenflucht aus der Sowjetzone," *Gewerkschaftliche Monatshefte* (Cologne), April, 1953; article, "Fluechtlinge," in *SBZ von A bis Z* (Bonn, 1963), pp. 146ff.

6. Compare especially the methodical Dutch study by C. Beijer and G. H. L. Zeegers, "Quelques aspects demographiques de l'Allemagne Orientale," in *Remp* (The Hague), May–June, 1953; also in *Ost-Probleme* (hereafter cited as *OP*), V, No. 26 (June 25, 1953), 1068–69, which attributes age and sex imbalances largely to defection.

7. A speech delivered by Ulbricht before a Berlin rally of activists on May 12, 1960, under the title: "The United Working Class Has Led the People from Disaster." It was not without political significance that the speech was not published until five years later in *Neues Deutschland* (East Berlin), April 17, 1965; Wolfgang Leonhardt, who had been one of Ulbricht's early associates, has recently added to his earlier autobiographic account a vivid report on the Ulbricht group's early Berlin activities: "Es muss demokratisch aussehen . . . ," in *Die Zeit* (Hamburg), May 14, 1965.

8. From the abundant literature available see: Fricke, *Selbstbehauptung und Widerstand, passim;* Carola Stern, *Portraet einer Bolschewistischen Partei* (Cologne, 1957), pp. 138ff.; W. Ruehmland, *Mitteldeutschland, Moskaus westliche Provinz* (Stuttgart, 1959), pp. 99ff., 133ff., 227ff., in addition to numerous studies published in the *Bonner Berichte aus Mittel-und Ostdeutschland* series, especially since 1952. For a broad perspective in terms of general Eastern European development see Andrew Gyorgy's essay "The Internal Political Order," in Stephen Fischer-Galati, *Eastern Europe in the Sixties* (New York, 1963), esp. pp. 166ff.; Zbigniew K. Brzezinski, *The Soviet Bloc* (rev. ed.; New York, 1962), Chapters 5–7.

9. Quoted from *Neues Deutschland,* January 25, 1952, by Jaenicke, *Der Dritte Weg,* p. 226, n. 4.

10. Robert Havemann, *Dialektik ohne Dogma?* (Reinbeck/Hamburg, 1964), pp. 153ff.

11. See A. Leutwein, "Betriebskollektivvertraege nach Diktat," *SBZ Archiv,* May 5, 1953, pp. 132ff.; A. Leutwein, "Ursachen und Folgen der administrativen Normenerhoehung," *ibid.,* June 20, 1953.

12. Hermann Axen, "Der Beschluss der II. Parteikonferenz und die Aufgaben auf dem Gebiet der Kaderpolitik," *Neues Deutschland,* April 30, 1953; also in *OP,* V, No. 21 (May 21, 1953), 872ff.

13. "Important Resolutions," *Neue Rundschau,* June 13, 1953.

14. S. Gruen and Kaethe Stern, "Es wird Zeit den Holzhammer beiseite zu legen," *Neues Deutschland,* June 14, 1953; also in *OP,* V, No. 26 (June 25, 1953), 1073ff.

15. On these matters see C. Stern, *Ulbricht*, pp. 165ff.; also Schenk, *Im Vorzimmer der Diktatur*, p. 185, from the perspective of the planners; C. Stern, *Portraet*, pp. 158ff.

16. It has been suggested that in the course of these developments a parallelism can be noted between the enhancement of the role of the governmental apparatus in Moscow (Malenkov) and the corresponding emergence of Grotewohl in the G.D.R. elite.

17. C. Stern, *Ulbricht*, pp. 165ff.

18. See Jaenicke, *Der Dritte Weg*, pp. 34 and 228, n. 42; Anonymous, "Die Sowjetische Deutschlandpolitik," *SBZ Archiv*, V, Nos. 1 and 2 (January 25, 1954), p. 4; much significant information on the whole complex is contained in an unpublished memorandum by Heinz Brandt (at the time a well-connected SD functionary in Berlin), which the present author has seen and from which *Der Spiegel* (Hamburg, No. 26 [1964]) has published some sections; Fricke, *Selbstbehauptung und Widerstand*, p. 117, refers to a speech by Khrushchev of March 8, 1963, which touched on it; also Flora Lewis, "Did Reds Nearly Jettison East Germany in 1953?" *The Washington Post* (Outlook section), October 3, 1960.

On this point Richard Lowenthal's lucid observations in his introduction to Baring II should be noted concerning the Malenkov-Beria preoccupation with an international *détente*. He points to its connection with internal power struggles and sees the cause of its withering in the events of June 17 as well as in the coolness of the Western chancelleries.

19. *Neues Deutschland*, August 6, 1952; also in *OP*, IV, No. 35 (April 30, 1952), 1143–144.

20. This was the gist of a patronizingly pedagogic article in *Die Arbeit* (East Berlin), December, 1953; also in *SBZ Archiv*, January 25, 1954, p. 31.

21. The *Tribüne* article can be found in Bundesministerium fur Gesamtdeutsche Fragen (BMFG) (ed.), *Der Volksaufstand vom 17. Juni 1953* (Bonn, 1953), pp. 44–45.

22. Schenk, *Im Vorzimmer der Diktatur;* the pertinent section on the events of June 16 and 17 is available in *SBZ Archiv*, XIII, No. 10 (May, 1962), pp. 150ff.

23. Much has been said about the role of RIAS in these events. For the full record see RIAS' own activities report for the week of June 16–27, 1953: *Der Aufstand der Arbeiterschaft im Ostsektor von Berlin und in der Sowjetischer Besetzungszone Deutschlands* (n.d.). The report declares (p. 38) that "as a matter of course, the management of RIAS subordinated its entire program to the events in East Berlin and the Soviet Zone. The RIAS broadcasts were for at least five days altogether dominated by the workers' uprising." Hence RIAS was attacked as interventionist from one side and as do-nothing from the other.

24. BMGF, *Es Geschah im Juni 1953, Fakten und Daten,* is the source for this data. Unfortunately, it does not explain how "uprising" was defined.

25. Paul Kecskemeti, in his remarkable study of the Hungarian uprising of 1956, comments on the same phenomenon: *The Unexpected Revolution* (Stanford, Calif., 1961), p. 111.

26. Schenk, *SBZ Archiv*, XIII, p. 150. For some interesting observations see the RIAS report, *Der Aufstand der Arbeiterschaft*, pp. 27, 29.

27. Schenk, *SBZ Archiv*, XIII, p. 152, reporting a conversation of Selbmann, Minister for Iron Ore Mining and Processing, with Leuschner.

28. *Ibid.*, p. 151. Schenk also reports the gloom of members of Leuschner's staff after having watched the demonstrations on the 17th. Most members in

one particular group, he believes, would have preferred to join the strikers but were convinced that the Russians would before long squash the revolt. It was their belief that without Soviet intervention the uprising was likely to succeed and would rapidly attain reunification—a prospect about which they were dubious.

29. Some of these questions have been more fully considered in my paper, "East Germany" (June, 1953), which is to be published in 1966 as part of a symposium by the Special Operations Research Office, Washington, D.C.

30. There are some inconsistencies in the statistics concerning the number of victims. West German official sources speak of 267 killed and over a thousand wounded. Baring (*Der 17. Juni 1953*, p. 58) speaks of 21 killed—a figure which is close to one released in 1953 by the SED Ministry of State Security (19 killed, 126 wounded). These figures do not take into account the victims of subsequent trials and liquidations.

31. See Schenk, *Im Vorzimmer der Diktatur*, p. 158, n. 26.

32. Kecskemeti for Hungary: *The Unexpected Revolution*, p. 116.

33. See Rutgers University, Department of Sociology, *Soviet Reporting on the East German Uprisings of June 1953* (New Brunswick, N.J., n.d.). For examples of factory rallies with SED leaders after June 17 see BMGF, *Der Volksaufstand*, pp. 71ff.

34. An early study, W. Zimmermann, "Die Traeger des Widerstandes," *SBZ Archiv*, October 20, 1953, pp. 309ff.; an unpublished and undated memorandum by Ernst Riemschneider, *The People of June 17, 1953*, an analysis of a sample of 1200 participants; Baring, *Der 17. Juni 1953*, pp. 43ff.; for some details see my study, "East Germany" (June, 1953), n. 27.

35. I have benefitted from the following: Kecskemeti, *The Unexpected Revolution*, esp. Chapter 9, pp. 119ff.; Andrew Gyorgy, "The Internal Order," in *Eastern Europe in the Sixties*, esp. pp. 190ff., his paper for the present conference, and a paper on "East Germany" for an unpublished symposium edited by Gyorgy and Stambuk; H. G. Skilling, *Communism, National and International* (Toronto, 1964); Frank Gibney, *The Frozen Revolution, Poland* (New York, 1959); Ferenc A. Váli, *Rift and Revolt in Hungary* (Cambridge, Mass., 1961); Paul A. Zinner, *Revolution in Hungary* (New York, 1962); Hugh Seton-Watson, "Five Years after October," *Problems of Communism*, X, No. 5 (September/October, 1961), 15ff.; Robert Bass, "The Post-Stalin Era in Eastern Europe," *Problems of Communism*, XII, No. 2 (April/May 1963), 70–71.

36. Kecskemeti, *The Unexpected Revolution*, p. 157.

37. The speech is cited by Gibney, *The Frozen Revolution*, pp. 57ff.

38. Váli, *Rift and Revolt*, p. 494. Nonetheless, one should recall the early June, 1953, disturbances among Pilsen workers as well as the ferment in Hungarian villages in response to the regime's currency reforms.

39. Shrewd observations on the social composition of the German rising in general and on the make-up of the strike leadership may be found in Baring II, pp. 66ff. and 83ff.

40. See P. C. Ludz's review of Jaenicke, *Der Dritte Weg*, in *SBZ Archiv*, XVI, No. 6 (April, 1965), 122.

4. Poland's Role in the Loosening of the Communist Bloc*

Adam Bromke

I

The shift in the communist orbit from monocracy towards polycentrism has been brought about by several overlapping events. Clearly the major catalyst of change has been the Sino-Soviet dispute.[1] However, various other developments—the independent course followed by Yugoslavia since the late 1940's, the reforms introduced after Stalin's demise in the U.S.S.R., the outbreaks in Poland and Hungary in 1956, Albania's dispute with the Soviet Union in the early 1960's, the second de-Staliniza-tion campaign undertaken by Khrushchev in 1961, and most recently the widening of Rumania's autonomy within the Soviet bloc—also played important roles.

All the changes in the communist world tend to reinforce themselves. Reforms in one communist country generate pressures for similar changes in the others. As a result, there is a tendency on the part of the backward states to eventually catch up with the more advanced ones. As Professor Robert Havemann put it, in advocating the reforms in East Germany: "What has been possible for a long time in other socialist countries should also prevail in the GDR."[2]

The more widespread the changes in the communist orbit, however, the more complex the interdependence among the various states becomes. In experimenting with reform, the more advanced countries tend naturally to adopt measures which correspond to their own particular needs. Thus, as reforms proliferate they diverge increasingly along national lines. At the same time the less advanced countries, having more models of reform to follow, select those measures which best fit their specific cir-

* The original version of this paper appeared in the *International Journal*, Autumn, 1965. The author would like to express his thanks to his research assistant, Miss Eva Balogh, for her able help in collecting the materials used in this paper.

cumstances. In so doing they contribute further to the growth of polycentrism. A Hungarian writer in effect admitted this in 1965 in the observation that the more communist countries there are "with conditions substantially differing from those of the first dozen countries, the less possible it is simply to take over the experiences of the latter."[3]

To sort out the role of a single country from the criss-crossings of change in the communist world is becoming an increasingly difficult task. First of all, since the starting point of reform in all the communist states is essentially the same, namely the Stalinist system, they all tend to pass through somewhat similar stages. The similarity, then, stems from the same initial situation rather than from one country's conscious imitation of another. With the growth in variety of national models of reform, moreover, the example of a single state is rarely followed lock, stock, and barrel. More frequently, before being accepted, it is blended with the relevant experiences of some other countries. Last but not least, even where there is a virtual copying of the reforms in one state by another, this is usually not admitted by either side. For the ideological rationalization of the whole process of change—the doctrine of different roads to socialism—precludes recognition of the universal validity of the experiences of any communist country other than the U.S.S.R. The changes thus have to be presented simply as local variations of the Soviet model.

To evaluate Poland's contribution to the changes in the communist orbit is particularly difficult. For one of the cardinal tenets of Gomulkaism has been the disclaiming of any universal validity of the reforms in Poland. On various occasions Gomulka went out of his way to argue that the changes introduced in Poland in 1956 were peculiar to that country and of no relevance at all to the other communist states.[4] Indeed, he came out strongly against the writers in *Po prostu* who openly depicted the events in Poland in 1956 as a model for all communist countries, "the turning point in the international workers' movement."[5] Gomulka apparently felt that such an assertion would hurt rather than help the reforms in Poland. By juxtaposing the Polish and Soviet experiences, it virtually amounted to advancing a Polish claim to leadership of the communist world—a direct challenge to Moscow.[6] Gomulka's program was far less ambitious.

He presented the changes in Poland as merely a manifestation of her "own road to socialism," differing in some particulars but in essence following closely the universal Soviet model.

All Gomulka's denials of the validity of Poland's experiences for the other communist states notwithstanding, there seems little doubt that the developments in that country have exerted a considerable impact outside its boundaries. The special importance of the changes in Poland lay, above all, in their timing. The upheaval in Poland took place eight years after the outbreak of the Soviet-Yugoslav dispute, but four years before the Sino-Soviet rift came into the open. The Poles stood up to the Russians in a particularly difficult situation. They could not count on the kind of support which had been extended to the Yugoslavs from the West in the late 1940's, nor on support of the kind that was given the Albanians and Rumanians by China in the early 1960's.[7] The consequences which the Poles escaped only by a hairsbreadth in 1956 were amply illustrated by the tragedy which befell the Hungarians. Considering the circumstances in which the reforms in Poland were carried out, even though their scope was modest, they amounted to a considerable achievement. The Poles actually succeeded in changing several aspects, both internal and external, of the communist system which hitherto had been regarded as sacrosanct. The reforms in Poland went beyond those in any other communist country except Yugoslavia.

In terms of setting a pattern of change for other communist states, the experiences of Poland in 1956 appear to be more important than those of Hungary. For if the Hungarian example was negative, in pointing out the limits which could not be crossed without provoking the wrath of Moscow, the Polish example was positive: It proved that within those limits it is possible to win concessions from the Soviet Union. Indeed, although the Poles were impressed with the Yugoslav example, Poland's experiences appear in some respects to be even more significant than those of Yugoslavia. For while the Yugoslav-Soviet quarrel preceded the period of Sovietization (Stalin's attempt to impose such a course on Yugoslavia representing the main bone of contention between him and Tito), the Polish-Soviet dispute took place after Poland had been subjected to

Sovietization for nearly a decade. Thus Poland's situation was more directly relevant for the other countries in Eastern Europe which had undergone a similar process.

In the late 1950's the scope of the reforms in Poland was gradually tightened. Had the new changes in the communist orbit not come in time, it is likely that her differences with the other countries would have ultimately been eliminated. In such an event the impetus of the Polish upheaval of 1956 would probably have spent itself without bringing about any further significant consequences. History, however, took a different course. In the early 1960's the Sino-Soviet dispute broke out into the open, and shortly thereafter the second de-Stalinization campaign was launched by Khrushchev. Since at that time Poland still remained much freer than any other communist country,[8] her experiences acquired new importance. The other communist states in Europe had a ready-made model which now, in more favorable circumstances, they could follow. And, indeed, Poland's example appears to have contributed to the spread of both de-Stalinization and de-satellitization throughout Eastern Europe.

II

As a model of reform after the changes which had been brought about by the upheaval of 1956, Poland had a good deal to offer. Her position in the communist orbit was unique. She was the sole country in the bloc which had carried out a thorough de-Stalinization; and she was the only state in Eastern Europe which enjoyed a measure of independence from Moscow. This status was achieved through a succession of interconnected pressures, each operating at a different level but at the same time largely reinforcing all the others.

First of all there was the pressure from the people. The ferment among the masses reached its climax in 1956—in the Poznan revolt in June, and in the demonstrations staged in Warsaw and some other cities in October and November. In the subsequent years its intensity declined; but as the occasional students' riots, the workers' strikes, and the Catholics' outbursts demonstrated,[9] it was by no means extinguished. At the same time, the discontent among the populace took the form of a widespread mood of "non-violent non-cooperation," ignoring or even deliberately defying particularly objectionable communist measures.[10]

The masses pressed for reforms in the direction of both de-Stalinization and de-satellitization. The slogans advanced in the Poznan revolt were: "We want freedom and bread!" and "Down with the Russians!" And on several occasions the popular pressures were successful in throwing the communist regime into retreat. The severe punishment with which Cyrankiewicz threatened the participants of the outbreak in Poznan in June[11] was never meted out; in fact, the workers arrested on that occasion were set free later in the summer. In October, 1956, in a speech at a closed meeting with journalists, Gomulka admitted that he was personally against the removal of Marshal Rokossovsky from the command of the Polish armed forces, but that he had to bow to the will of the people on this issue.[12] And Jedrychowski openly acknowledged that the dissolution of collective farms in 1956 had not been a result of the communist policy but had been "brought about by the pressure of antisocialist elements [which] the party was not able to resist."[13] The relations between the communist regime and the Catholic church have represented almost a continuous tug of war. The 1956 agreement by the communists to introduce religious instruction in the schools was a sign of their extreme weakness, while their backtracking in the late 1950's marked a consolidation of their position. However, the Catholic hierarchy's outright refusal to accept government control over the teaching of religion in the parishes was a setback to the communist party.

Various less conspicuous but nevertheless important concessions to the popular sentiments have been made by the communist regime, especially in the realm of personal liberties. Freedom of movement, private meetings and conversations—including the right to criticize the communist government—have been respected. Western-style entertainment—movies, theater, jazz, and cabaret satire, often flavored with political accents—has been tolerated. Music, painting, and art in general have remained lively and controversial. Jamming of Western broadcasts has been discontinued, and a limited access to the Western press has been made possible. Travel to the West on a relatively large scale has been permitted. All of these small freedoms have considerably transformed the atmosphere in the country. "One can walk for hours here," reported an American newsman in 1963, "and remain unaware of communist rule."[14]

The second main source of pressure came from the nonconformist intellectuals. The intellectual ferment preceded and actually in large part prepared the way for the upheaval of 1956. The literary thaw was already well under way in Poland by mid-1955; the celebrated Adam Wazyk's "Poem for Adults" appealing for "bright truth and the corn of freedom" appeared in *Nowa Kultura* in August of that year.[15] By the spring of 1956 the two channels of pressure merged, with the intellectuals largely assuming the role of spokesmen for the masses. In the summer the prominent sociologist Professor Jozef Chalasinski took advantage of his appearance as a witness at the trial of Poznan workers to articulate the reasons for their discontent. The newspapers, notably *Po prostu,* aired the grievances of the people, searched for their sources, and suggested remedies. Clubs of the young intelligentsia—especially the famous Club of the Crooked Circle, which drew together the Warsaw intellectual elite[16]—and clubs of the Catholic intelligentsia sprang up throughout the country to debate and formulate the proposals of reform. It was in the press and in these discussion groups that the concrete program of the "Polish October" was put forward.

The unrest among the intellectuals continued well beyond 1956. In some respects it only reached its peak in 1957. It was in that year that the most shattering attacks aimed at the intellectual foundations of the communist system were made. Leszek Kolakowski in philosophy, Stanislaw Ossowski and Jan Sczepanski in sociology, Stefan Kurowski and Wlodzimierz Brus in economics, and many other writers subjected hitherto sacrosanct tenets of Marxism-Leninism to open criticism. It was also in 1957, however, that the communist regime moved to curb the freedom of the written word in Poland. In May Kolakowski's writings were singled out by Gomulka as an example of attempted revisionism.[17] In October *Po prostu* was suppressed, and in January, 1958, a drastic purge was carried out in the editorial board of *Nowa Kultura.* Censorship of the entire press was greatly increased, and in 1958 communist control of the Writers' Union was tightened.

As with the popular discontent, the ferment among the intellectuals was curbed but by no means stamped out. Late in 1961 it flared up anew. A discussion in *Przeglad Kulturalny* on the relationship between ideology and science had strong political overtones.[18] The debate signaled the revival of pressures in the other spheres of intellectual activity. The meeting of the Union of Writers in December, 1961, was turned into a demonstration against communist restrictions, and early in 1962 the Club of the Crooked Circle stepped in with two lively debates on the issue of freedom under socialism. The communist regime responded swiftly. Discussion in the press was brought to an end and the Club of the Crooked Circle was closed. Even more repressive measures were taken in the following year. In June, 1963, *Przeglad Kulturalny* and *Nowa Kultura* were shut down and replaced by a new weekly, *Kultura,* proclaiming as its main objective "the struggle against reactionary ideology."[19] These measures still failed to bring the restive intellectuals into line. They responded with a boycott of *Kultura,* and in March, 1964, thirty-four leading writers, journalists, and scientists dispatched a letter of protest against the curtailment of freedom of expression to Premier Cyrankiewicz.[20] The government, in turn, accused the signatories of the letter of instigating "a campaign of lies"[21] and launched a countercampaign to collect signatures in support of the party. Many writers, however, including several well-known communist party members, refused to support the counterprotest. In desperation, the communist authorities resorted to crude repression. They arrested and tried one of the signatories of the letter to Cyrankiewicz, the elderly writer Melchior Wankowicz, on trumped-up charges of passing information abroad that was detrimental to the government. Wankowicz was sentenced to three years' imprisonment, but apparently the widespread manifestations of sympathy for him throughout the country made the communist regime change its mind, for enforcement of the punishment was left in abeyance. Thus the tug of war once again shifted to the side of the nonconformist intellectuals.

The major impact of the ferment among the nonconformist intellectuals on the government, however, was not direct but rather indirect—through those intellectuals who had conformed with the communist line and by virtue of this fact had frequently been placed in positions of authority. In a small and relatively closely knit intellectual community such as exists in Poland, where its members participate in the same associations, write in the same newspapers, and patronize the same Warsaw cafés, this process proved to be quite effective. The stubborn refusal of the leading journalists, writers, and scientists—the people who command great prestige in the country—to submit to the orthodox communist doctrine created an intellectual climate where the people who adhered to it were placed on the defensive.[22] At the peril of impairing their reputations, they had to explain their stand with arguments meeting at least minimum intellectual standards. Since no such arguments could be found in the traditional body of Marxist-Leninist dogma, the conformist was compelled to devise them by tampering with various communist tenets. In this way, what has been termed "orthodox revisionism,"[23] representing the third main source of change in the country, came into existence.

The Polish "orthodox revisionists" have shown a good deal of ingenuity in their efforts to make the communist ideology more palatable. While loudly proclaiming their unswerving allegiance to Marxism-Leninism, they have explained away or at least modified several of its particularly objectionable aspects. The general justification for what was presented as a creative revision of communist doctrine was advanced by the senior Marxist philosopher Professor Adam Schaff. This opened the valves for the widening of freedom of scientific inquiry in the various disciplines. Tadeusz Kotarbinski in philosophy, Jerzy Wiatr and Zygmunt Bauman in sociology, Oskar Lange in economics, Leopold Infeld in physics, and many other writers—all in one way or another have contributed to the erosion of various tenets of Marxism-Leninism. They have occasionally run into criticism, but their dialectical abilities, coupled with their high standing in the Polish United Workers' Party, has generally protected them from more serious trouble.

As a whole the "orthodox revisionists" have also made an important contribution to the changes in Poland. On the one hand, they bridged the chasm between the communist regime and the nonconformist intellectuals. By using their positions of influence they have often been able to assist or at least to moderate the communist sanctions against critics. On the other hand, the conformist intellectuals have exerted a moderating influence on the government, especially in the realm of cultural policy. They have helped to preserve fairly wide freedom of scientific inquiry at the universities and research centers and, if only because they themselves were interested in it, have advocated cultural exchanges with the West. Sociology in particular has flourished under their auspices. They have upheld a relatively tolerant attitude toward literature and arts, permitting the occasional publication of nonconformist works. They have also tried to maintain some reasonable standards in journalism. The major organ of the "orthodox revisionists," *Polityka,* has remained lively and at times even controversial. And the Catholic press, notably *Tygodnik Powszechny,* continued in existence, although with reduced circulation. The "orthodox revisionists" have also tried to influence communist economic policy. In 1957 the Economic Council, headed by Professor Oskar Lange, came out with recommendations for the overhaul of the entire economic system through the replacement of administrative directives with material incentives. At that time the Council's proposals were not accepted. But by 1963–64 at least some of them were revived.[24]

The combined pressures from the masses and the intellectuals culminated in far-reaching changes in the nature of the communist regime itself. By the spring and summer of 1956 several leading Stalinists had been eased out of posts in the party and the government. At the same time, the rule of terror was curbed. In October, 1956, the top leadership of the communist party was taken over by Wladyslaw Gomulka and his followers, who in the Stalinist period had been disgraced and persecuted. Once in power Gomulka not only continued to cleanse the Polish United Workers' Party by removing the unrepentant Stalinists, but he also extended his hand to the non-communists. "The communist party," he declared in November, 1956, "has no intention of preventing any of the former enemies of socialism from joining in the program of democratization of our political, social, and economic life."[25] To give concrete expression to this offer, although over-all control was firmly retained in communist hands, broader participation by non-communists in the political life of the country was permitted. Many responsible posts in the administration have been given to non-party specialists. The universities have been opened to young people irrespective of their class origin. More authority has been given to local government. The role of the parliament, at least in debate on legislative measures and the venting of popular grievances, has been strengthened. A new system of elections has been introduced, permitting a larger number of candidates than there are seats to be filled. And a reduction in the number of communist deputies has produced a corresponding increase in the representation of the two non-Marxist parties, the United Peasant Party and the Democratic Party, as well as the various Catholic political groups.

To be able to carry out the reforms in the country—both the ones he had personally endorsed and those which he had adopted only under pressure—Gomulka had to get a free hand from Moscow. Consequently, soon after his return to power, he pressed for changes in Poland's relations with the Soviet Union. In his first public speech he stressed that in relations among communist states "each country should possess full independence, and the right of every nation to sovereignty should be fully respected."[26] In asserting this position for Poland, however, Gomulka moved cautiously. He avoided the fatal mistakes of the Hungarians and upheld both Poland's membership in the Soviet bloc and her preservation of the communist political system. It is only within these limits that he sought greater internal freedom, which he termed "Poland's own road to socialism." He supported his claims by ostentatiously emphasizing his continued adherence to the communist doctrine and by invoking the authority of Lenin. In an article in *Pravda* on the eve of the meeting of communist leaders in Moscow in November, 1957, Gomulka wrote: "Lenin had a profound understanding of the specific character of the Polish workers' movement . . . [and of] the sensitivity of the Polish worker over the issue of Poland's independence."[27]

Gomulka's efforts to widen Poland's autonomy have been at least partially successful. The various inequities in Polish-Soviet relations which had been imposed on Poland during the Stalinist era were removed in 1956. Soviet overseers in the Polish government were relieved of their posts and sent home. The Soviet troops stationed in Poland were made subject to at least the formal control of the Polish authorities. And Poland was even partially compensated for losses suffered in the past in her trade with the U.S.S.R.

The relations between the two communist parties, however, posed great problems and led to serious friction between Gomulka and the Soviet leaders. The Russians emphasized their preference for multilateral rather than bilateral ties among the communist parties and underscored the leading place of the CPSU in the international communist movement, implying that this entitled the Soviet party to the position of arbiter in the matters of ideology. In 1957 they apparently considered the possibility of formalizing such relations by reviving an international organization of communist parties. Gomulka opposed the Soviets on all these issues. Although he did not explicitly challenge the Soviet party's leading role, he avoided confirming it. At the same time, he emphasized his preference for bilateral ties among the communist parties and his dislike of a formal international organization. At the meeting in Moscow in November, 1957, apparently under strong pressure from the other communist leaders, he conceded on the first two issues, but remained adamant in his opposition to the resurrection of the Comintern. "The practice of directing all parties from one center," he declared bluntly after his return from the conference, "is frequently harmful."[28]

In 1956 Poland also secured a modicum of freedom in her foreign policy. Serious disagreement between the Polish and Soviet communists was revealed in their evaluations of the revolution in Hungary. The Russians claimed that the Hungarian upheaval represented a counterrevolution, while the Poles placed the responsibility for the outbreak in "the errors and even crimes of the Stalinist period."[29] The Polish communists clung to their opinion of the nature of the Hungarian revolution for some time, even after the uprising had been suppressed. Indeed, in November, 1956, Poland took a step hitherto unprecedented for a member-country of the Soviet bloc. She failed to support the Soviet position in the vote on admission of United Nations observers to Hungary and instead abstained from voting, as did Yugoslavia. Although early in 1957 Gomulka reversed his stand on the issue of Hungary, other differences in foreign policy between Poland and the U.S.S.R. remained. In 1957 Poland developed close co-operation with Yugoslavia. During his visit to Belgrade in September, Gomulka came close to endorsing the concept of "active coexistence," which represents the crux of Yugoslavia's neutralist foreign dispute: Warsaw has preserved closer ties with Belgrade than with any other communist capital. At the same time, Poland's relations with the West, notably with the United States, underwent a marked improvement. Her trade with several Western countries was expanded, amounting to roughly 40 per cent of her total foreign trade. The Polish communist government applied for and received American economic aid. Gomulka presented this step as part of the general policy of peaceful coexistence with the West. The political aspect of American credits, he declared, "is not unimportant, for we believe that the economic relations between states with different social systems contribute to the improvement of the international situation."[30]

The Sino-Soviet rift in the early 1960's has helped Gomulka to consolidate Poland's precarious autonomy vis-à-vis Russia. With the two giant communist parties at odds, the position of the Polish Communist Party—which, after all, rules in the third largest country of the communist orbit—has been considerably enhanced. In exchange for their support against the Chinese, the Poles could now try to extract concessions from the Russians. And, indeed, Gomulka has taken advantage of this situation to reiterate the independence of the Polish communists. In 1961 he emphasized that the plan for establishment of an international communist organization had been abandoned. "There exists no center," he said, "which directs the activities of all communists and workers' parties. It is not needed."[31] In the same year he asserted that each communist party is "fully independent and bears full responsibility for the country where it is in power."[32]

III

The multilevel nature of the changes in Poland has made her particularly attractive as a model of reform. The Polish experiences have appealed to the various segments of Eastern European societies—the masses, the intellectuals, both nonconformist and conformist, and even the ruling communist elites. As a result, although nowhere has Poland's example been followed completely, there is substantial evidence that at different times and at different levels it has contributed to changes in several of the Eastern European communist states. Indeed, in some cases a paradoxical situation has emerged. Reforms which had been discontinued and ideas which had been rejected outright by the Gomulka regime in Poland have taken root in some other communist countries.

The changes in Poland had their first impact abroad in a

country with which Poland had traditionally maintained close ties of friendship: The success of the popular upheaval in Poland in October, 1956, exerted an immediate influence over the restive populace of Hungary. The news of the developments in Warsaw was received in Budapest with "enthusiasm over what was considered a magnificent victory of Polish nationalism over Soviet Russian domination . . . [and] did not fail to create an atmosphere of satisfaction and aggressive confidence among the enemies of the regime. . . ."[33] And it was a mass demonstration in sympathy for Poland (symbolically staged at the statue of a hero of the Hungarian revolution of 1848, Polish General Bem) which turned into an open revolt against the communist regime in Hungary.[34]

At the same time, though at a different level, the influence of the events in Poland was felt in East Germany. In November, 1956, a group of intellectuals in that country led by Wolfgang Harich came out with a program of reforms which followed the Polish pattern in several respects. The similarity was by no means accidental. Harich kept in touch with the Polish nonconformist intellectuals and derived some of his ideas from them.

Indeed, the intellectual ferment in Poland even had some impact in the Soviet Union. For some time after the upheaval of 1956, Polish papers were in considerable demand in the U.S.S.R. The Polish delegates to the Moscow Youth Festival in the summer of 1957 were eagerly questioned by the Russian youth about the nature of the changes in Poland. "There is a great hunger for knowledge about Poland in the Soviet Union . . . ," reported the organ of the Polish journalists, *Prasa Polska,* in July, 1957.[35]

In 1956–57, however, any open signs of Polish influence in the other Eastern European countries were obliterated. The Hungarian revolution was suppressed by Soviet troops. The Harich group in East Germany was dispersed by the Ulbricht regime and Harich himself was arrested and sentenced to ten years of imprisonment in March, 1957. A virtual ban was imposed on the Polish press in Czechoslovakia. At the same time, attacks on the changes in Poland were mounted by foreign communists, with the Soviets, Czechs, and East Germans taking the lead. The criticisms were aimed at the transformations in Poland at all levels. Thus, after his visit to Poland in April, 1958, Voroshilov criticized Poland for lagging behind in collectivization of agriculture.[36] In

September, 1957, *Voprosy Filosofii* launched a scathing attack against Kolakowski, at the same time warning Gomulka that "the consequences of tolerating thoughtless treatment of ideological problems are clearly illustrated by the events which took place in the autumn of last year in Hungary."[37] The revival of authority in the Polish parliament was denounced in December, 1957, by the Czech journal *Tvorba* as a tendency to abandon the dictatorship of the proletariat.[38] Poland's preference for bilateral over multilateral bonds among the communist parties was condemned in December, 1956, by another Czech paper.[39] At the same time, *Pravda* censured Poland for moving close to some Yugoslav views.[40] And in May, 1958, the same Soviet paper implicitly rebuked the Poles for accepting American credits. Although the charges were ostensibly brought against Yugoslavia, they obviously also applied to Poland: "The imperialists," the *Pravda* article said, "do not give anything to anybody for nothing. Everybody knows that American aid to any country is by no means disinterested and that it leads in one form or another to economic and political dependence."[41] The attacks against the changes in Poland continued essentially unabated well into 1958. They were brought to an end only later that year when Gomulka (after his prolonged stay in the Soviet Union in the fall) executed a major retreat from the program of reforms.

There were significant abstentions, however, from the chorus of denunciations of the reforms in Poland. The Hungarian communists, while showing little restraint in denouncing the Yugoslavs, generally refrained from similar attacks against the Poles.[42] Indeed, in the early months after the suppression of the revolution it appeared that Kadar, while repudiating Nagy's brand of "national communism," was also trying to avoid reversion to Rakosi-like Stalinism. In the second half of November, 1956, he negotiated with the leaders of non-communist political parties to establish a coalition government; in December he offered various concessions to the national sentiments of the people—lifting the ban on national emblems, for example, and giving up the compulsory teaching of Russian in the schools—and even raised the hope of an early withdrawal of Soviet troops. In so doing, Kadar was taking a position largely similar to Gomulka's stand in Poland. When, however, Kadar was given to understand by the Soviets "that Hungary and her communist party had to be aligned to the 'faithful' People's Democracies . . . it became clear to him that he should not imitate even Gomulka . . . ,"[43] and early in 1957 he abandoned all attempts at an independent policy. Yet Gomulka's example apparently had not lost all attraction for the Hungarian communists, for soon after Moscow brought to an end its anti-Polish campaign, they showed revived signs of interest in his policies. In March, 1959, one of the most trusted lieutenants of Kadar, Gyula Kallai, drew a direct parallel between the difficulties which faced the communist parties in Poland and Hungary and praised Gomulka as a "dynamic leader" maintaining the middle course between the Scylla of abandoning communism and the Charybdis of returning to Stalinism.[44]

The Rumanian communists, too, abstained from any drastic criticisms of Poland—just as, incidentally, they refrained from any sharp denunciations of Yugoslavia. This was openly acknowledged by the Poles. In July, 1957, *Polityka* asserted that in the Rumanian press one cannot find "the slightest critical reference to the current political trend of events in Poland."[45] This attitude of the Gheorghiu-Dej regime toward Poland and Yugoslavia coincided with two developments in Rumanian-Soviet relations which, though scarcely appreciated in the West, were of great importance. First of all, in mid-1958 the Soviet troops were withdrawn from Rumania. Although the timing of this move suggests that its immediate objective was to enhance Rumania's prestige when she undertook a peace offensive in the Balkans,[46] its origin appears to date back to the changes in Polish-Soviet relations in the autumn of 1956. The issue of the stationing of Soviet forces in a foreign communist country was for the first time made the subject of negotiations in the Polish-Soviet agreement concluded during Gomulka's visit to Moscow on November 18, 1956. After this concession was granted to Poland, the Russians could not readily deny it to the other communist regimes in Eastern Europe. A similar Rumanian-Soviet agreement was thus signed on December 3, 1956, during Chivu Stoica's visit to Moscow. Little is known about the subsequent negotiations which culminated in the withdrawal of Soviet troops from Rumania in 1958.[47] It is likely, however, that the opening of the matter in the fall of 1956 provided the initial impetus. It was also in 1958 that the Rumanians came out with clearly formulated arguments in favor of industrialization of their country, regardless of the outcome of discussions, already under way, about specialization among communist countries within the framework of CEMA. In April, 1958, *Probleme Economice* published an article by M. Horovitz which contained, "barely cloaked in Marxist terminology . . . , the basic arsenal of protectionism in underdeveloped countries. . . ."[48]

IV

If in the late 1950's the Hungarian and Rumanian sympathies with the changes in Poland were manifested in a negative way, by abstention from attacks on the Poles, in the early 1960's they were given positive expression after the open outbreak of the Sino-Soviet dispute and the new de-Stalinization campaign in the U.S.S.R. Both the Hungarian and the Rumanian communist regimes in some respects followed the Polish example. In each case, however, the impact of Poland took a different form. Where the Kadar regime imitated some features of Gomulka's domestic course, the Gheorghiu-Dej regime adopted certain aspects of Gomulka's foreign policy.

Poland's influence on Hungary was more obscure in the early 1960's than it was in 1956, for it was blended with the impact of the new de-Stalinization campaign in the Soviet Union. In view of the Kadar regime's complete dependence on Moscow, the changes in the U.S.S.R. seemed to represent a natural model for the Hungarian communists to follow. Still, there is evidence that "Hungary, although in the main hewing to a course similar to that of the Soviet Union under Khrushchev, has adopted some procedures more 'Polish' than 'Russian' in character."[49] The reforms in Hungary were initiated early in 1961, several months before the new de-Stalinization campaign was launched in the U.S.S.R. toward the end of that year. And after the Twenty-second CPSU Congress, Kadar's "new course" still surpassed in its scope the reforms which had been carried out in the U.S.S.R. and brought the political system in Hungary closer to that of Poland.

The main feature of Gomulkaism which Kadar adopted as his own seemed to be exactly what had impressed Kallai so much in 1959, namely, the "centrist" course of upholding communism but repudiating Stalinism. Kadar, like Gomulka, had strongly emphasized Hungary's faithful adherence to the Warsaw Treaty and the internal communist system. The Hungarian communist regime has closely followed the Soviet line in foreign policy, while the communist party has retained its monopoly of political power in the country. At the same time, however, Kadar in 1961–63 introduced various domestic reforms which bore strong resemblance to those of Gomulka in Poland. The hard-core Stalinists have been removed from leading posts in the government and the party. Widespread terror has been abandoned, and a general amnesty has been granted to political prisoners. Noncommunists have been invited to co-operate with the government. In 1962, much in the vein of Gomulka's conciliatory pronouncements of 1956, Kadar declared: "We must bear in mind that many people of different pasts and points of view have remained and now live in our People's Democracy. They live peacefully and work honestly. What shall we do? Live on a war footing with them? We only want to fight those who want to overthrow the people's power. . . ."[50] And indeed, several concessions closely resembling those which had been won by the Poles have been offered to the Hungarian populace. Broad freedom of conversation has been tolerated. Western-style entertainment has been permitted. Artistic freedom and freedom of scientific inquiry have been considerably widened. Sociology has been re-established as a separate discipline, with Hungarian sociologists maintaining close contacts with their Polish colleagues. Relations between the communist government and the Catholic church have improved, Hungary being the first communist country to conclude a formal accord with the Vatican. Responsible administrative posts have been given to non-party specialists. Some attempts have been made to revive the activities of the parliament. Restrictions on travel to the West have been eased. Cultural exchanges with the West have been undertaken and commerce with the non-communist countries has been expanded to roughly 30 per cent of Hungary's total foreign trade. All in all, there has been a major change in the political climate of the country, "placing Hungary next to Poland among the most liberalized East European communist countries."[51]

Poland's impact in Rumania in the early 1960's was even more difficult to discern than in Hungary, for it was blended not with one but with two other foreign influences. In the efforts to widen their independence from Russia, the Rumanians ably exploited the Sino-Soviet rift. Paradoxically, they moved closer to neighboring Yugoslavia at the same time. Poland's example (especially since Warsaw took a stand closer to Moscow than to Bucharest in the dispute over specialization in CEMA) seemed in fact to be the least important of the three influences. Yet it clearly played some part, particularly in the early stages of the dispute. "The Romanian attitude toward the Soviet Union . . . resembled the Polish attitude in 1957 on the basic issue of the position of Moscow in the socialist camp."[52]

In executing his "Rumania first" policy, Gheorghiu-Dej followed closely the cautious tactics of Gomulka. Like the Polish leader in 1957, he did not repudiate membership in the Soviet bloc, nor participation in the Warsaw Treaty and CEMA. He did not even totally reject the principle of specialization within CEMA. What he initially strove to attain was, in effect, recognition by the Soviet Union of Rumania's own road to socialism— and, above all, her right to carry out the policy of industrialization free from interference by CEMA. This stand strongly resembled the position which had been taken by Gomulka in 1957 toward the proposal to revive the Comintern. What was at stake in both cases was the restricting of the national sovereignty of a smaller communist country by a supranational organization dominated by the Soviets. In opposing such a plan, Gheorghiu-Dej invoked the authority of Lenin as Gomulka had done in 1957. The April, 1964, resolution of the Central Committee of the Rumanian Workers' Party stressed that "the distinctive national and state features, which, as Lenin pointed out, will prevail for a long time even after the victory of the proletariat on a world scale, will make it an extremely complex task to find the organizational forms of economic cooperation."[53]

It was only after winning the argument over the nature of specialization in CEMA that Rumania's policy vis-à-vis the Soviet Union, encouraged by the continuance of the Sino-Soviet dispute, became more assertive and moved beyond its "Polish" into a "Yugoslav" phase. However, even in this latter stage, especially since Rumania still has not left the Soviet bloc, some parallels between her actions and those of Poland in the 1950's could easily be observed. In November, 1963, as Poland had done seven years before, Rumania failed to support the Soviet position in the vote in the General Assembly of the United Nations on the establishment of a nuclear-free zone in Latin America. At the same time, Rumania's cultural and trade relations with various Western countries, notably the United States, were considerably expanded. That in following this course the Rumanians were aware of the Polish precedent was confirmed by Radio Bucharest in a response to Soviet criticism of Rumania's efforts to expand commerce with the West. The Rumanian speaker pointedly asked if the criticism also referred "to Poland, in whose foreign trade capitalist countries have a share of approximately 40 per cent."[54]

In the early 1960's, however, the impact of Poland's example was not confined to Hungary and Rumania, the two countries which had shown some sympathies toward it from the start. It also made some inroads in those communist states where in 1956–58 it had been bitterly opposed: Czechoslovakia, East Germany, and the U.S.S.R. In these cases, of course, Polish influence did not operate directly through adoption of Gomulka's policies, but made itself felt indirectly through its appeal to the masses and particularly to the intellectuals, who in turn pressed their respective communist regimes to emulate the Polish reforms.

The Polish example seems to have contributed indirectly to far-reaching domestic changes in Czechoslovakia. As in the case of Rumania, Poland's impact in Czechoslovakia was blended with two other foreign influences and appeared to be the least important of the three. The popular pressure for reforms in Czechoslovakia which erupted into the open in 1963 was in the first place brought about by the new de-Stalinization campaign in the Soviet Union. It was subsequently intensified greatly by the changes in neighboring Hungary—what was labeled in Czechoslovakia as "Kadarism."[55] The interest in the Polish model of reforms, however, was also present among the Slovaks and the Czechs. In May, 1963, immediately after the appearance of an article in *Kulturny Zivot* about the Hungarian reforms, readers requested that a similar report be written on Poland.[56] There was, in fact, a good deal of similarity between the events in Czechoslovakia in 1963 and those in Poland in 1956. For if the changes in Czechoslovakia paralleled those in Hungary in that they were carried out without drastically interrupting the continuity of the communist leadership, they were brought about, as in Poland, only under strong pressure coming especially from the intellectuals.

The intellectual ferment in Czechoslovakia in 1963 in several respects resembled that in Poland in 1956. The writers and journalists assumed the role of spokesmen for the masses, the self-styled "conscience of the nation." They submitted the various aspects of the communist system to criticism and demanded reform. The Slovak Writers' Congress in April, 1963, and the Congress of the Union of Czechoslovak Writers a month later were used as forums for denouncing the continued Stalinist course of the Novotny regime. The two literary journals, the Slovak *Kulturny Zivot* and the Czech *Literarni Noviny,* played a role similar to that of their Polish counterparts in airing the grievances of the people and searching for remedies. The attempts on the part of the communist leaders, notably Novotny himself, to silence the nonconformist intellectuals proved of no avail. Miro Hysko, Radoslav Selucky, Roman Kalisky, and many others boldly pressed their attack. Faced with signs of growing popular discontent, as signaled by the students' demonstrations in Prague in May, the communist regime gave in. Various reforms akin to those in Hungary and in Poland have been introduced. Although President Novotny himself weathered the storm, several leading Stalinists, including Premier Siroky, have been relieved of their posts in the party and the government. Victims of terror have been rehabilitated. The scope of personal liberties has been considerably widened, and fairly broad freedom of expression and research has been tolerated. The position of the Catholic church has been ameliorated, Cardinal Beran having been released from imprisonment and allowed to leave the country for Rome. An extensive overhaul of the economic system—surpassing the changes in this sphere both in Poland and Hungary—has been undertaken. Travel to the West by Czechs has been made easier; and Czechoslovakia has been widely opened to Western tourists. As a result of these reforms the political atmosphere in the country has markedly improved, placing Czechoslovakia next to Poland and Hungary as the most liberalized communist state.

If in Czechoslovakia the Polish influence has affected the non-conformist intellectuals, in East Germany and the U.S.S.R. it has been felt among the "orthodox revisionists." It has been manifested above all in the demands for widening the freedom of scientific inquiry and in the proposals for economic reform. The revival of sociology in Poland has clearly assisted a similar development in the Soviet Union. By the early 1960's, although still, as a whole, more primitive in its research methods, sociology has asserted itself in the Soviet Union as a separate discipline. Some Polish influence has also been felt in the Soviet natural sciences. In November, 1961, Professor Leopold Infeld, the former disciple of Albert Einstein, came out with an article in *Przeglad Kulturalny* in which he upheld his master's theories,[57] and this soon found an echo in the U.S.S.R. In March, 1963, the distinguished Soviet physicist Pyotr Kapitsa (who had also been trained in the West) published an article in *Ekonomicheskaya Gazeta* in which he joined in the defense of Einstein's theories.[58] Gradually, especially since the ouster of Khrushchev in 1964, freedom of inquiry in the Soviet natural sciences has been widened. In the realm of economic reforms, some of the proposals advocated by Professor Oskar Lange, which, paradoxically, had been turned down in Poland, reappeared in the early 1960's in both the G.D.R. and the U.S.S.R. The "new economic system" introduced in East Germany in 1963 "began to realize many ideas of the Polish economic reformers."[59] And in the Soviet Union various proposals strikingly similar to those of Lange could be found in the Liberman program, which by now has largely been adopted.[60]

V

With the growth of polycentrism the special importance of the Polish model of reform has gradually declined. The greater the number of communist states experimenting with reform, the more the relevance of Polish experience has been diluted. Poland's example has been overshadowed by the more recent and in some respects more profound changes in several other Eastern European countries. The Hungarians have surpassed the Poles in widening the scope of cultural freedom. The Czechs have taken the lead in rationalizing the economic system. And of all the members of the Warsaw Treaty Organization, the Rumanians have secured the greatest measure of independence in foreign policy. Although in terms of over-all liberalization Poland's position still compares favorably with that of the other communist states (her unique feature being the abandonment of collectivization), she has clearly lost her undisputed primacy in the several spheres of reform.

The spread of de-Stalinization and de-satellitization throughout Eastern Europe has helped the Poles to consolidate the reforms which they have managed to maintain since 1956. A leveling off among various countries of the Eastern European bloc has removed Poland from her former vulnerable position as the lone outpost of reform. And the Poles have taken advantage of this new situation. Pressures for change have been intensified at various levels. Gomulka has emphasized the independence of the Polish Communist Party from Moscow and has given new assurances that there will be no forcible collectivization. Discussion of reform of the economic system has been revived. The intellectuals have made demands for widening freedom of scientific inquiry as well as of expression; and the Catholics have appealed for an improvement in the position of the church. As a whole, however, the renewed pressures have been rather weak. At the most they have been aimed at restoring the situation which existed in 1956, but have not gone beyond that. Certainly there has been no attempt on the part of the Poles to continue in the present circumstances as an *avant-garde* of the program of reforms in the communist world.

Poland's reluctance to exploit the situation which developed in the early 1960's in the same way that she exploited the situation in 1956 may be attributed to a breakdown in the series of interconnected pressures at two crucial levels. First, the communist regime has had no reason to be dissatisfied with the existing status quo. With the spread of polycentrism Gomulka has been assured of Moscow's recognition of Poland's internal autonomy in line with the concept of different roads to socialism. He has never had any intention of moving beyond that, for to do so would be contrary to his beliefs as a communist and, moreover, could well spell trouble for him as leader of the ruling party. To sever Poland's alliance with the U.S.S.R. would seriously undermine the very rationale for the communist party and thus Gomulka's continuance in power. Gomulka, therefore, has made it quite clear that he will not submit to any pressures pushing him in that direction. "The Soviet Union," he declared in 1963, "is the decisive main strength of the socialist camp, without which no socialist state could hold out against imperialism. No communist party . . . should forget that."[61]

Gomulka has been spared a test of strength with his people on the issue of the Polish-Soviet alliance, for in the early 1960's no strong pressures to repudiate it came from the Poles. The mood of the country has been one of political realism.[62] The memories of the abandonment of Poland by the West and the futility of her unaided efforts to preserve her independence from Russia in the late 1940's are still vivid in the minds of the Poles. Moreover, the Polish people have been restrained from pressing for complete emancipation from the Soviet Union by their fear of West Germany. The German territorial claims to Poland's western provinces, which so far have not been disavowed by the United States, have made the Poles look to Russia for protection. In the final analysis, Western policy has contributed to the transformation of Poland from a restive satellite into an unenthusiastic but basically reliable ally of the Soviet Union.

As long as the present international situation persists, the prospects in Poland for changes of the magnitude of those of 1956 seem remote. The Poles apparently feel that in view of the realities of their country's external position they have done everything that they possibly can. Thus they are unlikely to press for any drastic changes in the near future. The impetus of the Polish upheaval of 1956 has largely spent itself. As a model of reform, Poland no longer has much to offer the other communist states. Indeed, if the present trends continue, she might in the end turn from a progressive into a retrogressive force in the communist orbit—her policies checking rather than advancing the spread of polycentrism in Eastern Europe.

NOTES

1. For the author's views on the impact of the Sino-Soviet dispute on the communist orbit see: *The Communist States at the Crossroads* (New York, 1965) ; and *Eastern Europe in a Depolarized World* (Toronto, 1965) .

2. *Echo am Abend*, March 11, 1964. (Translation, "Professor Havemann's Views," *East Europe*, April, 1964, p. 21.)

3. I. Harsanyi, "The Universality of Marxism-Leninism and the Uniform Strategy of the International Working Class," *Tarsadalmi Szemle*, February, 1965. (Translation, *Hungarian Press Survey*, Research Department of Radio Free Europe, February 16, 1965, p. 8.)

4. In particular in his exposition of the "Polish Road to Socialism" at the meeting of the Central Committee of the Polish United Workers' Party in May, 1957, and in an article published in *Pravda* on November 5, 1957. See Wladyslaw Gomulka, *Przemowienia, 1956–1957* (Warsaw, 1958), pp. 264–71, and *Przemowienia, 1957–1958* (Warsaw, 1959), pp. 101–13.

5. Edda Werfel in "O 'komunizmie narodowym,'" *Po prostu*, February 24, 1957.

6. Significantly, in view of Poland's vulnerable position vis-à-vis Russia, various non-communist writers agreed with Gomulka in this regard. For instance, one of the leading exponents of the program of reform, Stefan Kurowski, in an article written in 1957, called in an euphemistic fashion for concentration on resolving the problems "on a local scale . . . without getting involved in larger conflicts." "Apatia-czyli poszukiwanie celu," in *6 lat temu* (Paris, 1962), p. 162.

7. This does not exclude the possibility that in October, 1956, the Chinese approached Moscow urging restraint. Indeed, an astute Western observer of communist affairs believes that this was the case. See Zbigniew K. Brzezinski, *The Soviet Bloc: Unity and Conflict* (Cambridge, Mass., 1960), p. 257.

8. "Life is much freer in Warsaw," observed a British journalist who travelled extensively throughout Eastern Europe in the early 1960's, "than in any other Soviet bloc capital." Anthony Sylvester, "Poland Observed—1963," *East Europe*, October, 1963, p. 17.

9. For instance, the strike of electric tram drivers in Lodz in 1957, the students' riots in Warsaw after the closing of the newspaper *Po prostu* in the same year, and the disorders over the religious issue in Krasnik Lubelski in 1959, in Nowa Huta and Zielona Gora in 1960, and in Torun in 1961.

10. For illustrations of the mood of "non-violent non-cooperation" see the author's *A Visit to Poland: Impressions of a Political Scientist* (Cambridge, Mass., July, 1961), p. 23 (mimeographed).

11. *Trybuna Ludu*, June 30, 1956. (English translation in Paul E. Zinner [ed.], *National Communism and Popular Revolt in Eastern Europe* [New York, 1956], p. 135.)

12. In *6 lat temu*, pp. 72–73.

13. *World Marxist Review, Problems of Peace and Socialism*, February, 1959.

14. Max Frankel, "Poland's Marxist Path," *The New York Times*, August 31, 1963.

15. *Nowa Kultura*, August 19, 1955. (English translation in Zinner, *National Communism and Popular Revolt*, pp. 40–48.)

16. For a detailed account of the activities of the Club of the Crooked Circle see Witold Jedlicki, *Klub Krzywego Kola* (Paris, 1963); for an English summary see *East Europe*, June–July, 1963.

17. *Przemowienia, 1956–1957*, pp. 318–24.

18. For a detailed account of the debate see the author's "Poland: A Matter of Timing," *Problems of Communism*, May/June, 1962.

19. *Kultura*, June 16, 1963.

20. For the text of the letter in English see *East Europe*, May, 1964, p. 48.

21. "Nie uda sie przeciwstawic," *Polityka*, April 25, 1964.

22. Gomulka himself acknowledged this when he complained in July, 1963, that among the party ideologists "participation in the party indoctrination is not regarded as *bon ton*." *Nowe Drogi*, August 31, 1963.

23. Zbigniew A. Jordan, "The Philosophical Background of Revisionism in Poland," *East Europe*, June, 1962, p. 14.

24. For a penetrating discussion of economic revisionism in Poland see Michael Gamarnikow, "The Growth of Economic Revisionism," *East Europe*, May, 1964, pp. 20–21.

25. *Przemowienia, 1956–1957*, p. 110.

26. *Ibid.*, p. 38.

27. *Przemowienia, 1957–1958*, p. 107.

28. *Ibid.*, p. 150.

29. *Trybuna Ludu*, October 28, 1956.

30. *Przemowienia, 1956–1957*, p. 158.

31. *Przemowienia, 1961* (Warsaw, 1962), p. 517.

32. *Ibid.*, p. 79.

33. Ferenc A. Vali, *Rift and Revolt in Hungary: Nationalism versus Communism* (Cambridge, Mass., 1961), p. 261. In comparing the post-1956 developments in Poland with those in Hungary, the author profited not only by perusing this penetrating study, but also by the valuable comments of Professor Váli, offered to him for the purposes of preparing the present paper.

34. The Poles, incidentally, reciprocated the warm feelings of the Hungarians by subsequently manifesting their sympathy with the Hungarian revolution.

35. Quoted in *East Europe*, October, 1957, p. 49.

36. Radio Moscow. (For excerpts in English see *East Europe*, June, 1958, p. 28.)

37. S. I. Mikhailov and K. A. Komarov, "Starye Pagubki na Noviy Lad," *Voprosy Filosofii*, September, 1957, p. 112.

38. *Tvorba*, December 10, 1957, from Brzezinski, *The Soviet Bloc*, p. 360. For the account of several other attacks against the Poles see the same author, pp. 274–77.

39. *Rude Pravo*, December 8, 1956; Brzezinski, *The Soviet Bloc*, p. 275.

40. A. Azizian, "O proletarskom internatsionalisme," *Pravda*, December 23, 1956.

41. *Pravda*, May 8, 1958.

42. Brzezinski, *The Soviet Bloc*, p. 373.

43. Vali, *Rift and Revolt*, p. 391.

44. *Nepszabadsag*, March 29, 1959. (Summary in Vali, *Rift and Revolt*, pp. 480–81.)

45. *Polityka*, July 24, 1957, quoted by Brzezinski, *The Soviet Bloc*, p. 373.

46. This interpretation is offered by Ghita Ionescu in *Communism in Rumania, 1944–1962* (London, 1964), p. 289.

47. The withdrawal "in the near future" was announced in a communiqué issued in May, 1958, by the Warsaw Pact Conference in Moscow, and on July 25, 1958, the Bucharest radio announced that the Soviet forces had already left the country.

48. John Michael Montias, "Background and Origins of the Rumanian Dispute with Comecon," *Soviet Studies*, October, 1964, p. 132.

49. H. Gordon Skilling, *Communism, National and International: Eastern Europe after Stalin* (Toronto, 1964), p. 38.

50. *Nepszabadsag*, December 3, 1961. (Translation by George Mueller and Herman Singer, "Hungary: Can the New Course Survive," *Problems of Communism*, January/February, 1965, p. 33.)

51. Ferenc A. Vali, in *The Communist States at the Crossroads*, p. 71.

52. J. F. Brown, "Eastern Europe," *Survey*, January, 1965, p. 71.

53. *Scinteia*, April 26, 1964. (Translation in *East Europe*, June, 1964, p. 28.) The resolution, incidentally, implicitly emphasized the coincidence of Ru-

mania's view with those of Gomulka over the issue of supranational organization, for it also criticized the record of the Comintern.

54. *East Europe*, July, 1964, p. 10.

55. *The New York Times*, October 23, 1963.

56. Rudolf Hoffman, "Struggle for the Return of Leninism in Poland," *Kulturny Zivot*, May 18, 1963. *(Czechoslovak Press Survey*, May 25, 1963.) In one of his subsequent essays Hoffman explicitly linked the developments in Poland and Hungary by pointing out the impact which the events in Warsaw had in Budapest in the fall of 1956. "The Strange Hungarian Autumn," *Slovansky Prehled*, No. 1 (1965) *(Czechoslovak Press Survey*, March 13, 1965) .

57. *Przeglad Kulturalny*, November 23, 1961.

58. *The New York Times*, April 15, 1962.

59. Hansjakob Stehle, "Polish Communism" in William E. Griffith, *Communism in Europe* (Cambridge, Mass., 1964) , I, 167.

60. Lange's *Political Economy*, published in 1959, subsequently appeared in several translations, but not in Russian. When in 1962 the present author asked Professor Lange why this was so, Lange answered: "You see, the new ideas have to come from Rome and not from a local bishop." The book, however, was circulated in the Soviet Union in mimeographed form; and in 1961 Professor Lange visited the U.S.S.R. to discuss it with the Soviet economists.

61. *Trybuna Ludu*, January 18, 1963.

62. For a detailed discussion of the historical background and contemporary manifestations of political realism see the author's "Political Realism in Poland," *Survey*, April, 1964, and "Nationalism and Communism in Poland," *Foreign Affairs*, July, 1962.

5. The Rumanian National Deviation: An Accounting

R. V. Burks

As Professor Montias has pointed out in a brilliant essay, Western observers were slow to recognize that the communist regime in Bucharest had begun to pursue an independent policy based on Rumanian national interests.[1] Astonishment at this development could scarcely have been more profound. Not only had no one foreseen such an eventuality, but many could not even believe the evidence of their senses. At Radio Free Europe, where events in Rumania are closely watched, only in mid-1962 was there hesitating recognition that something out of the ordinary was going on.

Thus in June, 1962, the RFE Daily Guidance, in connection with the visit of the Soviet party first secretary to Rumania, declared that "Khrushchev's remarks concerning Comecon seem designed to reassure smaller countries that international division of labor will not be disadvantageous to their national objectives." Two weeks later, on July 6, the Daily Guidance commented as follows on the relations between Rumania and the Council for Economic Mutual Assistance (CEMA or COMECON): "Rumanian Broadcasting Department domestic radio service continues to cover in press review question of all-round national industrial development versus industrial specialization within Comecon framework. Our use of press review will thus indicate to audience that Western observers sense Soviet-Rumanian conflict over this issue, but that experts are not fully agreed as to the nature of conflict." That was putting it mildly, to say the least. Nonetheless, some editors and researchers found it extremely difficult at this juncture to accept even this mild formulation.

As Montias points out, signals of the conflict had been available since 1958, but by 1961–62 "the messages were coming in virtually *en clair*."[2] Radio Free Europe did not begin systematic coverage of the conflict between Moscow and Bucharest until

March 13, 1963. At this time a plenum of the Rumanian Central Committee reaffirmed the correctness of the instructions Barladeanu had taken with him to a preceding CEMA conference in Moscow, expressed the Committee's pleasure with the way in which he had implemented these instructions, and reasserted Rumanian adherence to the principle of the socialist division of labor, subject to the sovereignty, equality, and special circumstances of each socialist nation.[3] Such a statement was, in itself, without precedent. It was followed some thirteen months later by a Central Committee declaration which openly rejected Moscow as the ideological center and command post of the world communist movement.[4]

If any of the experts had been asked, say in 1958, to rank the East European satellites in the order of the probability that they would issue such a declaration, he would no doubt have rejected the request as too speculative to merit serious consideration. If our expert had nonetheless been prevailed upon to produce such a list, he would most probably have placed Rumania next to the bottom, immediately above the so-called German Democratic Republic (G.D.R.).[5]

If asked to defend his choice, our typical expert would have assembled a truly impressive array of arguments. Other than the Soviet Union there are only two independent communist countries, he would have said. Of these, China is independent because of her enormous size and, in any case, co-ordinates her foreign policy very closely with the Soviet Union's. The other, Yugoslavia, is independent for reasons which cannot apply to Rumania. The Yugoslavs have direct access to the West by sea, as well as land frontiers with both neutral Austria and a weak Italy, whereas the Rumanians have a lengthy common frontier with the U.S.S.R. and are virtually surrounded by communist states. The Yugoslavs have a long tradition of heroic resistance against almost hopeless odds: the first successful rising against the Turks in 1804; the Bosnian insurrection of 1875; the retreat to Corfu in the winter of 1915–16; the partisan war of 1941–44. The Rumanians, on the other hand, have a long tradition of dealing with conquering oppressors by subtler means: transhumance, diplomatic resilience, and corruption.

Above all, the Yugoslav communists fought their way into

power. They emerged as victors in a bloody three-way civil war. Their power was based on a *Hausmacht* of their own, the partisan army. Soviet forces entered Yugoslavia only after the partisans had seized power. Furthermore, the Yugoslav Communist Party had in the one free election in all of Yugoslav history, that of 1920, captured 12 per cent of the popular vote, thus becoming the second or third strongest party in the country.

The Rumanian party, by contrast, had never earned as much as 2 per cent of the total vote. At the time of the liberation of Rumania by the Soviet army in 1944, it had a mere 884 members, most of whom were not ethnic Rumanians at all, but representatives of the minorities. The party was thrust into power in 1945 by Soviet fiat, the defeated country being occupied by the Soviet armed forces. From the very beginning, the Rumanian party pursued an extremist course through such measures as the use of terror by a powerful security police and the hermetic isolation of the population from the outside world. The failure of the regime to de-Stalinize after 1956 would constitute evidence for our expert that the party could not afford to relax its controls.

Sound reasoning, we all would have said! Yet in the event, quite wrong.

The Rumanian surprise is, of course, not the first of its kind. There is a long list of such surprises: the February (1948) events in Prague; the Berlin Blockade; the secret denunciation of Stalin in February, 1956; the return of Gomulka to power; the flash rising in Hungary; the Sino-Soviet schism; the Cuban missile crisis; the overthrow of Khrushchev.

In view of the length of this list, the question is bound to arise: How expert are the experts? The fact that none of these events was foreseen is not the crucial point, though most of us would have been happier if there had been contingency planning for Berlin or Korea. What is important is the belatedness of the experts in reading the evidence when it was already there. In the Yugoslav case, responsible officials were maintaining as late as 1951 that it was all a trick by means of which the Soviet generals hoped to get possession of the latest American weapons. From time to time ever since, there have been those who predict the return of Yugoslavia to full membership in the bloc. In view of the experts' record of failure, it may be worthwhile to review the Rumanian case in the hope of finding some of the reasons for which we were so wrong.

THE RUMANIAN DEVIATION AND THE GREAT SCHISM

In retrospect, one thing is clear. The Rumanian deviation was made possible by the existence of the Sino-Soviet schism, so that in one sense our surprise is the result of an underestimation of the effects of this schism. The existence of two centers in a totalitarian movement is almost the equivalent of the existence of any number of centers, or of none. The Rumanian Central Committee declaration of April 22, 1964, is a recognition of this fact expressed in Marxist terms. Faced with a significant difference of views between itself and Moscow, the Rumanian satellite had the possibility of shifting to another orbit. It could imitate Albania. By taking a neutral position in the Sino-Soviet dispute, and by attempting to serve as mediators, the Rumanians threatened in effect to do so.

In the circumstances of schism, the options open to the Soviet Union were not particularly attractive. If Moscow proclaimed a ban of excommunication, the likely result would be a round of ideological mudslinging. This would profit no one but the "imperialists." If Moscow resorted to economic sanctions, Bucharest would go to Peking or to Washington (or to both) for help and would probably get it. If Moscow ordered troops into the country, she would probably find herself in armed conflict with a regime which many communists regarded as more *linientreu* than that in the Kremlin. Only with the greatest difficulty could the Gheorghiu-Dej regime be pictured as in league with reaction. The rumor circulated in Bucharest that Khrushchev attempted to organize a conspiracy against Gheorghiu-Dej to unseat him but that Gheorghiu-Dej discovered the plot in time and took appropriate countermeasures. There is at present no way of knowing whether there is anything to this story. In short, there was nothing the Kremlin could do which did not carry worse risks than those involved in the recognition of an independent communist Rumania. Moscow had to choose between an independent communist Rumania, which would co-operate with her communist neighbors on such matters as she deemed in her

national interest, and a second European communist state joining the Chinese camp. The first alternative probably seemed the
more acceptable, partly because it offered no great contrast with
official doctrine, partly because a second Albania would represent
for the U.S.S.R. a catastrophic loss of prestige.

Our Rumanian problem is thus of a twofold nature. There is
the minor problem of how a basic conflict of interest could
develop between the regime in Bucharest and that in Moscow.
And there is the major problem of how a regime so clearly the
creature of Moscow, one dependent on Moscow for its very
existence, could find the inner sources of strength to defend its
interests at the risk of an open quarrel with its sponsor.

The Rumanian-Soviet Conflict of Interest

As everyone is now aware, the conflict of interest concerned
the industrialization of Rumania. The Soviet leaders, working
within the framework of CEMA, wished the Rumanians to implement the principle of the socialist division of labor by concentrating on the development of petrochemicals, synthetic ferti-
lizers, food processing, and agriculture. The Rumanian leaders,
on the other hand, wished to develop a "heavy" industry, producing iron and steel, complex machinery, and the like. Their principal project was a huge iron and steel combine (ultimate capacity, 4,000,000 tons of steel per annum) to be built at Galati on
the lower Danube.

There were some subordinate issues—reflections, at least in
part, of the primary conflict. For obvious reasons, the Rumanians
proposed to enlarge the membership of CEMA by the addition of
the communist states of Asia. They objected to the Soviet proposal according to which the state plans of CEMA members
should be co-ordinated through a central organ. They rejected
the establishment of bilateral Soviet-Rumanian governmental
commissions for supervising the implementation of long-term
bilateral agreements. The Rumanians also opposed the development of joint companies among CEMA members.[6] But the immediate and central issue in the quarrel was the question of all-
round versus specialized industrialization.

The ideological implications of this argument must have been
somewhat confusing to the participants. The Rumanian position

was strictly Stalinist: emphasis on group "A," or the pursuit of autarchy, and on the need to create an industrial base upon which a socialist political superstructure could be built. For Galati there were many precedents: *Die Schwarze Pumpe* in East Germany, Stalinvaros (Dunapentele) in Hungary, Nowa Huta in Poland, the East Slovak Iron Works at Kosice, and Kremikovtsi in Bulgaria, all of these except the last having been undertaken in Stalin's time. The Soviet position was pragmatic and revisionist. The leaders in the Kremlin were bent upon vitalizing CEMA, partly to offset the increased pull of the emergent Common Market and partly to reduce the host of irrationalities which had grown up in the bloc economies because of Stalinist policies of autarchy. The socialist division of labor was not a new principle, but as of June, 1962, a summit meeting of CEMA decided upon its far-reaching implementation and upon the establishment in the future of a central organ for the co-ordination of state plans.

At the same time, it was the Rumanians who were taking a nationalistic position, whereas the Soviet posture was internationalistic. The Rumanians wished to build up and modernize their own country. They could point to the fact that national income per capita in 1958 equalled $340 in Rumania as compared with $795 in East Germany and $833 in Czechoslovakia.[7] Modernization and industrialization meant to the Rumanians the construction of a steel industry. Advanced countries, both large and small, had steel industries, in their view. The Rumanians put forward the traditional arguments of underdeveloped countries, such as the need for protecting infant industries and the problem of a negative balance of payments, scarcely bothering to clothe these arguments in Marxist terminology. They also pointed out that prices of raw materials were declining. Thus, for a preponderantly agricultural country, the terms of international trade were steadily becoming worse.

The Soviets, for their part, could lean heavily on strictly economic considerations. It was nonsense to subsidize the construction of a Rumanian steel capacity when there was elsewhere in the bloc a relative surplus of such capacity; the U.S.S.R. was even cutting back on its rate of investment in this field. It was even greater nonsense to transport both the fuel and the ore nearly 500 kilometers overland from Krivoi Rog to Galati.[8] Such a haul would involve a major expansion of the Soviet railway system, not to mention the existence of adequate processing facilities in the eastern Ukraine itself. It would be much more economical for the Rumanians to industrialize in those products for which they possessed the raw materials. A fine plastics industry, the Russians argued, could be based on Ploesti oil.

The reader will recognize that this kind of confrontation was not new to communist annals. The Yugoslav state had been wracked by the quarrel between backward and advanced republics, the former demanding to be industrialized with capital assets provided by the latter. This quarrel had contributed to faction-building within the party, hard-line elements from the southern republics pressing for a continuation of the subsidies and revisionist elements in the northern republics advocating their elimination. This intra-Yugoslav quarrel has still to be resolved.

The Sino-Soviet schism itself had a similar altercation among its causes. This was the significance of the continuing Chinese attacks on the Soviet program of aid to underdeveloped countries. The Chinese could not understand why Soviet long-term credits should be given to a reactionary Egyptian regime which persecuted Egyptian communists while a communist country such as China was struggling to industrialize herself in forced marches and at great human sacrifice. In particular, the Chinese did not understand why India, which was not only non-communist but also China's principal competitor for influence in Asia, should be awarded credits (as distinguished from deliveries) the sum total of which was greater than those proffered Peking.

The Rumanians, moreover, had developed a special sense of grievance in this respect. At the conclusion of hostilities they had been saddled with a heavier burden of reparations in relation to population and income than had either the Hungarians or the Bulgarians. The joint companies had not been dissolved in Rumania until 1954–55, substantially after they had disappeared in the other satellites. Such exploitation had clearly impeded the industrialization of Rumania. And at the very time the Soviet leaders were opposing the construction of Galati, they granted the Bulgarians a credit of 650 million rubles (December, 1960) for the expansion of the Kremikovtsi steel works. The Rumanians must also have been well aware of the fact that Soviet aid for the years 1945–62 came in their case to $10.00 a head, whereas the corresponding figure for Poland was $33.00, for Hungary $38.00, for Bulgaria $73.00, and for the G.D.R. $78.00.[9]

RUMANIAN NATIONALISM AND INTERNATIONAL COMMUNISM

For our purposes, the key element in this confrontation is the fact that the Rumanian communist leaders were placing the national interests of Rumania, as they understood them, above the interests of international communism, as interpreted by the Russians. Patriotism was taking precedence over the communist faith. How, we may ask, was this possible? How could a party which before the war advocated the cession of Transylvania to Hungary, of Bukovina and Bessarabia to Soviet Russia, and of Dobrudja to Bulgaria end up after the war as the palladin of Rumanian nationalism?[10]

One of the principal clues may be found in the Central Committee plenum held toward the end of November and at the beginning of December, 1961. This rather lengthy plenum devoted its attention to the history of the party. One after the other the speakers rose to repeat one version or another of the same theme: The history of the Rumanian party is the history of a struggle between cadres who had spent long years in the Soviet Union and cadres whose party life, especially the war years, had been spent in Rumania. Until 1952 the Muscovites, according to the speakers, had held the upper hand, and this fact explained all the evil things that had come to pass: the admission of Iron Guardist elements into the party, the arrest of masses of peasants in the course of the collectivization of agriculture, the confiscation of savings by currency reform, and the like. The Muscovites were repeatedly referred to as alien elements. There was Foris, the Hungarian who had been imposed on the party as first secretary by edict from Moscow in 1940. There were Stefanov, the Bulgarian from Dobrudja, who was party first secretary from 1935–40; Chisinevschi, the Jew from Bessarabia; and, above all, Ana Pauker. The heroes of party history, on the other hand, were people like Gheorghiu-Dej, Apostol, Draghici, and Stoica, most of whom were ethnic Rumanians. The Muscovites had persecuted the nativists and particularly the Spaniards among them.[11]

What Gheorghiu-Dej and his colleagues were telling us was that there had been a Rumanization of the party leadership, and that as soon as this transformation had been completed there was an end to Soviet interference in the internal affairs of the Rumanian party. The November-December plenum took place shortly after the Twenty-second Congress of the Soviet Party, at which the Albanians had been expelled from the bloc. The November-December plenum should thus probably be interpreted as a declaration of Rumanian communist independence addressed to the initiated, whereas the later Central Committee declaration of April 22, 1964, was a declaration of independence addressed to the world at large. It was subsequent to the Twentieth Congress of the CPSU, at the March, 1956, plenum, that the altercation between Gheorghiu-Dej, on the one hand, and Constantinescu and Chisinevschi, on the other, took place. This led to the purge of the latter in July, 1957, and the final victory of the nativists. From what we know of the March plenum, it is a reasonable inference that Constantinescu attempted to force the adoption of a policy of de-Stalinization on the Soviet model, while Gheorghiu-Dej took the position that there would be no serious de-Stalinization in Rumania regardless of what the Soviets did. Failure to de-Stalinize was also a sign of growing independence. Montias argues that it was probably the plenum of November, 1958, which decided upon a major orientation of Rumanian trade away from the Soviet bloc and toward the West. The share of the Soviet Union in total Rumanian trade dropped from 51.5 per cent in 1958 to 47.3 per cent in 1959, to 40.0 per cent in 1960.[12] The last Soviet troops were withdrawn from Rumania in 1958.

Of course, the Rumanization of the leadership is only a statistical verity. There were such people as Lucretiu Patrascanu, an ethnic Rumanian from Transylvania who spent the war years under arrest in his native country and who was shot on Gheorghiu-Dej's orders in 1954, just as there are such cadres as Emil Bodnaras, who was born in the Bukovina of a Ukrainian father and a German mother, resided in the Soviet Union most of the time between 1933 and 1944, and who remains to this day a prominent member of the nativist leadership.[13] But conflict between Muscovites and nativists was a fact and has not been limited to the Rumanian party. The strongest nativist leaderships have been precisely those in Yugoslavia, Albania, and China, where they fought their way to power in command of guerrilla armies. It is also true that the anti-Titoist purges of 1948–51 struck heavily those communists who had taken part in the underground resistance: Rajk in Hungary, Slansky in Czechoslovakia, Kostov in Bulgaria, and Gomulka in Poland.

THE RUMANIZATION OF THE PARTY

The Rumanization of the leadership was accompanied by the Rumanization of the party. This was to begin as a purely physical consequence of accession to power. As of August 23, 1944, there were less than a thousand party members, most of them probably from the minorities. The country could simply not be governed by a group of this size and composition. In fact, the years 1946 and 1947 were witness to shameless mass recruitment. The whole of the Tudor Vladimirescu Division, for example, was enrolled. This division had been formed from Rumanian prisoners of war in Soviet camps and had entered Rumania as part of the Soviet command. The forcible fusion of the Communist and the Social Democratic Parties in 1948 brought the party, which henceforth bore the name of Rumanian Workers' Party, to a total membership of something over nine hundred thousand.

The bulk of these new members could not possibly have been Marxists, let alone Marxist-Leninists. In fact, shortly after the fusion congress, the leadership prescribed a period of mass education and indoctrination. Some 249,000 were sent to school in 1949–50 and an additional 324,000 in 1950–51, or more than 90 per cent of the total membership at the later date. Even so, this education must have been on the whole superficial, since the bulk of the courses lasted no longer than six months and many were given in the evening after work.[14] In short, it seems doubtful that the majority of the members ever developed more than a perfunctory acquaintance with communist doctrine. It seems reasonable to assume that with the passage of time the leadership found it could best control and motivate the membership by stressing the industrialization and modernization of the country, and that in the end the policy of across-the-board industrialization, particularly since it was opposed by Soviet Russia, came to be the bond which held the party and the leadership together. In

1965, 64 per cent of party members were under forty years of age, while 99 per cent had entered the party after World War II.[15]

The membership in 1955 was substantially less than that in 1948 as a consequence of the systematic purging of unreliable elements. But party membership began to grow after 1955, especially following the adoption of new party statutes in April, 1962.

Membership in the Party[16]

1948	*ca.*	900,000
1955		595,398
1960		834,600
1962	*ca.*	900,000
1963	*ca.*	1,100,000
1964		1,377,847
1965		1,450,000

Thus, in a decade, the size of the party more than doubled, rising from approximately 3 per cent of the population in 1955 to almost 7 per cent in 1964.[17] The party was moving from cadre to mass status.

The 1962 statutes reduced the length of the probationary period of candidate members, permitted direct admission to the party as full members in some cases, recommended greater restraint in the expulsion of party members, and, above all, provided for the admission of the former members of the late "bourgeois" political parties. The plenum which adopted the statutes also decreed that in the future all key posts were to be allocated to party members who were professionally qualified. Thus there was less emphasis on ideological and more on professional qualifications. The 1965 statutes went even further in this direction. They abolished candidate membership altogether and ruled that date of party rank would no longer necessarily be determined by the date of admission to the party. Date of rank could start with membership in the Social Democratic Party or with the commission of some other "progressive act."[18]

At the same time, the party's image of itself was changing. The principal vehicle of this change was a reinterpretation of the events of August 23, 1944, when King Michael had overthrown the Antonescu regime in a *coup d'état,* following which the

Rumanian army deserted the Nazis and joined the Soviet side. As early as the 1955 anniversary of the coup, Gheorghiu-Dej asserted —in the presence of Khrushchev—that the coup, far from being undertaken by the king, was the "work of the leading forces of the anti-Hitlerite Patriotic Front, the Communist Party of Rumania."[19] Subsequently this enormous prevarication was repeated at appropriate intervals. "The king and his entourage," said Gheorghiu-Dej, "were compelled to accept the plan of action which was established by the Rumanian Communist Party. . . ."[20] At the November-December, 1961, plenum Gheorghiu-Dej declared that the Muscovites had disapproved of the coup, maintaining that it was a "big mistake" because it made necessary a period of collaboration with the bourgeois political parties. He asserted further that Pauker and company would have preferred the final defeat of the Rumanian Army at Soviet hands and the devastation of the country, thus permitting an immediate transition to the dictatorship of the proletariat.[21]

The new myth was further developed when in December, 1962, the Rumanians suddenly attacked an obscure Soviet historian, B. V. Ushakov, for presenting the view—up to that time accepted as standard—that the coup of August 23 had been made possible by the advance of the Soviet armies.[22] Ushakov, it appeared, was guilty of underestimating the role of indigenous forces in the liberation of Rumania and particularly of the role played by the party. A new national monument was dedicated to the "Heroes of the Struggle for the Freedom of the People and the Fatherland, for Socialism," with socialism obviously coming in a poor second. In addition to the communists interred there, the monument contained the remains of Petru Groza, a non-party man and former Transylvanian landowner who was prime minister from 1945 to 1958, thus suggesting that the regime had a multiclass basis.

The Central Committee declaration of April 22, 1964, with its ringing asseveration of the party's independence from Moscow, is well known. There is in the bloc, says the declaration, no center authorized to issue instructions to other parties, to depose or install party leaderships, to excommunicate or liquidate whole parties, or to determine what is sound doctrine. Every party in power is free to decide how it shall reach socialism.[23] In a socialist state, sovereignty over the national plan is the prerequisite of national sovereignty. It comes as no great surprise that new party statutes, released to the press in May, 1965, abandon all reference to the Great October Revolution, heretofore the ultimate source of legitimacy of all communist regimes, and expressly state that it is the patriotic duty of all party members to defend the fatherland and its frontiers.[24]

THE RUMANIZATION OF CULTURE

Simultaneously with the transformation of the party into a national and patriotic body, a whole new approach to cultural life has developed in Rumania. This consists of three related movements: a rejection of Russian and Soviet sources and models; a return to national traditions; and a restoration of cultural contact with the West.

Rumanian historians, for example, now deny that Marxism was imported into Rumania from the East. They argue that it has indigenous origins stretching back many centuries before 1917. Russian place names have been changed to Rumanian; streets and factories have in many instances reverted to their precommunist names. The Russian language has been dethroned from its royal place in the nation's school system, a variety of Western languages being given equal or greater emphasis. The orthographic reform of 1952, which had sought to give the Rumanian language a Slavic appearance, has been abandoned and stress has again been laid on the Latin origins of the language and of the people who speak it. The great figures of the Rumanian past have been, in one degree or another, rehabilitated: Titelescu in diplomacy, Iorga in history, Gusti in sociology, Octavian Goga in poetry, Lovinescu in the drama, and so on. The plays of the exile Ionescu have begun to be staged in Bucharest as the works of a great Rumanian playwright. For the first time new editions of Rumanian classics have become available on a large scale.[25]

At a meeting of the Writers' Union in March, 1964, virtually the entire corpus of contemporary Western literature was granted an ideological imprimatur. Western works, decreed the Union, should be divided into three classes: those which were consciously anticapitalist (Dreiser, Hemingway); those which were unconsciously capitalist (Rolland, Joyce, Sartre); and those which were conciously procapitalist (sole example—the French antinovel). A major effort to translate and publish works in the first two categories has been made. Subsequently, the poet Michael Beniuc, epitome of Stalinism in literature, was toppled from his post as president of the Writers' Union. Socialist realism has been mentioned less and less frequently. For the first time abstract paintings have been placed on public exhibition. Ceausescu, who succeeded Gheorghiu-Dej as party first secretary in March, 1965, addressed the writers in May and spoke in terms of a Rumanian realism, derived from the national past, which would assist the party in the building of socialism.[26]

THE REVIVAL OF MINORITY AND FRONTIER ISSUES

In the prewar days the party had been made up largely of minority elements. Perhaps as many as half of all party members were of Hungarian origin, a fact which accounts for the early prominence of the Hungarians in the leadership.[27] The Szekely minority in central Transylvania was granted an autonomous district in 1952, perhaps as part of a bargain in which the Hungarians sought to protect their interest against the emergent Gheorghiu-Dej leadership. Meanwhile, Hungarians throughout Transylvania were granted equal status in schools, theaters, language, and the like.

The situation of the Magyars began to change in the late fifties, however, after the minority had become involved in the literary ferment which, in Hungary itself, preceded the flash uprising of October, 1956. The Hungarian and Rumanian universities at Cluj were merged in July, 1959, and thereafter Hungarian was strongly de-emphasized as a language of instruction, both at the university and at the secondary level. In December, 1960, the boundaries of the Hungarian autonomous district were redrawn and its official title changed so as to dilute its Hungarian character. More and more the key officials in the district came to be Rumanians. It was clearly the intent of Bucharest to assimilate the Hungarians by quiet but unrelenting pressure. The minority reacted to the new policy with anger and contempt. Tension rose.

The country's other numerically significant minorities, the Jews and the Saxons, were by the late fifties permitted to emigrate in small numbers. No doubt the time will come when both minorities will have virtually disappeared.

In 1964 the Rumanian minority in the Soviet Union evidently became the subject of discussion, if not of negotiation, between Bucharest and Moscow. In January, 1964, a high-level delegation from the Moldavian S.S.R. suddenly undertook to return a Bulgarian visit made in 1956, eight years earlier. The Moldavians were received in Sofia with great attention and toured the country for two weeks.[28] In February, Todor Zhivkov returned to Sofia from Moscow by train and stopped off in Kishenev for official ceremonies—an unprecedented act.[29] It was almost as if the Bulgarian party wished to underline the Soviet character of the Moldavian Republic. At about the same time as the Zhivkov stopover, Chinese-Soviet border negotiations got under way in Peking.

In June, 1964, an obscure Soviet journal, *Vestnik Moskovskogo Universiteta,* carried an article by E. B. Valev, a Soviet geographer of Bulgarian extraction, suggesting the establishment of supranational regional industrial complexes within the framework of CEMA. One such complex might consist of parts of the Ukraine, southern Rumania, and northern Bulgaria. The Rumanian press seized upon this article violently, presenting it as an attempt to partition Rumania, even implying that Transylvania was involved.[30] On July 4, *Izvestia* carried a repudiation of the Valev article. Two days later Prime Minister Ion Gheorghe Maurer, at the head of a powerful delegation, arrived in Moscow for a surprise visit. Six days later, while rumors circulated in London that Maurer had broached the subject of Bessarabia, Mao Tse-tung gave an interview to a delegation of Japanese socialists.[31] In the course of the interview the Chinese leader suggested that the Soviet imperialists continued to occupy territories not rightfully theirs, having been acquired in the past as the consequence of the imposition of unequal treaties. Among the territories mentioned by Chairman Mao was Bessarabia.[32]

In December, 1964, there appeared in the bookshops of Bucharest a collection of hitherto unpublished essays by Karl Marx entitled *Notes on the Rumanians.* In these essays Marx criticized Russia for annexing Bessarabia in 1812 even though the majority of the population spoke Rumanian.[33] Appropriately enough, the Institute of Party History managed to dig up a letter written by

Engels to the Rumanian socialists on January 4, 1888. Said Engels: "You have suffered much as a result of Kiselev's Organic Rule, the crushing of the 1848 Revolution and the twice repeated annexation of Bessarabia, not to mention the innumerable Russian invasions of your country, situated as it is on the route to the Bosphorus."[34] On the other hand, the new first secretary of the Rumanian party, Nicolae Ceausescu, paid a first official visit to the Soviet Union in September, 1965. The official communiqué issued on the occasion of the visit revealed that "both sides declare for the inviolability of the frontiers existing in Europe."[35] At about the same time the official Hungarian tourist agency began a series of unprecedented, regularly scheduled bus trips to Transylvania, thus reinstituting a measure of family contact with the minority across the eastern frontier.

In sum, communist Rumania had raised a territorial claim against Soviet Russia, was putting assimilationist pressure on its Hungarian minority, and was permitting the systematic exit migration of its Germans and its Jews.

THE METHODOLOGICAL PROBLEM

All of this is very strange behavior for a satellite communist regime, especially one originally imposed upon a recalcitrant population by a foreign army. So strange is this behavior that the experts had great difficulty in recognizing it for what it was. This brings us back to the methodological problem with which we started.

It is no explanation of our failure to recognize major communist developments early or to allege the sparsity of facts. Communist regimes are totalitarian in character in part to deny outsiders (and even insiders) essential elements of information. But the experts are supposed to be able to read whatever evidence is available because they have a picture of how the system works and have learned to follow the esoteric communication of the communists. In the Rumanian case there must have been something wrong with the experts' picture, for there was more evidence than usual that something extraordinary was going on.

As of the early 1960's, the following information was available:

1. There were no longer any Soviet troops in Rumania.
2. The Sino-Soviet quarrel had become irreparable, and Albania had successfully defied Moscow and joined the Chinese side.
3. The proportion of Rumanian trade with the U.S.S.R. had dropped from 51.5 per cent of the total in 1958 to 40.0 per cent in 1960.[36]
4. The Rumanians were involved in a dispute with their CEMA partners over their program of industrialization. There were generous Soviet credits for Kremikovtsi but none for Galati; indeed, no Soviet source had made any reference to Galati since July, 1960.
5. The party had grown in size by 70 per cent between 1955 and 1960.
6. The policy of cultural autonomy for the Hungarians had been reversed and Jewish and Saxon emigration was being permitted.
7. Since 1955 the regime had gradually changed its interpretation of the events of August 23 so as to minimize the Soviet role in the acquisition of power by the Rumanian party. At the November-December, 1961, plenum the Muscovite faction was attacked as the agent of a foreign (and, by inference, inimical) power.

Yet a search of the newspapers and of the learned literature of the period would probably reveal that no one thought anything unusual was going on in Bucharest.

There are no doubt many causes for what was obviously an inadequate picture of the functioning of the bloc and its regimes. Of immediate relevance is our inability to conceive of the Rumanian regime as capable of a national deviation. To put the point in the form of a question: Does not the fact of national deviation in Rumania suggest that all communism in power tends to become national communism?

Consider the following propositions:

1. A principal result of the Bolshevik seizure of power was the industrialization of Russia by forced marches. Partly as a consequence, Russia survived the German invasion of 1941 and came back to conquer the eastern half of Europe

and become the second most powerful state on the face of the globe.

2. Tito's partisans emerged victorious from the Yugoslav civil war of 1941–44 because they alone stood for the idea of a Yugoslav nation in a Yugoslav state. All the other contestants stood for particularist solutions—the Ustashe of Pavelic for an independent Croatia, the Chetniks of Mihailovic for a Serb-dominated Yugoslavia, the Macedonian communists for union with Bulgaria.

3. In seizing power in 1949, the Chinese Communists aimed to imitate the Bolsheviks, i.e., they intended (with Soviet help) to industrialize and modernize their nation of seven hundred million souls and to make of it the third superpower. The task before the Chinese Communists is even more formidable than that which faced the Bolsheviks. To impose the sacrifices and maintain the discipline called for by their situation, the Chinese Communists must maintain a situation of national emergency, which they do by promoting and dramatizing international tension.

4. In rebelling first against Yugoslav domination in 1948, then against Soviet patronage in 1961, and in joining the Chinese, the Albanian communists appear to have been primarily concerned with preserving the existence of Albania as a sovereign state.

The bloc is undergoing structural change. The Rumanian regime, after falling into the hands of a nativist leadership, now pursues a policy which involves: (*a*) rapid, all-round industrialization, (*b*) defiance of Russia, a hereditary enemy, and (*c*) compensation for the loss of Moscow's support in an enlarged base of domestic co-operation (and in increasing co-operation with the Western powers). Moscow had protected its vassal from the wrath of the people; now the people (and the West) were to shield the regime from the fury of the Kremlin.

If the analysis presented in the foregoing pages is correct, then any other East European regime, with the exception of the G.D.R., could successfully defy Moscow—that is, provided the regime were motivated to take the risk by the emergence of a major conflict of interest between itself and the U.S.S.R. What constitutes such a conflict is in considerable part, of course, a question of how the regime evaluates its own interest. There are, to be sure, strong cases of mutual national interest, e.g., Poland, the U.S.S.R., and the Oder-Neisse line. Defiance of Moscow also involves an act of political will, a readiness to exchange Muscovite patronage for domestic support, in the political conditions of Eastern Europe a somewhat hazardous enterprise. But it seems safe to say that a regime with a reason and a will can accomplish what the Rumanians have done, and with less risk.

In this connection, *nota bene:* a partisan faction in the Polish party which presents itself as possessing a strong nationalist orientation and which, in the last few years, has built up a major power position such as would allow it to wield decisive influence in determining the succession to Gomulka. And on the night of April 7–8, 1965, the Bulgarian police (with the help of Soviet security authorities?) crushed a conspiracy, no doubt the first of its kind in communist annals, based on the army and on ex-partisan elements. The aim of the conspirators was evidently that of establishing a regime on the Rumanian pattern: communist, but independent of Moscow.

What we need, in sum, is a new understanding of the relationship between communism and nationalism. To be more precise, we need a theory of the parochial uses of a universal faith. We tend to approach communism from an international standpoint, as a faith which absorbs and transforms particularisms. This approach has real merit. But we can also look at the reverse side of the picture: how parochial groups seize upon the communist view of the universal because it is useful to them in their immediate situations. This second approach has even greater merit. It might be helpful if we would remember that our own democratic faith combines a claim to universality with distinctly local uses.

NOTES

1. John Michael Montias, "Background and Origins of the Rumanian Dispute with Comecon," *Soviet Studies*, XVI (1964), 125–51. For a good account, see J. F. Brown, "Rumania Steps out of Line," *Survey*, October, 1963, pp. 19–34.
2. Montias, "Background and Origins of the Rumanian Dispute with Comecon," p. 149.
3. Brown, "Rumania Steps out of Line," p. 25.
4. Central Committee Declaration of April 22, 1964, *Scinteia*, April 26, 1964.
5. The G.D.R. would have been last because it is not a national entity, but

only a part (the smaller part) of a nation. Any attempt on the part of the G.D.R. to follow a policy opposed to that of Moscow would threaten its rapid transformation along national lines and its ultimate absorption by the larger, more powerful, and more prosperous part of the nation.

6. Although rejecting Soviet or CEMA joint companies, the Rumanians proposed at one point to establish analogous relationships with the West. Private Western firms would provide the equipment, the industrial know-how, and the managerial experience, while state-owned firms in Rumania would provide the plant, the labor, and the raw materials. Profits would be paid in dollars and marketing in third countries would be a joint operation. "Situation Report," *RFE Research: Rumania,* November 25 and December 15, 1964. On the other hand, Alexandru Barladeanu, speaking at the Nineteenth Party Congress in July, 1965, stated flatly that Rumania did not wish to be host to foreign investment capital.

7. According to an unpublished Czechoslovak computation cited by Montias, "Background and Origins of the Rumanian Dispute with Comecon," p. 130, n. 20. Writing from Belgrade, Harry Schleicher gives somewhat different figures. If the industrial production per capita of the G.D.R. be taken as 100, then the corresponding figures are 110 for Czechoslovakia, 60 for Poland, 55 for Hungary and only 36 for Rumania. Harry Schleicher, "Statt Arbeiterpartei wieder KP," *Süddeutsche Zeitung,* July 17–18, 1965, p. 9. Ultimately, of course, Soviet internationalism reflected Soviet national interests, e.g., the beefing up of CEMA was an endeavor to substitute economic controls of the satellite area for political controls which had either snapped or had become dangerously frayed.

8. In 1958 the Poles calculated that it cost them 40 million export zloty per annum to transport the slag content of Soviet iron ore from Krivoi Rog to Nowa Huta. See *Gospodarka Planovana,* January, 1958.

9. Montias, "Background and Origins of the Rumanian Dispute with Comecon," p. 127, n. 8.

10. Sandor Korosi-Kriszan, Political Secretary of the Rumanian Party from 1920–28, himself drafted a CC resolution according to which the national minorities had the right of secession. Conversation with Korosi-Kriszan, Munich, August 3, 1965.

11. The proceedings of the plenum are to be found in *Scinteia,* December 7, 1961. The bulk of the Spaniards, however, were from the minorities.

12. "Situation Report," *RFE Research: Rumania,* February 27, 1963; *Anuarul Statistic 1964,* p. 434. In 1964, the proportion of Rumanian trade with the U.S.S.R. was approximately 42 per cent. See "Rumania's Foreign Trade in 1964," *Information Bulletin* (Bucharest), No. 6 (June, 1965), p. 1.

13. The rumors concerning Khrushchev's attempt to unseat Gheorghiu-Dej assert that the Soviets approached Bodnaras, who at once reported the incident to Gheorghiu-Dej.

14. Ghita Ionescu, *Communism in Rumania 1944–62* (London, 1964), pp. 206–7.

15. *Scinteia,* July 20, 1965.

16. Gheorghiu-Dej in *For a Lasting Peace, for a People's Democracy* (Bucharest), June 23, 1950; *Scinteia,* December 25, 1955, June 20, 1960, and May 17, 1962; *Lupta de Clasa,* July, 1963, p. 5; *Agerpress,* April 17, 1965; *Scinteia,* July 20, 1965.

17. For these figures see *Scinteia* of December 25, 1955, and July 19, 1965.

18. For the April, 1962, plenum see *ibid.,* May 17, 1962; for the draft party statutes, *ibid.,* June 6, 1965.

19. *Ibid.,* August 23, 1955.

20. *Ibid.,* December 7, 1961.

21. G. St. Dumitrescu, "Gheorghiu-Dej on the '23 August 1944' *coup* in Rumania," *RFE Research: Rumania,* December 15, 1961. Henry L. Roberts, who was in touch with key Rumanian communists in 1944–45, reports the views of the Pauker group as running along these lines. See Roberts' *Rumania: Political Problems of an Agrarian State* (New Haven, Conn., 1951), pp. 259–60.

22. Ushakov's book was entitled *The Foreign Policy of Hitlerite Germany.* See James Brown, "Soviet-Rumanian Relations," *RFE Research: Rumania,* March 23, 1963.

23. "Blick durch den Vorhang," *Hinter dem eisernen Vorhang* X (1964), IV–V (January–February).

24. *Scinteia,* June 6, 1965.

25. I. Gheigel, "Bucharest Maxim Gorky Institute Incorporated into New Institute," *RFE Research: Rumania,* September 24, 1963; E. Raphael, "The Changing Intellectual Scene in Rumania—a Survey," *ibid.,* July 6, 1965; G. St. Dumitrescu, "Wider Horizons for Rumanian Scholarship," *ibid.,* December 12, 1964; A. Burilianu, "Winds of Change on the Rumanian Literary Scene?" *ibid.,* December 4, 1964.

26. A. Burilianu, "The Rumanian Writers and Western Literature," *ibid.,* April 30, 1964.

27. Conversation with Korosi-Kriszan, Munich, August 3, 1965.

28. "Situation Report," *RFE Research: Bulgaria,* January 21, 1964.

29. *Rabotnichesko Delo,* February 22 and 23, 1964.

30. For both the Valev article and the Rumanian reply, see *Viata Economica,* June 12, 1964, pp. 5–12. The explosive character of the Rumanian reaction may have been due to the Soviets having raised the Transylvanian question in behind-the-scenes Comecon negotiations.

31. "Situation Report," *RFE Research: Rumania,* July 17 and December 23, 1964.

32. *Pravda,* September 2, 1964; *Sekai Sinko* (Tokyo), August 11, 1964; "Khrushchev Warns Mao on Revision of Frontiers," UPI dispatch, September 15, 1964.

33. "Situation Report," *RFE Research: Rumania,* December 22, 1964.

34. Cited in "Situation Report," *RFE Research: Rumania,* December 23, 1964.

35. RFE Central Monitoring Desk, "Full Text of Soviet-Rumanian Communiqué Issued in Moscow Following the Visit of Ceausescu to the USSR," September 11, 1965.

36. See n. 12.

National Minority Problems

Chapter III.

6. National Minorities under Communism
in Eastern Europe.
GEORGE A. SCHÖPFLIN

6. National Minorities under Communism in Eastern Europe

George A. Schöpflin

Marxist-Leninist policies on minorities stem from Lenin's belief in the primacy of class over nationality. Lenin recognized that the aspirations of national minority groups to autonomy or independence could be turned to good account in the revolutionary process (his context here was primarily czarist Russia), but purely as a short-run tactic. In the long term, nationality was fundamentally subordinate to class. Thus Lenin favored the maximum use of national language to purvey propaganda, and he was prepared to accept the organization of administrative units along ethnic lines. But the degree to which ethnic minorities in the new Soviet state were permitted an independent existence was wholly contingent on their usefulness to the communist cause. The fate of the Chechens, the Ingushes, and the Crimean Tartars attests to the ruthless suppression of such groups when their existence was judged a threat or a liability to the pursuit of regime policies or goals.

National minorities have been dissipated or suppressed in other, less violent, ways. The process of industrialization, for example, requiring the influx of technicians and administrators from outside the national area and the movement of members of the minority group from the country into the cities, had the effect of gradually disrupting traditional patterns of life. Uprooted and dispersed, cast into the melting pot of the urban centers, minority elements eventually tended to lose their national identities and become assimilated. Mass colonization of minority areas also served to suppress minority groups. Kazakhstan is the classic example of an area in which the ethnic minority was submerged by a colonizing majority. The case of the Buryat-Mongols and Outer Mongolia illustrates yet another process—that of isolating a minority from its kinsmen abroad. The Rumanians in Moldavia were similarly weaned from the culture of the Rumanian national state. The tools employed included

Russification of the language; the local language in Moldavia, Rumanian, is not only written in Cyrillic but has been gradually modified by the introduction of new words based on Russian rather than on the Latin mother tongue. Over and above the processes and tactics which, individually and in combination, have suppressed or dissipated national minorities in the Soviet Union, the process of assimilation has been served by the fostering of what might be called "State patriotism" and discouragement of the maintenance of the distinct cultural and historical traditions of the minorities.[1]

The situation has not changed dramatically under Stalin's successors. They have, it is true, admitted that the nationalities deported and broken up in the Soviet Union during the war suffered unjustly. In a recent development, the rehabilitation of the Volga Germans was announced early in 1965.[2] But the policy of assimilation—or, more precisely, Russification—has continued. Khrushchev made clear in a speech at Leipzig, on March 7, 1959, the unaltered ultimate Marxist-Leninist goal of eradicating national identities:

> With the victory of communism on a world-wide scale, state frontiers will become extinct, as we learn from Marxist-Leninism. Only ethnic frontiers will remain in being, in all probability for some time to come. . . . These frontiers will demarcate the historically established homelands of definite peoples or nationalities in a definite territory. That this will be so is shown by the process that is under way today in the Soviet Union, which is now a multinational state. . . . Within the Soviet Union, nations are already united into one family.[3]

Beyond the borders of the Soviet Union, Khrushchev envisaged a "coalescence of people into a single communist family when the question of frontiers, as it is understood today, will cease to exist."

The Eastern European communists have professed to adopt the principles of Marxism-Leninism in dealing with their minorities. The Rumanians and Yugoslavs copied the Soviet tactics by establishing autonomous areas for some of their minorities, which should in theory foster the survival of variant cultural patterns. In practice, however, the communist governments have on the whole sought first and foremost to safeguard the integrity of their national states. The Czechs and Rumanians at first favored a policy of conciliating their minorities. During the period of consolidating communist rule they could not afford the additional source of disaffection which a dissatisfied minority would represent. Moreover, the proportionately larger communist party membership among the minorities would seem to have dictated conciliation during the initial period. In Yugoslavia, a country which could make no pretensions at all to being a unitary state and which had an exceptionally large number of nationality groups of various sizes, the problem was approached differently. From the outset, Belgrade attempted to reconcile the national minorities to their existence in Yugoslavia, and on the whole the cultural rights of minorities there have not been seriously infringed. Yugoslavia's special situation, however, was conditioned by two factors: First, in the immediate aftermath of the war, Belgrade's prestige was immeasurably enhanced by the fact that the Yugoslav communists had won power independently of the Red Army, unlike all the other East European communist regimes except that of Albania. Second, after the break with the Cominform in 1948 and the shift to internal liberalization in the years that followed, the position of the minorities was given more favorable consideration with a view to counteracting the hostile, disruptive propaganda of Yugoslavia's communist neighbors—particularly Hungary and Albania. But the long-term aim of assimilating the minorities, though violent means were to be excluded, was never abandoned.[4]

After 1956, with the rise of polycentrism and the concomitant upsurge of nationalism, the position of the minorities in Rumania and Czechoslovakia tended to deteriorate. This development was closely connected, at least as far as the Hungarian minorities were concerned, with the revolution of October, 1956, when the attitude of the Hungarian minorities was clearly one of sympathy with their conationals in Hungary. The potential threat to Rumania of a gradual "democratization" in Hungary, and the effect this might have on the Hungarians in Translyvania, encouraged Bucharest to strive more openly for a unitary state. A similar development took place in Czechoslovakia, though less explicitly and more gradually. Only in Yugoslavia did the Hungarian minority remain more or less contented. In all three countries the administrative machinery, ostensibly at the disposal of the minorities, was watered down by keeping the minorities in a numerical minority, even in areas where they would normally form a clear majority. A device that amounted to gerrymandering was employed to insure that the minorities did not find themselves in a position in which they might exercise political control in their own areas: Administrative districts were so delineated that the minorities remained minorities. This technique is hardly foreign to Western Europe. It is certainly being employed in the South Tirol, for example.

The assessment of the position of a minority under communist rule is complicated by the problem of gauging the extent to which repression is directed particularly and with special force at the minority group, as distinct from repression that falls on all sections of the population, including the minorities, with more or less equal force. The problem can be compounded when the standard of living of a minority is higher than that of the majority, as in the case of the Hungarians in Transylvania; the fact that their lands are confiscated and assets nationalized is not primarily determined by their nationality, but the effect is nonetheless to weaken their position as a nationality group. As the *Bulletin of the International Commission of Jurists* points out: "In a communist state the denial of freedom to any particular group must be examined in the context of the entire social and political outlook of the state, since many rights and freedoms as understood in liberal democracies are denied to the whole population. If it be that a particular group resists the process of socialization more vigorously than another, it is not easy to see the line between discrimination against that group and the employment of greater force to deal with greater resistance."[5]

Some Country-by-Country Statistics

It would be virtually impossible, in this brief paper, to deal in detail with all the minorities in the Eastern European communist states. There are innumerable small ethnic splinter groups in these countries, and virtually no reliable information about some of them is available. An idea of the multiplicity of nationalities in the region may be gleaned from the tables below, compiled primarily from census figures supplied by the countries themselves but with data from other sources, as indicated, where census statistics are lacking.

It may be noted, in regard to religious minorities, that the chief problem is to determine when a religious group feels itself to be a separate and distinct ethnic minority and when its members consider themselves to be nationals of the country in which they reside, distinguished from their conationals only by their religion. This problem exists notably in regard to the Jews of Rumania and the Moslem Pomaks of Bulgaria.

A distinction must also be drawn between more or less coequal nationality groupings (such as the Czechs and Slovaks in Czechoslovakia and the Serbs, Croats, and Slovenes in Yugoslavia) which make up multinational states and the smaller ethnic groups which compose genuine minorities.

Further, in scanning these tables, account must be taken of the sources—or, more properly speaking, the lack of sources. Census figures provided by the communist governments may understate the figures for particular minorities for a variety of reasons. Western sources may be just as unreliable in that they frequently

TABLE 6–1:

YUGOSLAVIA: BREAKDOWN OF POPULATION BY NATIONALITY, 1953 AND 1961

Nationality	1953	1961
Serbs	7,065,923	7,806,213
Croats	3,975,550	4,293,860
Slovenes	1,487,100	1,589,192
Macedonians	893,247	1,045,530
Montenegrins	466,093	513,833
Yugoslavs	998,698	317,125
Moslems	—	972,954
Shqiptars	754,245	914,760
Hungarians	502,175	504,368
Turks	259,535	182,964a
Slovaks	84,999	86,433
Rumanians	60,364	60,682
Bulgarians	61,708	62,624
Italians	35,874	25,615a
Czechs	34,517	30,331
Others	256,545	142,627
Total	16,936,573	18,549,291

a Loss through emigration.

SOURCE: *Statisticki Godisnjak SFRJ 1964* (Belgrade), Table 103–4.

emanate from *émigré* groups with their own axes to grind. Thus one must resort to something like a balancing act between sets of possibly slated figures—a risky process at best. Tables 6–1 through 6–6 accordingly provide an over-all picture of the com-

Table 6–2:

Rumania: Breakdown of Population by Nationality, by Birth and Mother Tongue, February 21, 1956

Nationality	By Birth		By Mother Tongue
Rumanians	14,996,114		15,080,686
Hungarians	1,587,675		1,653,700
Germans	384,708[a]		395,374
Jews	146,264[a]	Yiddish	34,337
Gypsies	104,216[a]		66,882
Ukrainians, Ruthenes	60,479		68,252
Serbs, Croats, Slovenes	46,517[a]		43,057
Russians	38,731[a]		45,029
Czechs, Slovaks	35,152[a]		25,131[b]
Tartars	20,469		20,574
Turks	14,329[a]		14,228
Bulgarians	12,040[a]		13,189
Others	42,756		29,011
Total	17,489,450		17,489,450

[a] These nationalities have declined in number since the census of 1930.
[b] Slovak by mother tongue, 18,935; Czech by mother tongue, 6,196.
Source: *Rumanian Statistical Pocket Book* (Bucharest), 1965, Tables 10 and 11.

Table 6–3:

Czechoslovakia: Breakdown of Population by Nationality, 1930, 1950, and 1959

Nationality	1930	1950	1959
Czechs	7,426,284	8,383,923	8,921,195
Slovaks	2,295,067	3,240,549	3,826,080
Hungarians	596,861	367,733	415,951
Germans	3,306,099	165,117	162,522
Ukrainians, Russians	118,440[a]	67,615	76,506
Poles	99,712	72,624	79,197
Others	156,034	40,889	41,363
Total	13,998,497	12,338,450	13,522,814

[a] This figure includes the population of Sub-Carpathia, which was ceded to the Soviet Union in 1945.
Source: *Czechoslovakia—Statistical Abstract* (Prague), 1963, Table S.

TABLE 6–4:
POLAND: BREAKDOWN OF POPULATION BY NATIONALITY[a]

Nationality	Number
Ukrainians[b]	180,000
Byelorussians[c]	165,000
Germans[d]	140,000
Slovaks	21,000
Russians	19,000
Gypsies	12,000
Lithuanians	10,000
Greeks, Macedonians	10,000
Czechs	2,000

[a] All figures are estimates. Polish official statistics do not provide breakdowns by nationality.

[b] The Ukrainians are largely diffused throughout the Polish population and do not appear to have a separate national consciousness. Many of them are refugees from the territories which were ceded to the Soviet Union in 1945.

[c] The Byelorussians tend to be concentrated around Bialystock.

[d] The figure for the Germans is that given by Bonn. With somewhat dubious validity, it includes the Masurians of the Olsztyn (Allenstein) area and the bilingual Polish-German inhabitants of parts of Silesia.

NOTE: The population of Poland, according to the census of December 6, 1960, was 29,776,370 (*Concise Statistical Yearbook of Poland* [Warsaw, 1964]). The above figures, with the exception of the ones for the Germans, are taken from Leszek Kosinski, "Poles among their neighbors," *Polityka*, October 30, 1965, Radio Free Europe, and Polish Press Survey, No. 1928. The figure for the Germans is taken from Guy Heraud, *L'Europe des Ethnies* (Paris, 1963), p. 238.

TABLE 6–5:
HUNGARY: BREAKDOWN OF POPULATION BY NATIONALITY[a]

Nationality	Number
Germans	220,000
Slovaks	110,000
Serbs, Croats	100,000
Rumanians	25,000

[a] Here, too, the figures are estimates. Hungarian official statistics do not provide breakdowns by nationality.

NOTE: The total population of Hungary in 1963, estimated on the basis of the census of January 1, 1960, was 10,071,715 (*Concise Statistical Pocket Book of Hungary* [Budapest, 1964]). The above minorities, about 450,000 in all, form approximately 4.5 per cent of the total population of Hungary.

None of these minorities forms a compact group; all tend rather to be scattered throughout the country; they live by and large in villages and are employed in agriculture. Education is guaranteed in their mother tongues, both at the primary and at the secondary level. In addition, there are teacher training facilities for each minority. Each group has its own newspaper: Germans, *Neu Zeitung;* Slovaks, *Ludové Noviny;* Yugoslavs, *Narodne Novine;* and Rumanians, *Foaia Noastra*.

SOURCE: MTI report, July 29, 1964.

plex of nationalities, big and small, that make up the ethnic patchwork quilt that is Eastern Europe, rather than a precise and systematic breakdown of reliable statistics on each individual group.

TABLE 6–6:

OTHER COUNTRIES: BREAKDOWN OF POPULATION BY NATIONALITY[a]

BULGARIA	
Nationality	Number
Turks	500,000
Gypsies	150,000
Pomaks[b]	300,000
Macedonians[c]	300,000

ALBANIA

There are Greek and Kutuzo-Vlach minorities totaling about 35,000.

EAST GERMANY

The number of Lusatian Sorbs was estimated at about 30,000 in 1961. The Sorbs have a measure of local autonomy and bilingual administration, as well as educational facilities.

[a] All figures are approximate.
[b] The Pomaks are Bulgarian-speaking Moslems.
[c] It is questionable whether the Macedonians of Pirin are a minority, properly speaking. They probably tend to identify themselves with Bulgaria.
SOURCE: Guy Heraud, *L'Europe des Ethnies* (Paris, 1963).

FIVE IMPORTANT ETHNIC MINORITIES

A close look will be taken here at a selected group of ethnic minorities which are of sufficient size to represent sources of political concern to the majority nationalities of the countries in which they reside. These are the Hungarians in Slovakia, the Hungarians and Germans (Transylvanian Saxons and Donau-schwaben) in Rumania, and the Albanians and Hungarians in Yugoslavia.

Czechoslovakia's Hungarian Minority. In contrast to the prewar situation, the only significant ethnic minority in Czechoslovakia today is the Hungarian population of southern Slovakia. According to the census of 1955, it was 392,056 strong. This figure, however, must be regarded with some caution. According to the census of 1930, the number of Hungarians at that time was about

572,000; even taking into account the population exchanges and expulsions of the immediate postwar period, which affected some 100,000 people, the 1955 figure fails to account for 100,000 people. Clearly, the "re-Slovakization" campaign initiated by the postwar government must have had some effect if that many persons who would have been bilingual came to declare themselves of Slovak nationality.

The constitutional position of the Hungarians, as of the Ukrainians and Poles, is laid down in Article 25 of the 1960 Constitution. This article provides: "For the citizens of Hungarian, Ukrainian, and Polish nationality the state guarantees all possibilities and means for their education in their mother tongue and for their cultural development." In the draft text of the constitution there was also a sentence guaranteeing the minorities "full participation in the life of the society of working people," but this was deleted. The omission was explained by Novotny during the debate on the new constitution at the Party Congress of July 5–7, 1960. He stated that the right of full participation was guaranteed to all Czechoslovak citizens in any event; hence its repetition in this context was superfluous. (In connection with minorities policy Novotny also stated that citizens of German nationality, unlike the others mentioned above, no longer constituted an ethnic unit in Czechoslovakia and that therefore the right to education in their mother tongue was not guaranteed them in the constitution.)

One can trace three principal phases in the Prague government's policy toward the Hungarian minority since the war. The first was from 1945 to 1948. During this time the avowed policy of the Czech government was to eliminate Czechoslovakia's national minorities on the ground that they had materially contributed to the internal weakness of the country during the inter-war period. Following the Košice Program of 1945 a number of measures discriminating against the Hungarians were introduced. These included (1) loss of citizenship, on the ground that "Hungarians were enemies of the state";[6] (2) the trial of all persons who may have been connected with the Hungarian administration between 1938 and 1944; (3) a ban on the organization of national committees in the Hungarian areas; (4) the confiscation of property and no compensation for war damage; and (5) the closing of Hungarian schools and frequently imposed bans on Hungarian-language religious services. The concept which underlay this policy was that of collective guilt of the minority.

In addition to the measures cited above, the Prague government proposed an exchange of populations with the Hungarian government in Budapest. After the war there were about 100,000 Slovaks living in Hungary, and in exchange for these people the Prague government wished to return Hungarians on a one-for-one basis. An agreement was signed with the Budapest government on February 27, 1946, which the Hungarians, however, did a good deal to sabotage. In the end, about 53,000 Hungarians were exchanged and some 39,000 more were expelled on various grounds. A further measure instituted by the Prague government, not specifically directed against the minorities, was that of compulsory labor in the Sudetenland. Several thousand Hungarians were thought to have been affected by this measure, but most of them returned to Slovakia after 1948.

After the communist takeover, the new government claimed that it would solve the minority problem according to the principles of Marxism-Leninism, and certainly the new policies curbed most of the excesses of the precommunist period. In the period after 1948, Hungarians had their citizenship rights restored, and facilities for education and cultural life were freely granted—to some extent even encouraged. Thus Karol Bacilek, the first secretary of the Slovak Party, stated that he opposed the excesses of Slovak "bourgeois nationalism."[7] He pronounced himself against the Slovakization of Hungarian place names and instead encouraged the Hungarians to demand use of "the fine old Hungarian place names."[8] Apart from a general desire to settle the problem of the Hungarian minority, which was potentially restive, the Czechs saw in the Hungarians a possible counterweight to the Slovaks, whose opposition to Prague centralism, whether communist or not, was well recognized. It is also significant that the Czechoslovak Communist Party was proportionately stronger among the Hungarians than among the Slovaks and that several of the higher communist functionaries—notably Siroky—were of Hungarian origin.

The policy favoring the Hungarian minority lasted from 1948 until about 1960. In that year there existed some twenty Hungarian-language journals and newspapers; thirty-three literary works were published; and there were some eighty thousand pupils in

Hungarian schools, with about three thousand teachers.[9] There can be little doubt that the ensuing change in tactics and the decision to press more vigorously for the assimilation of the Hungarians was at least partially motivated by the events of the autumn of 1956. During the Hungarian revolution the Slovakian minority was extremely restive. It must have become crystal clear to the Prague government, if there had ever been any doubt, where Hungarian sympathies lay. It was judged that the minority represented a potential danger to the state in that the minority would never be fully reconciled to incorporation in Czechoslovakia.

The policies initiated during the third phase, from 1960 to date, rested on three bases: There was, first, a loosening of the compactness of the Hungarian-inhabited areas, partly by Slovakization and Slovak "colonization," partly by industrialization requiring the influx of Czech technicians and functionaries, and finally through administrative reorganization. Second, stress was placed on the principle of "socialist patriotism" in educational and cultural policy, as well as on "loyalty to the Czech homeland." All aspects of cultural life—education, theaters, libraries, and the publication of books—were affected. Third, the teaching of Slovak to the Hungarians was intensified. References to the importance of the Hungarians having a better command of Slovak recurred with increasing frequency in the speeches of various functionaries after about 1960.[10] This aspect of the policy toward the Hungarians bears a strong resemblance to the Magyarization policies of the Budapest government at the end of the nineteenth century.

The administrative reorganization took place early in 1960. It was justified on the grounds that "the development of our society requires that we further strengthen the role of the national committees in their task of realizing the building of socialism. We must broaden the effectiveness of the national committees and entrust them with the direction of economic, cultural, and social organization. . . . All this demands that we change the heretofore existing organization of the administrative divisions of the state, which in relation to the stage of development of our society has become outdated."[11]

In practice the reorganization took the form of altering the boundaries of Hungarian administrative areas so that the proportion of Slovaks residing there would be increased and the Hungarians, reduced to a smaller proportion, would be forced out of administrative and other positions; ultimately, Hungarian was to be excluded as an administrative language.

During this phase, the Czechoslovak Communist Party was still insisting that it was following the principles of Marxism-Leninism in its minorities policy, but evidently the means by which the policy was to be implemented had been re-evaluated. Thus it was stated in a book on the Party's nationalities policy that the problem of the minorities was secondary in importance to that of building socialism. Although Marxism-Leninism guaranteed minorities the right to manage their own affairs, even including the right of secession, this did not mean that the enforcement of this right was guaranteed. Hence in the post-1960 phase the problem of nationalities became secondary to the struggle for the attainment of socialism, and it is this fact which explains the omission of the guarantee of full rights to the minorities from the 1960 Constitution, which granted at best some privileges.[12]

The place of the Hungarian minority in the "Czechoslovak homeland" was defined by Jan Uher in an article in *Új Szó* entitled "Certain Questions Concerning the Life of the Citizens of Hungarian Nationality in the CSSR."[13] This article stated that the party was still following the principles of Marxism-Leninism in its minorities policy, but that schools must deepen the consciousness of Czechoslovak patriotism among the minorities. This was to be accomplished first of all through a complete understanding of the language (Slovak), a complete mastery of the language being in the primary interests of the minority because only thus could its members participate fully in the life of the country.

It would appear from this brief survey of the position of the Hungarian minority in Slovakia that the Prague government, almost certainly with the full approval of Bratislava, is intent on pursuing a policy that will ultimately lead to assimilation. In this it is tacitly abetted by the policy of the Budapest government, which has made it quite clear that it has no intention of intervening on behalf of the Hungarian minority—a reversal of the irredentist policies of the Horthy regime. The Hungarian government probably has little alternative. One can also appreciate the viewpoint of Prague. The Hungarians inhabit a strip of land contiguous to the frontier and would certainly welcome a reversal of the Trianon settlement. This, however, would leave Slovakia weakened and economically poorer, and it is in any event something which no Prague government could contemplate. The fact that "democratization" is much further advanced in Hungary than in Czecholslovakia is a further factor likely to induce Prague to tread circumspectly and discourage its Hungarians from looking across the frontier. All in all, the prospects facing the Hungarian minority in Slovakia are not encouraging.

Rumania's Hungarian and German Minorities. According to the census figures of 1956, there are 1,587,675 Hungarians in Rumania, together with another 66,025 people who give their mother tongue but not their nationality as Hungarian; the same census categorizes 384,708 people as Germans by nationality and a further 10,666 having German as their mother tongue. The Hungarians are concentrated partly along the border with Hungary, with a center at Oradea (Nagyvarad), and in the Mureş-Magyar Autonomous Area, the capital of which is Tîrgu-Mureş (Marosvásárhely). There are also significant numbers of Hungarians in most of the towns in Transylvania, and it is estimated that there may be about 10,000 Hungarians in Bucharest. The Germans divide into the Transylvanian Saxons, centering around Sibiu (Hermannstadt), and the Donauschwaben in the Banate.[14]

Policy on Minorities. The Preamble to the Constitution of 1952 grants the following rights to the minorities: "The national minorities of the Rumanian People's Republic enjoy rights absolutely equal to those of the Rumanian people. In the Rumanian People's Republic, administrative and territorial autonomy is guaranteed to the Hungarian population of the Szekler *rayons*, where this population forms a compact group."[15]

Article 82 states: "In the Rumanian People's Republic the national minorities are assured full freedom to employ their mother tongue, the right to education at all levels in their mother tongue, and to books, newspapers, and theaters in their mother tongue. In *rayons* inhabited equally by peoples of other than the Rumanian nationality, all organs and institutions will make equal use, orally and in writing, of the language and way of life of the local population.

These provisions, however, should be viewed in the light of Article 17: "The people's democratic Rumanian state—a unitary, sovereign, and independent state . . . assures the development of the culture of the Rumanian people and the culture of the national minorities, socialist in content and national in form."[16]

In his report on the draft constitution to the General Assembly of the Rumanian People's Republic on September 23, 1952, Gheorghe Gheorghiu-Dej had the following to say regarding minorities: "The people's democratic state . . . has granted equality of rights to the national minorities residing in Rumania and has created the most favorable conditions for their development in all fields. . . . The draft constitution provides a democratic solution at the highest level to the nationalities question in Rumania in envisaging the establishment of a Hungarian autonomous region in the territory inhabited by a compact population of Szekler Hungarians."[17]

Similar clauses were inserted into the Peace Treaty of 1947 between Rumania and the Allied powers.[18]

The draft constitution of 1965, published at the end of June, mirrors the significant changes in policy towards the minorities which have taken place in the intervening years. Article 1 provides that "the Socialist Republic of Rumania . . . is sovereign, independent, and a single entity. Its territory is inalienable and indivisible."[19] Article 17 deals with the minorities in passing, together with Article 22. Article 17 states: "The citizens of the Socialist Republic of Rumania, regardless of nationality . . . , enjoy equal rights in all fields of economic, political, legal, social, and cultural life. . . . No limitation of these rights and no discrimination in their exercise for reasons of nationality . . . are permitted. Any manifestation aimed at establishing such limitations, nationalistic-chauvinistic propaganda, and incitement to racial or national hatred is a punishable offense."

And Article 22: "In the Socialist Republic of Rumania the resident nationalities are insured the free use of their mother tongue, as well as of books, newspapers, magazines, theater, and education at all levels in their own tongue. In *rayons* with nationals other than Rumanians, all the organs and institutions shall also use, orally and in writing, the language of the respective nationality and appoint employees from its ranks or other citizens who know the language and the way of life of the local population."

Article 102, corresponding to Article 68 of the 1952 Constitution, permits the use of languages other than Rumanian in the courts for those who do not speak it. The most important difference between the 1952 and the 1965 Constitutions is the omission in the latter of the provisions dealing with the compact mass of the Szekler population (Preamble and Article 19 of the 1952 Constitution). There is also a certain difference between Article 82 of the old and Article 22 of the new constitution in that the latter speaks of "the resident nationalities," the adjective "resident" implying that the nationalities have no fundamental right to be considered full-fledged Rumanians, but are merely tolerated.

These changes, especially the downgrading of the special status of the Hungarians, in effect no more than formalize an already existing state of affairs. The new constitution underlines the fact that Rumania has little time for its minorities.

The Hungarian Minority. After the war and the reversal of the Vienna Award of 1940, which involved the return of northern Transylvania to Rumania from Hungary, there was a period when the Bucharest government did take certain measures to conciliate the Hungarian minority, and possibly also the regime in Budapest.[20] Probably the presence of Petru Groza at the head of the Rumanian government influenced this, since he was a Transylvanian and could speak Hungarian. Apparently under pressure from Moscow, the 1952 Constitution provided for a Magyar Autonomous Area, which included about one-third of the Hungarian minority. The privileges granted to the Hungarians at this time were certainly extensive. They included numerous Hungarian-language schools, a medical institute at Tîrgu-Mureş (Marosvásárhely), and the Bólyai University at Cluj (Kolozsvár), where Hungarian was the language of instruction. As in Czechoslovakia, the larger proportion of communists among the Hungarians constituted a certain safeguard against possible Rumanian nationalistic excesses.

The Constitution of 1952 was in many ways a high-water mark of the policy of conciliation toward the Hungarians. It was in

1952 that the Rumanian wing of the party consolidated its power against the Muscovities—who included Vasile Luca, a Hungarian by origin—and that Gheorghiu-Dej assumed control with the liquidation of the Pauker-Luca-Georgescu faction.[21] From then on the party, and presumably its policy too, were to be "Rumanianized."

The new policy did not become evident, however, until after 1956. The Hungarian revolution of that year did not pass without certain disturbances among the Hungarians in Transylvania. There were meetings and demonstrations at Tîrgu-Mureş (Marosvásárhely), Timişoara (Tenmesvár), and Cluj (Kolozvár), and it was reported that those units of the Rumanian Army which were composed of Hungarians were restive.[22] Bucharest did not move against the Hungarians immediately. The measures taken against them were unfolded slowly from 1957 onward and may to some extent have been delayed until after the death of Petru Groza in 1958. Most important, they included a declaration by Kádár in February, 1958, that Hungary held no claim to those Rumanian territories inhabited by Hungarians. In effect, he could have done nothing else at that time, since his domestic position was still very weak and he had received a considerable amount of aid from Rumania. After this, a mass purge got under way in Transylvania; Bucharest was determined to liquidate the state-within-a-state which the Hungarians represented. There were widespread arrests of intellectuals and other measures of intimidation which culminated in the merging of the (Hungarian) Bólyai University with the (Rumanian) Babeş University in Cluj (Kolozsvár) on July 3, 1959, after a meeting of professors and students had unanimously "approved" the scheme.[23] This was followed by the "Rumanianization" of secondary education. The measures included the introduction of parallel Rumanian sections into purely Hungarian schools, the abolition of Hungarian sections in mixed schools, and a decree permitting only the eldest child of a family to receive his education in Hungarian.

The next move came against the Autonomous Area in December, 1960. Symbolically, its name was changed from the Magyar Autonomous Area to the Mureş-Magyar Autonomous Area, implying that it should no longer be considered an area where the Hungarians form a compact mass of the population.[24] This was also justified in the fact by the administrative reorganization of the Area. The reorganization involved the transfer of the purely Hungarian districts of Sfantu Gheorghe (Sepsiszentgyörgy) and Tîrgu Secuesc (Kézdivásárhely) to the province of Braşov (Brassó) and the attachment of the Rumanian districts of Tirnaveni (Dicsöszentmarton), Şarmaşu (Kissármás), and Luduş (Marosludas) to the Autonomous Area. By this maneuver the number of Hungarians in the Area dropped from 564,510 to 473,154, while those of the Rumanians increased from 146,830 to 266,403. The introduction of the reform, whatever its national aspects, certainly served to strengthen the Area economically, as the newly transferred districts possessed important industrial concerns. Ceauşescu stressed the important financial saving which would accrue from the reorganization and emphasized that it would create stronger and more viable economic units.

That the situation of the Hungarian minority had deteriorated considerably was indicated by a memorandum, in all probability genuine, which was smuggled out to the West and was reported in several Western newspapers.[25] This document, although it may to some extent have exaggerated the picture of oppression, was revealing in its description of wide-scale arrests, deportations, and in some cases even executions of Hungarians suspected or involved in what the authorities considered activities hostile to the state. It was stated that several members of the Bólyai University faculty committed suicide after the enforced merger with the Babeş University. This last statement has been borne out by other evidence. It appears that one of the pro-rectors of the Bólyai University, László Szabédi, his wife, and five other university professors committed suicide. The impact of seven suicides on such a relatively small town as Cluj was devastating and may well have been one factor prompting Bucharest to carry out its policies more circumspectly.[26]

There is little doubt that Bucharest is working for the total fragmentation and assimilation of the Hungarian minority. Recent reports from Transylvania indicate that an atmosphere of terror is strongly in evidence there. Transylvania is probably the only place now under communist rule where one still finds such manifestations—once characteristic of the Stalinist era—as fear of contact with foreigners. Pressure on the Hungarians to "denationalize" themselves is intense and unremitting. For instance, there is an absolute ban on Hungarians wishing to settle in any urban area in Transylvania; conversely, Rumanians from the Regat, especially Oltenia, are encouraged to immigrate. Another practice is the insistence that Hungarians spell their names according to the Rumanian orthography; it seems that to use the Hungarian orthography has become a declaration of national allegiance. The teaching of history, of course, makes no mention of the independent role of Transylvania during the Turkish occupation; and although a fair amount of material is published in Hungarian, this is frequently translated from the Rumanian. Although a Hungarian-Rumanian cultural agreement provides for the import of a certain number of books and periodicals from Hungary, it is believed that much of this material never finds its way to Transylvania, but rather is put on sale in the Regat, where there are no Hungarians. Because Hungary is also a communist country, Rumania cannot very well jam Hungarian broadcasts; nevertheless, listening to the Budapest radio is frowned on and may in certain circumstances be regarded as evidence of chauvinism or unreliability.[27]

It is questionable whether the recent changes in the composition of the government to include a number of ethnic Hungarians, such as the nomination of Ion Fazekas to be a deputy premier, represent an improvement for the Hungarian minority. Those ethnic Hungarians who have been appointed are either people who have entirely sold out to the Rumanians or are in such a delicate position vis-à-vis the Rumanians that they dare not take any action which might be cited as evidence of pro-Hungarian sympathies. As a result, Hungarians often prefer to deal with Rumanian officials, who do not have to bend over backwards to prove their loyalty to the state.

The blame for the bad relations between Hungarians and Rumanians should not be ascribed entirely to the latter. The attitude of the Hungarians tends to be one of contempt and non-co-operation towards the Rumanians and suggests that they have learned little since 1918.[28] The tragedy of the situation is perhaps best summed up in a comment ascribed to "a member of a linguistic minority": "I'm genuinely fond of the Rumanians, but I'll never get them to believe it."[29] However, even discounting factors such as these, it is difficult not to subscribe to the conclusion spelled out by the International Commission of Jurists: "Too many individual items which could be capable of other explanations than discrimination, if taken singly, point unmistakably, when viewed as a whole, toward a pattern of conduct. In short, as far as the Hungarian people in Rumania are concerned, they appear in the give and take of living together to lose on both the swings and the roundabouts. When this happens to a minority group, it is difficult to resist the conclusion that they are being subjected to discrimination."[30]

The German Minority. In contrast to its policy toward the Hungarians, Bucharest appears to have reached a *modus vivendi* with the German minority. Although immediately after the war there were expulsions and deportations, including forced labor in the Soviet Union, these measures were in many cases taken at the initiative of the Russians and there was no policy of wholesale expulsion of the Germans as in Czechoslovakia and Poland. Consequently, the Transylvanian Saxons and the Banater Schwaben form the largest single German minority in Europe. In contrast to the Hungarians, the Germans have never really posed a serious problem for Bucharest, and the question of *irredenta* never arose to menace the integrity of the state. The Germans are not a compact geographical group, but are for the most part scattered throughout southern Transylvania. They live principally in the province of Brașov (Kronstadt), where they constitute 16.4 per cent of the population; around Timișoara (Tenmesvár), 14.6 per cent; Hunedoara (Eisenmerkt), 6.4 per cent; and Oradea (Grosswardein), 1.2 per cent.

The people whose land and property had been confiscated after the war received compensation in 1956, either through actual return of the property involved or in the form of monetary repayment.[31] The decision to grant compensation was taken "to end the policy of national discrimination." Similarly, in 1956–57, negotiations were initiated between Rumania and West Germany to permit the repatriation of those Germans who had close relatives in the latter country. This agreement, which was concluded through the good offices of the Red Cross, permitted some thirteen thousand persons to emigrate to West Germany. When subsequently the Rumanians appeared to have second thoughts on the matter and failed to permit the agreed repatriations, West Germany replied with economic sanctions. West German trade, which in 1958 had been valued at DM seventy-one million, fell by DM twenty-one million in 1959 after the imposition of import restrictions in January of that year. The lifting of these restrictions in October, 1959, was followed by revival of the issue of exit visas for Germans in Rumania. There has since been a steady trickle of Germans emigrating from Rumania, although it appears that one of the conditions for this emigration is that it receive no publicity.

Although relations between the Germans and the Rumanians are incomparably better than between the Germans and the Hungarians, there is little doubt that they, too, have been affected by the upsurge of Rumanian nationalism in the last few years. The number of German-language secondary schools in Rumania has tended to decline, as has the number of children attending them. In 1955–56 there were 132 secondary schools in which the language of instruction was exclusively German, with another 18 which had German sections; by 1958–59 the figures were 85 and 34, respectively.[32] The drop in the number of German school children receiving education in their mother tongue is also indicated by the fact that by the 1956 census Germans formed 2.2 per cent of the population of Rumania, while only 0.87 per cent of the school children were being taught in German.

Nevertheless, since a large proportion of the Germans in Rumania tends to be composed of skilled craftsman with a generally high educational level, the economic value of the Germans to the Rumanian state more than outweighs any political disadvantage which may stem from their presence in the country. Moreover, since the Germans form no compact group and have neither a strong organized political movement nor external support, the Rumanians can hardly regard their presence as a threat to the security or integrity of the state.

Yugoslavia's Minorities.   In view of its diverse national composition, Yugoslavia has been forced to devote somewhat greater attention to the problem of intranational relations and minorities policy than the other communist states. The communists who took over at the end of the war found several minorities disaffected and strongly hostile toward Belgrade. The policies adopted and pursued in the postwar period succeeded in keeping the minorities reasonably reconciled to the idea of remaining in

—or being reincorporated into—Yugoslavia. Immediately after the war the communists ruthlessly punished all those who had collaborated; they expelled most of the Germans, threatening at one stage to do the same to the Hungarians, while at the same time making it clear that revenge on the minorities by the rest of the population was not to be tolerated.[33] This policy came to be tested in 1948 after the break with the Cominform, and it was vindicated. Despite the efforts of both Budapest and Tirana— Bucharest and Sofia were involved to a lesser extent—to exploit the minority issue and turn it against the security of Yugoslavia, the overwhelming bulk of the minorities remained loyal to Tito. Having eliminated the potential threat to the country which the presence of the minorities posed, the Yugoslavs turned their attention to positive measures designed to integrate the minorities into the mainstream of Yugoslav life. This included the establishment of schools in which instruction was provided in minority languages, as well as cultural organizations, publications, theaters, and so forth to serve the minorities. Functionaries were recruited from the minorities, and autonomous administrative areas were erected in the Vojvodina and the Kosmet.

This far-reaching cultural autonomy helped to entrench the isolation of the minorities, however, and during the 1950's a reexamination of the minorities policy brought Belgrade to the conclusion that this isolation would have to be broken down. Proceeding cautiously, the various local cultural organizations, set up on a purely national basis, were gradually dissolved and replaced by cultural groups organized by local "people's committees" in which all minorities were to participate together with the majority nationality in each republic. In education, too, there has been a shift in emphasis, with greater stress placed on the teaching of the official languages. Minority schools have tended to be merged with Yugoslav schools in mixed areas, though bilingual teaching has been retained.

The objectives of the Yugoslav regime's minorities policy are reflected in the following passage, however much wishful thinking it may involve:

> In conditions of dynamic economic development and intensive production and communications, the citizen of Yugoslavia, as a contemporary producer with a defi-

nite level of production and general culture, is less and less tied to his place of birth. In conditions of full equality, he is primarily guided by material interests in choosing his working organization—i.e., the social community in which he will live. He is less interested in the question of the nationality to which the majority of the population in this social community belongs, the more so since the languages spoken by the peoples of Yugoslavia, including even Slovene, are similar and easily understandable. . . . In such conditions, marriages between citizens of different nationalities are most frequent, and their children belong, in fact, to two rather than to one nationality. . . . Citizens born of such marriages no longer feel a need to declare themselves nationally, but only socially, as citizens of a definite socialist social community.[34]

The 1963 constitution guarantees extensive cultural rights to the minorities (or rather to the "nationalities-national minorities," as they are now defined), who, are, however, to be distinguished from the "peoples of Yugoslavia." One major privilege granted to the latter is withheld from the minorities: The majority "peoples"—the Serbs, Croats, Slovenes, Montenegrins, Macedonians, and Yugoslavs—retain the right to education in their own languages.[35] The constitution of the Serbian Republic, which includes both the Autonomous Province of Vojvodina and the Autonomous Oblast of Kossovo-Metohija (Kosmet), contains detailed provisions regulating the rights of the minorities.[36] In practice, the Yugoslav record in educational and cultural treatment of the minorities has been good and even generous, especially when compared with the prewar situation and with the policies of other communist, or for that matter non-communist, countries.

The over-all result of this policy is that there has been comparatively little discontent among the minorities. The Albanian Shqiptars, potentially by far the most dangerous, have remained by and large unaffected by the barrage of propaganda directed at them from Tirana since 1957. On February 13, of that year Hoxha made a speech in which he accused the Yugoslavs of carrying out a policy of "denationalizing" the Kosmet.[37] This attack came as something of a surprise, since as late as the autumn of 1956 Tirana had assured the Yugoslavs that it was not interested in the Shqiptar minority. Furthermore, an attack on out-and-out irredentist grounds was a departure from the existing communist line and had no precedent even during the worst days of the Cominform dispute. The attempts made by the Albanians and Hungarians during the dispute to sow disaffection amongst the minorities had never entailed an actual questioning of Yugoslavia's territorial integrity. Hoxha's attack drew a protest from Belgrade and the withdrawal of ambassadors, and there has since been a steady barrage of recriminations between the two capitals.

The real salvation of the Yugoslav policy toward the Shqiptars is that the minority is backward and almost wholly apolitical. Despite the trials of Albanians on charges of disseminating propaganda endangering the security of the state, the vast mass of the population remains too poor to care. But once the generation of Shqiptars which is now being educated starts to have an impact on the Kosmet, the situation is likely to become potentially explosive, especially in view of the fact that on the personal level relations between the Shqiptars, Serbs, and Montenegrins are traditionally bad.[38] In a sense, Belgrade will have brought its troubles on itself, through the massive efforts directed at raising the Kosmet out of its medieval backwardness. The best safeguard against such an explosion in the future would be to make Yugoslavia a more attractive place to live in than Albania, and it is precisely such thinking which seems to underlie Yugoslavia's present policy.

The principal problem with respect to the minorities, as seen from Belgrade, is that they do not want to be integrated into the mainstream of Yugoslav life. Communism alienates them from authority far more than the Yugoslav nationalities do, since the minorities regard communism as a purely Slavic tool. The problem of reconciling the minorities to their position in Yugoslavia is still not solved, but the communists have been far more successful than their predecessors.

NOTES

1. For an exhaustive treatment of this subject see Walter Kolarz, *The Peoples of the Soviet Far East* (London, 1954).

2. The decree announcing this was published in January, 1965, dated August 29, 1964. Unlike the other deported ethnic minorities, however, the Volga Germans were not permitted to return to their homelands.

3. Cited in Elliot R. Goodman, "Die künftige Verschmelzung der Völker," *Osteuropa*, October, 1961, p. 738.

4. Paul Shoup, "Yugoslavia's National Minorities under Communism," *Slavic Review*, March, 1963, p. 64.

5. "The Hungarian Minority Problem in Rumania," *Bulletin of the International Commission of Jurists*, No. 17 (December, 1963), p. 35.

6. János Ölvedi, "Magyarok Szlovákiában," *Új Látóhatár*, November-December, 1961, and January-February, 1962.

7. *Új Szó* (Bratislava), December 22, 1963, cited by Ölvedi in "Magyarok Szlovákiában."

8. *Új Szó*, June 5, 1951, cited by Ölvedi, *ibid.*

9. Cited by Ölvedi from *Új Szó*.

10. For instance, Bacílek, speaking in 1962 to the Eighth General Assembly of the Cultural Union of Hungarian Workers in Czechoslovakia (Csemadok): "Work in the organizations (national committees, trade unions, etc.) should not be divided on ethnic lines, and [on] no account must separate Hungarian and Slovak groups be established. This would alienate us from one another and prejudice our joint aims. . . . First and foremost we must establish the principle of bilingualism in areas with a mixed population." Cited in "Chronik: Tschechoslowakei," *Osteuropa*, August-September, 1962, quoting *Pravda* (Bratislava), April 15, 1962.

11. *Új Szó*, January 16, 1960, cited by Ölvedi in "Magyarok Szlovákiában."

12. Ölvedi citing M. Hájek and O. Stanková, *Národnostni Otázka v Lidově Demokratickém Československu* (Prague, 1956).

13. June 8, 1961, cited by Ölvedi in "Magyarok Szlovákiában."

14. Figures from *Rumanian Statistical Pocket Book*, 1965, Tables 10 and 11.

15. *Constitution de la République Populaire Roumaine* (Bucharest, 1952).

16. *Ibid.*

17. Gheorghe Gheorghiu-Dej, *Rapport sur le projet de Constitution de la R.P.R.* (Bucharest, 1952), p. 33.

18. Details in "The Hungarian Minority Problem in Rumania," *Bulletin of the International Commission of Jurists*.

19. Text of the draft constitution in B.B.C., *Summary of World Broadcasts*, Part 2 (Eastern Europe), EE/1899/B/1–12.

20. J. F. Brown, "The Age-Old Question of Transylvania," *World Today*, November, 1963, p. 500.

21. Ghita Ionescu, *Communism in Rumania 1944–1962* (London, 1964), p. 208.

22. Elek Telegdi, "Position of the Hungarian Minority in Rumania," *The Review* (Brussels), No. 2 (1963).

23. J. F. Brown, "The Age-Old Question of Transylvania," p. 503.

24. As described in the Preamble to the 1952 Constitution.

25. *The Observer*, April 14 and May 5, 1963.

26. Judith Listowel, "The Case of A Minority," *The Listener*, November 4, 1965, pp. 692–93.

27. "Levél Erdélyből," *Irodalmi Ujág* (Paris), November 1, 1965.

28. Viktor Meier, "Rumäniens Selbständigkeit im Ostblock: Machtrealismus des Regimes von Bukarest," *Neue Zürcher Zeitung*, May 25, 1965.

29. Quoted by François Bondy in "Rumanian Travelogue," *Survey*, April, 1965, p. 30.

30. "The Hungarian Minority Problem in Rumania," *Bulletin of the International Commission of Jurists*, No. 17 (December, 1963), p. 41.

31. *Süddeutsche Zeitung*, June 13, 1956.

32. Wilhelm Reiter, "Die Nationalitätenpolitik der rumänischen Volksrepublik im Spiegel ihrer Statistik," *Osteuropa*, March, 1961, p. 189.

33. Shoup, "Yugoslavia's National Minorities under Communism," p. 72.

34. Koca Joncic, "Man and Intra-national Relations in Yugoslavia," *Review of International Affairs* (Belgrade), No. 322 (September 5, 1963), p. 26.

35. Article 42, *The Constitution of the Socialist Federal Republic of Yugoslavia* (Belgrade, 1963).

36. Joncic, "Man and Intra-national Relations in Yugoslavia," p. 28.

37. *Neue Zürcher Zeitung*, February 21, 1957.

38. Shoup, "Yugoslavia's National Minorities under Communism," p. 76.

Observations on Eastern European Economy

Chapter IV.

7 The Development of the East German Economy in the Framework of the Soviet Bloc

Karl C. Thalheim

East Germany's position as the second largest industrial producer in the Council for Economic Mutual Assistance (CEMA) rests on an industry marked by a high level of technological development and the availability of a large skilled labor force.

With the notable exception of chemicals, basic industries had been largely underdeveloped before World War II in the territory now forming the "German Democratic Republic" (G.D.R.). The eastern part of Germany was dependent for basic industrial products on deliveries from what is today the Federal Republic of Germany (F.R.G.), while some branches of the East German consumer-goods industries—particularly textiles—had a capacity sufficient to supply the western parts of the country. Since 1951, however, East Germany's national economic planning has put great emphasis on developing such branches of heavy industry as coal mining, metallurgy, and chemicals, and on the production of capital investment goods (engineering, electrotechnical, precision tool, and optical industries), while expansion of consumer goods industries has been relatively neglected.

East Germany's present contribution to the over-all industrial capacity of the CEMA states can be seen from the figures compiled in Table 7–1. Comparable statistics are unavailable for some important branches of industry, especially those producing capital investment goods, but the available information is sufficient to demonstrate the importance of the G.D.R.'s role in CEMA.[1] Despite the G.D.R.'s limited size, its integration into the East European *Grossraumwirtschaft* has enhanced the economic potential of the bloc as a whole to a remarkable degree, especially if one bears in mind that East Germany's main efforts have been directed toward the production of capital investment goods since 1951, the first year of the First Five-Year Plan.

TABLE 7–1:

THE POSITION OF EAST GERMANY AS AN INDUSTRIALIZED COUNTRY WITHIN THE CEMA AREA[a]

(1963 production figures)

Energy (billion kilowatts)		Carbonate of Soda (1,000 tons NA_2CO_3)	
CEMA Total	555.3	CEMA Total	4,178
U.S.S.R.	412.1	U.S.S.R.	2,417
G.D.R.	47.5	G.D.R.	653
Poland	37.0	Poland	526
Czechoslovakia	29.9	Rumania	327
Iron (million tons)		Caustic Soda (1,000 tons $NaOH$)	
CEMA Total	74.9	CEMA Total	1,882
U.S.S.R.	58.7	U.S.S.R.	965
Poland	5.4	G.D.R.	356
Czechoslovakia	5.3	Poland	192
G.D.R.	2.2	Rumania	166
Steel (million tons)		Nitrogen Fertilizer (1,000 tons N)	
CEMA Total	105.5	U.S.S.R.	1,360
U.S.S.R.	80.2	G.D.R.	340
Poland	8.0	Poland	330
Czechoslovakia	7.6	Czechoslovakia	154
G.D.R.	4.1		
Sulphuric Acid (1,000 tons)		Lime Phosphate (1,000 tons P_2O_5)	
CEMA Total	10,296	U.S.S.R.	1,321
U.S.S.R.	6,887	Poland	270
G.D.R.	919	Czechoslovakia	203
Poland	888	G.D.R.	196
Czechoslovakia	725		
Cement (million tons)		Trucks (1,000 pieces)	
CEMA Total	87.7	U.S.S.R.	413.9
U.S.S.R.	61.0	Poland	26.8
Poland	7.7	Rumania	13.8
G.D.R.	5.5	Czechoslovakia	13.1
Czechoslovakia	5.2	G.D.R.	10.1
Cutting Machine Tools (1,000 pieces)		Tractors (1,000 pieces)	
CEMA Total	316.2	CEMA Total	405.1
U.S.S.R.	182.7	U.S.S.R.	325.4
G.D.R.	56.4	Czechoslovakia	28.5
Poland	27.3	Poland	17.8
Czechoslovakia	26.7	G.D.R.	16.5
Railroad Passenger Cars (pieces)		Household Refrigerators (1,000 pieces)	
CEMA Total	4,282	CEMA Total	1,622.4

U.S.S.R.	1,986	U.S.S.R.	911.0
G.D.R.	1,202	G.D.R.	245.1
Poland	531	Czechoslovakia	221.1
Hungary	521	Poland	120.0

Railroad Lorries (pieces)		*Household Washing Machines (1,000 pieces)*	
CEMA Total	66,883		
U.S.S.R.	37,214	CEMA Total	3,622.0
Poland	15,540	U.S.S.R.	2,282.0
Czechoslovakia	5,580	Poland	536.0
Rumania	4,219	G.D.R.	255.5
G.D.R.	2,601	Czechoslovakia	174.5

Automobiles (1,000 pieces)		*Television Sets (1,000 pieces)*	
CEMA Total	338.5	CEMA Total	4,001.4
U.S.S.R.	173.1	U.S.S.R.	2,473.0
G.D.R.	84.3	G.D.R.	580.0
Czechoslovakia	56.5	Poland	366.0
Poland	18.3	Hungary	251.3

Woolen fabrics (million square meters)		*Beer (1,000 hectoliters)*	
CEMA Total	864.7	U.S.S.R.	28,088
U.S.S.R.	471.0	Czechoslovakia	16,580
Poland	117.0	G.D.R.	13,180
G.D.R.	106.0	Poland	7,255
Czechoslovakia	70.6		

Cotton Fabrics (million square meters)		*Margarine (1,000 tons)*	
CEMA Total	7,354	U.S.S.R.	566
U.S.S.R.	5,070	G.D.R.	195
Poland	639	Poland	130
Czechoslovakia	473	Czechoslovakia	125
G.D.R.	371		

Paper (1,000 tons)		*Foreign Trade (turnover in million rubles, 1963)*	
CEMA Total	4,898		
U.S.S.R.	2,866	U.S.S.R.	12,898
G.D.R.	590	G.D.R.	4,536
Poland	587	Czechoslovakia	4,160
Czechoslovakia	471	Poland	3,374

[a] The four or five leading countries in each category are listed.
SOURCE: *Statistisches Jahrbuch der Deutschen Demokratischen Republik* (1965), 5–8, 11, 43, 45.

THE GAP BETWEEN PLANNED AND ACTUAL ECONOMIC GROWTH

Despite all its efforts, the G.D.R. has failed to achieve the rate of industrial growth realized in the Federal Republic. Although the official East German production index represents the G.D.R.'s growth rate as having surpassed the F.R.G.'s, the East German rate of growth in absolute volume of industrial output could not possibly have surpassed that of West Germany unless industrial labor productivity in the G.D.R. had increased much more rapidly than in the F.R.G. And this was clearly not the case. In a study conducted at the East European Institute of the Free University of Berlin,[2] Dr. Gert Leptin concludes that between 1936 and 1962 the total number of persons employed in industry increased by 95 per cent in Western Germany as against 42 per cent in the East. That labor productivity has increased more slowly in the G.D.R. than in the F.R.G. is acknowledged by East German sources themselves. Walter Ulbricht, Chairman of the State Council and First Secretary of the SED Central Committee, admitted in his report to the SED's Sixth Congress in January, 1963, that East German industrial labor productivity was approximately 25 per cent lower than the corresponding West German figure.[3] This is, of course, only a rough figure. But Ulbricht's statement did make it clear that his own statisticians consider the G.D.R. to be lagging considerably behind the F.R.G. in this regard. As Dr. Leptin points out, the East German claim to more rapid industrial growth is incompatible with Ulbricht's productivity figure unless one assumes that in 1936 the productivity of East German industrial labor was lagging behind that of West Germany by 45 per cent.[4] And this would be completely unrealistic. Regional differences in labor productivity, if any, cannot have been of that order of magnitude.

The over-all objective of "overtaking and surpassing" West Germany was emphasized by Ulbricht at the Fifth Party Congress in July, 1958. His formulation of the so-called *Ökonomische Hauptaufgabe* (main objective of economic planning) read as follows: "Within a few years the national economy of the GDR is to develop in such a way as to definitely prove the superiority of the socialist economic system as opposed to the rule of the imperialist forces of the Bonn republic and consequently to overtake and surpass West Germany with respect to per capita consumption of food and consumer goods."

The *Ökonomische Hauptaufgabe* was supposed to be attained by 1961—that is, during the first half of the Seven Year Plan launched on January 1, 1959. This objective was unrealistic, and the *Ökonomische Hauptaufgabe* was not in fact achieved. Unfortunately, the available statistical information allows exact comparisons of per capita consumption for a very few items only. Comparing the development of real industrial wages seems, therefore, a more practical approach. Though not necessarily a representative gauge of living standards of the entire population, the figures assembled in Table 7–2 provide at least some insight into the economic situation of a majority of the people. It should be noted that the columns for the G.D.R. and the F.R.G. are not wholly comparable. The East German wage statistic in the table covers only (1) fully employed workers, (2) workers employed in socialist enterprises (on the whole, wages in socialist enterprises are slightly higher than in private enterprises that have remained in East Germany), and (3) workers employed in industries belonging to the so-called sphere of material production. The inclusion of all the workers who are excluded under this statistical procedure would have the effect of decreasing the figure on the average wage level. It is an open question whether the decrease in the cost-of-living index for the period 1958–60 that is claimed by the East German authorities corresponds with reality, and a fair allowance for the increasing West German cost-of-living index may be taken into account. Nevertheless, the statistical comparison leads to the conclusion that the difference between the levels of consumption in West and East Germany were widening rather than diminishing during the period from 1958 to 1960.

Since 1961 this trend has taken on additional momentum as a result of two factors: (1) rapid increases of real wages in West Germany, and (2) the erection of the Berlin Wall on August 13, 1961, facilitating the imposition of a much tougher wage policy by the East German authorities and further reducing the already slow pace of wage increases. Nineteen sixty-five was the last year of the Seven Year Plan—a plan which had been intended to bring about a dramatic increase in the G.D.R's Gross National Product. It is certain that some important objectives of the plan remained unrealized at the end of 1965.[5] Investments, one of the factors determining growth, have been lagging behind the planned figures. According to the plan, 142 billion DM (34 billion U.S. dollars) were earmarked for gross investments in fixed assets during the seven-year period. The figures for investments realized during the period are as follows:[6]

TABLE 7–2:

THE DEVELOPMENT OF WAGES IN EAST GERMANY AND THE FEDERAL REPUBLIC OF GERMANY[a]

	1958	1959	1960	1961	1962	1963	1964
GDR							
Index of nominal and real wages of fully employed workers and employees (apprentices excluded) of socialist enterprises in material production:							
Index of net wages	100	107.9	112.2	116.6	117.6	119.4	—[b]
Cost-of-living index	100	98.0	96.7	97.0	97.7	97.6	97.5
Index of real wages	100	110.1	116.0	120.2	120.4	122.3	126.0
Average monthly labor income (in East Mark) of fully employed:							
Workers and employees in socialist enterprises	494	531	555	578	583	592	610
Workers in material production	484	526	554	572	573	580	599
FRG							
Index of gross labor income in industry (all workers) gross wages per week	100	105.1	115.1	126.7	139.6	149.1	160.8
Index of the average gross income per month of employees in industry, trade, banking, and insurances (all commercial and technical employees)	100	—	111.7	121.3	131.7	140.3	149.5
Cost-of-living index	100	101.0	102.4	105.0	108.7	112.1	114.7

[a] *Statistisches Jahrbuch der Deutschen Demokratischen Republik,* IX (1964), 55–56, and X (1965), 18, 67, 429; *Statistisches Jahrbuch für die BRD* (1964), pp. 489, 500, 511, and (1965), pp. 497, 505, 513.
[b] No comparable index for all spheres of material production have been published for 1964.

	Billion DM (East)
1959	14.11
1960	15.57
1961	15.57
1962	15.86
1963	16.72
1964	18.18
1965	19.60

Especially important is the stagnation of investments in the 1960–62 period. West German gross investments in fixed assets increased during that period from 70.6 billion DM (17.6 billion U.S. dollars) to 90.0 billion DM (22.5 billion U.S. dollars). In East Germany, investments fell short of the planned figure by 26 billion DM in 1965. With economic growth to a large extent dependent on the volume of investments, it is difficult to escape the conclusion that the failure to meet investment targets— certainly one of the key ingredients of the plan—means failure to meet a good many other planned targets as well. In addition, one must bear in mind that East Germany has concentrated its efforts on industrial development. As a result, plan fulfillment looks much better in industrial investments than—for example—in housing.

One of the reasons for the gap between planned and actual investments is the relatively high standard of living in the G.D.R. Long an industrially highly developed country, East Germany has a standard of living surpassing that of almost all the other CEMA states by a wide margin. Political and psychological factors prevented the communist leaders from reducing it below the level at which it had long been established; the result was that limitations were placed on funds available for investments in producer-goods industries. At the Sixth SED Congress, Ulbricht called for an increased share of the national income to be channeled into the production of capital investment goods. He complained, in evident contravention of the facts, that a philosophy of consumption had developed during recent years— even a philosophy of "waste"—and he stressed the need for production and efficiency. There is now a clear tendency toward directing increases of the GNP into the production of capital investment goods.

CAUSES OF ECONOMIC DIFFICULTIES

The economic difficulties yet to be overcome in the G.D.R. stem from a variety of causes, the most important of which may be grouped in four categories: (1) consequences of the reparations system of 1945–53; (2) the economic division of Germany; (3) the economic integration of East Germany into the CEMA area; and (4) the adoption of the Soviet economic system in the G.D.R.

1. Discussion of the consequences of the reparations system of 1945–53 can be brief. The facts about this period of economic history are well known. Dismantling of industry and transportation, the transfer of a large number of factories to the U.S.S.R. in order to "secure reparations deliveries," open and disguised reparations deliveries, and the impressment of East German labor into the service of the Soviet Union, especially in uranium mining, were the predominant features of the system. The aftereffects of the reparations system were considerable. The G.D.R.'s first long-term plans were aimed at directing an important share of the available investment funds into the reconstruction of facilities damaged by the war and by the process of dismantling. In addition, one must bear in mind that East Germany was deprived of the benefits that accrued to the F.R.G. through participation in the Marshall Plan. The reparations system ended in 1953 (dismantling ended some years earlier), when the U.S.S.R. canceled remaining reparations claims and converted property that had been sequestered to secure reparations deliveries into East German *Volkseigentum* (people's property). The economic exploitation of East Germany by the Soviet Union was subsequently limited to adjusting trade terms in favor of the U.S.S.R.—a practice deriving from the Soviet Union's status as the *économie dominante* within the CEMA area. After the Polish and Hungarian events of 1956, this practice, too, appeared for the most part to have ceased. More than a decade has passed since the reparations system came to an actual end. Its aftereffects have not entirely been erased, but they cannot be regarded as the prime cause of the G.D.R.'s present economic difficulties.

2. The consequences of the economic division of Germany[7]

are a more important factor. The transformation of the demarcation line between the three western and the Soviet occupation zones of Germany into an economic dividing line—especially after the separate currency reforms of June, 1948—had more serious effects on the G.D.R. than on the F.R.G., for three principal reasons: (*a*) East Germany's mineral resources were much less diversified. Among the more important basic materials, only lignite and potash were avaliable in adequate quantities; there was virtually no coal and oil; (*b*) East Germany depended on deliveries from West Germany for basic industrial items, especially metallurgical products; (*c*) East Germany, as the smaller part of the country, provided a correspondingly smaller internal market. As a consequence, the reallocation of production facilities that would become necessary after the division of the country was a more difficult task in East than in West Germany.

From the viewpoint of rational economic policy, all three considerations should have led East Germany to make serious efforts to preserve German economic unity. Just the opposite took place, chiefly because of political considerations and the U.S.S.R.'s efforts to integrate "its" Germany into the CEMA bloc. As a result, large investments became necessary to develop facilities that could compensate for the loss of former West German deliveries. Similar efforts were made in West Germany, but the capital required for this was much smaller in the F.R.G. West German compensatory development of new capacities concentrated chiefly on consumer goods and to a smaller degree on capital-investment goods, while East Germany put the emphasis on investments in heavy industry (coal mining, metallurgy, basic chemicals). In addition, East Germany did not have favorable sites for most of these branches of industry; permanent subsidies from the state budget were thus needed to keep the new industries "profitable." To be sure, this has not been the only reason for such subsidies. They have been dictated in part by a price policy that has kept the prices of raw materials and power irrationally low—a price policy that followed the Soviet model very closely. In the F.R.G. the solution to the problem of developing substitute capacities was made easier by the fact that displaced East German entrepreneurs re-established their lost enterprises in the West. An impressive illustration of the consequences is the fact that the East German share in total German employment in the textile industry dropped from 42 per cent in 1936 to 33 per cent in 1962. The creation of capacities to substitute for prewar mutual deliveries between East and West Germany is one of the reasons for the very small volume of East-West German trade compared with the commodity exchange before the war. Obviously the present interzonal trade constitutes only a small fraction of the flow of goods and services that would have taken place in an undivided Germany.

3. After the reparations ended, the Soviet Union's main economic interest in East Germany was to develop those branches of industry that produced industrial equipment in short supply both in the U.S.S.R. and in the CEMA area as a whole. These branches were not necessarily the most efficient from the point of view of an optimal allocation of the G.D.R.'s productive forces. A striking example was the effort to develop a shipbuilding industry in East Germany. Before the end of World War II, shipbuilding was negligible in the territory that was to form East Germany. Its development began in 1946, on Soviet orders, as an export industry oriented to the Russian market. For a long time the shipyards were unprofitable, and this is very likely still the case. On balance, the development of the shipbuilding industry, requiring large amounts of capital, has produced losses rather than gains for the East German economy.

As an exporter the G.D.R. supplies the U.S.S.R. and the East European bloc countries with machinery and equipment, the most important items being transport equipment, machine tools, precision tools, electrotechnical and electronic equipment, and optical instruments. Chemicals constitute another important category of export commodities. Based on a favorable resource endowment, this branch of industry had been traditionally strong in East Germany. Because of the predominance of capital investment goods in the East German commodity structure, the G.D.R.'s exports have constituted an important factor in the industrial development of the CEMA area as a whole. On the other hand, the G.D.R. is heavily dependent on imports of raw materials, the bulk of which are obtained from other CEMA countries—especially the Soviet Union and Poland (on which the G.D.R. relies for coal).

The commodity structure of East Germany's exports to other socialist countries can be described as "not unfavorable," the only exception being the somewhat limited export of consumer goods. Clearly unfavorable, however, are the regional bounds in which East Germany's foreign trade is confined. The G.D.R. conducts only a very small proportion of its trade with countries outside the CEMA bloc (see Table 7–3). The most important

TABLE 7–3:

THE REGIONAL STRUCTURE OF EAST GEMANY'S FOREIGN TRADE

| | REGIONAL SHARES[a] | | | | | |
| | Export | | | Import | | |
Region	1950	1960	1964	1950	1960	1964
Socialist Countries......	68.2	75.7	77.5	75.9	73.9	75.2
CEMA Countries......	68.2	68.7	73.4	75.9	66.7	71.2
All Other Countries.....	12.3	13.3	13.4	11.2	16.6	15.1
Interzonal Trade.......	19.5[b]	11.0	9.0	12.9[b]	9.5	9.7

[a] In percentages.
[b] Difference to 100 per cent.

result of East Germany's orientation toward the CEMA countries is the negative influence of this orientation on over-all foreign trade volume.[8] Being the smaller part of the former Deutsches Reich, and having by far the less diversified resource endowment, East Germany should be relying on foreign trade to a much greater extent than the F.R.G. and should be increasing its trade volume at a much more rapid pace. The actual situation has been just the reverse:

Foreign Trade per Capita[9] in U.S. Dollars (1964)

	F.R.G.	G.D.R.[10]
Export	279	172
Import	252	153
Turnover	531	325

Rapidly increasing exports were one of the decisive factors in West Germany's favorable economic development after the war. East Germany, cut off from such an expansion of exports by its entanglement with the CEMA countries, has had a strong interest in improving and intensifying economic co-operation among CEMA members and has vigorously supported Moscow's designs for a supranational economic plan for the entire CEMA area.

4. The three basic elements of the Soviet economic system (socialist ownership of the means of production, substitution of the market economy and the price mechanism by central planning, and maximizing economic growth as the objective function

TABLE 7-4:

NATIONALIZATION AND COLLECTIVIZATION IN EAST GERMANY[a]

		SOCIALIST ENTERPRISES			
	Total	"People's"	Co-operative[b]	Semi-state Enter-prises[e]	Private Enter-prises
Industry and Handicraft (except construction handicraft)					
1950	70.7	69.0	1.7	—	29.3
1955	78.9	76.0	2.8	—	21.1
1960	84.5	79.4	5.1	6.5	9.0
1964[d]	85.4	80.2	5.2	7.8	6.8
Construction					
1950	31.6	31.6	—	—	68.4
1955	56.0	55.8	0.2	—	44.0
1960	78.0	64.4	13.6	8.1	14.0
1964	82.0	68.4	13.6	8.0	10.0
Agriculture and Forestry					
1950	12.6	12.6	—	—	87.4
1955	25.0	12.6	12.4	—	75.0
1960	80.1	16.3	63.9	—	19.9
1964	90.4	16.2	74.2	—	9.6
Trade					
1950	62.1	29.1	33.0	—	37.9
1955	83.8	50.5	33.3	—	16.2
1960	86.6	57.4	29.1	4.6	8.8
1964[d]	88.8	62.5	26.3	4.6	6.6

[a] Percentage share of property types in the formation of the gross product broken down by economic branches.

[b] Mainly agricultural production co-operatives (LPG), producing handicraft co-operatives (PGH), and retail co-operatives.

[e] Semistate enterprises in the G.D.R. are enterprises in which there is participation of state capital (for instance, via the Deutsche Investitionsbank or a "people's" enterprise). This category also includes private trading enterprises which have an exclusive agreement with a state trading enterprise.

[d] Preliminary figures.

SOURCE: *Statistisches Jahrbuch der Deutschen Demokratischen Republik*, X (1965), 29

of economic policy) have been taken over almost completely in the G.D.R. (see Table 7–4) .[11] Deviations that remain (a small residue of private enterprises, private handicraft, privately owned land, and some features of the taxation system) simply indicate an East German lag behind the Soviet model, not a fundamental divergence from it. Thus East Germany has taken over, along with the basic elements of the Soviet system, the problems, difficulties, and shortcomings inherent in that system:

a. The elimination, or at least strict limitation, of the individual quest for economic gain as a basic economic motivation. This has produced the most negative consequences in industries characterized by a wide range of differentiated products (such as consumers goods) , in trade (especially wholesaling) , and in agriculture.

b. The absence of a basis for exact economic accounting. Prices are fixed by bureaucratic procedures (exceptions being very rare) and normally fail to provide a proper reflection of relative scarcities of commodities and factors of production. Administrative determination of prices is based on the calculation of costs. But even assuming these calculations to be correct, prices cannot fulfill their economic function under such a system. The cost calculations are not correct in any case, the main deficiency being the failure to take capital costs (such as depreciation and interest) into account. The lack of reliable indicators of commodity scarcities makes it particularly difficult to arrive at wise investment decisions. As a consequence, it seems fair to conclude that the economic efficiency of investments in the F.R.G. surpasses that of the G.D.R.

c. The dominance of political and ideological rather than purely economic considerations in economic decision-making. Some striking examples are the economically irrational collectivization of East German agriculture in 1960, the regional orientation of East German foreign trade to the CEMA area, and the relative neglect of the production of consumer goods, housing, and services, as compared with the production of capital investment goods. Structural disproportions have been produced by the system of central planning despite the existence of the so-called law of planned and proportional development. The system of central economic planning makes it possible to concentrate on developing certain branches of industry. But a concomitant of this policy is that other branches remain relatively underdeveloped. The G.D.R. and the U.S.S.R. have both been classic examples of unbalanced economic growth.

d. *Difficulties created for planning by the entanglement of the various economic factors.* Experience has shown that the so-called technological coefficients, designed to relate the economic activity of various branches and enterprises, do not work. This leads to a situation in which plans can be developed only on paper.

e. *The difficulty of properly allocating decision-making responsibilities* in a situation where, for purely administrative reasons, nothing less than a fairly high degree of decentralization will suffice. There have been problems in allocating decision-making powers to an optimum degree among branch, regional, functional, and other authorities throughout the planning hierarchy, from the top organs of the party through the ministry, VVB (associations of people's enterprises), and *Bezirk* (district) level down to the factories.

f. *The preference given to planning in terms of direct commodities exchange, and the corresponding neglect of the performance of the enterprises in terms of monetary profit.* One of the main consequences of this approach is the dissipation of capital.

g. *Insufficient incentives to technological progress.* Again the similarities between the Soviet Union and the G.D.R. are impressive. Predicting technological progress has proved to be an extremely difficult task, as has its inclusion in the formulation of national economic plans. Directors of socialist enterprises always seek "easy plans," and innovations will never become "easy." The Schumpeterian relation between innovations and profit—or, more generally speaking, economic success—not existing in the socialist society, the impetus for technological progress has been reduced below the level prevailing in market economies.

The listing above, though not complete, sums up the principal difficulties East Germany has faced in adopting the Soviet socioeconomic system. They have probably proved to be the more serious in view of East Germany's higher level of economic development. This is especially true with respect to difficulties originating in interindustrial relations mentioned under (d) above.

These difficulties will multiply as economic development increases and industrial diversity grows. This holds true especially for the production and distribution of consumer goods. The larger the income at the disposal of regime planners, and the wider the range of choice, the more difficult it is going to be to anticipate consumer choices properly.

These difficulties and the failure to meet the main targets of the Seven-Year Plan provide the background for public discussions on economic reform that have been under way since the fall of 1962 in East Germany. Time and again, participants in these discussions have pointed to the competition between the "two world systems" and the necessity to improve the methods of planning and directing the national economy in order to withstand competition from the West. According to Herbert Wolf,[12] it is especially necessary to keep up with technological progress. In order to understand these debates one must recall the discussions on economic reforms in the U.S.S.R. popularized by the well-known Liberman essay in the September 9, 1962 issue of *Pravda*. After a short period of reluctance, a similar public discussion was permitted by the SED leaders. These discussions resulted in the "New Economic System of Planning and Directing the National Economy" (NÖS), the main principles of which had already been framed by Walter Ulbricht at the Sixth Party Congress in January, 1963. After having been finally accepted by the economic conference of the SED Central Committee and the G.D.R. Council of Ministers on June 24, 1963, it was promulgated as a decree of the Presidency of the Council of Ministers on July 11, 1963.

THE "NEW ECONOMIC SYSTEM OF PLANNING AND DIRECTING THE NATIONAL ECONOMY" (NÖS)

Emulating the procedure in the Soviet Union, the New Economic System was tried out first in four VVB (associations of people's enterprises) and ten VEB (people's enterprises) before it was promulgated.[13] It is impossible to discuss the NÖS in full detail here. The decree promulgating it covers forty-three large-size pages. In addition, dozens of decrees, resolutions, and other documents relating to it have been promulgated. We will concentrate on the basic features: (1) the redistribution of powers within the hierarchy of economic and planning administrations; (2) the expansion of the functions of the VVB as socialist trusts; and (3) the creation of the system of economic incentives (*System ökonomischer Hebel*) as a substitute for directing enterprises by administrative order.

The first feature is of an administrative and organizational rather than a purely economic nature. Of special interest are (*a*) the redistribution of powers between the State Planning Commission and the National Economic Council, and (*b*) the expansion of the powers of the District Economic Councils. According to the new regulation, the Planning Commission is restricted solely to planning and has jurisdiction over planning for the entire national economy, while the National Economic Council is a planning and directing organ for industry only.[14] Its directing function derives from the competency of the departments of the industrial branches to select and appoint the managerial personnel of the enterprises. The District Economic Councils are the East German counterpart of the Russian *sovnarkhozy*. Their function is to plan and direct the local industry.

The expansion of the functions of the VVB is much more important. The VVB are the central organs of enterprises belonging to the same branch of industry. At present there are eighty-three VVB in industry and ten more in construction, forestry, and trade. As early as January, 1963, Walter Ulbricht stated in his report to the SED congress that the VVB were to be developed from administrative institutions into centers to manage the subordinate enterprises in some kind of socialist trust. To that end, powers resting with the central authorities have been transferred to the VVB. These associations are now held responsible for the investment policy of their subordinate enterprises and they share responsibility for marketing their products. In addition, VVB are responsible for international technological and scientific co-operation, especially within the organizational framework of the standing commissions of CEMA. Finally, they have been transformed from budgetary organizations into *khozraschet* organizations—that is, socialist enterprises.

Most important is the NÖS's third feature, the so-called interlinked system of economic incentives. The public discussions of this concept have clearly reflected the influence of the earlier Soviet debate, though Liberman's name was not mentioned either by Ulbricht or in the decree on the NÖS. The first paragraph of Liberman's celebrated article in *Pravda* reads as follows: "It is necessary to find a sufficiently simple and at the same time reasonable solution for one of the main tasks that has been put forward by the program of the CPSU: to develop a system of planning and evaluating the performance of enterprises in such a way as to mobilize their self-interest in the highest possible planning targets, in introducing new techniques, in improving the quality of products—in a word, in the highest possible efficiency of production."

This is a fair description of the main objectives of East Germany's NÖS as well. It is designed to permit the central authorities to concentrate on basic problems and to transfer detailed decision-making to the VVB and VEB level.

One of the keys to achieving this goal is profit. Profit is to become the basic measure for evaluation of the economic performance of enterprises and VVB, though not the only measure. Other criteria, such as increasing labor productivity and diminishing costs, are supposed to perform auxiliary functions. The principle of material incentives is to be linked to the predominant role of profits in two ways: (1) by relating the payments into the *Betriebsprämienfonds* (bonus funds) to profits, and (2) by partly relating formerly guaranteed salaries of socialist managers to economic performance. Failure to achieve norms of performance may result in salary reductions of up to 20 per cent for the top management and 10 per cent for supervisory or middle-level white collar workers. In determining whether or not the performance has met the norm, the fulfillment of the profit plan plays an important though not an exclusive role. The decisive criterion is the complex fulfillment of public obligations. Moreover, profit is meant to finance planned investments in the respective branch of industry. This principle, in turn, is limited by the rule that realized profits exceeding planned investments must be transferred to the state budget.

The *Produktionsfondsabgabe* (PA) that was announced in the decree may become another important economic device. The PA is a tax raised as a fixed percentage of the effective average balance of productive funds. Since these productive funds are practically identical to the capital of capitalist enterprises, the PA is in fact nothing more than interest on capital, the only real difference being that the communists dislike the term because of its ideological connotations. The PA is supposed to enforce the economical use of capital by the socialist enterprises. Two years after the promulgation of the NÖS, the PA has not yet been introduced on a nationwide scale, but is still being experimented with in some VVB and VEB. This can be taken as an indication of the rather inflexible nature of the East German economic system. It is also still undecided whether the PA is to become part of costs or is to be treated as distribution of profits. A legal regulation to relate all profit-oriented economic incentives in the VVB and VEB to "profit minus PA" favors the cost version.

The rationality of using profits as indicators of economic performance depends on the rationality of the price structure and cost calculations. The architects of the NÖS are fully aware of this fact. A decree of July 12, 1962, provided regulations for cost calculations which showed some improvements as compared with former periods but was still far from meeting Western standards. The role of the PA in this connection has already been mentioned. Depreciation was another critical problem. Rates had formerly been stable and insufficient, and they have been replaced by more realistic ones. In addition, a revaluation of fixed assets has taken place.[15] Both measures were designed to improve cost calculations.

Again, the revaluation of fixed assets required a rational price system if it was to make sense economically. And here we come to one of East Germany's most critical problems. East German economists are fully aware of the adverse effects of the country's distorted price structure. "To organize the price system in such a way as to reflect socially necessary labor and to avoid subsidies" is a goal of the party program adopted at the Sixth Party Congress. A practical step toward developing a rational price system was the reform of industrial prices that began on April 1, 1964, and is supposed to be fully accomplished by the end of 1966. The intention is to abolish existing distortions by raising prices at least to the cost level. The reform has already produced some substantial price increases—notably in the case of raw materials and power. The price of lignite has increased by 150 per cent, for example, and the price of melting coke by as much as 200 per cent. At the same time, the government is trying to keep retail prices stable. Thus price reform is diminishing the state budget by decreasing subsidies (for enterprises formerly selling their products below cost) and decreasing revenues (from enterprises that had formerly profited by low prices) at the same time.

Although prices are likely to change to an appreciable degree as the reform progresses, this does not mean an alteration of the system as such. For one thing, the principle of administrative price-fixing remains unchanged, despite the assignment of some powers to the VVB in this field. Secondly, the principle of fixing prices on the basis of cost calculations also remains unaltered. For this purpose costs are normally defined as "average costs of the branch." In addition, the NÖS calls for the "establishment of proper price and profit relations between products." It is difficult to understand how such correct relations could be worked out by the existing methods. Moreover, the NÖS calls for price differentiations (1) between "old and new products," allowing for higher profits for new and better products, and (2) favoring the accurate anticipation of demands with respect to assortment and quality of goods and time of delivery.

The above measures apply to the VEB and VVB as economic units. A second category of measures is designed to favor the material self-interest of the workers. Although East German economic propaganda puts heavy emphasis on these measures, their actual importance is rather limited. If the principle of relating wages to efficiency, with special consideration for quality and volume, is stressed, only the inclusion of "quality" points to something new. More important are the considerations concerning bonus payments, influenced by Soviet discussions on economic reforms. (Liberman began with proposals to improve the bonus system.) Every enterprise is to get a uniform bonus fund. Payments into that fund are to be calculated on the basis of net profits realized by the PA. They are to be paid only as compensation for performance that is above average with respect to quantity and quality. Further, in addition to the regular (short) leaves of absence, employees can earn additional leave by special accomplishments. Workers' housing is to be made available especially for leading personnel, regular personnel, shift workers, and specialists. However, no real profit sharing is envisaged for employees within the framework of the NÖS on the order, for example, of the system in Yugoslavia. Material incentives for the majority of workers to increase profits are, therefore, very modest.

The NÖS in Relation to the Other CEMA Economies

An evaluation of the NÖS shows, to begin with, that it has not brought about a fundamental transformation of the economic system. The principle of "socialist" ownership of the means of production is left intact, and there is scarcely any change in the central aim of forcing economic growth. This remains true despite the more frequent use now of the slogan on "optimizing the national economy" and despite the reference in the 1965 national economic plan to "optimization of planning."

The NÖS in particular is counted on to contribute to realization of the coveted growth targets. But the NÖS is not designed to create a socialist market-type economy, either. Ulbricht has emphasized repeatedly that the principle of central planning will not be impaired and that there will be no development toward "a questionable self-administration of the economy and enterprises." Here Ulbricht alludes, of course, to the Yugoslav economic system. At the Sixth SED Congress he declared that the new measures would cut the ground from under revisionism because these measures "result not in a reduction of planning but rather in a strengthening and development of planning and in a strengthening of the authority of the socialist state." And at the Economic Conference in June, 1963, he said: "The plan is and will remain the decisive instrument of our economic policy." These statements must be taken seriously.

The aim of the NÖS, therefore, is to make East Germany's economic system more efficient without abolishing its essential elements. And this alone makes clear the limitations on the efficacy of the NÖS measures. Profit is the key aspect, and there are rather inaccurate ideas about this aspect in the West deriving from insufficient knowledge. Some Western commentators who speak of "adoption of capitalist economic methods" in the G.D.R. are guilty of a fundamental error. Such a description would be valid only if the choice of investments were to be based on the income anticipated from them and if enterprises had the right to plan their production programs according to anticipated profit. But it is emphasized in the G.D.R. that decisions on investments are made only "within the plan" and that no "market mechanism" is to be put into effect. The production program, too, is determined chiefly by the central plan for the national economy. Only with regard to the specialization and specification of production does a certain profit orientation seem to be possible, mainly in consumer goods production.

Account must also be taken of the fact that prices for input as well as for output are still fixed by central authorities, the enterprises themselves having only a limited say in the determination of these prices. Hence, the only way in which enterprises can influence profit is by rationalizing their internal organization. Although material incentives have had some effect in increasing profits, the incentives are limited and have been effective mainly among leading personnel of state enterprises. Their effect on the working personnel is quite small. The role of profit under the NÖS is thus entirely different from what it is in a market-type economy.

Considerable difficulties also arise over the position of the "people's own" enterprises and their managements. The basic aim of the NÖS is to strengthen the managements' responsibility and to delegate more decision-making power—the central idea of the Liberman-type Soviet reformers. On the other hand, essential powers are delegated to the socialist trusts (WB), which are to administer the respective branches of industry on the basis of state central planning. In a number of cases the powers of the enterprises and the VVB do not seem to be defined with sufficient clarity. The enterprise manager's freedom to make decisions is limited in two ways: (1) by the central plan and (2) by the manager's subordination to the general director of the respective VVB. It is difficult to see how under such circumstances the initiative of the enterprise managers can be increased as called for by the NÖS.

Similar analyses could be applied to all the other procedures set up under the NÖS. The conclusion would nearly always be the same. Some of the new methods are indeed suitable for increasing the efficiency of East Germany's economy and coping with some of the difficulties of her economic system. However, since all the basic ingredients of this economic system are unchanged, the difficulties and shortcomings remain; they can be lessened but not removed.

An example is the Decree on Preparation and Implementation of Investments of September 25, 1964. This decree makes frequent mention of the use of economic incentives. However, a close look at the voluminous decree (twenty pages, including appendices) reveals an abundance of administrative detail but very little about the economic problems of investment selection. Paragraph 37, for instance, reads: "After completion of the investment project, the economic gain is to be shown by means of '*Ist-Kennziffern*' (actual figures)." However, there are only general guidelines on how the economic gain in a Soviet-type economy can be determined. The statements on the use of economic incentives are inadequate and in any case no proof that economic incentives and economic means of direction will substitute for administrative direction in such an important area.

Many more examples could be cited to demonstrate that the methods prescribed by the NÖS are unsuitable to achieve its aims. A comparison of the NÖS with the system in the U.S.S.R. is especially striking, first because discussions about reform of the planning system began earlier in the U.S.S.R. and were in some respects more intensive, and second because in the past East Germany had taken over reforms and reorganizations from the U.S.S.R. (including Khrushchev's 1957 industrial reform with its regional decentralization, a very similar version of which was adopted in East Germany in 1958). The introduction of the NÖS marked the first time that East Germany had preceded the U.S.S.R. in the adoption of a large-scale reform. So far, the results of the discussions about reform in the U.S.S.R. have been confined to experiments in a limited number of enterprises. The East German action was almost certainly taken with the concurrence of the Soviet leadership. It may be that the much smaller but economically highly developed East Germany was chosen to provide a test of new planning and administrative methods in order to accumulate experience for the Soviet Union.[16]

On the other hand, the scope and pace of the reforms under the NÖS lag far behind reforms in Czechoslovakia. This holds true for the delegation of decision-making powers to the enterprise managements as well as for price reforms. Czechoslovakia projects for one group of prices a market price formation, for another group the introduction of prices within certain margins, and for a third group a free-market price formation. By contrast, there is still only central price formation in East Germany. Hungary, too, has gone beyond the G.D.R. in the general introduction of levies on fixed assets (PA). The delegation of management functions to "socialist trusts" seems also to have been introduced in other CEMA countries such as Poland and Bulgaria.

It is unlikely that the results of the New Economic System will fulfill the expectations of its originators. The plan-fulfillment report for 1964 states that the growth of national income was 4.7 per cent, which is almost as high as the figures for 1962 and 1963 together. However, this serves to demonstrate the stagnation of East German economic development in those two years.[17] The economic plan for 1965 is also characterized by relatively modest targets. Industrial commodity production is to be increased by 5.7 per cent and gross agricultural production by 4 per cent. These figures show that the responsible East German politicians do not expect favorable changes from a "further implementation of the New Economic System" as demanded in the economic plan for 1965.

Apparently it has not yet been possible to develop a consistent system of economic incentives. Thus, the chairman of the National Economic Council, Alfred Neumann, stated at the seventh session of the SED Central Committee in early December, 1964: "An important task for 1965 is the improvement of the system of economic incentives. For this purpose groups of specialists in the VVB must work out in scholarly fashion how, instead of isolated working economic incentives for partial operations, a consistent system of economic incentives for complexes of products and complete economic processes can be carried out."

Such a statement, coming a year and a half after the proclamation of the New Economic System, shows how difficult the introduction of large-scale reforms into the East German economic system has been. Even if the reforms are completely implemented, it is unlikely, for the reasons discussed above, that the fundamental difficulties of this economic system can be removed. But the effort will undoubtedly continue, and it is likely that there will be further reforms and reorganizations in the East German economic system in the not too distant future.

The Soviet - East German Treaty of June, 1964

Finally, a brief review of some aspects of the Treaty for Friendship, Cooperation, and Mutual Assistance signed between the U.S.S.R. and the G.D.R. on June 12, 1964, seems in order. The political content of this treaty—e.g., Paragraph 6, with its obligation to consider West Berlin "as an independent political unit" —is outside the scope of this paper. Section 1 of Paragraph 8, however, is especially pertinent in the economic sphere:

> The high contracting parties will, on the basis of mutual advantage and of interested fraternal cooperation and in accordance with the principles of CEMA, develop and strengthen intensively the economic and scientific-technical relations between the two countries. They will also, in accordance with the principles of international socialist division of labor, coordinate their economic plans, achieve specialization and cooperation in production, and guarantee a high level of productivity through a drawing together and adjustment of the national economies of the two countries.

The clear intent of this treaty provision is to establish a closer economic community between the U.S.S.R. and East Germany. The communiqué of the SED Politburo at the time emphasized the co-ordination of national economic plans and further specialization and co-operation in production. The long term of the treaty (twenty years, and if neither side repudiates it, an additional ten years) is significant for the adjustment of long-term planning. The late Dr. Erich Apel,[18] Deputy Chairman of the Council of Ministers and Chairman of the State Planning Commission, emphasized that East Germany would save its own investments by importing semimanufactures such as aluminum coils. Moreover, an intensification of technical and scientific co-operation in particular is planned. "The highest possible productivity is the basic condition for victory in the economic competition between socialism and capitalism," according to a resolution of the G.D.R. State Council in connection with the treaty.

None of these measures exceeds the scope of the co-operation which the U.S.S.R. strives to achieve with all the CEMA member countries. But there are probably two chief reasons why the G.D.R. is a special case:

1. A close link to the second greatest industrial capacity in the CEMA bloc is highly significant for the U.S.S.R. against the background of its own development plans. Mutual aid, mutual deliveries of complete sets of equipment for chemical plants, and an extension of the exchange of technical information in order "to secure a rapid development of the chemical industry" is especially emphasized in the official communiqué. To this end a government contract between the U.S.S.R. and the G.D.R. was concluded on June 12, 1964, the day the treaty was signed. This contract, for 1966–70, is an extension of a contract for 1959–65. It schedules the delivery to the U.S.S.R. of more than one hundred plants and equipment for the chemical and oil-refining industries. In exchange the U.S.S.R. is to deliver complete sets of equipment for the expansion of the *Eisenhüttenkombinat Ost* in Eisenhüttenstadt, equipment for new thermopower plants, as well as crude oil and other raw materials.

2. The special contract with East Germany is also traceable, in this writer's view, to the fact that Soviet proposals for unified planning within the CEMA area could not be carried out because of Rumania's resistance. It seemed desirable, therefore, for the U.S.S.R. to strengthen bilateral relations. And such relations with East Germany are not only especially important but particularly reliable. The SED leadership has declared itself emphatically in favor of the Soviet proposals for a stronger, more unified CEMA. Thus, Ulbricht stated at the seventh session of the SED Central Committee in December, 1964:

> The leading party and state organs, after having studied the problems of the technical revolution, came to the conclusion that some important questions cannot be solved by the GDR alone. The technical revolution points objectively toward an internationalization of economic and scientific-technical cooperation. From this, new great tasks arise for CEMA which at the present time are not yet being dealt with. . . .
>
> Our party leadership deems these urgent questions extremely important. The problems of the technical revolution are to be mastered by all socialist countries

together in order to carry out completely the resolutions
of 1960. . . .

It is necessary, to that end, to overcome formalistic
administrative elements in the conduct of economic
affairs within the individual socialist countries as well as
in their mutual relations. In our opinion, the time has
come to organize technical cooperation among the socialist countries on the basis of their national economies
and in the interest of the solution of economic and
technical problems of the national economies.

The careful formulation notwithstanding, Ulbricht clearly
supports Soviet plans for a tighter unification within CEMA. A
similar formulation was used in the official communiqué on the
negotiations for the Soviet-G.D.R. treaty: "The GDR and the
USSR confirm their untiring endeavor to increase by every means
the significance of CEMA in its efforts to develop and to improve
the economic relations among the socialist countries and to
deepen the international socialist division of labor, the specialization and cooperation in production in the interest of each of
these countries and for the benefit of the entire socialist community."

The treaty between the U.S.S.R. and G.D.R., as well as the
supplementary special contracts, will certainly be of importance
in East Germany in the years to come. They represent, however,
no more than a strengthening and intensification of the already
close economic relations between the two countries. They bring
no fundamental changes.[19]

NOTES

1. It is true that the number of employees in industry and handicraft is
higher in Poland; but the productivity of labor is higher in East Germany
than in Poland, and it seems certain that the industrial production of East
Germany surpasses that of Poland.

2. Dr. Gert Leptin, *Berichte des Osteuropa-Instituts an der Freien Universität Berlin*, LXV.

3. From his report at the Sixth Congress of the SED, quoted from *Neues
Deutschland*, January 16, 1963.

4. *Berichte des Osteuropa-Instituts an der Freien Universität Berlin*, pp. 18,
19.

5. See Bruno Gleitze: "Die Industrie der Sowjetzone unter dem gescheiterten Siebenjahrplan," *Wirtschaft und Gesellschaft in Mitteldeutschland* (Berlin, 1964), II.

6. See *Statistisches Jahrbuch der Deutschen Demokratischen Republik, 1965*, p. 43; and for 1965: Report of the Staatliche Zentralverwaltung für Statistik on economic development in 1965.

7. The Declaration of the Potsdam Conference, July–August, 1945, did not anticipate such a division. On the contrary, it is stated in II A 2: "So far as is practicable, there shall be uniformity of treatment of the German population throughout Germany"; and in II B 14: "During the period of occupation Germany shall be treated as a single economic unit."

8. See Karl C. Thalheim, *Die Wirtschaft der Sowjetzone in Krise und Umbau* (Berlin, 1964), Chapter IX: "Die Entwicklung der aussenwirtschaftlichen Beziehungen und die Wirtschaftsintegration des Ostblocks."

9. Trade between East Germany and the F.R.G. excluded.

10. Converted by the official exchange rate for the Clearing (Verrechnungs) Dollar.

11. See Karl C. Thalheim: "Die Rezeption des Sowjetmodells in Mitteldeutschland," in *Die Wirtschaftssysteme der Statten Osteuropas und der Volksrepublik China* (Berlin, 1961), I.

12. Wolf is deputy director of the *Ökonomisches Forschungsinstitut bei der Staatlichen Plankommission.*

13. It is questionable whether such isolated experiments in an economy which remains centrally planned in all other respects can really prove anything.

14. The abolition of the National Economic Council and the restoration of nine ministries for the industry were announced at the December, 1965, session of the SED Central Committee.

15. By the decrees, "Über die Abschreibungen für Grundmittel und die Bildung eines Fonds für Generalreparaturen," and "Über die Umbewertung der Grundmittel," of January 30, 1964.

16. On October 4, 1965, the Council of Ministers of the U.S.S.R. issued a decree on the socialist production enterprise of the state. The meaning of this decree is very similar to the New Economic System of East Germany.

17. According to the *East German Statistical Yearbook for 1965*, p. 116, the growth of industrial gross production in 1964 as compared with 1963 was 6.1 per cent. In the same period the growth of industrial net production in the F.R.G. was 8.4 per cent. The contrast between the two parts of Germany has, therefore, further increased.

18. Dr. Erich Apel committed suicide on December 3, 1965.

19. On December 3, 1965, a commercial treaty between the U.S.S.R. and East Germany for 1966–70 was signed in East Berlin. The fixed volume of the turnover in this period is 60 billion East-Marks—not much above the annual average for 1964 (10,898 billion) but, according to the official declaration, 43 per cent higher than the turnover in the period of the last treaty (1961–65).

8. Economic Nationalism in Eastern Europe: Forty Years of Continuity and Change*

John Michael Montias

Although the five nations at the heart of Eastern Europe that form the subject of this retrospective study occupy a territory only the size of Venezuela, or of France and Italy combined, the natural endowments, the productive assets, the skills of the populations of Poland, Czechoslovakia, Hungary, Rumania, and Bulgaria are sufficiently varied to generate a large volume of trade in the region. But, as far back as we care to look into the history of Eastern Europe, we find man-made obstacles to trade depressing regional exchanges to levels much below those we might expect. Even the radical transformation of the economic systems of the region that took place under Soviet aegis after World War II did not alter that fact: The nature of the obstacles to trade was modified; on certain commodities, restrictions were lifted or reduced; on others they were tightened; the region's potential trade was still far from realized.

The first part of this paper describes the long-term trends in the region's trade, with separate consideration of the exchanges of machinery, foodstuffs, and manufactured consumer goods that have been taking place since the late 1920's. Since Czechoslovak data are available that make it possible to estimate approximately the volume of exchanges for various categories of goods in constant prices, the analysis will be concentrated on Czechoslovakia's trade with the nations of the area. In view also of Czechoslovakia's role as a major supplier of manufactured goods to the area both before and after World War II and of the systematic tendency on the part of the less-developed countries of Eastern Europe to protect their nascent industry, a close study of Czech trade is justified by the light it throws on the nature and the

---

* The author is grateful to Professor George Staller of Cornell University for his calculations of the post-war trade quanta for Czechoslovakia and for his advice on related points.

effects of restrictionist trade policies in this part of the world. The second part of the paper deals with the wider aspects of economic nationalism and of its relation to national sovereignty.

I

Many economists would invoke the free area of the Austro-Hungarian Empire dating back to the middle of the eighteenth century as evidence against the claim made above that obstacles to trade have persisted throughout the modern history of Eastern Europe. Actually the customs union comprised only a part of the area under discussion. Goods originating in Warsaw, Bialystok, Bucharest, or Sofia had to pay heavy customs duties to enter the Empire, which was protected by tariff barriers averaging 22.8 per cent ad valorem.[1] The Empire had a population of only fifty-five million people with a total income that amounted to little more than half of France's national income at the time.[2] If it had not been for the high barriers around the Union, Hungary probably would not have purchased three-quarters of her imports from the Austrian half of the Empire as it did in the first decade of the present century.[3] The breakdown of the Empire after World War I would not have been an unalloyed misfortune if the successor states and their neighbors had not proceeded to erect even higher barriers around their new territories than those that had surrounded the Empire.

At first, in the early 1920's, quotas and direct controls restricted trade. After 1925, after more normal economic relations had been re-established between the victor states and dismembered Hungary, tariffs exceeding prewar levels were mainly responsible for impeding exchanges.[4] In spite of high tariffs, a brisk trade went on during the 1920's among the nations of Eastern Europe, thanks to the favorable economic *Konjunktur* that counteracted these restrictive measures. In 1928 a little over 15 per cent of Czechoslovak exports—consisting mainly of manufactured consumer goods—went to Hungary, Poland, Rumania, and Bulgaria, which in return supplied Czechoslovakia with foodstuffs and raw materials.[5] Hungary's trade with Rumania and Bulgaria, consisting to a large extent of metal semifabricates and machines in exchange for mineral products and agricultural raw materials, was also substantial. Altogether Hungary sold a little more than a quarter of her total exports to Czechoslovakia, Poland, Rumania, and Bulgaria and bought about 35 per cent of her imports from these four countries.[6] Rumania's imports from the other four countries under consideration were slightly less than a quarter of her total imports in 1928.[7]

Unfortunately, the improvement in the late 1920's proved temporary. Even the guarded optimism of Leo Pasvolsky, who back in 1928 thought he could detect "the subsidence of the acute animosities aroused by the war" and welcomed recent trends in commercial policies that "would ensure greater and greater mutual benefits from international trade,"[8] was unfounded. Soon after the world depression set in, the region's trade collapsed. The panoply of beggar-my-neighbor policies adopted by the East European states toward each other, including tariff increases, discriminatory exchange controls, restrictive quota arrangements, and export subsidies, aggravated the crisis in the region as a whole. What happened to the physical volume of trade among the five East European countries, together with Germany, may be seen from the data in Table 8–1, based on Czechoslovak and Hungarian statistics.

The overwhelming importance of political considerations in determining the volume of trade between each pair of countries emerges clearly from the table, even if we allow for a considerable measure of error due to the approximative method adopted for deflating current values. Economic factors alone will not explain the dwindling of Czech-Hungarian exchanges to less than one-fourth of their predepression level, whereas Czech trade with Rumania, a fellow member of the Little Entente, fell by only a third at the bottom of the crisis and then bounced back to the 1928 volume by 1937. The political relations of Germany with Hungary and Czechoslovakia are clearly reflected in the diverging trends of Germany's exchanges with these two Central European powers. The deterioration of Hungary's relations with Rumania, due mainly to Budapest's determination to recover lost Transylvanian territory, led to the gradual curtailment of trade between the two countries after 1937. Even before the Axis Powers had sanctioned the Hungarian annexation of northern Transylvania in August, 1940, trade between the two antagonists had fallen to less than half of 1937 levels. By 1941 it had come to a virtual standstill.[9]

TABLE 8-1:

INDICES OF THE VOLUME OF RECIPROCAL TRADE AT CONSTANT PRICES BETWEEN
CZECHOSLOVAKIA, HUNGARY, RUMANIA, BULGARIA, POLAND, AND GERMANY

(1928 = 100)

Trade of Czechoslovakia with:		1933	1937	
Hungary	Imports	39	24	
	Exports	32	20	
Rumania	Imports	66	128	
	Exports	63	97	
Bulgaria	Imports	121	159	
	Exports	66	62	
Poland	Imports	30	28	
	Exports	49	47	
Germany	Imports	74	52	
	Exports	62	50	
Total Trade	Imports	60	74	
	Exports	69	73	
Trade of Hungary with:		1933	1938	1943
Czechoslovakia	Imports	20	18	31[a]
	Exports	43	27	38[a]
Rumania	Imports	43	75	16
	Exports	61	85	9
Bulgaria	Imports	21	37	265
	Exports	46	138	241
Poland	Imports	15	21	5
	Exports	29	36	6
Germany	Imports	45	95	254
	Exports	96	266	505
Total Trade	Imports	45	61	93
	Exports	102	115	100

[a] The Protectorate of Bohemia and Moravia together with Slovakia.

NOTE: In the absence of more detailed price data, the current values of trade carried on between each pair of countries were deflated by import and export price indices derived from data referring to the entire trade of Czechoslovakia and Hungary. The Hungarian price indices are based on an average of the year 1925–27. The Czech indices are linked to 1928. Differences between the trend in the value of exports from Czechoslovakia to Hungary and the trend in the

The economic disintegration of Eastern Europe in the 1930's is reflected in the decline in the combined share of Hungary, Rumania, Poland, and Bulgaria in the total trade turnover of Czechoslovakia and Hungary. In Czechoslovakia's trade this share fell from 15 per cent in 1928 to 10 per cent in 1933; in Hungary's it dropped from 32 per cent in 1928 to 15.5 per cent in 1933 and to 14 per cent in 1938. Also symptomatic was the parallel rise in Hungary's trade with Germany—from 20 per cent of turnover in 1928 to 53 per cent in 1938.

The impact of the recession in trade differed markedly according to the nature of the products exchanged. Exports of industrial consumer goods were hardest hit; exports of raw materials were least affected. The fate of machinery exports depended largely on political relations: Where these were bad—as between Czechoslovakia and Hungary—machinery exports fell drastically, though not as much as trade in manufactured consumer goods; where they were favorable—as between Czechoslovakia and Rumania—these exports quickly recovered their predepression level and then surpassed it in the late 1930's, both in current and in fixed prices. If we consider Czechoslovak trade with Bulgaria, which was not so politically engaged in Central European disputes at the time, we find that the current value of exports of manufactured consumer goods fell by two-thirds from 1929 to 1937, while that of machinery and equipment receded by only about 40 per cent.[10]

A further characteristic of the depression period is that agricultural protectionism played a major role in depressing trade in foodstuffs, particularly in Czechoslovakia where agricultural interests were politically powerful. In the spring of 1930, for instance, Prague approximately doubled the ad valorem import duties on wheat, flower, and rye and raised the duty on porkers

value of imports to Czechoslovakia from Hungary are mainly due to the disparities in the price deflators used to calculate the two indices.

Sources:

Czechoslovakia: *Statisticky obzor*, No. 2 (1959), p. 90; Státni úřad statistický, *Měsícní přehled zahranic ního obchodu*, December, 1928; *Statistisches Jahrbuch der ČSR 1936; Statistisches Jahrbuch für das Protektorat Böhmen und Mähren 1941.*

Hungary: András Nagy, "Magyarország külkereskedelme a második világháborúban," in *Magyarország külkereskedelme 1919–1945*, p. 179; A Magyar Királyi Központi statisztikai Hivatal, *Magyar statisztikai évkönyv*, 1933, 1938; *Magyarország 1930. Évi külkereskedelmi forgalma* (Budapest, 1931).

about fivefold. Budapest reciprocated by jacking up its tariff on sugar and by restricting imports of Czech consumer goods.[11] Thus began the tariff war, which within a few years came close to annihilating exchanges between the two countries.

The effects of the depression on Rumania, one of the less developed countries of the region, can be made out nicely from the indices of the volume of imports and exports in constant prices—the quantum indices—broken down by commodity groups that were publishd shortly before World War II by analysts of the National Bank in a detailed study of postwar Rumanian trade.[12]

The indices show that in 1932 the quantum of total imports into Rumania declined to a low of 59 per cent of the 1929 base, then went up again to 76.5 per cent in 1937. The quantum of imports of raw materials and semifabricates, however, never fell below 76 per cent (1931); in 1934 it had already surpassed the 1929 level by 13 per cent; by 1937 it was 45 per cent above the base year. Imports of manufactured products, also expressed in constant prices, hit bottom in 1935 when they were less than 50 per cent of the 1929 figure; they were still 30 per cent below the base year in 1937. The quantum of total exports, expressed on a 1930 base, fell to 85 per cent of base in 1934 but surged back to a level more than 10 per cent above the base year in 1936 and 1937. A comparison of total import and export quanta makes it evident that the barter terms of trade turned sharply against Rumania, as they did against most other exporters of primary products during this period.

The postwar trends in the quanta of trade may be contrasted with the fairly dismal record of the interwar years. To preserve comparability, an effort is made in this analysis to express the volume of trade at predepression prices, with full recognition of the very approximate character of the links relating prewar and postwar values. Geographic coverage is also limited. The only quantum data it has been possible to muster are for Czechoslovakia's trade with its present East European allies and with both halves of Germany. This is enough, fortunately, to throw into relief the crucial problem of industrial specialization in the bloc, as it manifests itself in the trading relations of an industrially advanced state, such as Czechoslovakia, with its Balkan partners.

It should first be noted that the over-all quantum of Czechoslovakia's trade did not recover its predepression level until 1957.[13]

If we examine Czech trade returns by countries, we find that this average date of recovery conceals wide differences: Trade with the U.S.S.R. already far exceeded the prewar high in 1948, whereas trade with Germany—taking both East and West together—was hardly greater in 1963 than in 1928. The share of total exchanges accounted for by the four East European countries we singled out for the prewar period—Rumania, Hungary, Bulgaria, and Poland—was greater than what it was in the late 1920's. It reached a peak, with respect to exports alone, of 32 per cent in 1953, as against 16 per cent in 1928, before the region's disintegration set in. It then fell back to 16.6 per cent in 1957, in connection with a trade recession which will be described presently. It finally climbed part of the way back to its 1953 high a decade later, when it came to 21.5 per cent of total exports.

The figures in Table 8–2 show the quantum indices of Czechoslovak trade with its principal partners in Eastern Europe, based, as in Table 8–1, on a 1928 base.

Some observations on the relation of imports to exports may throw light on these figures. In 1928 the value of Czech exports to Bulgaria was more than twice as great as the value of imports from that country; exports to Rumania were 62 per cent greater than imports. These positive balances were linked to the triangular nature of Czechoslovakia's trade with the Balkans—Rumania and Bulgaria exported most of their foodstuffs and raw materials to Western Europe, with which Czechoslovakia, in turn, had a trade deficit. The surpluses also corresponded in part to short- and long-term capital exports from Czechoslovakia to Bulgaria and Rumania. The trend toward the bilaterality of exchanges fostered by exchange controls and quota arrangements in the 1930's was accentuated in the entire postwar period. Discrepancies from strict equality in bilateral exchanges persisted, but they now resulted chiefly from the credits granted by one country to the other. When these credits were repaid as in the period 1953 to 1957, the excess balance in trade was reduced or even shifted the other way: A traditionally debtor nation, such as Bulgaria, accumulated surpluses with Czechoslovakia, her principal creditor in Central Europe in 1957 and 1958. Whereas Czechoslovakia exported 23 per cent more than she imported from her four East European partners in 1928, this surplus had diminished to 14 per cent in 1948. It rose to an all-time high in 1953 (38 per cent), fell back to 9 per cent in 1957 (the lowest relative surplus since

TABLE 8–2:

INDEX OF QUANTUM OF IMPORTS AND EXPORTS OF CZECHOSLOVAKIA'S TRADE WITH HUNGARY, RUMANIA, BULGARIA, AND POLAND IN 1948, 1953, 1957, 1960, AND 1963 (1928 = 100)

Trade of Czechoslovakia with:		1948	1953	1957	1960	1963
Hungary	Imports	35	136	139	189	268
	Exports	15	66	78	124	169
Rumania	Imports	72	105	80	202	170
	Exports	27	174	64	118	189
Bulgaria	Imports	199	409	981	1,237	1,534
	Exports	88	296	287	565	732
Poland	Imports	45	111	90	148	200
	Exports	62	160	139	246	374
Total Trade with above Countries	Imports	52	126	129	202	253
	Exports	34	129	102	177	232
Total Trade of Czechoslovakia	Imports	50	72	116	160	195
	Exports	36	65	97	150	191

SOURCES: Same as Table 8–1, plus the statistical yearbooks of Czechoslovakia for 1961 to 1964 and *Annuaire du Commerce Extérieur Tchécoslovaque* (Prague, 1962). The same method was used to deflate trade with individual countries as in Table 8–1.

1933), increased again to 12 per cent in 1960, and finally reached 32 per cent in 1963. In general, fluctuations in the positive balances of Czechoslovakia with the rest of Eastern Europe suggest that high levels of trade are associated with large surpluses and vice versa. Considering that a dominant part of these exchanges at present consists in Czech exports of machinery and equipment, the bulk of which must be sold on credit, this positive correlation is hardly surprising.

The relatively low surpluses in Czech trade with Hungary, Rumania, and Bulgaria in 1957 and 1960 are reflected in Table 8–2, the data of which show a much higher increase in the quantum of Czech imports from these countries since 1928 than in the quantum of exports. (Note that the quanta of Czech exports to Hungary and Rumania were only 24 per cent and 18 per cent greater, respectively, in 1960 than in 1928.)

If we compare the general evolution of the region's trade before and after World War II, we cannot but be struck by the abatement of the specific animosities that divided the region a generation ago; while protectionism is still rampant, politically motivated discrimination is no longer so flagrant. Nothing so drastic as the Czech-Hungarian tariff war of the early 1930's or the collapse of Hungarian-Rumanian trade of the late 1930's has so far occurred in Eastern Europe. The closest parallel that may be invoked is the great reduction in Rumanian purchases from Czechoslovakia in 1954 and 1955, but even here it may be argued that Rumania had no special quarrel with Prague at the time and was moved by economic considerations. We shall come back to this question of the relation between economic objectives and nationalistic biases at a later point.

The shortcomings of quantum indices linked to a far remote year are compounded when we attempt to measure the real volume of trade with individual countries broken down by commodity groups. The crude price indices at our disposal apply to the entire volume of Czech imports and exports; a significant error is likely to result from applying them to the value of bilateral exchanges in specific commodity groups. Such a procedure can at best yield a reasonable order of magnitude. It turns out, fortunately, that the trends are so marked that the roughest approximations will do to support our inferences:

1. In constant prices, Czech exports of industrial consumer

goods in the 1950's were a fraction of what they had been in the late 1920's. In the case of exports to Rumania, they amounted to an estimated 3 per cent and 10 per cent of their 1929 level in 1953 and 1960, respectively; the corresponding proportions for Poland were 13 per cent and 50 per cent, for Hungary 5 per cent and 24 per cent, and for Bulgaria 19 per cent and 37 per cent.[14]

2. Czechoslovakia's exports of machinery and equipment to her East European partners were anywhere from 8 to 21 times higher in 1953 than in 1928. They now made up the bulk of Czech exports, having usurped the dominant role played by manufactured consumer goods in the prewar period.

3. Czech imports of raw materials and semifabricates from Rumania, Bulgaria, Hungary, and Poland were some 50 per cent greater in 1953 than in 1929 and nearly double the 1929 level in 1960. The share of raw materials and semifabricates in total Czech imports from Rumania, Hungary, Bulgaria, and Poland was approximately the same in 1929 and in 1960.

4. Imports of food from the same four East European countries were more than 20 per cent lower in 1953 than in 1929. They had only reached 90 per cent of their 1929 level in 1960. Moreover, the geographic distribution of Czechoslovakia's food purchases was thoroughly different in the middle and late 1950's from what it had been before the depression. Imports of food from Poland in 1960 were a small fraction of what they were in 1929, while imports from Rumania were about twice as great as in 1929. From a negligible amount in 1929, Bulgarian food exports to Czechoslovakia increased to $22,000,000 (in current prices) in 1960, a sum only 20 per cent smaller than Czech imports of food from Hungary, her traditional source of supply. The share of foodstuffs and other agricultural products in total Czech imports from the four countries dropped from 52.7 per cent in 1929 to 25.2 per cent in 1960.

5. The rise in Czechoslovakia's machinery imports from Eastern Europe, both in absolute and in percentage terms, was even more spectacular than in her machinery exports. In 1929 these imports had been negligible, with the possible exception of imports from Hungary, 1.5 per cent of whose exports to Czechoslovakia were made up of machinery and equipment. In 1960 they totaled 31 per cent of Czechoslovakia's total imports from her

principal East European partners (19.3 per cent out of imports from Rumania and 22.4 per cent from Bulgaria!). Czechoslovakia, incidentally, was not the only industrially mature country in the bloc to buy large quantities of machinery from the Balkans. Machines made up some 30 to 40 per cent of East Germany's imports from Rumania and Bulgaria in certain recent years.

In fine, Czechoslovakia's trade with Eastern Europe was very slow to recover its 1929 level. During the postwar period Czechoslovakia's less developed partners adopted a systematic policy of substituting domestic for imported consumers' manufactures and curtailed Czechoslovakia's markets for those goods; on the other hand, their ambitious industrialization drives compelled them to buy enormous quantities of machinery, which Czechoslovakia was in a position to supply in the late 1940's and early 1950's. Payment for a part of these purchases was delayed to the extent that credits were made available; in large part, however, they were paid for by raw material exports; trade in foodstuffs among the five principal countries of Eastern Europe declined, both relatively and absolutely.

So far we have concentrated on the structural trends, disregarding the fluctuations in the level of exchanges, which are perhaps more revealing of nationalistic attitudes toward international trade than long-run policies. When we come to compare the trade recession of the mid-1950's with the depression of the 1930's, we step on to firmer statistical ground, since neither the magnitude nor the dispersion of price changes within a short span of years, particularly in the postwar period, is likely to produce the errors that comparisons over a third of a century will tend to generate.

We can assert with fair confidence that the quantum of Czech exports to Rumania fell by nearly two-thirds from 1953 to 1957, as compared with a one-third drop from 1928 to 1933.[15] With this important exception, the declines in the quantum of trade were all much smaller than those that occurred in the first years of the worldwide depression. Exports to Hungary slipped by 3 per cent from 1953 to 1955 and by another 7 per cent in 1956; but they rose to 119 per cent of their 1953 level in 1957, due in part to Czech aid in the recovery from the October Revolution's damage. Exports to Poland fell by 15 per cent from 1953 to 1957, which was an unusually adverse year for Czech-Polish trade. (Over the period 1954 to 1958, the quantum of Czech exports to Poland fluctuated between 85 and 107 per cent of their 1953 level.) If we except Czech-Rumanian trade, therefore, it is more proper to describe the trend of trade in the region in the mid-1950's as a slight retrogression rather than as a full-fledged recession, such as occurred in the early 1930's when the quantum of Czech and Hungarian exports to other East European nations went down by anywhere from 34 to 68 per cent (Table 8–1).

Nevertheless, the incidence of this mild recession on trade in specific commodity groups suggests some interesting comparisons with the situation of the 1930's. At that time, as we have seen, the full brunt of protectionist measures fell on manufactured consumer goods, while trade in machinery was spared the worst consequences of the crisis. On the import side, foodstuffs were more critically affected—especially in trade with Poland—than raw materials and semifabricates. In the course of the postwar retrogression, machinery exports were hardest hit. The less developed countries of the area were bent on developing their own engineering industries almost at any cost; when the demand for machinery fell, in conjunction with the decline or stagnation of investment activity associated with the New Course after 1953, these countries discriminated in favor of their own domestic machine-building industries and curtailed their imports. Thus, protectionist policies, which had mainly affected consumer goods in the 1930's and up to 1953, were now extended to capital goods; these new restrictions, in view of the nature of postwar development policies, probably had a more depressing effect on the potential level of trade than the protection of domestic consumer goods industries.

From 1953 to 1956 the quantum of Czech machine exports to Hungary, Rumania, Bulgaria, and Poland dropped by a little over 50 per cent, from 70.5 per cent of total exports to these countries to 49 per cent.[16] While, admittedly, machinery exports from Czechoslovakia were harmed somewhat more by the crisis than those of her competitors, the fact remains that the total machinery imports of her four partners must have dropped at least 40 per cent (by 43 per cent in current prices).[17] Table 8–3 illustrates the effects of the contraction of demand for machinery and equipment on Hungarian exports of a few typical items in this group.

Unfortunately, it is not possible to reconstruct the complete breakdown by commodity group for Czechoslovakia's trade with all four of her East European partners in 1956–57, the trough years of the recession. From the scattered data at our disposal, we can only infer that raw material imports from Eastern Europe stagnated or rose slightly from 1953 to 1957, while imports of foodstuffs underwent a fairly significant decline—of the order of 15 to 20 per cent both in current and in constant prices.[18]

Czechoslovakia's trade with Poland, for which we do have adequate information both in 1953 and in 1957 (see Table 8–4), may be used to illustrate the trends in the composition of trade between the two years.

The absolute and relative decline in Czech imports presents a striking parallel to the depression of the 1930's. The share of foodstuffs in total Czech imports from Poland fell from 42.2 per cent in 1929 to 7.8 per cent in 1937; during the New Course it fell from 13.4 per cent in 1953 to 2.8 per cent in 1957. To a varying extent, the same trend could be noted in trade between other East European countries.

Nevertheless, we should beware of matching like phenomena with like causes. During the depression the deflection of food exports by countries such as Poland and Hungary away from their traditional East European markets was due in part to protectionist measures adopted by their former customers and in part to their wish to avoid the accumulation of inconvertible currencies by countries exercising exchange controls. Food surpluses available for export dwindled after 1953, mainly by reason of the government decision, taken in line with the New Course, to allow domestic food consumption to rise at the expense of exports, particularly in Poland, Rumania, and Hungary.[19] However, clear violations of "proletarian internationalism"—violations that could not be exonerated by paramount domestic needs —did occur in 1956 and 1957 when Poland shunted part of her exports of raw materials and foodstuffs toward Western markets, which, as in the 1930's, offered the advantage of payment in convertible currencies.

It should be stressed again that intraregional trade in the first five years after Stalin's death suffered far more from the recession than the total trade of each of the East European countries separately. This was largely because the Soviet market continued

TABLE 8–3:

EXPORTS AND IMPORTS OF SELECTED MACHINERY PRODUCTS BETWEEN HUNGARY AND RUMANIA, BULGARIA, POLAND, CZECHOSLO-
VAKIA, AND EAST GERMANY, 1952 TO 1955

	Unit	1952	1953	1954	1955
Exports from Hungary to:					
Rumania					
Metal-working machines	Number	438	394	109	54
Trucks	Number	733	462	30	14
Ore flotation equipment	Millions of exchange forints	13	10	5.5	1.8
Bulgaria					
Steam turbines and parts	Thousands of exchange forints	323	117	160	564
Gas generators	Thousands of exchange forints	3,385	2,347	1,598	—
Poland					
Steam turbines and parts	Thousands of exchange forints	10,172	2,151	4,233	6,321
Hot water boilers	Square meters	8,900	21,353	3,686	—
Lifting and transportation equipment	Thousands of exchange forints	12,357	19,721	9,328	604
Compressed airtools	Number	3,463	8,307	2,364	3,404

Imports to Hungary from:
Czechoslovakia

Metal-working machines and parts	Thousands of exchange forints	14,169	28,727	7,566	4,960
Construction machines and parts	Thousands of exchange forints	2,016	751	4,546	1,051
East Germany					
Metal-working machines and parts	Thousands of exchange forints	16,790	24,365	15,424	15,508
Chemical-industry machines and equipment	Thousands of exchange forints	25,270	9,634	7,234	2,235
Antifriction bearings	Thousands of exchange forints	9,814	18,272	11,057	13,079

SOURCE: *Statistical Yearbook of Hungary, 1949–1955* (Budapest, 1957). (Translation issued by U.S. Joint Publications Research Service.)

to offer an outlet for machinery products which could not find buyers elsewhere, in return for food and raw materials other countries were unwilling to supply. From 1953 to 1956, for instance, when Rumania, Hungary, Bulgaria, Poland, and even

TABLE 8–4:

CZECHO-POLISH TRADE BY COMMODITY GROUPS
(millions of Czech crowns at current prices)

Trade	Value in 1953 (millions of Czecho-slovak Crowns)	Per Cent of Total	Value in 1957 (millions of Czecho-slovak Crowns)	Per Cent of Total
Czech Exports to Poland:				
Machinery and equipment	567	77.4	332	59.0
Raw materials and fuels	114	15.6	182	32.3
Food products	7	0.9	1	0.2
Manufactured consumer goods (excluding food products)	45	6.2	48	8.5
Total Exports	733	100	563	100
Czech Imports from Poland:				
Machinery and equipment	53	7.4	65	15.0
Raw materials and fuels	570	78.9	353	81.7
Food products	97	13.4	12	2.8
Manufactured consumer goods (excluding food products)	2	0.3	2	0.5
Total Imports	722	100	432	100

SOURCES: For 1953, Dušana Machová, *ČSSR v socialistické mezinárodní dělbě práce* (Prague, 1962); for 1957, *Statistický obzor*, No. 7 (1961), pp. 315–16. A relatively small percentage error in Machová concerning Czech exports of raw materials to Poland in 1953 was corrected with the aid of the data for 1960 published in *Statistický obzor*, No. 7, and the percentage increases from 1953 to 1960 given in Machová, *ČSSR*.

Albania reduced their purchases of Czech machinery and equipment, sales to the Soviet Union rose by about 50 per cent in current prices.[20] While Czechoslovakia's purchases of raw materials and semifabricates from the rest of Eastern Europe were stagnating, Soviet deliveries of these goods were about 55 per cent greater in 1957 than in 1953.[21] Food imports from the Soviet

Union also rose appreciably during this period—by 31 per cent—although they had to be supplemented by increases in purchases from capitalist countries.[22] The parallel with the 1930's that suggests itself here, *toutes proportions gardées,* is that a certain degree of disintegration in the region's trade was partly offset in both periods by increased dependence on a country outside the area with a wider market that could absorb the region's surpluses. In the mid- and late 1930's Germany was willing, mainly for political reasons, to take on Hungarian and Rumanian agricultural surpluses; in the mid-1950's the Soviet Union absorbed a significant part of the machinery surpluses of Czechoslovakia and Hungary, for reasons that may also have been to some extent political (although one should also keep in mind that the Soviet Union's investments in machinery did not stagnate in this period as they did in most East European countries).[23]

From 1958 on, trade activity in Eastern Europe changed radically for the better. The less developed countries of the area, including Rumania, again increased their purchases from the more developed—Czechoslovakia and East Germany. Trade in machinery, lubricated by generous credit facilities, soon topped the records attained in 1952 and 1953. The food and raw material exporting countries were both more willing and more able to import machinery than in the previous period, for four principal reasons: (1) They could afford to increase their imports because their export proceeds were no longer mortgaged to pay debts incurred in the 1949–52 period as they had been after 1953. (In the case of Rumania, the financial burden arising from the liquidation of the joint Soviet-Rumanian companies had reduced its import capacities until 1957.) (2) They succeeded in increasing their capacity to export raw materials and foodstuffs. (Rumania, for instance, had to import grain in 1956 and 1957, but from then on had large and increasing surpluses for sale abroad.)[24] (3) Both the more and the less industrialized countries of Eastern Europe raised the share of fixed investments in their national income from 1958 on. (The political turmoils of 1956 having subsided, there was no longer any urgency to raise consumption to ward off political disturbances.) The high and rising level of investment activity stimulated the demand for machinery products throughout the bloc. (4) The renewed vigor of regional exchanges in machinery products was also probably due to some degree to the intensified efforts of the Council for Economic Mutual Assistance to co-ordinate investment decisions and to promote specialization in the region's engineering industries.

Signs of another slowdown in the region's trade in machinery began to appear in 1963 and 1964, as Rumania and Poland, whose industrial expansion was decelerating, began to reduce some of their imports of equipment. But before we discuss this recent evolution and the prospects for the immediate future, we must take a broader view of postwar exchanges and of the nationalistic elements that conditioned their trends.

II

Our approach so far has been, for the most part, behavioristic. We have observed trends and patterns in East European trade, confining our comments on nationalistic policies to the most obvious inferences. This a priori discussion of the trading problems of the area may serve as an introduction to a more general analysis of economic nationalism, which I understand to be any commercial policy tending to harm the economic interests of a group of countries or "bloc" for the sake of pursuing some domestic goal.

We should try to distinguish two types of nationalistic policies which had their counterparts in Eastern Europe both in the prewar and in the postwar periods: The first is linked to the strategy of a country's development, while the second is more tactical in nature, stemming from political animosity or other non-economic considerations. Thus the policy of substituting domestic industrial products for imports—be they of consumer or of producer goods—clearly belongs to the first type of strategic decision.

Within the category of measures that can be traced to a country's strategy of development, we should perhaps further segregate direct from indirect effects. The decision to build up the production of machinery products in an underdeveloped nation has direct and easily observable consequences on its commercial policy in the way of tariff protection and restrictive quotas. Suppose, however, that the creation or the expansion of the nation's machine-building industry were to provoke a balance-of-payments crisis as a result of the additional raw material imports that it absorbed or by the diversion of domestically produced materials from exports to domestic consumption. Such a crisis can be invoked to justify almost any protectionist measure. An even more indirect implication of an initial strategic decision would involve an underdeveloped country's refusal to buy equipment from an exporting state that did not buy some of that country's newly produced machinery in return. Rumania's policies in recent years may be used to illustrate both of these indirect effects. According to a Czech author, Rumania in the mid-fifties had accepted a CEMA recommendation to specialize in the production of four-ton trucks. Instead of delivering these trucks to her partners according to schedule and buying other makes in return, the Rumanians advanced the pretext that the passivity of their balance of payments was forcing them to supply their country's entire needs from the types of equipment they were supposed to specialize in,[25] thereby undermining both their export and their import agreements. At about the same time, Rumania discriminated against Czechoslovakia in favor of East Germany and the U.S.S.R. in her imports of engineering products because the Germans and the Russians were more willing to buy large amounts of machinery from her than were the Czechs.[26]

The indirect effects, of course, are not the uniquely possible consequences of an initial strategic decision. Rumania, for instance, could have developed her trucking industry in the framework of the specialization agreement. She might also have used Czech equipment to develop her potential exports of raw materials or foodstuffs, thus releasing her own machinery products for domestic consumption; this policy need not have slowed down the expansion of her engineering industry. It must be conceded in this case that the fairly stringent requirement of bilateral balancing between trading countries in the communist bloc might have restricted the degree of freedom open to the Rumanian authorities to adopt less discriminatory policies.

Looking over the entire postwar period, we find that, with the possible exception of Rumania, most protectionist measures flowed fairly directly from strategic decisions. As has already been discussed, there seems to have been far less of the petty skirmishing between East European countries that led to the atrophy of trade before the war.[27] This should not be a matter for amazement, considering that these nations were close allies, governed by communists with more or less identical ideologies. Up to 1953, it may be surmised that any overt discrimination in trade by one satellite against the other would have drawn reproof from Moscow.

The political affinities of the rulers of Eastern Europe are not solely responsible for the closer integration of the area. It is manifest that the willingness to co-operate was vastly encouraged by the high trade *Konjunktur* that prevailed throughout the Soviet bloc in the postwar period, with the exception of the years 1953 to 1957. It may be useful, therefore, to review the mainsprings of trade and autarchy in the area for the light they may cast on the future prospects of integration.

The foundations of economic nationalism were laid when Stalin chose, or felt compelled, to maintain the nominal independence of the East European states rather than incorporate them into the Soviet Union, as he had done with the Baltic states. If the East European states and the U.S.S.R. had been fused into a single polity, the former international trade of the region would have assumed the form of regional trade, governed from a single center, with as much mobility of capital and labor among regions as the costs of redeployment permitted or defense considerations allowed. The failure to bring about this consummation implied, among other things, that labor was to be fixed in supply for each of the nation-states: The surplus labor of Poland or Rumania could not be assigned by central *ukaz* to work in Czechoslovak mines and foundries. Capital could be somewhat more mobile, since the wealthier countries of the area were free to sell on credit, if they found it to their advantage, to their less well-endowed partners. But these movements of capital were necessarily small compared with what they might have been if Moscow had set the level of "accumulation" in each formerly independent country and had distributed the total pool of investments among regions, regardless of previous national boundaries. The disparities in living standards among the countries of Eastern Europe would have been reduced in a superstate insofar as the richer among the constituent republics would have been compelled to contribute a much greater share of total saving than the poor. As it turned out, particularly after 1953, each state set its rate of accumulation with an eye to maintaining or improving traditional living standards. The less developed nations should not expect, as one Czech authority put it, that "socialism can be built with the hands of others." They should utilize their resources to the maximum extent and rely on the better-off nations as little as possible.[28] It was inappropriate, in any case, that the peoples of the poorer economies of the bloc should enjoy living standards that were out of line with their level of national income or productivity.[29]

Every independent state conducting trade through a monopoly must balance its international payments, the debits and the credits arising from its trade and capital transactions. The discipline imposed by the over-all balance of payments was reinforced in Eastern Europe by the necessity, introduced from the beginning of state trading in the area, of balancing accounts with each partner separately. The near impossibility of using the surpluses accumulated in trade with one socialist country to buy from another undoubtedly restricted the total volume of intrabloc trade.[30] Reciprocity could on occasion even be carried one step further: Officials of less industrialized nations have on occasion insisted on balancing not only total accounts but trade within each commodity group with each partner. The representatives of the less developed socialist countries attempted to raise the percentage share of manufactured goods in their exports to their more developed partners as near as possible to the share of these goods in their imports from the same countries, justifying these policies by the argument that the export of raw materials and foodstuffs in exchange for manufactures is characteristic of colonial exploitation and is incompatible with the equitable relations established among socialist countries. There was much room here for the exercise of discrimination against more developed nations.

A somewhat less obvious consequence of national independence may, in the end, be mentioned. Each nation-state sought to even out the disparities in development *within* its borders by establishing factories in previously underdeveloped regions. The communist authorities in Prague, for example, put forth great efforts to promote the development of Slovakia. Industries were set up in that part of the country which apparently duplicated, or were duplicated by, the factories set up (often with the aid of Czech documentation and equipment) in the less developed nations of CEMA.[31] This parallelism dampened trade; if we are to believe that trade accelerates the disappearance of international differences in levels of development, we must also believe that it has retarded this process. In a nutshell, "the incomplete equalization of development within states hampers the process of equalization among states."[32]

As we have seen, the years of intensive industrialization that followed post-World War II reconstruction in Eastern Europe witnessed a great upsurge in trade, even though the development programs of most of the countries concerned were oriented toward the diversification of their economies. To become more self-sufficient in industrial products the less developed nations of the bloc had to import machines, equipment, and whole factories from the more industrially advanced nations of the bloc. Czechoslovakia, especially in the years preceding East Germany's recovery from the joint effects of war damage and Soviet depredations, was slated to play a prominent role in this effort. Among the directives issued by the Central Committee of the Czechoslovak Communist Party for the First Five-Year Plan (1949 to 1953), it was stipulated that Czechoslovakia, "in keeping with the principles of proletarian internationalism," would become "the machine works for the entire socialist camp."[33] In point of fact, Czechoslovakia adapted the structure of her industry to provide not only the heavy equipment required for the industrialization of the less developed countries of the bloc, but also modern weapons for her allies and assistance in building up industries essential to their defense capacity.[34]

It was in this first period of intensive development throughout the communist bloc, after the stillbirth of the Council for Economic Mutual Assistance in 1949, that the foundations of autarky were laid in each of the industrialized nations. The blame for attempting to develop all branches of industry at once in disregard of the advantages of international specialization cannot all be laid on "the dogmatic application of Soviet experience in socialist industrialization" or on "remnants of bourgeois nationalism," although these factors, as the Czechs now assert,[35] cannot be ruled out. A more subtle contributing cause is to be found in the effects of the trend toward technological self-sufficiency in the bloc as a whole. Since the countries exporting equipment were to a large extent cut off from technical progress in the West, and the developing socialist countries were reluctant to buy licenses from "monopolists," the range of technical processes embodied in investment assemblies for export was quite narrow. Exporters sold relatively few types of machines; the machines that were sold were designed mainly for the manufacture of products that the exporters themselves were good at making. The underdeveloped importing nations, wishing to economize on their skilled manpower, reinforced this bias by concentrating their purchases mainly on plants and equipment with a standardized, easy-to-master technology—in order to produce such things as electric motors, standard lathes, trucks and tractors. These were also the items that could be produced with considerable economies of scale. The Czech machine-building industry is said to have contributed for these reasons to "the creation of parallel, superfluous, and at times unprofitable productions in a few socialist countries and thereby to the emergence of disproportions in the socialist world economy."[36]

Economies of scale did not present a problem when the bloc-wide demand for machine products was at its peak, but they led to a scramble for markets in the period after 1953 when the stagnant level of investments made it difficult for any East European economy to exploit these economies with a view exclusively to the satisfaction of domestic demand. By the time the investment projects launched in the Stalinist period had come into operation, almost every economy of Eastern Europe was producing more motors, lathes, trucks, and tractors than it could use at home—hence the efforts in the framework of the resuscitated Council for Economic Mutual Assistance, from 1956 on, to foster specialization by multilateral agreements.

The failure to co-ordinate the changes in economic policy associated with the New Course, in economies at different stages of development, created tensions in the bloc which had serious political consequences. Vladimir Kaigl, who was at that time the director of the Economic Institute of Czechoslovakia's Academy of Sciences, wrote in 1958 that the unsatisfactory progress of specialization prior to 1956

> played into the hands of bourgeois nationalists in individual countries who wished to bar the way along this path (the only correct path that could be taken), ena-

bling them to magnify shortcomings and distort them into the mendacious proposition about the exploitation of certain socialist countries by others. It also helped their efforts to misuse the correct tendencies to develop trade between socialist and capitalist countries in order to subvert the principles of international socialist division of labor . . . and to bring the people's democracies once again under the domination of imperialism. Along with political and ideological factors, economic shortcomings, in internal as well as in external relations, helped to launch the wave of bourgeois nationalism and revisionism that occurred in connection with the events of the fall of 1956.[37]

As we have seen, the latent contradictions of the 1949–53 era burst forth after Stalin's death; they did not disappear but again shrank from sight after 1958 when the simultaneous upsurge of investments throughout the bloc helped to keep exporters' capacities fully utilized. Despite the integrative efforts of CEMA, the share of imported machinery in total machinery consumption came to only 6.4 per cent in the CEMA bloc in 1961 (compared with an estimated 24 per cent in the European Economic Community).[38] As late as 1963, according to a Hungarian estimate, only 3 per cent to 5 per cent of total machinery production corresponded to the recommendations on specialization issued by CEMA.[39]

Among items exhibiting significant economies of scale, the achievements to date have been as poor or poorer than this average. The CEMA agreements on tractor production may be cited in this connection. There were 26 types of tractors produced in all the CEMA countries together, before specialization agreements were hammered out sometime in 1956. These agreements called for a reduction to 23 types; 6 types were to be eliminated and 3 new ones introduced. By 1964 only 2 had been eliminated, yet even these had not been replaced by imports: Their use was simply discontinued in the agriculture of the countries concerned.[40] According to the 1956 agreement, East Germany was to produce 17,700 tractors by 1960 and Rumania 6,000. The relative outputs turned out to be almost in inverse ratio: 9,076 tractors in East Germany and 17,102 in Rumania.[41] It is fair to conclude that the specialization agreements on tractors, as narrow in scope as they were, had not been able to overcome the autarkic bias of the member nations.

The dissensions among the CEMA nations, and particularly between Czechoslovakia and East Germany on the one hand and Rumania on the other, have already formed the subject of a fair amount of literature in English.[42] I shall not rake this ground over, except for one observation: The disputes came to a head between 1960 and 1963 when trade conditions were buoyant and the conflicts of interests between the developed and the underdeveloped economies of the Council were distinctly less acute than in the period 1953 to mid-1958. Since then, the industrialization programs of the less developed countries have shown signs of running out of steam, and the demand for machinery products has begun to flag.[43] A new note of resignation to the failure to achieve greater co-ordination can be detected in the writings of certain East European specialists in the affairs of the socialist commonwealth.[44]

These apprehensions are aroused by the prospect that the investments and skills devoted to the expansion of specialized industries or groups of products will be wasted if the client-countries do not curtail their own production of these goods. On the basis of past experience, this is a likely possibility. On the other hand, each country qua consumer is reluctant to curtail lines of production essential to the national economy for fear that specialized suppliers in the bloc will be unable to deliver required goods of the right quality and on schedule.[45] These misgivings are compounded when a developed nation must dovetail its production with that of an industrial latecomer, such as Rumania or Bulgaria.[46]

The lure of Western markets for primary commodities and the attractive prospects of obtaining "technologically progressive" capital goods from advanced capitalist countries also presents a serious challenge to the cohesion of the bloc. These magnets tempt members to cater to their national advantage at the expense of proletarian internationalism. The European Economic Community's pulling power is a case in point. The interests of CEMA members are so divergent, chiefly because of their disparities in development, that they cannot present a united front in negotiations with the West. A Czech official writes:

I consider to be refined science fiction the proposal to create a unified organization of the member states of CEMA for trading with the EEC. . . . It is clear that the less developed countries, in whose exports raw materials predominate, will be significantly less affected by the discriminatory measures of the EEC than the developed countries of CEMA which are capable of exporting to the advanced capitalist states much greater quantities of final—mostly machine-building—products to which the anti-import measures of EEC mainly apply.[47]

What makes the developed states in CEMA so sensitive on the subject is that when a less developed nation, such as Rumania, buys equipment in the West, in exchange for timber or corn, it hurts CEMA members in two ways: First, it cuts off an outlet for their production, and secondly, it reduces the total bloc supply of scarce raw materials or foodstuffs. Since, for reasons it is not feasible to explore in this paper, this writer believes that the ability of the less developed economies to produce and export surpluses of raw materials and foodstuffs to the Soviet bloc largely determines the level of exchanges in Eastern Europe, any deflection of these goods away from CEMA members to the West is likely to reduce the region's trade and thus to aggravate the recently observed slowdown in the region's trade.

The outlook for the next few years is not very bright. The combination of marketing difficulties for heavy industrial products, which will probably be reinforced by declining rates of economic growth, together with growing distrust and suspicion among the CEMA partners, arising partly from the unsatisfactory experience with co-operation in the years of trade prosperity, is likely to cause more of the indirect manifestations of economic nationalism to rise to the surface. Protectionism for the sake of protectionism, rather than protectionism focused on the specific goal of defending a particular development strategy, may become the order of the day. A striking example of the type of thinking that may be conducive to disintegration is provided by the recent theoretical article of the authoritative Rumanian economist Ion Rachmuth, who rejects the theory of specialization according to comparative advantage even in cases where it leads to greater output and consumption for both partners, if this specialization happens to widen the disparity in development levels between two countries at different stages of industrialization.[48] The animosities bred out of the unsuccessful negotiations in CEMA between countries wishing to enforce the recommendations of a supranational organization and those wishing to maintain their untrammeled sovereignty[49] may also give rise to discriminatory measures aimed against specific countries, which may not be even indirectly related to economic objectives. What makes this all the more probable is that there is much room for subjective evaluations in determining static and dynamic comparative advantage, the potential reliability of suppliers, or the likelihood that client-nations will follow the spirit and the letter of specialization agreements. Behind a developed country's unwillingness to trade or to enter into a long-run specialization agreement with a less developed country in the bloc, there may lurk political prejudice masquerading as "objective" justification, based in turn on a biased appraisal of past performance.

These speculations lean on a pessimistic reading of current trends. There are, however, some positive factors in the situation that augur well for the more distant future. As the disparities in levels of development in CEMA diminish—the marked slowdown in Czechoslovak and East German growth is accelerating this tendency—the newly industrialized countries will reach an acceptable level of industrial diversification from which they may become more willing to specialize in new products or new groups. As their industries mature, their partners may acquire more confidence in the quality and reliability of their exports. Finally, if market-type decentralization is launched in several of the CEMA countries, the advantages of trade will be easier to demonstrate on the basis of more reliable prices; this may remove impediments to trade due to lack of knowledge or to uncertainty as to its benefits. It would be unfortunate for the future integration of the region, however, if the more autarkic countries, such as Rumania, were to retain their centralized systems, while those already predisposed toward international specialization were to decentralize—as seems likely at the present time. In any case, if we take a long view of the process of integration, there is hardly any likelihood of a reversion to the extreme forms of commercial antagonism that accelerated the disintegration of Eastern Europe in the 1930's.

NOTES

1. Frederick Hertz, *The Economic Problem of the Danubian States: A Study in Economic Nationalism* (London, 1947), p. 72.

2. Antonin Basch, *The Danube Basin and the German Economic Sphere* (New York, 1943), p. 5.

3. József Buzás, "Magyarország külkereskedelme 1919–1938," in *Magyarország külkereskedelme 1919–1945* (Budapest, 1961), p. 51. In the late 1920's Trianon Hungary, bought about forty per cent of her imports from Austria and Czechoslovakia combined. This figure underestimates total imports from the old Austrian territories, since it excludes goods originating in Galicia (Poland) and Slovenia (Yugoslavia); but this is compensated to some extent by the inclusion of Slovakia, which was formerly part of Hungary.

4. For details see Hertz, *The Economic Problem of the Danubian States,* p. 72.

5. In 1929, out of total Czech exports to Hungary, Poland, Rumania, and Bulgaria, manufactured goods represented 56.2, 76.8, 91.7, and 95.7 per cent, respectively. Out of total imports, foodstuffs made up 74.7, 42.2, 48.6, and 7.5 per cent, respectively, for these four countries. The corresponding percentages for the share of imports of raw materials and semifabricates were 19.4, 54.0, 50.0, and 92.2 per cent, respectively. An exception to this pattern were the Czechoslovak exports of raw materials to Hungary, including coal and coke, which came to 42.1 per cent of the total exports to that country. Dušana Machová, *ČSSR v socialistické mezinárodní dělbě práce* (Prague, 1962), p. 86.

6. A Magyar Királyi Központi Statisztikai Hivatal, *Magyarország 1930. évi külkereskedelmi forgalma* (Budapest, 1931), p. 52.

7. Hertz, *The Economic Problem of the Danubian States,* p. 80.

8. Leo Pasvolsky, *Economic Nationalism in the Danubian States* (Washington, D.C., 1928), p. 574.

9. András Nagy, "Magyarország külkereskedelme a második világháború-ban," in *Magyarország külkereskedelme 1919–1945,* pp. 264–65.

10. Computed from data in Machová, *ČSSR,* p. 86.

11. Buzás, "Magyarország külkereskedelme 1919–1938," p. 109.

12. Serban Gheorghiu, M. Romaşcanu, and C. Săndulescu-Godeni, "Considerațiuni generale privitoare la comerțul exterior al României . . . ," in *Comerțul României 1928–1937* (Bucharest, 1939), I, 490, 540.

13. *Statisticky obzor,* No. 2 (1959), p. 90.

14. Trade in manufactured consumer goods in 1929, 1953, and 1960, broken down by country, was estimated by Machová, *ČSSR,* pp. 86, 210. She claims that she adjusted the coverage of the prewar statistics to make them as comparable as possible to the classification of the CEMA. Her data were deflated by the implicit price indices used in my previous calculations.

15. It should be noted, however, that Czech exports to Rumania in 1953 were blown up by extraordinary deliveries of equipment and armaments (see Machová, *ČSSR,* p. 127). Unfortunately, the level of these exports in 1952 could not be ascertained.

16. Czechoslovak machinery exports in 1953 were computed from percentages in Machová, *ČSSR,* p. 210. For 1956 the data are based on Jan Vaněk, *Ekonomicky a politický význam vývozu strojírenských výrobků z ČSSR* (Prague, 1960), pp. 189–91. The scattered data Vaněk supplies for 1953 show that his definition of machine-building exports coincides with Machová's.

17. Imports from Czechoslovakia made up 28 per cent of total Polish machinery imports in 1953 and only 22 per cent in 1956; the corresponding percentages were 24 and 19 per cent for Rumania and 20 and 17 per cent for Hungary; only Bulgaria increased the share of Czechoslovakia in its machinery imports, from 18 to 23.5 per cent between the two dates. (Vaněk, *Ekonomicky a politický*, pp. 196–99.) The absolute volume of imports of machinery into the four countries was calculated from the known data for Czechoslovak exports of machinery to the four countries and from the above percentages.

18. Czech trade in raw materials and foodstuffs with the communist bloc, excluding the U.S.S.R., may be calculated by subtracting trade with the Soviet Union (see the percentages in *Zahraniční obchod*, No. 9 [1959]) from the total imports and exports of these goods (*Razvitie ekonomiki stran narodnoi domokratii Evropy i Azii [Statisticheskii sbornik]* [Moscow, 1961], pp. 456–57). In addition to the four countries of Eastern Europe with which we are concerned, the data resulting from the above calculations include communist Asia and East Germany. In the case of raw material imports, we can eliminate communist Asia by making use of published statistics on raw material trade in CEMA for 1955 and 1958 (Jiři Novozámský, *Vyrovnávání ekonomické úrovně zemí RVHP* [Prague, 1964], p. 109) from which, as before, we may subtract trade with the Soviet Union. The following table summarizes the results (in millions of Czech crowns at current prices) :

Czechoslovakia:	1953	1955	1957
Imports of raw materials from communist bloc (excluding U.S.S.R.)	1,357	1,445	1,485
Imports of raw materials from CEMA (excluding U.S.S.R.)	1,165	1,268	1,244[a]
Imports of foodstuffs from communist bloc (excluding U.S.S.R.)	783	754	664

[a] 1958.

Note that food imports from China increased in this period, so that imports from East Europe must have fallen more than in the above data.

19. The consequences of the policy shift are described in some detail by Machová (*ČSSR*, pp. 134–35). Certain long-term agreements were violated by the traditional food-exporting countries in order to implement the new policy; at the same time, net food importers, such as Czechoslovakia, who also wished to abandon food rationing and to improve living standards, had to turn toward capitalist countries to supplement their purchases. The limited possibilities for redirecting trade made it awkward for them to increase consumption as rapidly as they would have liked. These difficulties are perhaps not unrelated to the popular riots of June, 1953, when the Czech government found itself compelled to carry out a drastic monetary reform in conjunction with the abolition of rationing.

20. This increase was calculated from percentage data in Machová, *ČSSR*, p. 210, and Vaněk, *Economicky a politický*, p. 193.

21. Computed from percentage data in *Zahraniční obchod*, No. 9 (1959).

22. According to Machová (*ČSSR*, p. 138), Czechoslovakia's food imports from capitalist countries rose 250 per cent from 1953 to 1955.

23. For candid comments on the greater reliability of the Soviet vent for

Czechoslovakia's machinery exports, compared to her markets in Eastern Europe, see Vaněk, *Ekonomicky a politický*, pp. 193–95. On the external dependence of Hungary, the words of a populist writer, published in 1943, deserve mention in this connection: "Since the death of Mátyás the Danube basin has always been [economically] dependent, and its peoples have always been unhappy. It would seem that this situation of dependence on big powers cannot disappear in the course of the evolution going on until now. It is probable that a totally new order will be needed for the peoples of the basin to find a happier future." J. Nagy, the discussant of this conference paper by L. Jócsik, asked whether it was likely that the abolition of capitalism would necessarily improve matters: "Wouldn't the Hungarian economy be exploited under a collective system, just as under capitalism?" (L. Jócsik, "A középdunamedence közgazdasága," in *Szárszó: Az 1943 évi Balatonszárszói Magyar elet —Tábor Elöadás—és Megbeszéléssorozata* [Budapest, 1943], pages 106–7.) I am grateful to Prof. Rudolf L. Tökés for drawing my attention to this interesting article on the economy of the Danubian basin.

24. For more details on Rumania's export problems in the mid–1950's see the *Economic Bulletin for Europe* of the United Nations Economic Commission for Europe, XI, No. 1 (1959), 52–53.

25. Machová, *ČSSR*, p. 155.

26. *Ibid.*, p. 201.

27. Excepted here, of course, are the drastic trade boycott of the Cominform countries imposed against Yugoslavia after 1948 and the relatively minor curtailment of East European, as distinguished from Soviet, trade with Albania from 1962 on, both of which fall outside the purview of this discussion.

28. Karel Pomaizl, "Proti škodlivým projevům nacionalismu" ("Against Harmful Manifestations of Nationalism"), *Nová myśl*, No. 5 (1962), p. 559.

29. See Jiři Novozámský in *Nová myśl*, No. 4 (1962), p. 430.

30. In 1961, 345,000,000 Old Rubles in trade, or 0.5 per cent of intra-CEMA trade, were cleared multilaterally. According to one estimate about a fourth of total trade in the capitalist world is so cleared (Novozámský, *Vyrovnávání*, p. 126). The creation of the Bank of CEMA in January, 1964, is not believed to have brought about any significant improvement in this regard. (See S. Albinowski's article in *Glos pracy*, May 17, 1965.)

31. After the First World War, on the other hand, certain Slovak factories, set up by Hungarians when Slovakia belonged to Greater Hungary, were said to have collapsed under the pressure of Czech competition. According to a precommunist Hungarian source, complaints about this state of affairs by a Slovak representative in Parliament in the 1930's fell on deaf ears: "The [Slovak] highlands became a graveyard for factories in Czechoslovakia." (L. Jócsik, "A középdunamedence közgazdasága," p. 99.) Quite the reverse policy was followed by the communist regime in Czechoslovakia, at least up to 1963 when the paramount urgency of eliminating waste and inefficiency made it necessary to close a number of factories in Slovakia.

32. Gustav Apetauer, "O aktuálních otázkách ekonomického rozvoje členských státu RVHP," *Plánované hospodářstvi*, No. 1 (1965), p. 72.

33. Machová, *ČSSR*, p. 99.

34. *Ibid.*, p. 100.

35. *Ibid.*, p. 124; Vaněk, *Ekonomicky a politický*, p. 213; and Novozámský, *Vyrovnávání*, p. 127.

36. Vaněk, *Ekonomicky a politický*, pp. 219–20.

37. *Nová myśl*, No. 6 (1958), p. 559.

38. Novozámský, *Vyrovnávání*, p. 113.

39. A. Balassa, "A gépipar szerkezete és a nemzetközi együtmüködés," *Közgazdasági szemle*, No. 11 (1964), p. 1274.

40. *Ibid.*, p. 1275.

41. C. Murgescu, "Cîteva observaţii pe marginea unei carţi privind relaţiile economice dintre ţările socialiste," *Viaţa economică*, No. 23 (June 5, 1964), reprinted in *Probleme ale relaţiilor economice dintre ţările socialiste* (Bucharest, 1964), p. 41.

42. Among recent publications, see Michael Kaser's *Comecon: Integration Problems of the Planned Economies* (London, New York, and Toronto, 1965), and John Michael Montias, "The Background and Origins of Rumania's Dispute with Comecon," *Soviet Studies*, October, 1964.

43. On Hungarian difficulties in marketing machinery products in the CEMA market in 1963, see United Nations *Economic Survey of Europe in 1963* (Geneva, 1964), Part I, Chapter I, p. 55. The increase in total Rumanian imports of machinery in 1963 over the preceding year was only 2 per cent, which, given Rumania's ongoing reorientation of its trade toward the West, may conceal an actual decline in purchases from CEMA members. The year-to-year increases in machinery imports were 52 per cent in 1960, 6 per cent in 1961, and 16 per cent in 1962 (*Anuarul statistic 1964* [Bucharest, 1964], p. 437).

44. Most notably in the articles already cited by Gustav Apetauer, a member of the Czechoslovak delegation to CEMA, and A. Balassa, an official of the Hungarian Planning Commission. According to Balassa, "the international cooperation among the CEMA countries and the analysis of the proximate future show that the preconditions for a significant reduction in the nomenclature of industrial production [in CEMA] have not developed," "A gépipar szerkezete és a nemzetközi együtmüködés," p. 1283; also pp. 1285–286.

45. *Ibid.*, pp. 1276–277.

46. This problem of industrial specialization between nations at different stages of development is related to one already referred to, namely, that the industrializing nation will wish to take on responsibility only for easy-to-produce items exhibiting economies of scale.

47. Apetauer, "O aktuálních otázkách ekonomického rozvoje členskych států RVHP," p. 75. The words *science fiction* are in English in the Czech text. The proposal referred to in the quotation was made by Novozámský in his book *Vyrovnávání*.

48. Ion Rachmuth, "Uncle aspecte ale acţiunii legii valorii pe plan international," *Probleme economice*, No. 9 (1963), pp. 9–11.

49. See C. Murgescu, "Concepţii potrivnice principiilor economice dintre ţărilor socialiste," in *Probleme ale relaţiilor economice dintre ţările socialiste*, pp. 22–29.

The Soviet-Eastern European Pact System

Chapter V.

9. The Warsaw Pact in Evolution

Thomas W. Wolfe

INTRODUCTION

During a three-day period in October, 1965, joint military exercises code-named "October Storm" and involving the armed forces of four Warsaw Pact countries (the Soviet Union, Poland, Czechoslovakia, and East Germany) were held in the wooded Thuringian countryside in the southwestern part of the G.D.R. opposite the West German border.[1] Witnessed by top-ranking Warsaw Pact military leaders, these exercises were given an unusual amount of publicity by the communist press and radio, which advertised them as an "object lesson to all who want to change the existing balance of power in Europe by military force."[2] Like joint military maneuvers carried out by various groupings of the Warsaw Pact countries during the preceding five years, the "October Storm" war games were said to have demonstrated again the "firm unity" and "growing strength" of the ten-year-old Warsaw Pact military alliance, which embraces the Soviet Union and six of its East European neighbors.[3]

Although one may regard the publicity as a demonstrative effort to impress the West with the military solidarity of the Soviet bloc at a time when the political unity of the communist world as a whole seems to be in some disarray, it would be a mistake to dismiss lightly the changes that have been taking place in the character and potential of the Warsaw Pact military alliance, especially over the past five years. Along with other important changes in the relationship of the Soviet Union with the countries of East Europe, there has been an interesting evolution in Soviet policy and attitudes toward the Warsaw Pact organization. The developments of the past four or five years, of which joint military exercises are but one, have both military and political implications that deserve attention. The trend toward closer military integration of the Warsaw Pact countries is of particular interest in light of NATO's approaching twentieth

anniversary in 1969. This occasion seems likely to be attended by
efforts, especially on the part of France, to convert the Western
alliance into a much more loosely knit association. Before taking
up the Warsaw Pact developments in the period from around
1960 to the present, it may be useful to recall briefly the main
lines of Soviet policy toward the Warsaw Pact military alliance
during the earlier years of its history.[4]

The Early Years of the Warsaw Pact

At its inception in May, 1955, the Warsaw Pact appeared to be
mainly a political and propaganda answer to the inclusion of
West Germany in NATO, rather than a working military alliance.[5] It did have some immediate military significance for the
Soviet Union, to be sure, such as providing an alternative basis
for the presence of Soviet troops in Hungary and Rumania after
the original justification, dating from the end of World War II,
was invalidated by the Austrian State Treaty on May 15, 1955—
just one day after conclusion of the Warsaw Treaty itself.[6] In the
long run, the Warsaw Pact also offered a means to advance the
military integration of the Eastern bloc countries on a multilateral basis under Soviet leadership, but this was only a potential
prospect. For at the time the Warsaw Pact came into being, the
Soviet Union already had bilateral military arrangements with
the various Pact countries,[7] and its own military forces—both
those garrisoning East Europe and those behind the borders of
the Soviet Union itself—were clearly counted upon to carry the
burden of any military undertakings in Europe in which the
Soviet Union might become involved.

From a military viewpoint, the tasks of the Warsaw Pact in the
early years of its existence were centered in the first instance on
perpetuation of prior arrangements which had made the East
European area in effect an extension of the Soviet early warning
and air defense system.[8] By the late fifties, the Soviets undertook
further improvement of the air defenses of East Europe by providing the Warsaw Pact countries with surface-to-air (SAM)
missiles, more modern interceptors, and so on, but comparable
modernization of the Pact ground forces lagged somewhat behind. While it can be said that the air defense role of East
Europe may diminish as the missile age advances, this task is still

an important consideration, and certainly was so in the early years of the Pact's life.

Apart from air defense, the East European area also was important in Soviet eyes for two other basic military reasons. First, the area served as a defensive buffer zone against a possible land invasion from the West. This factor might also be said to be of diminishing importance as it has become increasingly clear that a traditional military invasion of the Soviet Union is a remote contingency in the nuclear age. Nevertheless, traditional Russian fears rooted in past experience—and combined perhaps with apprehension about the growing power of Western Europe, especially Germany—have served to keep this buffer zone concept alive. Second, the East European area also had and continues to have an important place in Soviet military doctrine and planning as a glacis or springboard for an offensive theater campaign against Western Europe in the event of war.[9]

Notwithstanding the strategic importance which geography and history together have conferred upon the East European area, the actual contributions expected of the other Pact armed forces to military operations in the European theater—whether defensive or offensive in character—were apparently of secondary weight in Soviet planning. The development of command arrangements for conducting modern theater warfare on a joint basis received little attention; no joint exercises were held; and the Joint Command of the Warsaw Pact, headed by a Soviet officer, remained largely a paper organization with apparently even less real work on its hands than the Political Consultative Committee, the Pact's policy organ.[10] The latter seems to have functioned less as a genuine policy-making body than as a forum for presentation of the Soviet policy line of the moment.[11] Soviet propaganda treatment of the Warsaw Pact and the rare meetings of its formal organs, together with failure to flesh out these bodies in the first years of the Pact's existence,[12] all tended to support the view that its symbolic political role initially carried far more weight in Soviet thinking than its co-operative military aspects.[13]

There was, to be sure, some noteworthy progress toward military integration during the early period of the Pact, such as standardization of weapons and local arms production along Soviet lines, adoption of Soviet organizational forms and field doctrine, and broad definition of military tasks falling to the several national armies.[14] There was also co-ordination of disarmament policy as reflected, for example, in the moves for partial troop withdrawals and reduction endorsed at the May, 1958, meeting of the Political Consultative Committee.[15] On the whole, however, while the armed forces of the various Pact states had such obvious purposes as serving to support the communist regimes in East Europe, providing a school for political indoctrination and technical education, meeting certain traditionally felt needs for national prestige and the like, they were hardly a significant element in over-all joint military planning during the first five years or so of the Warsaw Pact.

Furthermore, even though a sense of common purpose may have lain behind the Warsaw Pact at its formation, the path to closer military co-operation between the Soviet Union and the East European countries was hardly smoothed by events in the earlier years of the treaty. The crushing of the Hungarian rebellion in 1956 by the Soviet Army certainly dealt a setback to the idea of a socialist military alliance based on common goals, and the apparently narrow margin of decision against applying similar treatment to Gomulka's defiance of the Soviet Union probably did not bolster a sense of common cause. At the same time, events in the fall of 1956 did have the effect of prompting the Soviet Union to negotiate a series of bilateral "status-of-forces" agreements with various East European countries,[16] and may also have led the Soviet Union eventually to conclude that tighter military integration under the aegis of the Warsaw Pact would help to forestall future problems like that of Hungary.

SHIFT IN SOVIET POLICY TOWARD THE WARSAW PACT IN THE EARLY SIXTIES

Changes in the Soviet conception of the role of the Warsaw Pact forces began gradually to appear toward the end of the fifties and by the summer of 1961 had become unmistakably evident. In this period the Soviet Union embarked upon a series of moves whose general effect over the next few years was to upgrade the Warsaw Pact publicly in terms of the common defense of the communist camp. Specifically, Soviet policy served to elevate the importance of the military contribution of the other Pact countries in over-all Soviet planning; to extend the mission of the East European Pact forces from primary emphasis on air defense to a more active joint role in defensive and offensive theater operations; and to promote joint training and re-equipment of the Pact forces commensurate with their apparently enlarged responsibilities.

The initial outward sign of change in Soviet - East European military relationships was a greater Soviet tendency in the late fifties to stress the joint strength of the Warsaw Pact forces and their combat co-operation,[17] at a time when Khrushchev was contemplating an overhaul of Soviet military policy designed to achieve economies by cutting back the size of the traditionally large Soviet theater ground forces. Soviet attention to the co-operative aspects of the Warsaw military alliance increased in the summer of 1961 as tension mounted over the Berlin issue. The Political Consultative Committee, called into session in Moscow in March, 1961, for its fourth meeting, issued a communiqué stating that the Pact countries had agreed among themselves on new measures deemed necessary for "further strengthening of their defensive capabilities."[18] In early September, 1961, the defense ministers of the Pact countries gathered in Warsaw for the first such publicly announced meeting devoted wholly to military matters.[19] This was followed in October by the first joint Warsaw Pact maneuvers,[20] in which Soviet, East German, Polish, and Czechoslovak forces participated in a major field exercise,[21] and which established the pattern of annual joint training and maneuvers that has continued to the present time.

Altogether, nine major joint exercises have been reported to date, involving Soviet forces in co-operation with all the East European Pact countries at one time or another, although the main emphasis has been on the northern tier of bloc states.[22] Soviet spokesmen have frequently extolled the value of these joint training activities. In 1964, for example, Marshal Grechko stated that the "great importance" of such exercises "lies in their contribution to further growth of the combat might of our joint armed forces, to higher standards of training, better coordination of forces and staffs, and elaboration of common views on methods of nuclear and conventional warfare."[23]

Along with joint exercises, which presented such novel departures from tradition as the mingling of troops from various East

European countries on each other's soil, went a program for re-equipment of the East European armed forces. Beginning in the early sixties, and focused mainly on the ground forces and their supporting tactical air strength, which had received lower priority than air defense forces in the preceding years, this program included substantial replacement of older T–34 tanks with more modern T–54 and T–55 tanks, provision of antitank missiles and self-propelled guns, and introduction of newer fighter-bomber models of such aircraft as the MIG–21 and the SU–7.[24]

During this process of modernization, the numerical strength of the East European armed forces appears to have remained relatively stable, totaling between nine hundred thousand and a million men, approximately the level to which they reportedly were reduced in the early years of the Warsaw Pact from 1955 to 1960.[25] These forces are organized in some sixty divisions, of which only about half are near combat strength, according to various Western accounts.[26] Poland, with ground forces of about fifteen divisions and the largest air force in East Europe (nearly 1,000 aircraft), appears to emerge with the strongest national armed forces among the non-Soviet Pact members, followed by Czechoslovakia with an army of fourteen divisions and an air force exceeded only by that of Poland.[27] The East German armed forces, while smaller than those of the other Pact countries, are among the best-equipped and have often received new items of ground armaments and aircraft from the Soviet Union before the others.[28] Only four of the East European Pact members have naval forces, all of which are small, with those of Poland topping the others.[29]

On the whole, the modernization program for the various East European countries and the training given their forces prepared them mainly for conducting conventional warfare, in contrast with the Soviet forces deployed in East Europe. The latter—comprising twenty divisions in East Germany, two in Poland and four in Hungary, plus sizeable supporting tactical air elements and tactical missile units[30]—possess dual conventional-nuclear capabilities, with doctrine for theater warfare which puts preponderant emphasis on operations under nuclear conditions.[31] This marked contrast between the essentially conventional posture of the East European forces and the nuclear-oriented posture and doctrine of the Soviet theater forces, the implications of which will be taken up later, was somewhat altered, however, when the modernization program of the early sixties began to include the furnishing of potential nuclear delivery systems to the East European countries in the form of tactical missiles with ranges up to about one hundred and fifty miles.[32] Nuclear warheads for these missiles presumably were kept in Soviet hands and probably remain there today. The missiles themselves are of little consequence without such warheads; but, missile acquisition by the East European armed forces marked a significant step toward possible nuclear sharing at some future point.

Precisely when decisions were made to take this initial step is not clear. As early as 1958, in a May 24 speech at the Political Consultative Committee meeting in Moscow, Khrushchev accused NATO of planning "to arm West Germany with atomic weapons" and declared that the Warsaw Treaty states were thus "compelled by force of circumstance to consider deploying missiles in the German Democratic Republic, Poland and Czechoslovakia."[33] Later, as the Soviet Union mounted an intensive diplomatic propaganda campaign to block the realization of the MLF project in NATO, numerous warnings were sounded that the Warsaw Treaty states "would be obliged to take appropriate measures" in return.[34] Although the MLF project bogged down, Soviet warnings did not. The first public confirmation that threats to make missiles available to other Warsaw Pact members had been carried out came in mid-1964, when Soviet-made tactical missiles were displayed in the hands of Polish forces in Warsaw.[35] Shortly thereafter, similar missiles turned up on parade with Rumanian and East German forces[36] and were subsequently reported in Czechoslovakia,[37] leaving out only Bulgaria, which also was said by some sources as likely to have such missiles.[38]

By the time Khrushchev's leadership came to an end in the fall of 1964, it was clear from developments of the preceding four or five years that substantial changes had taken place not only in the Soviet Union's policy toward the Warsaw Pact military alliance, but in the role that the Pact forces themselves were becoming capable of playing in both a military and political sense. Before turning to further developments since the new regime took over from Khrushchev, it may be appropriate to ask what the reasons may have been for the shift in Soviet policy in the first place.

Several major considerations appear to be involved. Perhaps one may begin with Khrushchev's own problem in the early sixties of defending a military policy that seems to have aroused a certain amount of disagreement within Soviet military and political leadership circles. In essence, this policy sought to achieve economies by reducing the size of the Soviet theater forces while emphasizing the deterrent effect of the new strategic nuclear forces upon which Khrushchev had chosen to place priority.

Different conceptions of the nature of a possible future war and of forces required for a European theater campaign lay at the root of disagreements over Khrushchev's policy, and found expression in a debate between "modernist" and "traditionalist" schools of thought. In general, the modernists felt that nuclear warfare would reduce the requirements for large ground armies and probably preclude a lengthy European theater campaign. The traditionalists, on the other hand, argued that massive theater forces were still needed to sweep to the sea and occupy enemy territory, and that war might entail bitter and protracted theater campaigning even in the nuclear age.[39] Khrushchev himself evidently thought more in terms of holding Western Europe "hostage" to Soviet military power than of actually fighting a war for Europe under nuclear conditions. To the extent that he took account of the possibility of war occurring, he seemingly felt that it would be over quickly after the initial nuclear exchanges, and that there would be little opportunity to employ large land armies; rather, only mop-up and occupation forces would be needed. These strategic notions took form in Khrushchev's January, 1960, speech to the Supreme Soviet, laying out his new military policy line.[40]

Given the need at that time to justify his position against what one may call a traditionalist-minded, theater-forces lobby among the Soviet marshals, Khrushchev seems to have found a handy rationale for reducing the Soviet Union's own theater forces in the idea of transferring some of the military burden—and perhaps the costs—to the other Warsaw Pact members. This would, of course, require that their forces be improved, re-equipped, and more closely integrated with Soviet forces in order to meet their added theater responsibilities, which is what subsequently happened. It is a point of interest, incidentally, that the Soviet traditionalist lobby, despite its stand for preserving strong theater capabilities, was slow to manifest much enthusiasm for an enlarged East European contribution in this field, since this would undercut the case for larger Soviet theater forces.[41] In any event, however, the strategic views and perhaps the pressures of economic necessity which informed Khrushchev's policy apparently prevailed over whatever internal objections were raised, and would seem to be among the basic factors in the post-1960 evolution of Soviet policy toward the Warsaw Pact forces.

Another factor, growing also out of modern military realities, was probably the concern of some Soviet professional leaders about the ability of the Soviet Union, in the event of war, to mobilize and deploy large-scale reinforcements to Europe under nuclear conditions. This problem, to which some attention has been given in Soviet military literature,[42] could not readily be met by the alternative of massive advance build-up of Soviet forces in East Europe without raising serious political complications, not to mention the economic burden of such a course over any prolonged peacetime period. Therefore, there was a solid professional argument to be made for greater reliance on the Warsaw Pact forces already "normally" in place in the European theater. Upon these forces—the combined Soviet and East European divisions of varying combat strength present in East Europe —along with their supporting air forces, plus medium-range strategic missile forces in the western U.S.S.R. itself, would fall the initial brunt of fighting a theater campaign in Europe if war should come.

In the immediate context of the international situation in the early sixties, other factors of a politico-military character may have counseled closer co-operation among the Pact forces. One of these was the need to present a strong posture toward NATO during the 1961 Berlin crisis, while at the same time keeping some sort of lid on Soviet military spending and troop levels. Another consideration, particularly relevant if local military action should flare up in Europe, was that closer integration of national armed forces would be likely to facilitate Soviet control over a potentially dangerous situation. With respect to Soviet policy interests elsewhere, it is notable also that Sino-Soviet relations deteriorated markedly from 1960–61 onward. In the Soviet view, a demonstration of "genuine" military collaboration between Moscow and its East European allies may have been considered a useful lesson in contrast for Peking, which apparently had objected to Soviet terms for military co-operation in the Far East area and had begun to insist on going it alone.[43] Moreover, an increase of co-operative efforts in the Warsaw Pact area stood as a rebuttal to Chinese charges that Moscow was a "splitter" and a disintegrating influence within the communist camp.[44]

Another problem not wholly unrelated to the Sino-Soviet rift probably had an important bearing on the Soviet decision to bring about closer military collaboration among the Warsaw Pact forces. This concerned the need for organizational means to maintain discipline and political unity among the communist countries of Eastern Europe, which by the early sixties had begun to manifest centrifugal political and economic tendencies at a growing rate.[45] Evidently the Soviet Union felt that the Warsaw Pact might serve as a useful instrument to offset such tendencies. In this sense, Soviet encouragement of closer joint arrangements in the military sphere seems to have had a function analogous to earlier attempts to repair discipline and political unity among the East European communist states through economic integration under the multilateral Council for Economic Mutual Assistance (CEMA). The latter, originally set up in 1949 but reactivated after the disruptive events of the fall of 1956, had not proved particularly successful as a unifying political instrument, whatever its economic benefits may have been.[46]

Finally, the garrison and control functions of Soviet forces in East Europe, as distinct from the more subtle kind of control implied above, can hardly escape mention in connection with Soviet policy toward the Warsaw Pact. After all, it was in the shadow of Soviet military power, to use George Kennan's term, that communist regimes were set up in these countries in the first place, and the only significant attempt to date to withdraw from the Warsaw community—that of Imre Nagy on November 1, 1956—was crushed by this same power.

Without going into the question of the residual potential for revolt in East Europe, one can say that the Soviet leaders probably came to feel that the garrison aspect of a Soviet military presence in the area could be less awkwardly managed under closer joint Pact arrangements than otherwise. While the Warsaw Treaty already gave collective sanction for the Soviet presence in the name of defense against the NATO threat, there was still room for friction and misunderstanding as to how far the Warsaw Pact might be stretched to cover Soviet policing actions.[47] The various bilateral status-of-forces agreements negotiated after the 1956 events in Poland and Hungary were doubtless meant to ease this issue, but a policy of closer joint collaboration may have seemed to offer the further advantage of fostering greater cohesion and a sense of belonging to the same team. Indeed, along with their military value, joint exercises are claimed to have opened up "significant possibilities for developing comradely bonds" among Warsaw Pact troops and to have provided an "excellent school of international indoctrination."[48]

Soviet Warsaw Pact Policy under the New Regime

Under Khrushchev's successors, the main lines of Soviet policy toward the Warsaw Pact appear to have gone essentially unchanged. The new regime has continued to stress more thorough integration of the East European armed forces into Soviet operational plans by means of joint military exercises and the like, and it is going ahead with re-equipment of the Pact forces to bring their capabilities more into line with their enlarged theater responsibilities. At the same time, there have been some signs that the policy of greater reliance on East European forces, which was intended in part to improve bloc unity and cohesion, may also be having the unintended effect of encouraging challenges to Soviet dominance and of giving the East European countries more leverage than before to influence Pact affairs.

Among the major problems of Soviet policy toward the Warsaw Pact which the new regime inherited from Khrushchev was the question of nuclear access and control within the alliance. This problem again came to the fore in January, 1965, when the seventh meeting of the Political Consultative Committee was convened in Warsaw to consider measures to counter NATO plans for a multilateral nuclear force. The meeting, held—according to a statement by Kosygin—at the initiative of the G.D.R.,[49] went on record to oppose a NATO nuclear-sharing arrangement "in any form whatsoever" on the grounds that this would "give West Germany access to atomic weapons." Should such plans be implemented, it was declared, the Warsaw Treaty states would be "compelled to take the necessary defense measures to ensure their security."[50]

While similar warnings had been sounded before, the situation was now somewhat different. For, having already provided the East European forces with potential nuclear delivery means in the form of tactical missiles and advanced fighter-bomber aircraft, the Soviet Union now faced the question whether it was also prepared to take the next step of furnishing nuclear warheads to its allies. As some observers have suggested, the Warsaw meeting in January, 1965, probably involved discussion of the knotty problem of East European access to nuclear weapons in the context of any new defense measures up for consideration.[51]

The Soviet Union, which has repeatedly declined to comment on its present procedures for controlling nuclear access within the Warsaw alliance,[52] presumably is reluctant to put warheads in the hands of its allies in peacetime, even under some sort of "two-key" control system. What arrangements the Soviets might be willing to make in wartime is another question. However, despite indications that the East European forces have had some training in nuclear warfare methods and have participated in joint exercises under simulated nuclear conditions,[53] and even that "joint nuclear forces" may formally exist,[54] the Soviets probably still have strong reservations about giving up the substance of their nuclear monopoly within the alliance. Pointed Soviet reminders since the January Warsaw meeting that "the security of the socialist countries is guaranteed by the nuclear-missile might of the Soviet Union"[55] would suggest continued resistance to any pressures within the Warsaw alliance for some more liberal form of nuclear sharing.[56]

Another question germane to Warsaw Pact affairs in the period since Khrushchev's ouster is the new regime's attitude toward the adequacy of the Soviet Union's own defense posture, especially in light of a deepening crisis in Southeast Asia and a general heightening of international tension. While the new Soviet leaders apparently decided by about mid-1965 that it would be unwise to "economize on defense" to the point implied by Khrushchev's latter-day military policies,[57] they have not manifested a willingness to accept the sort of major retrenchment in their domestic economic programs that would seem to be required if radical increases in defense expenditure were contemplated. This suggests, in turn, that they are probably disposed to ride along in the main with the Khrushchev-era policy of shifting part of the theater burden to the East European countries. Although they may find it necessary to make some concession to renewed arguments among the Soviet military for broad and well-balanced Soviet forces, the net result seems unlikely to reverse the trend toward greater reliance on joint Warsaw Pact forces.

Several other developments in Warsaw Pact affairs under the new regime deserve mention. One of these concerns the problem of getting the various Pact members to pull their proper weight within the alliance in return for closer integration and greater military responsibility. Some of the Pact members, most notably Rumania, have displayed a certain reluctance to accept the burdens entailed by larger Pact commitments. Rumania has reduced compulsory military service from twenty-four to sixteen months,[58] which could diminish her military contribution to the bloc, and has otherwise manifested expressions of dislike for the idea of military pacts in general.[59] Further, while the Rumanians have taken part in at least two joint military exercises, it was reported in the summer of 1965 that they had balked at sending troops out of their country for additional joint activities.[60] Two trips to Bucharest by Marshal A. A. Grechko, the Warsaw Pact commander, one in November, 1964, and the other in May–June, 1965,[61] may have been prompted by Rumanian obstructionism in the military sphere which has tended to parallel Rumania's recalcitrance in political and economic matters.[62]

A further hint that matters of military co-operation in the southern part of the Warsaw Treaty area may have needed untangling was provided by a nine-day gathering of senior military leaders in the Transcarpathian military region in May, 1965, at which "views were exchanged on various questions of military development." [63] This meeting came shortly after an abortive plot involving General Tsvetko Anev and several other Bulgarian army and party officials was disclosed in Sofia in April. While details of this internal conspiracy are lacking, it was apparently inspired by a nationalist-minded faction which hoped to orient

Bulgarian policy in a more independent direction, perhaps on the Rumanian model.[64] In any event, such a movement in Bulgaria, long considered the most conformist of the Soviet Union's Warsaw Pact allies, did not speak altogether well for the solidity of the alliance's southern flank. Memories going back to Hungary's errant behavior in 1956 were probably also stirred by these developments.

Perhaps partly as a hedge against soft spots in the southern sector of the alliance, which the Soviets recognized publicly only to the extent of asserting that imperialist "splitting" attempts against the bloc would prove futile,[65] a trend has emerged toward setting off the northern members of the Pact on a separate and somewhat more privileged basis. This has taken the form in public media of referring to the northern quartet—Poland, the G.D.R., Czechoslovakia, and the Soviet Union—as the "first strategic echelon" of the Pact,[66] a distinction reinforced not only by the more frequent participation of these countries in joint exercises and their stronger military forces, but also by renewal during the last year and a half of the postwar treaties of friendship and mutual assistance between the Soviet Union and the three northern Pact members.[67]

Both military and political considerations would seem to account for this emergent regional differentiation within the Warsaw Pact. For example, the territory of the three East European members of the northern quartet lies directly in line with what would in wartime be the main axis of a central European campaign, and these countries would probably be the first engaged, in the event of war. They are also the countries most immediately interested in the German question. As such, their adherence to Soviet interests may seem somewhat better assured by their concern over the "German threat" than is the case among other Pact members, although the G.D.R. and Poland may well look differently upon such matters as the terms of any future settlement of the German problem.[68]

On the whole, it can be said that the management of Soviet relations with other Warsaw Pact members has not grown notably smoother since Khrushchev's departure from the scene. The various questions mentioned above, many of which bear in one way or another upon how policy formulation and decision-making processes within a more closely integrated Warsaw alliance should be arranged, suggest that the Soviet leaders may be getting a bigger dose of coalition politics than they would like. In this connection, the Soviet party chief, Leonid Brezhnev, let fall a revealing remark at a Soviet-Czechoslovak friendship rally in September, 1965. Commenting on the need to strengthen bloc unity in meeting the problem of defense, Brezhnev said: "The current situation places on the agenda the further perfection of the Warsaw Pact organization. . . . We are all prepared to work diligently in order to find the best solution."[69]

This acknowledgement that the Warsaw Pact faces organizational problems that require new solutions would seem to testify to internal pressures for change, perhaps involving new forms of decision-making in areas of policy and strategy that once were the sole prerogative of the Soviet Union.[70] Although it would be stretching things to say that this foreshadows the development within the Warsaw alliance of open policy debate of the kind that takes place in the NATO forum, it may not be far from the mark to suppose that the East European members of the Warsaw Pact have begun to press for a more influential voice in matters affecting their own interests, such as the choice of alliance strategy, the sharing of military and economic burdens, and ultimately foreign policy issues bearing on the question of war or peace.[71]

SOME FURTHER IMPLICATIONS OF TRENDS WITHIN THE WARSAW PACT

The role and nature of the Warsaw Pact appear likely to be greatly conditioned by two closely related factors: the degree to which the Soviets are prepared to *rely* upon the other Pact forces and the extent of actual Soviet *dependence* upon them.

Many questions remain unanswered as to Soviet confidence in the reliability of the East European Pact members. As noted previously, there was some doubt in Soviet leadership circles in Khrushchev's time about the wisdom of counting on the East European forces in any war which the Soviet Union might have to fight in Europe. Judging from a continuing internal Soviet dialogue over the need for massive Soviet theater forces capable of waging a war in Europe,[72] this issue promises to remain a bone of contention under the new regime.

Soviet reluctance to share nuclear control with the Warsaw Pact allies is another index of doubt about their reliability, as is the Soviet attitude toward command and control arrangements in general. Despite an increased tendency in the past few years to erect a façade of coequal command authority by such devices as placing non-Soviet military men in nominal charge of some joint exercises,[73] there are reasonable grounds to assume that the substance of Soviet control is still jealously guarded. The supreme commander and the chief of staff of the Pact are Soviet officers, and control of its major operational elements appears to be also in Soviet hands.[74] Moreover, a special branch of the Soviet General Staff is known to serve as the planning and co-ordinating center for the Pact forces.[75] Probable Soviet reservations against any scheme for dual Soviet-East European control of joint forces in case of war were reflected in the 1962 and 1963 editions of Marshal Sokolovskii's *Military Strategy,* which suggested that command of joint operations in the major theaters of conflict would rest with Soviet officers, although allied units in some presumably less important areas might remain under national command.[76]

While one may thus suppose that the Soviets will attempt to retain operational and strategic direction of Pact forces in their own hands, despite the strain this may impose on intrabloc relations, Soviet willingness to rely more upon their Pact allies in the future may be influenced to some extent by other considerations. For example, historical alignments and antagonisms, such as the antipathy of Poles and Czechs toward Germany, or that of Bulgaria toward Greece and Turkey, might be counted on to ensure reliable performance by particular allies, depending upon whom they were stacked up against.[77] Indeed, there has been Soviet recognition of the diverse national backgrounds out of which the various Warsaw bloc forces have emerged, but which, given the unifying effect supposedly supplied by communist ideology and party discipline, are expected to enhance their reliability.[78]

How far the Soviets may be prepared to go in accepting any diminution of their authority within the Warsaw alliance will doubtless be dictated in some measure by the factor of Soviet dependence on the other Pact forces. In some respects, the advent of the missile age would seem, on the surface at least, to have somewhat reduced Soviet military dependence on the East European countries. Soviet strategic delivery forces, for example, particularly the sizeable medium-range missile forces trained against Western Europe from U.S.S.R. territory proper,[79] can serve either deterrent or war-waging functions without much regard for the belt of Warsaw Pact territory that lies in between. Other considerations, however, of both military and political character, suggest that on balance actual Soviet dependence on the Warsaw allies is probably becoming greater.

In the event of nuclear war, for instance, the difficulty of deploying substantial Soviet reinforcements from the U.S.S.R. would seem, as previously pointed out, to place a high premium on having effective Warsaw Pact forces already in place, close to the arena of European conflict. A bonus might also be seen in the effect that this disposition of forces might have in diverting some nuclear fire from the Soviet Union itself to targets in East Europe. In the event of non-nuclear hostilities, on the other hand, large East European forces essentially trained and equipped for conventional warfare would also represent an important asset.

One might even envisage the emergence of a concept under which East European forces would assume the main burden of conventional operations while nuclearized Soviet forces would remain uncommitted unless and until hostilities seemed likely to cross the nuclear threshold. Such a concept might not only give the Soviet Union considerable flexibility for crisis management or the conduct of low-key military operations, but might also seem to offer an answer to the problem of nuclear sharing.

The viability of such a concept, however, would rest in part on the attitudes of the East European Pact members. They have already moved along the road toward a nuclear posture themselves, which could bring further pressures for nuclear access, particularly if Soviet forces in East Europe should be reduced. The implication that a "cannon fodder" role was being allotted to the East European forces might also stand in the way of such a concept. There is another factor which might conceivably lead the East European countries to balk at the concept of a fixed conventional role for their forces and to press for nuclear weapons of their own. This is the possibility that the Soviet commitment to the defense of East Europe might in some circumstances come to be doubted, or—to put it in an idiom more familiar to the West—the credibility of the Soviet deterrent might come to be questioned by the Soviet Union's Warsaw Pact allies. In this connection, it has sometimes seemed easier for the nuclear powers to convince adversaries of the credibility of their deterrent posture than allies who depend upon it for protection. The Soviet case may be no exception.

Leaving aside the possibility that mutual obligations between the Soviet Union and its East European allies might come to be seriously questioned, and assuming that the general trend of intrabloc relations runs in the direction of a workable coalition, the Soviet Union might seek to turn a policy of greater military dependence on the Warsaw Pact countries to its own advantage in the area of disarmament negotiations and European security arrangements. Specifically, if convinced that the Pact countries can pull their own weight militarily under Soviet guidance, the Soviet Union may be able to contemplate some further withdrawal from East Europe of its own forces, using this prospect as leverage for reciprocal reductions or withdrawal of NATO forces. This approach, long adumbrated by various Soviet bloc proposals for collective security measures in Europe[80] and put in the form of a concrete troop withdrawal suggestion by Marshal Sokolovskii in February, 1965,[81] would fit logically into a Soviet foreign policy course aimed at promoting the dissolution of NATO when it comes up for renewal a few years hence.

On the other hand, a number of offsetting difficulties would attend such a Soviet policy line. Some of these might spring from military security considerations, such as probable opposition within the Soviet military and political leadership to placing the Soviet Union in what could appear to be a militarily disadvantageous position. But the more troublesome consequences might arise in the area of Soviet foreign policy. For example, by spreading the impression that the Soviet Union had abandoned hope of achieving communist goals with regard to Berlin and the German situation, Peking could seize upon further evidence of Soviet unfitness to lead the world communist movement.

Whatever precise shape the future may take, it can be said that the trends observable within the Warsaw Pact in the past few years have significant intrabloc political implications. Paradoxically, as the Soviet Union's partners have become capable of bearing a larger share of the Pact's military burden, they have at the same time apparently grown more determined to share in the management of the Pact's affairs. Tendencies at work within the alliance seem to pull two ways—toward closer military integration and interdependence, and toward assertion of separate national interests and a new balance of decision-making power among the Pact's members.

How this will affect the cohesion of the bloc remains a critical question. From the Soviet viewpoint, the Warsaw Pact continues to perform an essential political function. It provides not only the basic treaty obligation binding the East European states to the Soviet Union, but it also represents the most important multilateral institution tying the bloc together. As a cohesive factor, it may prove more successful than such institutions as CEMA, at least so long as the ruling regimes in East Europe remain persuaded that their ultimate security rests on the protection afforded by Soviet military power and influence.

Finally, from the viewpoint of the East European states themselves, the trends at work within the Warsaw Pact may seem to hold significant political promise. These countries—already on the way, albeit unevenly, to achieving greater autonomy in various spheres of economic, political, and cultural activity—may now find themselves in the process of acquiring a more meaningful voice in the development of Warsaw Pact military planning and strategy. If so, and one should stress the "if," this could mean the emergence of another attribute of national sovereignty among the East European Pact partners, and a further diminution of Soviet tutelage and control over their destinies. Although it certainly would be unrealistic to suppose that the Soviet Union will cease to play a predominant role in Pact affairs, the situation at least suggests that the Warsaw Pact is tending to evolve into an alliance of a more customary kind, subject in greater degree than hitherto to the interplay of coalition politics.

NOTES

1. *The New York Times,* October 20, 1965; *The Washington Post,* October 23, 1965. First announced in a TASS Moscow broadcast on September 25, 1965, the three-day joint exercises in East Germany were given a steady publicity build-up in the communist press, especially that of East Germany, until their conclusion on October 23. Soviet General P. K. Koshevoi, commander of Soviet forces in East Germany, directed the "October Storm" war games, which were

followed by a military parade of joint forces in Erfurt. One curious feature of bloc reporting on the exercises concerned the question of nuclear weapons. Some accounts in East German newspapers, cited in Western news dispatches, as well as East German radio broadcasts, stated that simulated nuclear strikes were employed by the joint Warsaw Pact forces after the assumed Western "aggressor" had used nuclear weapons. Soviet reporting of the exercises, however, studiously avoided any mention of nuclear weapons as such, but rather employed such circumlocutions as saying that the exercises were conducted "in accordance with all the demands of modern warfare" and with use of "the most modern arms."

Prominence was given in many accounts, on the other hand, to airborne landings at the rear of the "enemy" position by Polish troops airlifted in Soviet transports. It was also recalled that Soviet airborne troops from the U.S.S.R. had been similarly deployed into East Germany in connection with joint Soviet-G.D.R. exercises in the spring of 1965. See: serial eye-witness reports by Colonel A. Kulakov and Captain S. Gribanov, *Krasnaia Zvezda,* October 23 and 24, 1965; interview with General P. I. Batov, *Izvestia,* October 22, 1965; Guenter Seidel commentary, East Berlin radio, October 21, 1965; Warsaw radio broadcast, October 21, 1965; Von Frankenberg commentary, East Berlin radio, October 22, 1965; "Conclusion of Troop Exercises of the Warsaw Pact Countries," *Pravda,* October 23, 1965; "We Worked Shoulder to Shoulder," *Krasnaia Zvezda,* October 26, 1965.

2. *Neues Deutschland,* October 6 and 15, 1965; East Berlin ADN radio report, October 20, 1965; *Krasnaia Zvezda,* October 20, 22, 26, 1965; Ulbricht speech at Erfurt rally, East Berlin Intervision, October 23, 1965.

3. The six Warsaw Pact countries, in addition to the Soviet Union, are Poland, East Germany, Czechoslovakia, Hungary, Rumania, and Bulgaria. Albania, an original signatory of the Warsaw Treaty on Friendship, Cooperation and Mutual Assistance of May 14, 1955, has not been a participant in Warsaw Pact affairs since the Pact meeting of March, 1961. Although Albania has not been formally dropped, the Albanians protested several days after the Pact meeting in February, 1962, that they had been "excluded" from the meeting. *The New York Times,* February 9, 1962.

4. There is substantial literature on the Warsaw Pact, particularly on its earlier years. Among Western accounts of the origin and development of the Pact during the first five or six years of its existence, see: Zbigniew K. Brzezinski, "The Organization of the Communist Camp," *World Politics,* January, 1961, pp. 175–209; Hanns von Krannhals, "Command Integration within the Warsaw Pact," *Military Review,* May, 1961, pp. 40–52; Eugene Hinterhoff, "The Warsaw Pact," *Military Review,* June, 1962, pp. 89–94; Richard F. Staar, "How Strong is the Soviet Bloc?" *Current History,* October, 1963, pp. 209–15; J. M. Mackintosh, *Strategy and Tactics of Soviet Foreign Policy* (London, 1962), pp. 103ff; Boris Meissner (ed.), *Der Warschauer Pakt (The Warsaw Pact),* in the series *Dokumente zum Ostrecht (Documents on Eastern Law)* (Cologne, 1962), I. The Meissner work is the most comprehensive Western politico-legal analysis of the Warsaw Pact and includes a collection of relevant documents, but unfortunately it has not been published in English.

For some Western accounts covering Pact developments up to the recent past see: Richard F. Staar, "The East European Alliance System," *U.S. Naval Institute Proceedings,* September, 1964, pp. 27–39; the present author's *Soviet Strategy at the Crossroads* (Cambridge, Mass., 1964), pp. 210–16; Raymond L.

Garthoff, "The Military Establishment," *East Europe*, September, 1965, pp. 2–16. The latter is the best, concise, available review of the postwar development of the various East European armed forces and their integration under the Warsaw Pact.

For some representative Soviet descriptions of the Warsaw Pact see: G. P. Zhukov, *Varshavskii Dogovor i Voprosy Mezdunarodnoi Bezopastnosti* (*The Warsaw Treaty and Questions of International Security*) (Moscow, 1961); V. K. Sobakin, *Kollektivnaia Bezopastnost'—Garantiia Mirnogo Sosushchestvovaniia* (*Collective Security—the Guarantee for Peaceful Coexistence*) (Moscow, 1962); Colonel S. Lesnevskii, "Military Cooperation of the Armed Forces of the Socialist Countries," *Kommunist Vooruzhennykh Sil* (*Communist of the Armed Forces*), No. 10 (May, 1963), pp. 71–78; Marshal A. A. Grechko, "The Military Alliance of the Fraternal Nations," *Voenno-Istoricheskii Zhurnal* (*Military-Historical Journal*), No. 5 (May, 1965), pp. 16–25.

Current versions from a communist viewpoint of the postwar development of the various East European armed forces and their participation in the Warsaw Pact may be found in a series of articles which appeared in 1964–65 in the Soviet military journal, *Kommunist Vooruzhennykh Sil*. Some of these articles were anonymous; others were signed by East European military men. See: "The Polish People's Army" and "The Czech People's Army," No. 8 (April, 1964), pp. 77–80, 81–83; "The National People's Army of the German Democratic Republic," No. 9 (May, 1964), pp. 84–86; "The Bulgarian People's Army," No. 11 (June, 1964), pp. 80–82; "The Armed Forces of the Rumanian People's Republic," No. 14 (July, 1964), pp. 82–84; "The Hungarian People's Army," No. 15 (August, 1964), pp. 79–81; Lt. General N. Chernev, "Reliable Shield of the Revolutionary Accomplishments of the Bulgarian People," No. 17 (September, 1964), pp. 68–73; Lt. General V. Prchlik, "The Czechoslovak People's Army—20 Years," No. 19 (October, 1964), pp. 78–82; Major General C. Bratianu, "In a Military Family," Colonel General O. Rytirzh, "Together on Guard," and Colonel Gerhardt Amm, "On Guard for Peace," No. 8 (April, 1965), pp. 68–70, 72–73, 74–75.

5. See Hinterhoff, "The Warsaw Pact," p. 90; Wolfe, *Soviet Strategy at the Crossroads*, pp. 210–11. The former points out that in addition to being the Soviet response to failure of diplomatic efforts to block West Germany's integration into NATO, the Warsaw Treaty represents the only official obligation which binds the East European states to the Soviet Union. See also Brzezinski, "The Organization of the Communist Camp," p. 176.

6. Garthoff, "The Military Establishment," p. 13. See also William Lloyd Stearman, *The Soviet Union and the Occupation of Austria* (Bonn, 1960), p. 162.

7. For detailed analysis of the Soviet Union's system of bilateral agreements see Wladyslaw W. Kulski, "The Soviet System of Collective Security Compared with the Western System," *American Journal of International Law*, July, 1950, pp. 453–76, and Boris Meissner, "The Soviet Union's System of Bilateral Pacts in Eastern Europe," paper presented at the Fifth International Conference on World Politics at Noordwijk, The Netherlands, September, 1965, esp. pp. 5–7. The Soviet contention has been that the postwar bilateral agreements "played a big part in strengthening the defense capacity of the socialist countries," but that they proved "insufficient" for this purpose after West Germany's inclusion in NATO, and hence the Warsaw Pact was created to meet the need for "collective action" against the "growing military threat" of NATO. See Grechko, *Voenno-Istoricheskii Zhurnal*, May, 1965, pp. 21–22; unsigned article,

"The Armed Forces of the Socialist Countries and Their Military Alliance—Guarantee of Peace and the Security of the Nations," *Kommunist Vooruzhennykh Sil*, No. 13 (July, 1965), p. 66.

8. Garthoff, "The Military Establishment," pp. 14–15.

9. *Ibid.*, p. 15. See also by the present author, *Trends in Soviet Thinking on Theater Warfare, Conventional Operations, and Limited War* (RM–4305–PR) (Santa Monica, Calif., 1964), pp. 17–49.

10. For comment by a knowledgeable ex-Polish officer on the dormant state of the Warsaw Pact joint military staff in the 1955–58 period, see Pavel Monat, with John Dille, *Spy in the U.S.* (New York, 1962), pp. 188–89. The Political Consultative Committee was somewhat more active, although it met only three times during the first five years of the Pact, in January, 1956, May, 1958, and February, 1960. According to statements at the first meeting, the Committee was supposed to meet not less than twice yearly. The May, 1958, meeting was the most substantial during this period, dealing with decisions on withdrawal of Soviet troops from Rumania, troop reductions by the East European countries, and organizational questions concerning the joint forces. See *Izvestia*, January 29, 1956, May 27, 1958, and February 5, 1960.

11. Brzezinski, "The Organization of the Communist Camp," p. 177.

12. Besides the Joint Command itself, the only other element of the Warsaw Pact command structure that has been mentioned publicly is the Staff of the Joint Armed Forces, composed of representatives of national general staffs and seated in Moscow. On the political side, two subsidiary organs of the Political Consultative Committee were provided by the treaty—a Permanent Commission to deal with foreign policy questions and a Joint Secretariat. See Lesnevskii, *Kommunist Vooruzhennykh Sil*, No. 10 (May, 1963), p. 72.

13. Wolfe, *Soviet Strategy at the Crossroads*, p. 211.

14. Brzezinski, "The Organization of the Communist Camp," pp. 198–99; Garthoff, "The Military Establishment," p. 14; Staar, "The East European Alliance System," pp. 36–37; see also *Kommunist Vooruzhennykh Sil*, No. 13 (July, 1965), p. 67.

15. *Izvestia*, May 27, 1958. For further comment on this question see n. 25 *infra*.

16. Agreements were negotiated with Poland (December, 1956), the G.D.R. (March, 1957), Rumania (April, 1957), and Hungary (May, 1957). For analysis of these agreements and full texts see Meissner, *Der Warschauer Pakt*, pp. 67–80, 129ff. See also Brzezinski, "The Organization of the Communist Camp," pp. 183–86; Staar, "The East European Alliance System," pp. 34–36.

17. Wolfe, *Soviet Strategy at the Crossroads*, pp. 213–14.

18. *Izvestia*, March 31, 1961. To what extent the defense measures examined and agreed upon at the March meeting in Moscow concerned closer integration of the Warsaw Pact forces, as distinct from unilateral Soviet steps that were about to be taken, is not clear. In the succeeding months of the summer of 1961 the Soviet Union undertook such measures as an increase in the Soviet military budget, suspension of Khrushchev's troop reduction program initiated in January, 1960, recall to duty of Marshal I. S. Konev (who had been replaced in 1960 by A. A. Grechko as commander of Warsaw Pact forces) to take temporary command of Soviet forces in Germany, and on September 1 the resumption of nuclear testing. The first announcement that joint maneuvers were to take place in the fall of 1961 was made in Moscow in September. *Izvestia*, September 26, 1961.

19. *Izvestia*, September 12, 1961. The Defense Minister's Conference was held on September 8–9.

20. Marshal A. A. Grechko, "The Patriotic and International Duty of the USSR Armed Forces," *Krasnaia Zvezda,* October 6, 1961. Grechko noted, among other things, that "we attach great significance to these maneuvers of the Warsaw Pact armed forces staff and troops."

21. Garthoff, "The Military Establishment," p. 14; Staar, "The East European Alliance System," p. 38.

22. The location, dates, and participants in the joint exercises announced up to the present are: (1) G.D.R.—October, 1961, U.S.S.R., Poland, G.D.R., Czechoslovakia; (2) Czechoslovakia—September, 1962, U.S.S.R., Poland, Czechoslovakia; (3) Poland—October, 1962, U.S.S.R., G.D.R., Poland; (4) Rumania—October, 1962, U.S.S.R., Rumania, Bulgaria; (5) G.D.R.—September, 1963, U.S.S.R., G.D.R., Czechoslovakia, Poland; (6) Czechoslovakia—June, 1964, U.S.S.R., G.D.R., Czechoslovakia; (7) Bulgaria—September, 1964, U.S.S.R., Bulgaria, Rumania; (8) G.D.R.—April, 1965, U.S.S.R., G.D.R.; (9) G.D.R.—October, 1965, U.S.S.R., G.D.R., Poland, Czechoslovakia. In addition to these exercises dealing essentially with joint theater operations, and including in some cases airborne and amphibious landing maneuvers, there presumably have been other coordinated activities such as air defense exercises. The various national forces and the Soviet forces in East Europe also have held their own separate exercises in accordance with their annual training cycles. In the case of some of the joint exercises, East European military leaders have been placed in nominal command, with a good deal of attendant publicity. See *Izvestia,* September 26, 1961; *Kommunist Vooruzhennykh Sil,* No. 8 (April, 1964) , p. 80, No. 9 (May, 1964) , p. 86, and No. 9 (May, 1965) , p. 14; *Krasnaia Zvezda,* July 2, 1964; *Pravda,* September 21, 1964, and April 11, 1965; TASS international broadcast, September 25, 1965; *Neues Deutschland,* October 15, 1965; *Izvestia,* October 21, 1965; *Pravda,* October 23, 1965.

23. Marshal A. A. Grechko, interview in supplement to *Novosti (News)* , February 26, 1964. Also see similar remarks by Grechko in *Voenno-Istoricheskii Zhurnal,* May, 1965, p. 24.

24. Garthoff, "The Military Establishment," p. 14. See also *Voenno-Istoricheskii Zhurnal,* May, 1965, p. 24, and *Kommunist Vooruzhennykh Sil,* No. 13 (July, 1965) , p. 68.

25. *Ibid.* Garthoff states in the article cited that the East European forces were reduced about one-third in the period 1955–60. This figure can be arrived at from communist statements, although information publicly available on the size of the East European armed forces leaves something to be desired. Communist sources customarily have cited figures for claimed reductions but have avoided giving the strength left over after such cuts. In connection with the May, 1958, meeting of the Political Consultative Committee, it was announced that from 1955 up to that time the East European members of the Pact had cut their forces by 337,500 ("Declaration of the Warsaw Treaty States," *Izvestia,* May 27, 1958) . It was also announced separately ("Communiqué of the Political Consultative Committee," *Izvestia,* May 27, 1958) that decisions had been made for an additional reduction of 119,000 in 1958, bringing the total to 456,500. This roughly matches Garthoff's estimate of a one-third reduction—i.e., from around 1,500,000 to about 1,000,000 men. Later communist statements also indicated an aggregate cut of 500,000 in the East European forces from 1955–60. The Declaration of the Warsaw Treaty States accompanying the communiqué of the February, 1960, Warsaw Pact meeting in Moscow stated that the member states—including the U.S.S.R.—had cut their forces by 2,600,000 since the Pact's inception

(*Izvestia,* February 5, 1960). Figures given by Khrushchev in January, 1960 (*Pravda,* January 15, 1960), for Soviet reductions alone (since 1955) came to 2,100,000. Again, therefore, the reduction for the East European countries comes out at about 500,000.

26. Various published accounts in the West in the past few years have placed the number of East European divisions at from sixty to sixty-seven, plus twenty-six Soviet divisions deployed in East Europe. See, for example, Garthoff, "The Military Establishment," p. 14, Staar, "How Strong is the Soviet Bloc?" p. 213, and "The East European Alliance System," p. 32; *The Military Balance: 1963–64* (London, 1963), pp. 7–9. Beginning around early 1963, various U.S. officials (then Assistant Secretary of Defense Paul Nitze in a speech on March 2, 1963, and Secretary of Defense McNamara in a speech on November 18, 1963), began to qualify such numerical estimates of bloc divisions by calling attention to the smaller size and smaller divisional slice of these units in relation to NATO divisions, as well as to the fact that many of them were not maintained at full strength. For discussion of these qualifying factors see Timothy W. Stanley, *NATO in Transition: The Future of the Atlantic Alliance* (New York, 1965), pp. 248, 269, 273.

27. Garthoff, "The Military Establishment," pp. 6–10.

28. *Ibid.,* p. 10.

29. Besides Poland the G.D.R., Rumania, and Bulgaria have small navies. See *Kommunist Vooruzhennykh Sil,* No. 13 (July, 1965), p. 68. See also Staar, "The East European Alliance System," p. 32.

30. Garthoff, "The Military Establishment," p. 11; Staar, "The East European Alliance System," p. 32.

31. Wolfe, *Soviet Strategy at the Crossroads,* pp. 114, 172–76, and *Trends in Soviet Thinking on Theater Warfare,* pp. 17–34.

32. Garthoff, "The Military Establishment," p. 14.

33. *Pravda,* May 27, 1958.

34. Soviet note of July 11, 1964, to seven NATO governments in *Pravda,* July 13, 1964. See also a similar warning by Marshal Grechko, Commander of the Warsaw Pact forces, in *Krasnaia Zvezda,* August 2, 1964.

35. TASS international broadcast, July 22, 1964. See also *The Christian Science Monitor,* July 25, 1964.

36. At a military parade in Bucharest on August 23, 1964, celebrating the twentieth anniversary of Rumania's "liberation," the announcer called attention to the passing display of missiles and other equipment furnished by the U.S.S.R., commenting that "today, we have . . . a completely mechanized army which has every kind of equipment including rockets." Bucharest domestic broadcast, August 23, 1964; East Germany's Soviet-made tactical missiles were paraded for the first time on its fifteenth anniversary, October 7, 1964. *The New York Times,* October 8, 1964.

37. *Kommunist Vooruzhennykh Sil,* No. 9 (May, 1965), p. 85.

38. Fritz Ermath, "The Warsaw Pact on the Bloc Agenda," Research Report of Radio Free Europe, September 16, 1965, p. 3.

39. For a fuller discussion of the debate between "modernists" and "traditionalists" see Wolfe, *Soviet Strategy at the Crossroads,* pp. 25–37, *passim.*

40. *Pravda,* January 15, 1960.

41. In this connection, the removal of Marshal Konev as commander of the Warsaw Pact forces and his step-down into semiretirement in mid-1960 may have been related to a lukewarm attitude toward Khrushchev's new military policies. Konev was replaced by Marshal Grechko, a member of the "Stalingrad group" of officers who had been wartime associates of Khrushchev and

whose later careers prospered under Khrushchev's patronage. Presumably Grechko—whose public utterances warmly supported an important Warsaw Pact role—may have been more sympathetic to the Warsaw Pact aspects of Khrushchev's policy than his predecessor.

42. Marshal V. D. Sokolovskii, *Voennaia Strategiia (Military Strategy)* (2nd ed.; Moscow, 1963), p. 417; Major General V. Reznichenko and Colonel A. Sidorenko, "Tactics at the Present Stage," *Krasnaia Zvezda,* February 12, 1964. In connection with the problem of reinforcing the European theater, it is interesting that reports of joint maneuvers in the G.D.R. in the spring of 1965 placed great emphasis on the arrival of airborne troops from the Soviet Union.

43. There is circumstantial evidence that Khrushchev may have proposed arrangements for military collaboration with China in the Far East along the lines prevailing between the Soviet Union and its Warsaw Pact partners, which Peking apparently rejected. The evidence for this case is marshaled in an as yet unpublished paper by Malcolm Mackintosh, "Sino-Soviet Relations in a U.S.-China Crisis: The Soviet Attitude," pp. 22–26 in draft. The period between January and May, 1958, apparently was the critical one in this regard, particularly with respect to the matter of Soviet nuclear assistance to China. Up to January, 1958, the Chinese had spoken of drawing on Soviet nuclear experience, presumably on the basis of the "new technology" agreement of October, 1957. From May, 1958, on, the Chinese changed their tune, declaring that China was determined to make her own nuclear weapons.

In the interval between January and May the Soviets apparently began to have second thoughts about furnishing weapons and production facilities to Peking, and may have offered instead to provide only delivery means, with warheads to be kept in Soviet custody, perhaps along the lines of subsequent arrangements with the Warsaw Pact countries. The Chinese, however, seem to have balked at the strings attached to this presumed offer. Subsequently, for example, they charged that the Soviets in April, 1958, had proposed a joint Sino-Soviet command in the Pacific that was incompatible with Chinese sovereignty, and had sought to exercise military domination over China. At the end of May, 1958, the Soviets moved to open technical talks with the West on a test-ban treaty, further suggesting that some time in the preceding few months the Soviets had decided to try to curb Peking's nuclear aspirations. The next major Soviet moves, as subsequently charged (by Peking at least), were the tearing up of the October, 1957, "new technology" agreement in June, 1959, and the refusal to furnish China a sample atomic bomb. Thereafter, China increasingly showed that she intended to go it alone.

44. Wolfe, *Soviet Strategy at the Crossroads,* p. 216.

45. Among accounts discussing what has sometimes been described as the "polycentric" trend in East Europe in the past few years, see: George Kennan, "Polycentrism and Western Policy," *Foreign Affairs,* January, 1964, pp. 171–83; Richard V. Burks, "Perspectives for Eastern Europe," *Problems of Communism,* March/April, 1964, pp. 73–81; Zbigniew K. Brzezinski, "Russia and Europe," *Foreign Affairs,* April, 1964, pp. 428–44; Jeanne Kuebler, "Changing Status of Soviet Satellites," *Editorial Research Reports,* April 22, 1964, pp. 283–99; Richard Lowenthal, "Has the Revolution a Future?" *Encounter,* January, 1965, pp. 3–16, and February, 1965, pp. 16–21ff.; John Michael Montias, "Communist Rule in Eastern Europe," *Foreign Affairs,* January, 1965, pp. 331–48. Also see relevant articles in William E. Griffith (ed.), *Communism in Europe* (Cambridge, Mass., 1964–65), I and II.

46. Theodore Shabad, "Economic Plans Divide Red Bloc," *The New York*

Times (European ed.) , September 17, 1965. Open disagreements within CEMA had emerged by 1963, with Rumania leading the complaints against Soviet policy. See Staar, "How Strong is the Soviet Bloc?" p. 215; Montias, "Communist Rule in Eastern Europe," pp. 332–33; Burks, "Perspectives for Eastern Europe," pp. 74–79; Vaclav E. Mares, "East Europe's Second Chance," *Current History*, November, 1964, pp. 272–79; William E. Griffith, "The Revival of East European Nationalisms," Paper presented at Fifth International Conference on World Politics, Noordwijk, The Netherlands, September, 1965.

47. The Soviets have taken the position that Soviet military intervention in Hungary in 1956 was justified under terms of the Warsaw Pact, a view occasionally disputed by the Poles and Hungarians. See W. Morawiecki, "On the Warsaw Pact," *Sprawy Miezynarodowz (International Affairs)*, No. 5 (1958) , p. 29; Lesnevskii, *Kommunist Vooruzhennykh Sil*, No. 10 (May, 1963) , p. 73; Garthoff, "The Military Establishment," p. 16; Wolfe, *Soviet Strategy at the Crossroads*, p. 317. Among the bilateral Soviet agreements, the only one that contains a "safety clause" under which Soviet forces could presumably intervene to maintain security is the March 12, 1957, treaty with the G.D.R. See Staar, "The East European Alliance System," p. 35.

48. Grechko, *Voenno-Istoricheskii Zhurnal*, May, 1965, p. 24; see also *Kommunist Vooruzhennykh Sil*, No. 13 (July, 1965) , p. 69.

49. In a speech in Leipzig in early March, 1965, Kosygin, referring to the declaration of the Political Consultative Committee at Warsaw to "take necessary defense measures" in the event of creation of MLF by NATO, mentioned that the Warsaw meeting in January had been convened "at the initiative of the G.D.R." *Pravda*, March 2, 1965.

50. "Communiqué on the Meeting of the Political Consultative Committee of the Member States of the Warsaw Treaty," *Krasnaia Zvezda*, January 22, 1965.

51. Ermath, "The Warsaw Pact on the Bloc Agenda," pp. 4–5.

52. For example, the Soviets have failed to respond to frequent requests from the U.S. delegate at the Geneva disarmament negotiations that, "in view of East European possession of missiles capable of carrying nuclear warheads, the Soviets [should] make clear the manner in which the warheads are controlled." *Ibid.*, p. 4.

53. See, for example, a Soviet account of joint exercises in Bulgaria in 1964, which described landings following simulated nuclear strikes by the participating units. "Solidarity, Maturity, Mastery: Allied Troops Demonstrate High Combat Readiness," *Krasnaia Zvezda*, September 23, 1964. Articles and statements dealing with the various Pact armies have mentioned from time to time that they are prepared to fight with or without nuclear-missile weapons. See *Kommunist Vooruzhennykh Sil*, No. 8 (April, 1965) , p. 70; speech by Marshal Malinovskii, Moscow radio broadcast, May 14, 1965. As noted previously (see n. 1) , some dispatches on the October, 1965, joint maneuvers in the G.D.R. cited East German accounts that the Warsaw Pact forces carried out simulated nuclear strikes against an assumed "aggressor," although Soviet reporting of the exercises made no mention of nuclear weapons. This studied shunning of the term "nuclear" by Soviet commentators may have reflected newly aroused Soviet sensitivity to the question of nuclear control and sharing within the Warsaw alliance, as well as an effort to avoid compromising the Soviet stand against multilateral nuclear arrangements in NATO.

54. A rare Soviet comment indicating that some kind of formal joint organizational arrangement for nuclear purposes may have been set up within the Pact was made in May, 1965, by Marshal Grechko, commander of the Pact

forces. In a speech celebrating the tenth anniversary of the Warsaw Treaty, Grechko employed the term "the joint nuclear forces of the Warsaw Pact" in stating that these forces "are always ready to rebuff any aggressor." Moscow radio broadcast, May 14, 1965.

55. Marshal A. Grechko, "Military Alliance of Fraternal Nations," *Pravda*, May 13, 1965. See also Marshal A. Grechko, "Reliable Shield of Peace and the Security of Nations," *Kommunist Vooruzhennykh Sil*, No. 9 (May, 1965), p. 13; *ibid.*, No. 13 (July, 1965), p. 67; General P. I. Batov, chief of staff of the Warsaw Pact forces, "Reliable Shield for the Security of Nations," *Soviet Military Review*, No. 5 (May, 1965), p. 33; Marshal R. Malinovskii, "Powerful Guardian of the Security of Nations," *Krasnaia Zvezda*, May 13, 1965.

56. It has been suggested that intense Soviet opposition to any form of joint nuclear control in NATO may stem in part from Soviet concern that such arrangements would increase pressure within the Warsaw alliance for some comparable scheme of sharing in nuclear control and decision. See Ermath, "The Warsaw Pact on the Bloc Agenda," p. 5.

57. Speech at Volgograd by A. N. Kosygin, *Pravda*, July 12, 1965. For a discussion of the new Soviet leaders' approach to defense policy issues, including their largely noncommittal stand on the matter of how large Soviet theater forces should be, see the present author's article, "Military Policy: A Soviet Dilemma," *Current History*, October, 1965, esp. pp. 201–7.

58. Decree of the Rumanian National Assembly, November 14, 1964.

59. See David Binder, "Rumanians Quietly Reduce Role in Warsaw Pact," and "Rumania Affirms Independent Line," *The New York Times*, June 5 and July 20, 1965. The June 5 Binder dispatch also mentions a reported reduction in the size of the Rumanian Army from 240,000 to 200,000 men.

60. Reported to the author by a European student of East European affairs, who had talked with knowledgeable Rumanian officials during a visit to Rumania in the summer of 1965.

61. *The New York Times*, June 5, 1965. See also "Current Developments," *East Europe*, July, 1965, p. 32. Since this paper was written there have been increasing indications of Rumanian opposition to Pact military arrangements, paralleling in a sense De Gaulle's disapproval of military integration within NATO.

62. *The New York Times*, June 5, 1965. See also Max Frankel, "Rumanians Widen Independent Line," *The New York Times*, December 19, 1964; John Michael Montias, "Background and Origins of the Rumanian Dispute with Comecon," *Soviet Studies*, October, 1963, pp. 125–51; Richard V. Burks, "The Rumanian National Deviation: An Accounting," Paper presented at the Fifth International Conference on World Politics, Noordwijk, The Netherlands, September, 1965.

63. *Soviet News*, published by the Soviet Embassy in London, May 20, 1965, p. 1.

64. See dispatches in *The New York Times*, April 18 and 21, 1965; David Binder, "Bulgarians Find 9 Guilty of Plot," *ibid.*, June 20, 1965. See also J. F. Brown, "The Bulgarian Plot," *World Today*, June, 1965, pp. 261–68; "The Mystery in Sofia," *East Europe*, June, 1965, pp. 14–16; and Garthoff, "The Military Establishment," pp. 7–8, 15. The Bulgarian military figures involved in the plot along with General Anev, commandant of the Sofia garrisons, are said to have been members of the wartime Bulgarian partisan group which co-operated with Tito's partisan movement.

65. Grechko, *Voenno-Istoricheskii Zhurnal*, May, 1965, p. 25. Despite assertions that "imperialist" attempts to sow diversion within the Pact are bound

to fail, some Soviet writing still dwells on the need for resolute struggle against "surviving nationalist tendencies from the past," which are conceded to have important effects in view of the "multi-national character" of the Pact's armed forces. See editorial, "In the Spirit of Proletarian Internationalism," *Krasnaia Zvezda*, July 30, 1965.

66. See, for example, comments on the Warsaw Pact's "first strategic echelon," by the G.D.R. Defense Minister Heinz Hoffman, *Neues Deutschland*, April 22, 1965.

67. The treaty with Czechoslovakia was renewed in November, 1963, that with the G.D.R. in June, 1964, and that with Poland in April, 1965. See *Pravda*, November 29, 1963, and June 13, 1964; *Krasnaia Zvezda*, April 10, 1965.

68. The Soviet Union has diligently exploited fear of Germany as an element of common interest to bind the bloc together. However, Soviet dependence upon the "German threat" as a cohesive factor in the Warsaw Pact may also make it difficult for the Soviet Union to work out any settlement of the German problem that would tend to dispel this "threat" and loosen the Soviet hold upon Polish, Czech, and East German policy.

69. Moscow radio broadcast, September 14, 1965; see also Ermath, "The Warsaw Pact on the Bloc Agenda," p. 1.

70. It has been reported that in 1964 the Rumanians were already talking of the need for "new ways" of reaching decisions in the Warsaw Pact. See Frankel, "Rumanians Widen Independent Line."

71. Ermath, "The Warsaw Pact on the Bloc Agenda," p. 5.

72. Wolfe, "Military Policy: A Soviet Dilemma," pp. 205–7.

73. East European military leaders were in nominal command of four of the nine joint exercises reported to date. They were: Marshal Marian Spychalsky of Poland, October, 1962; General Heinz Hoffman of the G.D.R., September, 1963; General B. Lomsky of Czechoslovakia, June, 1964; and General D. Dzhurer of Bulgaria, September, 1964. See *Kommunist Vooruzhennykh Sil*, No. 8 (April, 1964), p. 80, No. 9 (May, 1964), p. 86, and No. 19 (October, 1964), p. 81; *Pravda*, September 21, 1964.

74. For example, Air Marshal V. A. Sudets, commander of the Soviet Union's air defense forces, was publicly referred to in 1964 as being also Commander in Chief of Air Defense of the Warsaw Pact. See Garthoff, "The Military Establishment," p. 14.

75. *Ibid.*, p. 13; see also Staar, "The East European Alliance System," p. 35. The important role played by Soviet military missions in the various Warsaw Pact countries as part of the Soviet control mechanism has been stressed by some observers. See Hinterhoff, "The Warsaw Pact," p. 93; Von Krannhals, "Command Integration within the Warsaw Pact," pp. 46–47. It should be noted that the various accounts of the Warsaw Pact command and control setup differ somewhat as to how far down into the national armies the presence of Soviet "advisors" extends today.

76. Wolfe, *Soviet Strategy at the Crossroads*, pp. 211–12; see also Marshal V. D. Sokolovskii *et al.*, *Soviet Military Strategy*, with Analytical Introduction and Annotations by H. S. Dinerstein, L. Gouré, and Thomas W. Wolfe of The RAND Corporation (Englewood Cliffs, N.J., 1963), p. 495 (in *Voennaia Strategiia* [2nd. ed.; Moscow, 1963], p. 475).

77. Staar, "The East European Alliance System," p. 39; Hinterhoff, "The Warsaw Pact," p. 93.

78. *Kommunist Vooruzhennykh Sil*, No. 13 (July, 1965), p. 67; *Krasnaia Zvezda*, July 30, 1965.

79. The number of MRBM (medium-range) and IRBM (intermediate-range) strategic missiles has been variously stated as from 700 to 800. See Stanley, *NATO in Transition*, pp. 115, 162; *The Military Balance: 1963–64*, Table III, p. 34.

80. The Warsaw Treaty itself, which was preceded by unsuccessful Soviet diplomatic efforts to engineer an all-European treaty of collective security, contained a stipulation that, if such a collective security system should be set up, bringing about the dissolution of NATO, the Warsaw Pact too would be dissolved. The various collective security proposals advanced at one time or another with the aim of holding back West German rearmament and of bringing about withdrawal of U.S. military power from Europe need not be recited here. It is of interest in terms of the policy line of the current Soviet regime, however, that the Warsaw Pact meeting of January, 1965, touched off a renewed round of such proposals as a nuclear-free zone in central Europe, a NATO-Warsaw non-aggression pact, renunciation of nuclear weapons by both German states, a conference on collective security in Europe, and so on. See Communiqué on the Warsaw Meeting, *Pravda*, January 22, 1965; I. D. Noerlund, "For European Peace and Security," *World Marxist Review*, March, 1965, pp. 3–7; Walter Ulbricht, "Vital Contribution to European Peace and Security," *ibid.*, May, 1965, pp. 3–5; editorial, "Peace and Security in Europe," *Sprawy Miezynarodowz*, No. 5 (May, 1965), pp. 3–6.

81. Marshal Sokolovskii's suggestion that manpower cuts and some withdrawal of Soviet troops from East Europe might be entertained if the West would reciprocate came in response to a question from an *Izvestia* reporter at a press conference held by Sokolovskii in Moscow on February 17, 1965. Some of the circumstances attending this conference, at which Sokolovskii took a position at variance with that of his military colleagues on the matter of Soviet over-all troop strength, are discussed by the present author in "Military Policy: A Soviet Dilemma," pp. 205–6.

10. The Soviet Union's Bilateral Pact System in Eastern Europe

Boris Meissner

Since 1956 the system of communist states which came into being after World War II has lost its monolithic character. Today it is a loose association of states, based upon an ideological alliance which has been shaken to its foundations by the conflict between Soviet Russia and Communist China.[1]

The rival claims to leadership by the two major powers within the "socialist world system," which includes not only the "socialist countries"[2] but also those communist forces not at present holding power, is expressed in the principle of "proletarian-socialist internationalism."[3] At the party level we meet it as "proletarian internationalism," at the government level as "socialist internationalism." But it is nothing more nor less than an ideological paraphrase of the concept of hegemony with which we have long been familiar.[4] The monolithic bloc has broken up into two hegemonic groups in which the degree of dependency in the relations of the individual subject state to its respective leading power varies constantly.

According to its basic motive force, hegemony is a concept of political organization which may, however, turn into a concept of legal organization should the dominating power make use of institutions of a legal nature in order to legalize its leadership under international law. In the Soviet sphere of power and interests the principles of "proletarian-socialist internationalism" constitute the general framework that is filled out by a complex system of pacts, which take both bilateral and multilateral forms.

The bilateral political treaties[5] will be discussed in greater detail below. Among the multilateral pacts the Warsaw Treaty Organization and the Council for Economic Mutual Assistance (CEMA or COMECON) are of particular significance.[6] Outwardly, these two multilateral bloc organizations differ only very slightly from the traditional forms of international groupings. In the communities of West European states the supranational features are far more pronounced. On the other hand, they lack —quite apart from the absence of links between political parties —the specific integrating effect produced by the bilateral pact system. Initially this system constituted the only tie under international law which amalgamated the Soviet sphere of power and interests into a legal and not merely a political unit. Today it is an additional means to screen off the European part of the bloc, and at the same time it forms the inner structure of the multilateral pact system.[7]

With the spread of polycentrism, spurred by "revisionism" and nationalism, the bilateral pact system is bound to grow in importance for the internal cohesion of the hegemonic association of states. Thus, in recent years the Soviet Union has endeavored not only to renew the treaties of alliance which form the core of the bilateral pact system, but also to extend them to include the Soviet-occupied zone of Germany.

The Bilateral Pact System under Stalin

The network of treaties which today spans Eastern Europe, the area which between the two World Wars exercised the function of a *cordon sanitaire* against the Bolshevik threat of a world revolution, has been spun from two sides—by the Soviet Union and by the Balkan communist powers, Yugoslavia and Bulgaria. The objectives of the two architects of the system were in some respects diametrically opposed to one another. Stalin's purpose in concluding the bilateral agreements was to consolidate and secure the predominance of the Soviet Union in Eastern Central Europe. Tito and Dimitrov, on the other hand, regarded them as "union agreements" which would first of all unite the Balkans and later the entire area lying between the Baltic Sea, the Black Sea, and the Adriatic into a federative unit.[8]

The starting point of the Soviet pact system in Eastern Europe was the treaty of friendship, co-operation, and mutual assistance in the postwar period concluded on December 12, 1943, in Moscow between the Soviet Union and Czechoslovakia. This treaty, as shown by the additional protocol, was originally conceived as a multilateral treaty envisaging the accession of other neighboring states which had become victims of German national socialist aggression. But the favorable course of the war placed the Soviet Union in the position of being able to exercise its influence beyond its immediate neighbors. It therefore decided to dispense with a multilateral treaty and instead to conclude bilateral agreements, which gave it a better opportunity to assert its natural ascendancy.

The other political pacts concluded by the Soviet Union shortly before the end of the war were the treaty with Yugoslavia of April 11, 1945, and the treaty with Poland of April 21, 1945. For reasons of propaganda the Soviet Union was glad to leave it to the other states of the projected eastern bloc to take further initiatives for extending the pact system. Since the Soviet Union did not appear as the sole driving force, the Soviet foreign ministry was able to expound in its official statements the thesis that the pact system did not constitute an emergent political bloc determined by the hegemony of a great power.

The treaties of alliance concluded by Yugoslavia with Poland (March 18, 1946), Czechoslovakia (May 9, 1946), and Albania (July 9, 1946) were followed by a treaty between Poland and Czechoslovakia (March 10, 1947). After the peace treaties with Hungary, Bulgaria, Rumania, and Finland were signed in Paris on February 10, 1947, Tito, supported by Dimitrov, actively set about extending the bilateral pact system still further. The treaties of alliance which Yugoslavia concluded with Bulgaria (November 27, 1947), Hungary (December 8, 1947), and Rumania (December 19, 1947) were supplemented by Bulgarian treaties with Albania (December 16, 1947) and Rumania (January 16, 1948), followed by a treaty between Rumania and Hungary (January 24, 1948).

Yugoslavia and Albania had agreed upon a customs union as early as November 27, 1946. At a meeting in Bled on August 1, 1947, Yugoslavia and Bulgaria concluded an agreement regarding an adjustment of customs duties which was intended as the preliminary step toward a customs union. A customs union was planned in connection with the treaty of alliance between Bulgaria and Rumania of January 16, 1948.

The plans for federation connected with the treaties concluded by Yugoslavia and Bulgaria, clearly expressed in a press interview given by Dimitrov on January 16, 1948,[9] were as unacceptable to the Kremlin as were the alliance clauses that deviated from the

Soviet pattern. By concluding treaties of alliance with Rumania (February 4, 1948), Hungary (February 18, 1948), and Bulgaria (March 18, 1948) Stalin endeavored to strengthen the ties between these former enemy countries and the Soviet Union and to isolate Yugoslavia in the Balkans. The treaty of alliance with Finland of April 6, 1948, secured the northern flank of the Soviet Union. It was followed by treaties of alliance between Czechoslovakia and Bulgaria (April 23, 1948), Poland and Bulgaria (May 29, 1948), and Poland and Hungary (June 18, 1948).

The Kremlin's hopes of being able to overthrow Tito's government with the aid of the opposition forces were not realized. Thus the only possibility left to the Soviet Union was to bind the people's democracies loyal to the Cominform more closely to it and to oust the federative People's Republic of Yugoslavia from the pact system. After the Cominform resolution against Tito's Yugoslavia at the end of June, 1948, the bilateral pact system was completed by the treaties of alliance between Bulgaria and Hungary (June 16, 1948), Czechoslovakia and Rumania (July 21, 1948), Poland and Rumania (January 26, 1949), and Czechoslovakia and Hungary (April 16, 1949). After that the Soviet Union had the people's democracies of Eastern Central Europe break off all relations with Yugoslavia. The economic and cultural relations were the first to be dissolved, after which the satellite states canceled the political agreements unilaterally. The only treaty of alliance severed by Yugoslavia itself was the one with Albania.

After the break between Moscow and Belgrade became final, Stalin endeavored to develop the hegemony of the Soviet Union into absolute power, indeed an imperium. This purpose was served on the one hand by an increased control over the subject states on a terrorist basis, and on the other by a further intensification of the bilateral pact system in the economic, scientific-technological, and cultural fields. The Council for Economic Mutual Assistance which was established on January 25, 1949, was hardly used at all by Stalin as a means for closer integration.

THE PACT SYSTEM UNDER KHRUSHCHEV AND HIS SUCCESSORS

The course of the negotiations conducted in February, 1948, in Moscow by leading Yugoslav and Bulgarian politicians showed that Stalin was pursuing far-reaching annexation plans with regard to the people's democracies of Eastern Central Europe.[10] But he made no attempt to incorporate the satellite states into the Soviet Union on the pattern of the incorporation of the Baltic states in 1940. Apparently such an undertaking appeared to him too risky, for reasons of domestic and foreign politics. After his death the Kremlin found itself obliged to grant the individual subject states an ever increasing amount of autonomy. At the same time, greater efforts were made to draw the European parts of the bloc closer together. After 1954–55, relations between the communist states were placed on a new basis through a reorganization of CEMA and the establishment of the Warsaw Treaty Organization. The former bilateral pact system was supplemented by an increasing number of multilateral agreements.

From the government declaration of October 30, 1956,[11] it became apparent that the Soviet Union was prepared to base relations among the bloc states not only on the "principles of proletarian internationalism," but also on the vaunted "five principles," with special stress on the principle of equality. The changeover in Poland and the popular uprising in Hungary in October and November, 1956, prompted the Soviet leadership to give greater prominence to the hegemonic and imperial aspects of "proletarian-socialist internationalism." In order to check the strivings for emancipation within the bloc, measures leading in two directions were taken by the Soviet leadership. Integration of the bloc was furthered in the military, economic, transport, communications, cultural, scientific, social policy, and law fields through the conclusion of numerous bilateral and multilateral agreements. The activities of the Warsaw Treaty Organization and of CEMA were stepped up. Other bloc organizations were instituted on a multilateral basis (nuclear energy, rail traffic, and shipping). The Soviet leadership did not confine itself to developing the pact system and creating a system of "international division of labor" which increased the economic dependence of the people's democracies on the Soviet Union. It also aimed at forming closer party relationships on a bilateral and multilateral basis.[12]

All these efforts did not produce the success for which Khrushchev had hoped. The conflict between Peking and Moscow gave great momentum to the centrifugal forces in the bloc. The trend toward emancipation in the East Central European area had become stronger. As illustrated by the case of Rumania, the satellites developed into vassals, some of them remarkably self-willed. This state of affairs induced Khrushchev to back up the Ulbricht regime by all possible means and at the same time, with the aid of Gomulka and Novotny, to prevent a further softening-up in Poland and Czechoslovakia. To that end a treaty of alliance between the Soviet Union and the "German Democratic Republic" (G.D.R.) was concluded on June 12, 1964. This was preceded, on November 27, 1963, by a renewal of the Soviet-Czechoslovak treaty of assistance of December 12, 1943. A renewal of the treaty of assistance between the Soviet Union and Poland took place on April 8, 1965.

The conclusion of all these treaties must be regarded as part of the Soviet effort to revitalize the bilateral pact system and tighten up the links between the people's democracies of Eastern Central Europe and the Soviet Union. They demonstrate that the Soviet attempt to consolidate the European part of the bloc into a firm unit on the basis of multilateral agreements has up to now not brought the expected results.

Soviet - East German Contractual Relations[13]

The establishment of a separate state in central Germany in October, 1949, in the form of the "German Democratic Republic,"[14] provided Stalin with an effective means of shoring up the bloc of European satellite states. Pursuant to a declaration by the Chairman of the Soviet Control Commission in Germany of November 11, 1949, the Soviet government handed over the administrative functions of the Soviet Military Administration to the government of the Soviet zone republic. Only after the Soviet Control Commission was converted into the Soviet High Commission in May, 1953, and the diplomatic mission of the U.S.S.R. became a Soviet embassy in October, 1953, were limited sovereign rights entrusted to the G.D.R., pursuant to a declaration of the Soviet government of March 25, 1954.

The gradual adjustment of the status of the Soviet zone republic to that of the East Central European satellite states found expression in the conclusion of long-term trade agreements and in the conversion of the diplomatic missions of the bloc states into embassies or legations. Apart from the East European bloc states, only Yugoslavia and Cuba (and temporarily also Zanzibar) have accorded full recognition to the G.D.R.

At first the G.D.R. was included in the Soviet Union's bilateral pact system merely through the agreement with Poland on June 6, 1950 (in contravention of the Potsdam Agreement), on the demarcation of the German-Polish frontier along the Oder-Neisse line, and through joint declarations with the major East Central European people's democracies. No further political treaties with the G.D.R. were concluded during Stalin's lifetime. Instead, as of September 29, 1950, the G.D.R. was accepted as a member of CEMA, which Albania had also joined.

After Stalin's death a transitional economic agreement was concluded between the Soviet Union and the G.D.R. on August 22, 1953, in which the Soviet government waived its claims to further reparations payments and agreed to return to the G.D.R. the remaining SAG enterprises, with the sole exception of Wismut-A.G.

A further strengthening of the ties under international law between the G.D.R. and the Soviet Union was effected by the agreement of September 20, 1955, on relations between the U.S.S.R. and G.D.R. Some Soviet international law experts regard this pact as equivalent to a treaty of alliance. In fact, it was directed toward co-operation between the contracting parties in the political, economic, and cultural fields, but not toward mutual military assistance.

The G.D.R. was first included in the military system of alliances through the Warsaw Pact of May 14, 1955[15]—that is, through a further multilateral agreement. Express reference is also made to this in the treaty of alliance between the Soviet Union and the G.D.R. of June 12, 1964.[16]

The treaty of alliance represented the contractual establishment of the principles of Khrushchev's policy on Germany. At the same time, it signified the return to a defensive status quo policy, as pursued by Molotov under Stalin and Malenkov. Thus the G.D.R. treaty marks the second stage of the retreat upon which Khrushchev had embarked with the erection of the Berlin Wall on August 13, 1961. The provisions of the treaty, whose contents in the light of international law will be dealt with later, indicated Khrushchev's readiness to break off the offensive which he had inaugurated with the Berlin ultimatum of November 10, 1958, and the draft peace treaty of January 10, 1959. He dropped the threat of a separate peace treaty, which was probably never meant particularly seriously. The Potsdam Agreement, which Khrushchev had intended to renounce, and the "international agreements" connected with it, were given special prominence. In connection with the two-state theory, the question is left open whether the entire German state continues to exist in the legal sense or not. It is emphasized that the restoration of national unity "can only be achieved through negotiations on an equal basis and an understanding between the two sovereign states." The possibility of the conclusion of a peace treaty by an all-German government is not excluded. A revision of the treaty of alliance in the case of reunification or upon the conclusion of a peace treaty (Article 10) is envisaged. The demand for a "free city of West Berlin" is not mentioned. The treaty merely refers to West Berlin as an "independent political unit" (Article 6). This wording provides the possibility to maintain the *de facto* situation and thus to let the three Western protective powers and the Federal Republic in practice represent the foreign policy interests of West Berlin in the future as well. It is noteworthy that the former Soviet and Soviet zonal thesis that West Berlin lay within the territory of the G.D.R. was not mentioned. We shall deal later in greater detail with the other provisions of the G.D.R. treaty, which are important for comparison with the other treaties of alliance.

The conclusion of the treaty with the G.D.R. took place shortly before the planned state visit of Khrushchev to the Federal Republic, which was intended to improve relations between Moscow and Bonn. Khrushchev's downfall intervened before the visit could take place. Statements made by his successors indicate a continuation of the Khrushchevian general line of Soviet policy on Germany. Khrushchev's successors also appear to regard close links between the Soviet zone republic and the Soviet Union as a decisive condition for the success of the far-reaching integration plans contained in the new program of the Communist Party of the Soviet Union, in which economic and political aspects are closely interwoven.[17]

Further developments will show whether the treaty of alliance with the G.D.R. was intended by the Kremlin as the starting point for incorporating the Soviet zone republic more fully into the bilateral pact system. The conclusion of agreements with the people's democracies could prove to be a means of countering the increased efforts of the Federal Republic to develop its relations with the countries of Eastern Central Europe.

THE BILATERAL POLITICAL TREATIES

The underlying structure of the bilateral pact system in Eastern Europe is provided by those political treaties which are termed "treaties of friendship, co-operation and assistance." They are, on the one hand, agreements of the *entente* and consultation type, and thus are agreements to prevent war; on the other hand, they are treaties of guarantee and alliance, and thus are treaties looking toward the eventuality of a war.[18] The alliance character predominates. Thus these treaties may be described as treaties of alliance or assistance.[19] As to their content, they may also be considered as integration agreements. In the course of development of the pact system, this inner function has grown in importance. Within the "socialist camp," economic, scientific-technological, and cultural co operation is effected exclusively on the legal basis of bilateral agreements of alliance.

Of the twenty-three treaties of alliance which were concluded in Eastern Europe under Stalin, sixteen remained in force after Yugoslavia left the bloc. The preamble to the additional protocol of November 27, 1963,[20] by which the treaty of alliance between the Soviet Union and Czechoslovakia of December 12, 1943, was renewed, has only slightly modified that treaty and thus brought it up to date. The treaty of alliance between the Soviet Union and Poland of April 8, 1965,[21] on the other hand, differs considerably from that of the former treaty of assistance of April 21, 1945. While it bears a certain resemblance in form to the treaty of alliance between the Soviet Union and the G.D.R. of June, 1964, its content differs in a number of respects.

Both the old and the new pacts center around the alliance clause in case of war. Differences in the wording stem in part from specific interests of the contracting parties and in part from the political situations prevailing at the time the treaties were concluded. In most of the old treaties the *casus foederis* takes effect should aggression be initiated by Germany or by a state "directly or in any other form" allied with Germany in its policy of aggression. There are also a number of treaties in which the *casus foederis* also arises in the case of aggression by any third state. It is significant that this group of treaties, in addition to the Yugoslav-Albanian treaty of alliance of July 9, 1946, includes all treaties concluded in the period between the meeting at Bled on August 1, 1947, and the Soviet objection to Tito's and Dimitrov's plans for federation in January, 1948. In the treaties of assistance concluded by Yugoslavia with Albania and Bulgaria, no mention at all is made of Germany in connection with the *casus foederis*. Of these treaties, those in which Yugoslavia did not participate are still in force today. By virtue of the alliance clause, for example, Rumania would have been obliged to give assistance to Hungary against the military intervention of the Soviet Union in 1956. The same obligation would arise for Hungary and Bulgaria should the Soviet Union go to the length of attacking Rumania.

In the treaty of alliance between the Soviet Union and the G.D.R. (Article 5, sentence 1), the *casus foederis*—as in the Warsaw Pact—applies "in the case of an armed attack on the part of any state or any group of states" upon one of the contracting parties. Assistance is to be given in conformity with the clauses of the Warsaw Pact. Pursuant to Article 4, paragraph 1, the decision as to the way in which the state attacked should be supported is generally left to the party rendering assistance. The G.D.R. constitutes an exception.[22] In the divergent original German text of the Warsaw Pact, the type, extent, and direction of help to be given by the G.D.R. is to be determined by the other member states of the Pact. According to the Polish, Russian, and Czech texts, each member state shall render the victim of an armed attack "assistance with all means which appear necessary to *it*." The German wording, on the other hand, stipulates "immediate assistance, individually and in agreement with the other member states of the treaty, with all means which they shall deem necessary."

In the case of the bilateral treaty of alliance, this means that the Soviet Union makes the decision as to the nature of the assistance which the G.D.R. must give. This discriminating clause shows that since 1955 the absolute dependence of the

G.D.R. upon the Soviet Union has in no way been lessened. Unlike the other bilateral alliance treaties, the alliance clause of the Warsaw Pact does not involve any commitment to automatic entry into a war on the part of the Soviet Union.

Under the new treaty of alliance with Poland (Article 7) the *casus foederis* becomes effective "in the case of an armed attack on the part of any state or any group of states." Reference to Article 6 shows that these potential aggressors are understood to be "the West German forces of militarism and revanchism, or attacks on the part of any other state allied with them."

The preamble to the Soviet-Czechoslovak protocol refers only to the commitments resulting from the Warsaw Pact, speaks of the danger of war from "forces which let loose the Second World War," and excludes the "peace-loving" Soviet zone republic as a possible aggressor. The latter was not the case with the older treaties, in which the alliance clause referred to the German state as a whole. It is interesting to note that, unlike the treaties with Czechoslovakia and the G.D.R., the alliance commitment is not regionally restricted to Europe in the treaty between the Soviet Union and Poland. This treaty is also directed against any possible allies of the "West German forces of militarism and revanchism" which is not to be found in the older treaties either, though it is contained in the Warsaw Pact.

The Finnish-Soviet treaty of alliance of April 6, 1948, which was renewed for 10 years in 1958, holds a special position in the bilateral pact system. In it the basic neutral attitude of Finland is specifically recognized and the *casus foederis* limited to an attack on Finnish territory.

Most of the treaties of alliance which are directed against Germany or a power allied with Germany contain clauses on the possibility of joint measures "against any threat arising from a new aggression." A distinction is thus made between the assistance to be given in the case of an armed attack and preventive actions, which may take not only a diplomatic but also a military form. In the treaty of alliance between the Soviet Union and Poland these two aspects of alliance commitment are very closely linked through the reference in Article 7 (commitment to assistance) to Article 6 (on preventive measures). The wording of the G.D.R. treaty (Article 4) does not include the limitation contained in Article 6 of the Polish-Soviet treaty to "West German forces of militarism and revanchism" and their allies. It refers to the necessity of taking measures "to prevent aggression on the part of those forces of militarism and revanchism which aim at revising the results of the Second World War."

Such forces need not mean West Germany alone. The clauses referring to special measures against the German state as a whole, or the Federal Republic of Germany, are based on the special provision of Article 53, paragraph 1, sentence 3, which, in connection with Article 107 of the United Nations Charter, allows preventive measures against former enemy states and thus constitutes an exception to the general prohibition of the use of force.[23] Article 107 is only to be regarded as a transitional provision and has become ineffective with the lapse of time. Moreover, the two-state theory is inconsistent with this special provision, which in the case of Germany presupposed an undivided Germany. To draw a distinction between an "aggressive Federal Republic" and a "peace-loving G.D.R." on the authority of Article 107 is not permissible.

All the new treaties contain a reference to "peaceful coexistence." Further, in the preambles to the new treaties (and in Article 3 of the G.D.R. treaty), as in most of the former treaties, reference is made to the "aims and principles of the United Nations Charter," which, in addition to the principles which were incorporated in the *Panch Shila,* also include the right of self-determination of nations and universal human rights. Article 1 of the G.D.R. treaty and Article 1 of the Polish-Soviet treaty both contain a list of principles which are related to the principle of "peaceful coexistence" and embodied in the United Nations Charter. Equality of rights is listed before respect for sovereignty and the obligation not to intervene in the internal affairs of another country. In the same article, however, reference is also made to the principles of "socialist internationalism." The most important principle of "socialist internationalism" is considered to be "fraternal mutual assistance." This is the actual wording with which it is referred to in Article 1 of the G.D.R. treaty, whereas the Polish-Soviet treaty uses the more noncommittal expression "mutual assistance," which is to be granted on the basis of the *Panch Shila* referred to above. The G.D.R. treaty does not contain this link. This is an important point, since from the Soviet point of view the principles of "proletarian-socialist internationalism" in every case take precedence over the "five principles." In the Soviet hegemonic grouping of states the latter in any case appear only in connection with "proletarian-socialist internationalism." "Peaceful coexistence" is mentioned only in the preambles and in the G.D.R. treaty in Article 3.

This means that the hegemonic character of the grouping of states led by the Soviet Union is contractually recognized not only by the Soviet protectorate called the G.D.R., but also by Poland. Czechoslovakia has skillfully evaded this stipulation.

It is especially significant in this connection that "fraternal mutual assistance" does not only mean the granting of economic and technical aid. It also involves the obligation to support the communist single-party domination, as well as national revolutionary movements of liberation and civil wars waged under communist tutelage.[24] The military intervention by the Soviet Union in Hungary in 1956 has been interpreted in this sense as fulfillment of the "international obligation" of the U.S.S.R. to give assistance to the workers of Hungary. The right of allied socialist states, and above all of the Soviet hegemonic power, to intervene for the purpose of upholding an existing communist regime is thus derived from the principle of "proletarian-socialist assistance."

This right of intervention resulting from "proletarian-socialist internationalism" competes with the obligation of non-intervention in the internal affairs of a country which is embodied in the principle of sovereignty and that of national self-determination. Most of the former alliance treaties contain, in addition to a reference to the "aims and principles of the United Nations Charter," a formula to the effect that the treaty shall be implemented in accordance with the principles of the Charter. In dealing with the *casus foederis*, Article 7 of the new Polish-Soviet treaty explicitly refers to the right of individual and collective self-defense contained in Article 51 of the United Nations Charter. It then goes on to state that the contracting parties shall inform the Security Council of the measures they are taking to fulfill their obligation of assistance, and that they will act in accordance with the spirit of relevant clauses of the United Nations Charter.

Article 5 of the G.D.R. treaty, which does not refer to Article 51 of the U.N. Charter, contains the additional assurance that these measures will be stopped immediately "as soon as the Security Council adopts the measures necessary to restore and maintain world peace." Article 51 extends the "inherent right of individual self-defense" to include the right to give assistance to a victim of prohibited aggression, which forms the basis of "collective self-defense." This is based upon the legal premise that an attack upon a third party is to be regarded as an attack upon oneself. The concept of "collective self-defense" means in this sense "assistance in case of emergency," not merely "self-defense."

The bloc's interpretation of international law regards the bilateral treaties of alliance as regional agreements within the meaning of Chapter VIII of the Charter of the United Nations.[25] According to the U.N. Charter, however, a regional pact must not only provide protection against attacks from outside states but must also serve the security within the region in question.[26] The bilateral pact system guarantees collective self-defense, but not collective security. An important point in this connection is that the Soviet bloc's pact system does not provide for a peaceful arbitration of disputes. Thus the Soviet pact system in Eastern Europe is an alliance with strongly marked hegemonic characteristics, but is not a regional pact within the meaning of the Charter of the United Nations.

All of the old treaties of alliance contain a clause prohibiting membership in alliances directed against the partner in the old treaty. The new treaties do not contain that clause. It may be derived, however, from cross-references to the Warsaw Pact, Article 7 of which contains the clause.

All the treaties of alliance contain a consultation clause. The contracting parties undertake to consult on all important international questions which affect the interests of the two countries.

The old treaties had already mentioned co-operation and friendship, which were to contribute to the further development of economic and cultural relations. In the new treaties (U.S.S.R.-G.D.R. and U.S.S.R.-Poland), this aspect is considerably reinforced, while referring to the interests of the entire "socialist commonwealth" and to the principles of CEMA. In the G.D.R. treaty, in addition, attention is drawn expressly to the principles of the "international socialist division of labor" (Article 8). These references may be taken as a counterweight to the strivings toward autarchy on the part of other people's democracies, such as Rumania.

The G.D.R. treaty (Article 8) puts special emphasis upon the bilateral interlacing of the Soviet and Soviet zonal national economies. This may also be seen in the demands "to develop and consolidate the economic and the scientific-technological links between the two states to the maximum degree" and to "effect the coordination of the national economic plans and of specialization and cooperation in production, and to ensure maximum productivity in both states through approximation and alignment of their national economies." In this connection, attention may be drawn to the protocol of May 30, 1961, "On the Further Development of Economic Relations Between the GDR and the USSR in 1962–1965." It provides for "the development of a close economic community between the two countries," thus aiming at far closer economic co-operation than had been effected up to then within the framework of CEMA. The Polish-Soviet treaty is far more reserved in regard to co-operation within CEMA (Article 2). Special emphasis is laid upon the principle of mutual advantage.

The development of cultural relations is now also dealt with in considerably greater detail in the new treaties (Article 8, U.S.S.R.-G.D.R.; Article 3, U.S.S.R.-Poland).

The two-state theory, which was developed under Khrushchev, finds expression in all the new treaties of alliance. It is stated most explicitly in the Czechoslovak-Soviet protocol, which says in its preamble that "two sovereign states have formed on the territory of the former German Reich." It is interesting to note that this wording, which presumes that the single German state has perished, was not adopted in the two subsequent treaties. This opens up the possibility of a modification of the two-state theory. In the preambles to the two treaties it is stated that the G.D.R., as "one of the two German states," or "the first state of workers and peasants in the history of Germany," has carried into effect the principles of the Potsdam Agreement. Mention is also made in the G.D.R. treaty (Article 7) of the "existence of two sovereign German states."

Both treaties place particular emphasis upon the guarantee of territorial integrity. According to Article 4 of the treaty with the

Soviet zone republic, "the inviolability of the national frontiers of the German Democratic Republic is one of the basic factors of European security." It is to be guaranteed jointly in accordance with the Warsaw Pact. Article 5 of the Polish-Soviet treaty states "that the inviolability of the national frontier of the People's Republic of Poland along the Oder and [Lausitzer] Neisse is one of the most important factors of European security." The Potsdam Agreement of August 2, 1945, which is referred to in both treaties, provides no grounds for a justification under international law of the institution of a separate central German state, nor of the annexation of the eastern German territories.[27]

The Potsdam Agreement is based upon the Berlin Declaration of June 5, 1945, which presumed the continued existence of the single German state within the frontiers of December 31, 1937. Soviet international lawyers formerly pointed out themselves that the German state as a subject in international law continued to exist also after the occupation by the four powers.[28] Accordingly, the Potsdam Agreement reserved the decision regarding the fate of the eastern German territories, which were handed over to Poland and the Soviet Union for temporary administration, for a peace treaty to be concluded with an all-German government. As a result the G.D.R. was not entitled under international law to agree to the annexation of the Oder-Neisse areas by Poland in the Görlitz frontier agreement of 1950.

Irrespective of the future determination of the frontier, the Potsdam Agreement expressed itself unequivocally in favor of the political and economic unity of Germany under four-power control. The attempt made in Article 2 of the G.D.R. treaty to split up this four-power responsibility contravenes the four-power agreements of 1944 and 1945 and therefore also the Potsdam Agreement, to which particular attention is drawn in Article 9. This is all the more true of the two-state theory.

It may be pointed out that with the exception of the Finnish-Soviet pact of assistance mentioned above, all the treaties of alliance within the Soviet pact system in Eastern Europe have been concluded for a period of 20 years. This also applies to the new treaties.

The forces agreements concluded by the Soviet Union with Poland (December 17, 1956), the G.D.R. (March 12, 1957),

Rumania (April 15, 1957), and Hungary (May 27, 1957) must be regarded as directly connected with the Warsaw Pact and the bilateral treaties of alliance.[29] Of these the forces agreement between the Soviet Union and Rumania expired in 1958 after the departure of the Soviet forces. A further legal basis for the stationing of Soviet troops is provided in the case of Poland and the G.D.R. by the Potsdam Agreement and the four-power agreements of 1944 and 1945 which constitute its basis. This follows indirectly from the preambles, which refer to the joint Polish-Soviet declaration of November 18, 1956, to the agreement on relations between the U.S.S.R. and the G.D.R. of September 20, 1955, and to the joint declaration of the U.S.S.R. and G.D.R. of January 7, 1957. Despite characteristics shared in common, the forces agreements display differences, which in the case of Poland indicate relative independence but in the case of the G.D.R. tend toward definite dependency.

Whereas the NATO Status of Forces Convention, which is the basis of the forces convention of the Federal Republic of August 3, 1959, can be denounced after four years, the Soviet forces agreements remain valid as long as Soviet forces stay in the country in question. They regulate not only the legal status but also basic questions of strength, deployment, and movement of the Soviet troops. Changes in the strength of the forces or of the garrison may only be effected through bilateral agreements on the part of the states affected. The inferior position of the G.D.R. compared with that of Poland and Hungary is obvious from two special provisions. In the case of movements of Soviet troops, the G.D.R. is only entitled to a vague consultative right, but not to an actual say in the matter. In addition, the Soviet Union has reserved the right of its forces to intervene if "their security is threatened" (Article 18). Contrary to Article 5 of the Bonn agreement of May 26, 1952, between the Federal Republic and the Western powers, the proclamation of a state of emergency is thus not made dependent upon objective conditions. On the contrary, the subjective decision of the High Command of the Soviet Forces suffices for the imposition of measures to dispose of the imminent danger.

A number of special questions which were not dealt with in the forces agreements—permission to enter and leave the coun-

try, application of the customs, tax, and currency regulations, etc.
—are still settled by special agreements on legal aid in military
matters.

The political treaties in the wider sense also include agreements on cessions of territory and on frontier and minority
questions which have been concluded since the end of World
War II.[30] Apart from the Görlitz frontier agreement concluded
between Poland and the G.D.R. on July 6, 1950, mention may be
made in particular of the treaty of June 29, 1945, between the
Soviet Union and Czechoslovakia on cession of the Carpathian
Ukraine and the frontier agreement of August 16, 1645, between
the Soviet Union and Poland on the delimitation of the Polish-
Soviet frontier along the Curzon line. The treaty of February 15,
1961, between the Soviet Union and Poland on the exchange of
parts of their national territories should also be mentioned.

The political treaties are supplemented by numerous bilateral
pacts which regulate relations between the Soviet Union and the
Eastern Central European countries in the fields of economy,
transport, culture, technology, social policy, and legal matters.[31]
The clauses on economic, scientific-technological, and cultural
co-operation in the bilateral pacts form, as it were, the foundation upon which rests this widely ramified pact system, which
extends far beyond the actual political sphere.

INTERPARTY RELATIONS AND THE BILATERAL PACTS

Interparty relations form an important complement to the
intergovernmental relations which have found expression in the
bilateral pact system.[32] These interparty relations result from
the dualistic structure of the communist states, characterized by
the preponderance of the party organization over the government organization under the "dictatorship of the proletariat."

Since 1956, interparty relations have become highly developed
both bilaterally and multilaterally. At first, joint party declarations were made separately in parallel with the government
agreements. Since the U.S.S.R. - G.D.R. joint party and government declaration of August 13, 1957, it has become customary, on
the pattern of the Soviet-Polish declaration of November 18,
1956, for government and party agreements to be produced in the
same document, which is termed a "declaration," "statement," or

"communiqué." Special importance has been attached to multilateral party relations since the end of 1957. It finds expression in the conferences of the first secretaries of the parties, of the heads of parties or governments, who generally meet before the conferences of the Warsaw Pact organization and those of CEMA, and who make the actual decisions. But even this supreme directive body of the Soviet hegemonic association has not remained free from polycentric tendencies. This has been shown particularly clearly by Rumania's rebellion against certain of CEMA's decisions. This trend has led to an upgrading of bilateral relations at both the party and the government level. Thus special importance is attached today to bilateral party agreements, apart from resolutions of multilateral party conferences, insofar as these conferences are restricted to the Soviet hegemonic association.

Since in communist states the bodies of the ruling party are government bodies in the widest sense of the word, both bilateral agreements and the multilateral arrangements must be regarded as agreements under international law. They reflect very clearly the hegemonic structure of the East European association of states under Moscow's leadership. In this sense party agreements constitute not only the political but also the legal core of the intergovernmental pact system in Eastern Europe.

NOTES

1. See Richard Lowenthal, "Bündnissysteme und nationale Interessen," *Politische Vierteljahresschrift*, V (1964), 95ff.

2. Kurt London, "The Socialist Commonwealth of Nations," *Orbis*, III (Winter, 1960), 424ff.

3. Boris Meissner, "Die interparteilichen Beziehungen im Ostblock und das Prinzip des proletarisch-sozialistischen Internationalismus," *Internationales Recht und Diplomatie*, VI (1961), 147ff.

4. See H. Triepel, *Die Hegemonie, Ein Buch von führenden Staaten* (new ed.; Aachen, 1961).

5. A complete collection of the treaties concluded under Stalin is to be found in Boris Meissner, *Das Ostpaktsystem* (Cologne, 1955).

6. Boris Meissner (ed.), *Der Warschauer Pakt* (Cologne, 1962); A. Uschakow, *Der Rat für gegenseitige Wirtschaftshilfe* (Cologne, 1962).

7. A. Uschakow, "Das bilaterale Paktsystem der europäischen Ostblockstaaten, die Vereinten Nationen und das sozialistische Völkerrecht," *Internationales Recht und Diplomatie*, VIII (1963), 91.

8. See the lecture by the author on "Sowjetische Hegemonie und Osteuropäische Föderation," which is to appear shortly in a collection published by the Otto Suhr-Institut of the Free University of Berlin.

9. Text of press interview given by Dimitrov, and comment by *Pravda* on January 28, 1948, in Meissner, *Das Ostpaktsystem*, pp. 15–16.

10. V. Dedijer, *Tito* (Berlin, 1953), pp. 315–16; M. Djilas, *Gespräche mit Stalin* (Frankfurt-on-Main, 1962), p. 225.

11. Text of the Soviet Government Declaration of October 30, 1956, "On the Bases for the Development and Further Consolidation of Friendship and Cooperation: Between the Soviet Union and the Other Socialist States," in *Internationales Recht und Diplomatie*, III (1958), 63ff.

12. Meissner, "Die interparteilichen Beziehungen," pp. 151ff.

13. A complete collection of the agreements concluded between the U.S.S.R. and the D.D.R. is to be found in *Internationales Recht und Diplomatie*, IV (1959), and X (1965).

14. Boris Meissner, *Russland, die Westmächte und Deutschland* (Hamburg, 1953), pp. 213ff.

15. Text of the agreement and complete documentation of the Warsaw Pact organization in Meissner, *Der Warschauer Pakt*, pp. 97ff.

16. See H. H. Mahnke, "Der Beistandspakt zwischen der Sowjetunion und der 'DDR' vom 12. Juni 1964," *Internationales Recht und Diplomatie*, X.

17. Boris Meissner, *Der Parteiprogramm der KPDSU 1903 bis 1964* (Cologne, 1962), p. 48.

18. For a closer conceptional definition of these types of treaties see P. Barandon, *Das System der politischen Staatsverträge* (Stuttgart, 1937), pp. 189 and 211ff.

19. See: Wladyslaw W. Kulski, "The Soviet System of Collective Security Compared with the Western System," *The American Journal of International Law*, XLIV (1950), 453ff; N. V. Zacharova, "Dvustoronnie dogovory o družbe, sotrudničestve i vsaimopomošči" ("Bilateral Agreements of Friendship, Cooperation and Assistance"), in V. M. Šuršalov (ed.), *Meždunarodno-pravovye formy sotrudničestva socialističeskich gosudarstv* (*Forms of Cooperation between Socialist States under International Law*) (Moscow, 1962), pp. 78ff.

20. Original Russian text: *Vedomosti Verchovnogo Soveta SSSR* (*Gazette of the Supreme Soviet of the U.S.S.R.*), No. 1 (1964) Article 1 (hereafter cited as *VVS SSSR*).

21. Original Russian text: *VVS SSSR*, No. 21 (1965), Article 327.

22. Meissner, *Der Warschauer Pakt*, p. 42.

23. V. K. Sobakin, *Kollektivnaja bezopastnost'—garantija mirnogo sosuščestvovanija* (*Collective Security—the Guarantee of Peaceful Co-existence*) (Moscow, 1962), pp. 373–74; R. Yakemtchouk, "Sowjetunion und regionale Sicherheitsabkommen," *Osteuropa-Recht*, II (1956), 192–93; Uschakow, "Das bilaterale Paktsystem," pp. 81ff.

24. Boris Meissner, *Sowjetunion und Selbstbestimmungerecht* (Cologne, 1962), pp. 83ff.

25. Uschakow, "Das bilaterale Paktsystem," p. 84.

26. N. Scheuner, "Kollektive Selbstverteidigung," in *Strupp-Schlochauer, Wörterbuch des Völkerrechts* (Berlin, 1961), II, 241.

27. Boris Meissner, "Deutschland war nicht vertreten," *Die Welt*, July 17, 1965; G. Meyer-Lindenberg, "Germany's Frontiers: The Evidence of International Law," *Internationales Recht und Diplomatie*, IX, 19ff.

28. A. A. Anisimov, "K voprosu o suverenitete Germanii" ("On the Question of the Sovereignty of Germany"), *Sovetskoe gosudarstvo i pravo* (*Soviet State and Law*), No. 5 (1949), pp. 14ff.

29. Text of the forces' agreements in Meissner, *Der Warschauer Pakt*, pp. 117ff.

30. Text in Meissner, *Das Ostpaktsystem*, pp. 51ff.

31. See contributions by E. T. Usenko and A. T. Poltorak in Šuršalov, *Meždunarodo-pravovye formy sotrudničestva socialističeskich gosudarstv*, pp. 164ff. and 318ff. On the legal aid conventions see V. S. Tadevosjan (ed.), *Pravovoe sotrudničestvo meždu socialističeskimi gosudarstvami (Legal Cooperation between the Socialist States)* (Moscow, 1962).

32. Meissner, "Die interparteilichen Beziehungen," pp. 151ff.

Eastern Europe, Asia, and the Sino-Soviet Conflict

Chapter VI.

11. Rumania and the Sino-Soviet Conflict

Stephen Fischer-Galati

On March 24, 1965, Nicolae Ceauşescu delivered the principal funeral oration at the grave of Gheorghe Gheorghiu-Dej. The eulogy of his predecessor as head of the Rumanian Workers' Party contained, *inter alia,* an unequivocal restatement of the fundamental principles of Rumanian foreign policy spelled out in the now celebrated Statement of April, 1964.[1] These very principles—unity of the socialist camp, peaceful coexistence among states with differing social orders, respect for national independence and sovereignty, equality of all peoples, nonintervention in internal affairs—have been interpreted by Kremlinologists and other students of international affairs as expressions of the nationalistic, anti-Russian tendencies of a Rumanian leadership determined to turn the contradictions in the communist world to its own advantage.

The exponents of this interpretation have emphasized the growing friction between Russia and Rumania over economic integration under CEMA, the historic Russo-Rumanian antagonisms, and the effects of the Sino-Soviet conflict as the determining factors in the adoption of the so-called independent Rumanian course.[2] They have repeatedly cited the *de facto* Rumanian rejection of CEMA decisions in March, 1963, and subsequent anti-Russian manifestations—particularly those with a pro-Chinese character—as evidence to support their theory. The purpose of this paper is to evaluate these contentions, primarily in the light of the Sino-Soviet conflict.

There can be little doubt that the Rumanian course is essentially one of independence from the Soviet Union. Numerous intricate factors, however, modify this broad generalization. For instance, any invocation of the "historic tradition" requires a careful definition of terms.[3] The stereotyped view that the Rumanians have always been anti-Russian and that Russia has always sought the incorporation of Rumanian territories into her empire is incorrect. The nationalistic, revisionist trends, particularly evident after the reannexation of southern Bessarabia in 1878, did not reflect the sentiments of the Rumanian masses. Indeed, throughout the nineteenth century and as late as 1945 a substantial segment of the peasantry, working class, and urban intelligentsia looked upon Russia—csarist or Bolshevik—as a source of inspiration for their own efforts to free themselves from domestic or foreign oppression. The emancipation edict of Alexander II in 1861 served as a prototype for Alexandru Ion Cuza's three years later; the Russian revolution of 1905 did influence the timing of the Rumanian peasant revolts of 1907. The events of 1917 did trigger the uprisings that forced the Rumanian monarchy to promise drastic land reform at the end of the war. These interrelationships were understood by the peasantry. Similarly, the rising industrial working class was sympathetic toward the Soviet Union during the interwar years even after the dissolution of the Rumanian Communist Party in the 1920's. And it is well known that a substantial segment of the intelligentsia regarded the Soviet Union as a possible savior from German domination in the thirties and early years of World War II. To these social groups the issues of territorial revisionism which became the principal *raison de guerre* of the Antonescu regime in 1941 were of virtually no significance. The noteworthy fact is that the Rumanian population at large became anti-Russian only after the "liberation" of their country in August, 1944, and, most significantly, through association of the detested Rumanian communist regime with Soviet sponsorship. A "historic" justification for the current Rumanian course cannot be based on an assumed popular anti-Russian tradition. Thus, any meaningful analysis of the current "nationalist" trends must revolve around the postwar relationship between the Rumanian and Russian parties.

THE INTERNAL POWER STRUGGLE

The origins of the conflict between the current Rumanian leadership and the Kremlin have been traced to a series of events dating back to the end of World War II. The latest theory, advanced by the Rumanians themselves, is that pro-Stalinist elements of the illegal Rumanian Communist Party sought the assassination of Gheorghiu-Dej and his imprisoned associates in the spring of 1944.[4] It was subsequently revealed that the leaders of this conspiracy, designed to eliminate the hard core of the Rumanian organization and to allow complete control of the movement by a Moscow-trained group, were connected in one way or another with the "antiparty group" purged in 1952. Whether true or not, the story is indicative of a struggle for power which started shortly after the installation of the communist-dominated Groza government in 1945 and lasted at least until 1957.

There is general agreement among students of the Rumanian Party that the Moscow group, headed by Ana Pauker, enjoyed more power between 1945 and 1952 than the so-called Rumanian group led by Gheorghiu-Dej. The precise nature and extent of the conflict between these factions remains, however, obscure. According to recent Rumanian statements, Ana Pauker and her associates betrayed both the principles and long-range plans contained in the party statutes, program, and resolutions adopted at the first postwar Conference of the Rumanian Communist Party in 1945.[5] The documents of 1945 are now recognized as the expression of the party's historic aims, as the blueprint for the attainment of national and communist goals: the construction of socialism in Rumania. Significantly, in 1952 Gheorghiu-Dej accused Ana Pauker and the "antiparty group" of violating the principles adopted in 1945. More significant, however, is the exclusion to this day of errors in foreign policy from the long list of "deviations" attributed to the deposed clique. The Rumanians have been most reticent about providing any information that would substantiate the view that Gheorghiu-Dej had favored Dimitrov's schemes for reorganization of the bloc, or displayed pro-Titoist tendencies, or shown any inclinations toward closer economic contacts with the West before 1955. While it is possible that Gheorghiu-Dej and his close associates were more resentful of Rumania's economic exploitation by the Soviet Union than Ana Pauker and her colleagues were, it would appear that the principal element in the struggle for power between the "Rumanian" and "Moscow" groups was the seizure of control of the party apparatus.

In terms of Gheorghiu-Dej's subsequent actions and statements it is certain that the coup, although long contemplated, was staged only at a time when the "objective conditions" for success were assured. The "objective conditions" were not favorable for the adoption of any course essentially different from the Pauker group's, but they did permit the substitution of one set of leaders for another. Stalin's preoccupation with the Korean War and the assurances given by Gheorghiu-Dej of even closer economic, political, and cultural Russo-Rumanian co-operation insured approval of the change of leadership in 1952. One major unresolved question remains: Were Gheorghiu-Dej's later policies formulated to any extent in 1952?

The evidence is inconclusive. Considered retrospectively, a better case may be made for a potentially Titoist position. Discounting, but not necessarily rejecting, the validity of later rumors to the effect that Stalin was contemplating the purging of Gheorghiu-Dej in 1948 for alleged pro-Titoist proclivities, the positive case can best be based on the political indictment of Ana Pauker and her associates. Gheorghiu-Dej justified the purges in terms of deviations from the party program of 1945 and proclaimed the attainment of the goals formulated in that year as the *raison d'être* for the new leadership and the party in general.[6] Specifically, two fundamental concepts of what may be described as "communist nationalism" emerged: first, that the Rumanian party was the democratic political organization of all Rumanians, no longer divorced from the masses; second, that the democratic party was dedicated to the construction of socialism in the Rumanian People's Republic through the industrialization of the country and the socialist transformation of agriculture. In short, the attainment of socialism was the *national* goal of a party representing and acting for all the inhabitants of Rumania.

On the other hand, there is no evidence to prove that in 1952 Gheorghiu-Dej regarded dependence on the Soviet Union as incompatible with the attainment of these goals. It could be demonstrated convincingly that the change in the international "objective conditions" following Stalin's death determined the Rumanian course to an infinitely greater extent than Gheorghiu-Dej's actions or inclinations. In fact, it is clear that until 1955 the new leadership was far more concerned with consolidation of internal power and carrying out inherited domestic economic policies than with exploitation of the international consequences of Stalin's death. The liquidation of the suspect intellectual wing of the party once headed by Lucreţiu Pătrăşcanu, further elimination from the party ranks of pro-Pauker cadres, and the strengthening of the Gheorghiu-Dej coterie through promotion of the technocratic intelligentsia—all carried out between 1952 and 1955—had priority over the belated adoption of the "new economic course" in 1953 and manifestations of ever-so-slight independence from the U.S.S.R.

The current Rumanian views on the events of 1952–55 tend to suggest that Gheorghiu-Dej was merely clearing the decks for later action. While this explanation is plausible in terms of post-1955 developments, it presupposes exceptional farsightedness by an untested leadership not known for its sophistication. Still, whether Gheorghiu-Dej had been actually awaiting the right moment or whether he merely recognized it when it came, the evidence irrefutably supports the contention that he and his associates formulated the essential arguments of 1964 in 1955.

THE PARTY CONGRESSES OF 1955 AND 1960

At the Rumanian Communist Party's second Congress in December, 1955, Gheorghiu-Dej stated unequivocally that the national goal of the socialist transformation of Rumania would have to be attained in co-operation with members of the socialist camp rather than through subordination of the interests of individual national communist states to those of the camp as a whole. The socialist community would have to develop "relations of a new type based on mutual respect for state sovereignty, equality of rights for all countries, and respect for national characteristics." Relations with non-socialist countries would also have to be altered and be based on the principles of "respect for national sovereignty, equality of rights of all nations, non-aggression and peaceful settlement of all problems, peaceful coexistence among countries with different social systems, and non-interference in internal affairs."[7]

It has been suggested that these statements and ensuing actions —most notably the *rapprochement* with Yugoslavia and the cautious search for economic ties with the West—were possible only because of the liberalization of Soviet views on peaceful coexistence, on intercamp relations, and on the Yugoslav "heresy." There can be little doubt that the "spirit of Geneva," the establishment of friendly relations "of the new type" between Moscow and Belgrade, and Khrushchev's views as expressed at the Twentieth CPSU Congress were all exploited by the Rumanian leaders. However, a careful chronological review of Rumanian speeches and actions would indicate that Gheorghiu-Dej's formulae antedate Khrushchev's and that their timing may indeed have been influenced by contemporary Chinese positions. Indeed, the Chinese view that "communist-governed states should be free from Soviet interference in their internal affairs and should make their voices heard in matters of common concern, but should acknowledge the primacy of the Soviet Union in the making and execution of a common policy" was given extensive Rumanian press coverage in 1956.[8] Rumania's rejection of Peking's condemnation of Titoism would not necessarily invalidate that supposition, for Gheorghiu-Dej consistently thereafter selected only those elements of Chinese doctrine that could strengthen his own position vis-à-vis Moscow. The essential fact, however, is that between December, 1955, and October, 1956, Gheorghiu-Dej and his lieutenants repeatedly stressed the importance of national and historic conditions in socialist construction, of co-operation among members of the socialist camp, and of the extension of friendly relations "of the new type" with all nations. The principles of non-interference in Rumania's internal affairs and equality of all nations were underlined on every occasion.

It is demonstrable that even during the period of temporary depolycentrization following the Hungarian revolution, the Rumanian regime did not abandon the principles enunciated in 1955. As early as December, 1956, Gheorghiu-Dej reiterated the necessity of attaining the national goal of socialist construction as rapidly as possible in accordance with the policies adopted at the Second Congress of 1955.[9] If anything, faced with the threat of renewed interference in internal affairs under the aegis of a reactivated CEMA, and consequent frustration of the goals of 1955, the Rumanians were seeking new avenues for independent action within the limits of maneuverability afforded by the principles of "peaceful coexistence" and "unity of the socialist camp." It can also be demonstrated that these actions were essentially anti-Russian, even though superficially Gheorghiu-Dej continued to be a faithful supporter of Khrushchev's policies.

The formulation of the so-called Stoica Plan for peaceful multilateral co-operation among Balkan nations in the fall of 1957, the conclusion of extra-CEMA agreements with non-committed and even West European nations in 1958, and the seemingly unrelated but most significant final elimination of the vestiges of the "Moscow group" in the party in 1957 and securing of the withdrawal of the Russian armed forces from Rumania in 1958 provided the "objective conditions" for the eventual implementation of the goals of 1955. The concurrent intensified drive for more rapid industrial development, with resultant improvement in the standard of living, was ultimately aimed at preventing the country's economic exploitation by Moscow for the benefit of the U.S.S.R. and her more industrialized satellites. The same motive prompted the refinement of the doctrines of 1955 at the Third Party Congress in 1960; but the "objective conditions"—partly created by the Rumanian leadership, partly by Russia's relations with the West, and partly by the Sino-Soviet conflict—made their reformulation possible at that time.[10]

The essential difference between the views contained in Gheorghiu-Dej's report to the Third Congress from those propounded in the Second was assignment of the paramount role in the socialist transformation of Rumania since 1945 to the Rumanian Workers' Party. Attributing Rumania's impressive achievements to the co-operative efforts of the Rumanian people and the nationally oriented communist leadership, the Workers' Party in effect assumed the mantle of executor of, and heir to, a historic legacy identified with the construction of an economically powerful, independent Rumania.[11] The national interest was clearly placed above that of the socialist camp, all statements referring to the unity of the socialist community notwithstanding. The strength of the camp, according to Gheorghiu-Dej, was measured in terms of the strength of its members. And the leadership of each member-country was best qualified to determine the potential of each nation and to seek the realization of that potential for the ultimate benefit of each nation and consequently of the socialist community in general. The execution of the necessary policies had, of course, to be conducted according to the blueprint drawn in 1955—relations of the new type, peaceful coexistence, non-interference in internal affairs.

The nationalistic, anti-Russian position contained in Gheorghiu-Dej's report surpassed its antecedents to the extent that the Rumanian leaders sought to stimulate the anti-Russian sentiments of the population and to exonerate themselves of any complicity with the "Moscow group," now violently condemned and held responsible for the retardation of the process of socialist construction in Rumania by and for the Rumanian people. It must be emphasized, however, that this declaration was one of socialist interdependence rather than of independence from Russia and the bloc, and that it was restricted to "socialist"-nationalist rather than "bourgeois"-nationalist aspirations. Such bourgeois aspects of nationalism as establishment of closer cultural and political ties with the non-socialist world or territorial revisionism were actually condemned by Gheorghiu-Dej and his associates in 1960. But even such a limited doctrine of national communism could not have been formulated and implemented without correct appraisal of the external "objective factors."

THE FACTS AND OPPORTUNITIES OF INTERNATIONAL LIFE

It is now evident that the Rumanians acted on the basis of a conclusion reached as early as 1957: that the Russo-Chinese rivalry and Moscow's policies of peaceful coexistence with the West were both unalterable facts of political life. Those opportunities, compatible with the Rumanian party's interests which could be derived from these two conditions, were to be exploited. It is also evident that between 1957 and 1960 the Rumanian party was too concerned with its own security to allow more than economic contacts with an essentially hostile West. Thus, pending the development of better relations between party and masses on the one hand and, on the other, the West's readiness to recognize the legitimacy and permanency of the Rumanian communist regime, and to engage in economic exchanges the Rumanian leaders could take only limited advantage of the possibilities for economic contacts with non-CEMA nations afforded by the doctrine of peaceful coexistence.

The opportunities to be found in the rapidly developing Sino-Soviet conflict between 1957 and 1960 were also limited: The existence of ideological differences permitted some maneuverability but aroused no expectation of deriving direct and far-reaching benefits from supporting either Russia or China. The most that can be said for Rumanian policies in these years is that the regime, while fundamentally unsympathetic to the Chinese posi-

tions, took advantage of Peking's opposition to Russian domination of the socialist world and Russia's unwillingness to allow the
splitting of the camp into two or more factions to pursue its own
policies in line with its own reading of the Moscow Declaration
and Statement of 1957 and 1960.[12] The Rumanian interpretation
of these fundamental statements of international communist policy was clearly closer to Moscow's than to Peking's, although it
was anti-Russian to the extent to which the aims of Rumanian
national communism were incompatible with Khrushchev's plans
for CEMA integration.

Gheorghiu-Dej, however, was too much of a realist to delude
himself into believing that Moscow would alter its economic
plans for Eastern Europe merely because of ideological conflicts
with the Chinese. Nor would Rumanian support of the basic
Russian policies vis-à-vis the West and condemnation of Chinese
dogmatism sway the Kremlin. The only factor that could possibly
result in an acceptance of the Rumanian position by Moscow was
recognition of the growing industrial power of Rumania. Such
industrial growth would also strengthen Rumania's political
voice in the socialist camp and permit it to play a more decisive
role in determining policies affecting the socialist community as a
whole and in any case Rumanian policies per se.

Thus, the decisions of the Third Party Congress of 1960,
reinforced by the Moscow Statement of that year and the Rumanian interpretation of it, were designed to transform Rumania into a powerful member of the socialist camp—perhaps
even of the international community as a whole—through rapid
construction of socialism. But while the regime assigned priority
to the gaining of a leading role within the socialist community,
choosing—also for internal political reasons—to limit its contacts with the West, it is evident that the leadership clearly
envisaged the alternative of increasingly closer ties with the West
in the event that its intercamp maneuvers failed. As long as the
Rumanian economy was overwhelmingly dependent on Russian
resources and equipment and was generally bloc-oriented, independent action was clearly circumscribed. And China had nothing
to offer economically. By 1961 the Rumanian course had undergone further alterations, whose full significance did not become
evident until two years later.

Although Rumania's freedom of action was severely restricted by the Berlin crisis of 1961 and the intensification of the Cold War prior to the Cuban confrontation in 1962, Gheorghiu-Dej's regime resisted as best it could the growing Russian, Czech, and East German pressures for economic integration of the bloc under a formula detrimental to Rumania's national interests. But the constant reiteration of the Rumanian views favoring loose co-ordination through integration of the national economies of member-nations, as opposed to tightly co-ordinated economic development through CEMA, failed to convince Khrushchev and his more advanced economic partners.[13] It may indeed be stated that the CEMA communiqué of June, 1962, stressing subordination of national to bloc interests—a position reiterated by Khrushchev following an "inspection" of Rumania's new industries at the end of that very month—was regarded by the Rumanian leadership as proof that economic progress alone would not be a determining factor in the formulation of bloc policies. In anticipation of these developments the Rumanians had intensified their search for potential and actual economic partners in the West since 1961 and had redoubled their efforts to win the support of the masses through political and economic concessions and reaffirmation of the party's paramount role in the struggle for attainment of the national goal. The gradual release of political prisoners, the re-establishment of cultural ties with the West, most notably with France, and the rewriting of the history of Rumania's "liberation" and subsequent evolution in a manner designed to arouse the nationalist and potentially anti-Russian sentiments of the population were all calculated to strengthen Rumania's position in a possible showdown with Moscow.[14] It is noteworthy, however, that as long as the Gheorghiu-Dej regime still entertained some expectation of reaching a satisfactory compromise with its CEMA partners and believed that Khrushchev might be influenced by Bucharest's loyalty when making a final decision on Rumania's role in the camp, no attempt was made to exploit the Sino-Soviet conflict beyond endorsing current Russian positions in 1961 and 1962.[15]

Two major events crystallized the course of Rumanian policy in the following few months: the Cuban confrontation, with the consequent exacerbation of the Sino-Soviet conflict and polycentric tendencies in the socialist community, and Russia's continuing insistence on pursuing its plans for CEMA in a manner contrary to Rumanian interests. Apparently convinced that Moscow's retaliatory power was weakened in the aftermath of Cuba, the Rumanians intensified their efforts to seek closer economic ties with the West. At the same time, they veered more and more into a position of neutrality in the Sino-Soviet conflict in the expectation of becoming mediators in a dispute that threatened to disrupt the unity of the camp. Both policies were clearly designed to strengthen their leverage on Moscow. Thus, when the Russians refused to accept the Rumanian position on CEMA integration in March, 1963, the Rumanians publicly denounced the decision of the majority as incompatible with theirs. And as the Russian efforts to placate Gheorghiu-Dej were deemed too little and too late, the Rumanians embarked openly on the pursuit of what has now come to be known as the Rumanian independent course.

Since 1963 the evolution of this course, rooted in ideas and actions developed from at least as early as 1955, has been more tortuous than is generally assumed. It must be noted that even after the showdown of 1963 the Rumanians attached priority to the attainment of a powerful position within the socialist camp. The now well-known actions of 1963 and 1964, characterized by renewal of correct, even friendly ties with ostracized Albania, publication of the anti-Russian "25 Chinese Points," and finally, the overt but unsuccessful attempt to mediate the Sino-Soviet conflict, were all determined not by any sympathy with the Chinese ideological positions—other than those challenging Russia's domination of the camp—but by the belief that if successful, Rumania would become the leader of a "third force" in the international communist movement.[16] The unwillingness of the Chinese to reconcile their differences with Moscow and accept the Russian-backed proposals submitted by the Rumanians in March, 1964, led directly to the issuance of the Statement of April, 1964, and to the redefining of the means whereby Rumania could attain its national communist goals. Indeed, the Chinese rebuff of the Rumanian plan for reconciliation lessened her usefulness to the Soviet Union and virtually precluded the possibility of wresting meaningful concessions from Moscow and Moscow's faithful allies. Russia's partners in CEMA, who generally endorsed the Russian plans and resented Rumania's policies as those of an opportunistic upstart, became, if anything, more reluctant than ever to subscribe to Rumania's views on economic integration, to accept her as a leading member of the bloc or of a "third force" in the socialist camp. Thus, faced with the possibility of economic retaliation and isolation, the Rumanian Communist Party issued the now well-known declaration proclaiming its independence in the formulation and conduct of domestic and foreign affairs—albeit as a loyal member of the socialist community—and accelerated its efforts to "build bridges" to a much more responsive West.

The coolness in Russo-Rumanian relations, evident after Rumania's rejection of Khrushchev's plans for economic integration, became more acute after April, 1964. The strains were aggravated by the stimulation and exploitation of the anti-Russian feelings of the masses and the pursuit by the Gheorghiu-Dej regime of a campaign of denigration of csarist Russia's historic relations with Rumania with a view to establishing a claim for the restitution of Bessarabia.[17] For indeed, the Rumanian regime having decided to embark on a policy of close economic and cultural relations with the West and having become convinced that its internal security would not be jeopardized by a population endorsing an independent and in effect anti-Russian course, Gheorghiu-Dej felt sufficiently secure in the post-Cuban atmosphere to curtail all ties with the U.S.S.R. and extend his concept of the party's heritage of the Rumanian historic tradition to include even that of the territorial revendications previously identified with "bourgeois nationalism."

The reopening of the Bessarabian question in 1964, the most daring manifestation of the Rumanian course, is also most illustrative of its nature. Whether the question was raised in response to Russian encouragement of Hungarian revisionism in Transylvania, whether the regime is seeking the total fulfilment of the national historic legacy, or whether—as has been suggested—it tries to link Rumanian with Chinese revisionism in the expectation of eventual territorial adjustments in the communist world, its significance lies in its ever having been raised at all. Indeed, this overt challenge to the Soviet Union would have been inconceivable had not Gheorghiu-Dej and his associates felt immune from retaliation, ultimately because of the "objective conditions" created by the Sino-Soviet conflict.

While the Rumanians are in reality defying both Peking and Moscow, they realize that as long as the Soviet Union is unwilling to break with China they are safe from meaningful retaliatory action. In fact, the defiance of the U.S.S.R. and her East European partners is not based on the expectation that the West would bail out Rumania in the event of a showdown with Moscow, but rather on the belief that the Kremlin would not act because of certain Chinese reaction against any drastic measures directed against a member of the socialist camp sharing anti-Russian interests. Thus the Rumanians can afford to keep the territorial issue alive. Similarly, Russian toleration and the matching of extensive Western investments in an independent Rumanian industrial economy, in the face of continuing Rumanian resistance to simultaneous Russian counterpressures, even during the current Vietnamese crisis, can best be explained in terms of the Sino-Soviet conflict.

It may seem paradoxical that the socialist nation which renders the least assistance toward the attainment of Chinese goals in Asia and which is most closely connected with the mortal enemies of Peking, the "Western imperialists and capitalists," should be the greatest beneficiary of that conflict. It may seem as paradoxical that the supreme defier of the principle of the unity of the socialist camp should be its foremost theoretical advocate. But this is hardly a paradox at all: Under the umbrella provided by the Sino-Soviet conflict and its repercussions, the Rumanians have found the way to derive the greatest benefits. Gheorghiu-Dej's diagnoses of 1955, 1957, 1960, and 1962—that peaceful coexistence and the unity of the socialist camp are by no means incompatible with Rumania's interests, but rather should be exploited to the hilt—are still valid after his death. And Rumania will benefit, whatever her ultimate choice—either as a friend of China or of the West, or as a supporter of Moscow's views on peaceful coexistence and the unity of the international communist movement. The objective conditions, international and national, have been masterfully exploited by Gheorghiu-Dej and his successors and provide the ultimate explanation for Rumania's unique position in the socialist camp.

NOTES

1. Ceauşescu's speech in *Scînteia*, No. 6569, March 25, 1965. Cf. *Statement on the Stand of the Rumanian Workers' Party Concerning the Problems of the World Communist and Working-Class Movement* (Bucharest, 1964).

2. The best and most comprehensive statement to date is by Ghita Ionescu, *Communism in Rumania 1944–1962* (London, 1964).

3. No entirely satisfactory account of the historic relations between Russia and Rumania is available. N. Iorga's chapters in *Istoria Românilor* (Bucharest, 1936–39), generally regarded as the definitive statement by a prewar historian, suffer from strong anti-Russian bias. The once authoritative communist interpretation contained in P. Constantinescu-Iaşi, *Relaţiile culturale romîno-ruse din trecut* (Bucharest, 1954) has been substantially revised by Rumanian historians in recent years. The latest Rumanian version—covering, however, only the period through 1878—is most explicitly stated in Volumes II, III and IV of *Istoria Romîniei* (Bucharest, 1960–   ).

4. Most clearly expressed in *Formarea statului naţional român. Lupta poporului român pentru independenţa naţională* (Bucharest, 1964), pp. 58–65.

5. This version was first made known in substantial detail by Gheorghiu-Dej himself in his "Report to the Central Committee of the Rumanian Workers' Party, November 30–December 5, 1961," *Scînteia*, No. 5371 (December 7, 1961). The original indictment of Ana Pauker and her associates may be found in Alexandru Moghioroş's article in the June 6, 1952, issue of *For a Lasting Peace, for a People's Democracy*.

6. Gheorghe Gheorghiu-Dej, "Bericht über den Entwurf der Verfassung der Rumänischen Volksrepublik vor der Grossen Nationalversammlung am 23 September 1952," *Artikel und Reden* (Berlin, 1955), pp. 361ff.

7. Gheorghe Gheorghiu-Dej, "Raportul de activitate al Comitetului Central al Partidului Muncitoresc Romîn la Congresul al II-lea al Partidului din 23 decembrie 1955," *Articole şi cuvîntări (decembrie 1955-iulie 1959)* (Bucharest, 1959), p. 18. Gheorghiu-Dej's complete report to the Second Congress, containing a penetrating review of post-1952 conditions and problems, may be found in the same publication on pp. 6ff.

8. G. F. Hudson, Richard Lowenthal, and Roderick MacFarquhar, *The Sino-Soviet Dispute* (New York: Frederick A. Praeger, 1963), pp. 2–3. See also the very revealing editorial, "Salut frăţesc Congresului Partidului Comunist Chinez," *Scînteia*, No. 3701 (September 15, 1956).

9. Even more interesting than Gheorghiu-Dej's statement is the penetrating editorial contained in *Scînteia*, No. 3792 (December 31, 1956), entitled "Pentru contnua imbunătăţire a traiului oamenilor muncii."

10. On these points consult Gheorghiu-Dej's fundamental statement contained in his report presented to a special session of the Grand National Assembly on August 30, 1960, "Situaţia internaţională şi politica externă a Republicii Populare Romîne," *Articole şi cuvîntări (august 1959-mai 1961)* (Bucharest, 1961), pp. 208–29.

11. Gheorghiu-Dej, "Raportul C. C. al P. M. R. cu privire la activitatea partidului în perioada dintre congresul al II-lea şi congresul al III-lea al partidului, cu privire la planul de dezvoltare a economiei naţionale pe anii 1960–1965 şi la schiţa planului economic de perspectivă pe 15 ani," *ibid.*, pp. 97ff.

12. Consult two basic statements by Gheorghiu-Dej: "Dare de seamă prezentată la plenara C. C. al P. M. R. din 19–20 decembrie 1960 asupra lucrărilor

consfătuirii partidelor comuniste şi muncitoreşti de la Moscova din noiembrie 1960," *ibid.*, pp. 337–45, and "Lagărul socialist—forţa conducătoare a dezvoltării internaţionale," *Probleme ale păcii şi socialismului*, No. 1 (29) (January, 1961).

13. The Rumanian position is clearly stated in the editorial "Bun sosit, dragi oaspeţi sovieticii," *Scînteia*, No. 5562 (June 17, 1962). Khrushchev's views are equally clearly expressed in a speech made in Rumania on June 24, in *Scînteia*, No. 5570 (June 25, 1962).

14. Almost every issue of *Scînteia* after July, 1962, contained articles or editorials on one or another aspect of "liberalization."

15. Most revealing is Gheorghiu-Dej's speech on the occasion of the "Fifteenth Anniversary of the Rumanian People's Republic," contained in *Scînteia*, No. 5758 (December 30, 1962).

16. Apart from Gheorghiu-Dej's summary statement contained in his speech "A XX-a aniversare a eliberării României de sub jugul fascist," *Scînteia*, No. 6357 (August 23, 1964), extremely valuable bits of information may be found in the issues of *Scînteia* immediately antedating the "Twentieth Anniversary of Rumania's Liberation," in August, 1964.

17. Most striking in this connection was the publication in the fall of 1964 of Karl Marx's *Insemnări despre romăni* (Bucharest, 1964) under the editorship of the distinguished Marxist historian A. Oţetea. The volume, containing Marx's critical views on czarist imperialism, was designed to justify Rumania's claims to Bessarabia. It is also noteworthy that nearly thirty thousand copies of the book were sold within forty-eight hours after publication.

12. Eastern Europe's Relations with Asian Communist Countries

Ernst Kux

The communist grand design of a "socialist commonwealth," a "comity of fraternal socialist parties and countries," and a socialist world market" from the Elbe to the Pacific Ocean has remained a dream expressed in ideological propaganda slogans, at best a patchwork of disjointed organizational measures. The integration of communist countries with different national settings into a "World Soviet Socialist Republic"[1] was conceived at the outset as an important part of the communist utopia. Lenin was convinced "that the trend in the direction of establishing a unified world economy as a whole, regulated by the proletariat of all nations according to a common plan, would be further developed under socialism and brought to fulfillment."[2] Khrushchev forecast at the height of his power the ultimate emergence of a socialist world system without borders or economic barriers and with a common language.[3]

These grandiose expectations are further than ever from realization. Efforts at co-operation and co-ordination even among the neighboring communist states in Eastern Europe have foundered, and the gap between the East European and the Asian communist countries has widened. To weld together countries with such divergent national, economic, social, cultural, and religious roots and traditions into a unified communist camp, with a billion inhabitants, one third of the globe's population, and an anticipated share of more than half of the world's production, was from the beginning no modest undertaking. The unity of all the disparate communist states in Eastern Europe and Asia could be imposed neither by a process of *Gleichschaltung* from above under Stalin nor by assimilation through convergent economic development as attempted under Khrushchev. The concept of "new relations between states," unmarred by the disunity and "contradictions" that characterize capitalist state relations, has remained in the realm of theory, and the practical results of the

efforts to bring the "new relations" into being were Tito's break
with the Cominform and, in the recent period, a progressive
alienation of the communist countries of East and West under
the impact of the Sino-Soviet schism. The communist take-overs
in Asian countries and the emergence of the People's Republic of
China (C.P.R.), the Democratic People's Republic of Korea
(D.P.R.K.), and the Democratic Republic of Vietnam (D.R.V.)
did not in fact enlarge the power and influence of the communist
camp, but became in the event a decisive factor for disunity and
disruption within the bloc. The emergence of communist countries in Asia played an important role in shaping the relations of
the East European communist countries with one another, with
the Soviet Union, and with the West—a role at least as significant as those played by the Yugoslav example and Togliatti's
agitation for polycentrism. The Sino-Soviet conflict and the separation of the Eastern from the Western part of the communist
camp was a product also of the evident incompatibility between
European and Asian forms of communism.

We witness today on the one side a greater differentiation
among the East European communist countries, their growing
independence from Moscow, their response to the attractive force
of West European progress and an increase in their economic,
cultural, and even political ties with the West. On the other side,
the Asian communist countries have been drawn more tightly by
"silk threads" into Peking's orbit and have begun to reorient
their political and economic interests toward their Asian neighbors under the concepts of Asian-African solidarity, the "new
emerging forces," and anticolonialism, all with a certain racist
coloration and with purposeful exclusion of their "white" comrades from Soviet Russia and Eastern Europe. Neither Moscow
nor Peking, of course, in the power struggle for the leading role
in the communist bloc and the international communist movement, has given up its efforts to win adherents in the European
or Asia area: Moscow is backing its satellite Mongolia against
Chinese designs, is courting North Korea with some success
and still hopes to strengthen its influence in Hanoi. Peking, with
Albania as its miniature bridgehead and mouthpiece on the
European shore of the communist camp, is cultivating the image
of protector of Rumania's independence and is openly encouraging the assertion of national interests by the East European

communist countries against Soviet "great power chauvinism." The communist empire is thus disintegrating under the force of its inner contradictions, and its components are reorienting their relationships or looking toward the creation of new structures.

MONOLITHIC UNITY UNDER STALIN

The emergence of new communist states in Europe and Asia after World War II brought with it the problem of integrating these countries into a cohesive relationship with the Soviet Union. Stalin's concept of "monolithic unity" was an application of the *Gleichschaltung* of the Soviet republics in Central Asia, the Caucasus, the Ukraine, and the Baltic area into the multinational Soviet state. The mold of "people's democracy" was superimposed on the East European and the Asian communist states. A uniform system of one-party rule, centralized state power, economic planning with priority for heavy industry, monopoly of foreign trade, and "socialist realism" as the cultural guideline was forced upon these countries with conformity as the objective. A corresponding organizational pattern was adopted in the Asian communist countries, including China, which spoke with considerable fanfare in its propaganda about following the Soviet model. But the more or less identical "people's democratic" orders did not draw the East European and Asian countries closer together. Stalin, in order to secure his authority over the bloc, favored a system of bilateral relationships among the communist countries with Moscow as focal point. And the center of gravity of Stalin's interests was in Europe.

The network of interstate relationships had been firmly established in Stalin's East European empire before the advent of the communist states in Asia and their absorption into the communist bloc. The Democratic People's Republic of Korea was founded in September, 1948, the People's Republic of China came into being in October, 1949, and the Democratic Republic of Vietnam, constituted in October, 1946, was recognized by Peking and Moscow in January, 1950. Stalin had already concluded bilateral treaties of friendship and mutual aid with the East European countries—with Czechoslovakia in December, 1943, Poland in April, 1945, Hungary and Rumania in February, 1948, and Bulgaria in March, 1948. The treaty system was extended through similar bilateral treaties among the East European people's democracies themselves during 1948 and 1949 and through friendship treaties concluded by these countries with East Germany. Albania, less integrated in the system, signed a pact only with Bulgaria in December, 1947.[4] The Sino-Soviet treaty of friendship, alliance, and mutual assistance, signed in Moscow in February, 1950, was basically modeled after the East European pacts but remained apart from the pact system centered in Europe. The Chinese did not sign similar treaties of friendship and mutual aid with the European communist countries; they concluded only trade agreements with Czechoslovakia, Poland, and East Germany (1950), Hungary (1951), Bulgaria and Rumania (1952), and Albania (1954) and cultural agreements with Poland (April, 1951), Rumania (May, 1952), and Bulgaria (October, 1952).

During these years the Asian communist states played a secondary role in the bloc, not only in state relations but in party and economic relations. The Asian communist parties were not represented at the conference in Poland in September, 1947, which brought the Communist Information Bureau into being. The European states were bound together in the economic sphere in January, 1949, when the decision was taken to establish the Council for Economic Mutual Assistance (CEMA). The main clauses governing CEMA's activities—the "promotion of planned development of the economies of the member-countries"—were adopted at an economic conference in Moscow attended by representatives from Bulgaria, Hungary, Poland, Rumania, the Soviet Union, and Czechoslovakia; Albania became a member in February, 1949, and East Germany in September, 1950. Membership was available to "other European countries accepting the principles of CEMA." The Asian communist states were later associated with CEMA, but only in a passive role as observers. The members of Moscow's European bloc were linked militarily in the Warsaw Treaty Organization, established in May, 1955, with Albania, Bulgaria, East Germany, Hungary, Poland, Rumania, the Soviet Union, and Czechoslovakia as members. Thus, while organizational ties were tightened in the state, party, economic, and military spheres in Europe, the Asian "members of the socialist world system" followed Stalin's political course in internal and foreign policies but remained organizationally outside the core of the system during Stalin's lifetime.

THE SOCIALIST COMMONWEALTH

Stalin's death in 1953 and the ensuing power struggles in the Kremlin shattered the Soviet power structure in Eastern Europe and Asia and hastened the process of erosion of the monolith. Stalin's heirs were forced progressively to abandon Stalin's totalitarian control system and method of unification by *diktat* from above. The convulsions in the Soviet Union and its East European satellites on the one side and the temporary calming of the Asian scene with the cease-fires in Korea and Indochina in 1953–54 on the other side led to a growing presence and growing influence of the Asian countries within the communist camp. Khrushchev's visit to Peking and the withdrawal of Soviet controls in Manchuria and Sinkiang in accordance with the new Sino-Soviet treaty signed in Peking on October 12, 1954, underlined Peking's new stature as a more or less equal partner in a Sino-Soviet duumvirate. China's new role in the bloc came strikingly to the fore during the upheavals in Poland and Hungary in October, 1956, with Chou En-lai's trip to Warsaw, Budapest, and Moscow as would-be arbiter between the Soviet Union and its rebellious East European satellites. There remains some doubt as to the real influence of the Chinese in Eastern Europe during the developments in 1956, and the Chinese "help" probably existed more in the wishful imagination of the Poles and Hungarians than in fact. Yet the impact of "de-Stalinization" was felt in both the European and the Asian sectors of the communist world, and similar reactions produced popular unrest on both sides of the camp. Polish intellectuals were as much excited about the Chinese "hundred flowers" as were the Chinese and Vietnamese students by the articles in the Polish *Po Prostu.* The uprisings of 1956 did not stop in Poznań or Budapest; the reverberations were felt with no less violence in China and North Vietnam.[5]

Faced with the spector of far-reaching convulsions and a progressive dissolution of "monolithic unity" and party rule, all the communist power centers turned their energies toward stemming the further disintegration of the bloc. At the Meeting of Representatives of Communist and Workers Parties in Moscow in November, 1957, an attempt was made to reunify the communist parties and countries on the basis of "proletarian international-ism" and the "leading role of the Soviet Union." The ruling parties acted in concert as signers of the Moscow Declaration. But Chinese proposals for a new organization of the ruling parties and Mao Tse-tung's concept of "non-antagonistic contradictions" as an explanation and solution for the differences among commu-nist countries were not accepted. The only concrete step toward closer co-operation among the bloc parties was the inception in 1958 of the joint publication of *Problems of Peace and Socialism.*

Khrushchev, having consolidated his power at home with the purge of the "antiparty group," inaugurated a new concept of unification of the communist countries through assimilation of their economic development and a withering away of their na-tional differences by a leveling-off of their economic substruc-tures. In his speech in Bitterfield on July 9, 1958, Khrushchev presented—in "vulgar Marxist" terms—a euphoric forecast of co-operation and convergence of the communist countries:

> In order to speed up the advance of all socialist coun-tries to communism, we must do everything possible for each socialist country to develop its economy and in-crease its labor productivity more rapidly. . . .
>
> In the process of building communism, all socialist countries will equalize their economies, eliminate differ-ences in level of development, without taking the rela-tively underdeveloped countries as their criterion. . . . The equalization should and will proceed through the more rapid advance of the countries that are relatively less developed economically by bringing them up to the level of the most developed countries. Thus all the socialist countries will march in a common united front along the road of socialism, along the road of building a communist society.[6]

Also on the basis of converging economic development, the relations among communist countries were to take on a new form in what amounted to a "socialist commonwealth," as defined in 1955 in *Kommunist:*

A new, socialist type of international relations arose with the formation of the commonwealth of socialist states. These are relations of fully equal rights, genuine friendship, fraternal co-operation in the sphere of politics, economics and culture, and mutual assistance in the building of a new life. These relations are determined by the nature of the social-economic system of the countries of the socialist camp; by the unity of their fundamental interests and ultimate great aim, the building of communism; and by the single Marxist-Leninist world view of the communist and workers parties.[7]

As the new concept of a "socialist commonwealth" took root, the question of reconciling the differing economic conditions in Europe and Asia became operative. On the one side, the Chinese embarked on their own "road" of people's communes—a course they claimed would enable China to accelerate its entry into full communism, bypassing the conventional stages and outdistancing the economically more developed communist countries in Europe; on the Soviet side, the theory was pressed "that the European socialist countries, united in CEMA, will build a special economic zone and be the first to reach communism. The Asian socialist countries, which have much in common in their economic and cultural development, will build a second regional zone and reach communism together."[8] Khrushchev adjusted this concept at the Twenty-first CPSU congress in 1959 into one of "advancing shoulder to shoulder," and it became accepted theory that "the socialist countries, equalizing the levels of their economic and cultural development, in fact have the opportunity to pass over to communism more or less simultaneously."[9]

There began after the 1957 Moscow meeting a revitalization of the existing multilateral organizations, CEMA and the Warsaw Treaty Organization. The Warsaw Treaty of Friendship, Co-operation, and Mutual Aid, signed in May, 1955, had marked a first step away from Stalin's bilateral pact system toward a multilateral alliance of the Soviet Union and the East European countries.[10] It was in the same period, in April, 1955, that China and North Vietnam had participated in the Bandung Conference, which was to emerge as a significant turning point in the development of divergent European and Asian orientations within the bloc.[11] It is true that CEMA and the Warsaw Pact had not basically been designed as special instruments for developing a higher form of socialist unity. They had been conceived in the first instance as the Soviet bloc's response to Western economic and political developments—CEMA as the answer to the Marshall Plan and the beginning of West European economic integration, the Warsaw Pact as the answer to NATO. But both were to play key roles in the realignments within the bloc.

The starting point of the post-1957 efforts to revitalize the multilateral organizations was the Conference of Representatives of the Communist Parties of the CEMA Member States, held from May 20 to 23, 1958. With observers present from the Chinese, North Korean, and Mongolian CP's, the conference discussed "questions connected with the further development of economic co-operation among the socialist countries on the basis of gradual implementation of an international socialist division of labor and of rational specialization and co-ordination of production." It also heard reports on the work done by the socialist countries' state planning agencies in the drawing up of "long-range plans for the development of basic branches of the economy." The conference recognized a "need for further increasing the role of the Council for Economic Mutual Assistance," and the representatives of the Asian parties expressed their "readiness to participate actively in the economic co-operation among the socialist countries and also to strengthen this mutual co-operation in appropriate forms by implementing measures corresponding to the concrete conditions of their own countries."[12]

At about the same time, the Conference of the Political Consultative Committee of the Warsaw Pact was held in Moscow on May 24, 1958, with the participation of party first secretaries, prime ministers, and foreign and defense ministers of the member states. A high-ranking Chinese observer was present in the person of Politburo member and Deputy Premier, Chen Yun. The proposals adopted at this conference, with the consent of the Chinese Communist government, for the establishment of peace zones in Central Europe and in the Pacific area may well have been envisaged as first steps towards a closer co-operation between Communist China and the Warsaw Pact and an integration of their defenses.

Groundwork for closer co-operation between East European

and Asian communist countries on a multilateral basis had been laid in 1956 and 1957 through specialized international organizations:

1. The Joint Institute for Nuclear Research in Dubna was founded in March, 1956, by representatives of the eleven communist countries—North Vietnam became the twelfth member in September, 1956—to engage in joint research in peaceful uses of atomic energy. The costs were divided among the original eleven member-states as follows: the Soviet Union, 47.25 per cent; China, 20 per cent; East Germany and Poland, 6.75 per cent each; Rumania and Czechoslovakia, 5.75 per cent each; Hungary, 4 per cent; Bulgaria, 3.6 per cent; Albania, North Korea, and Mongolia, 0.05 per cent each. Some 200 scientists and technicians from all the member-countries are still working together in the institutes and laboratories in Dubna.[13]

2. The Railway Co-operation Organization (RCO) was established in June, 1956, in Sofia for co-ordination of rail and automotive transport, dealing especially with questions of construction norms, tariffs, routing, frontier-stations, etc. The leading and directing body of RCO is the assembly of the transportation ministers of Albania, Bulgaria, Hungary, North Vietnam, East Germany, China, North Korea, Mongolia, Poland, Rumania, Czechoslovakia, and the Soviet Union; the executive apparatus is directed by the committee for Railway Transport. A special commission is responsible for automobile transport and roads.

3. The Communications Co-operation Organization (CCO), in existence since December, 1957, promotes economic, scientific, and technical co-operation and co-ordination in the field of postal and telegraphic communications. This organization has no governing organs and functions as an annual conference of the communications ministers of the twelve communist countries in Eastern Europe and Asia. Cuba became a member in July, 1965.

A new relationship between East European and Asian communist countries began to grow. Treaties of friendship and co-operation were signed between China and East Germany in December, 1955, China and Czechoslovakia in March, 1957, Mongolia and Czechoslovakia in April, 1957, and China and Hungary in May, 1959. Consular and cultural agreements, goods exchanges, protocols for technical and scientific co-operation, exchanges of medical aid, and so forth were concluded between East European and Asian communist countries from 1958 on. Friendship societies came into being to promote cultural and visitors' exchanges. Swarms of delegations began to travel between Eastern Europe and Asia, and visits to the Asian countries became fashionable among members of the ruling strata in East Europe. Czech and Polish government delegations visited China, North Korea, North Vietnam, and Mongolia in March and April, 1957, followed by a Rumanian parliamentary delegation in May and a Bulgarian party-government delegation and a Czech parliamentary delegation in September–October, 1957. North Vietnamese leader Ho Chi Minh visited Eastern Europe in July–August, 1957, and a Mongolian state delegation was sent in September–October of that year. A Rumanian government delegation went to Asia in March, 1958, a Bulgarian party delegation in October, 1958, an East German government delegation in January, 1959, a Hungarian party-state delegation in June, 1959, and a Czech government delegation in October, 1959; a Korean party-state delegation traveled to the Soviet Union and Eastern Europe in April, 1959. Moves toward closer military co-operation were also manifest in exchanges of military delegations: military delegations from the Soviet Union, Poland, Albania, and Hungary visited the Asian communist countries in 1958, and a Chinese military delegation led by Defense Minister Peng Te-huai went to the Soviet Union and Eastern Europe in the spring of 1959.

The real basis for the new atmosphere of "togetherness," however, was the extension of economic co-operation. In harmony with the "objective law of the development of world socialism," initial steps were taken toward "international specialization of production and ever closer cooperation of national economies, coordination of the national means of production and national labor power of the socialist countries, and an exchange of goods and experience." A co-ordination of national economic plans for fifteen- to twenty-year periods was attempted. The international economic co-operation was based on the "state monopoly of foreign trade as a means of planned linkage of their economies, their credit agreements, joint construction in industry and in transport, mutual aid in surveying and exploiting natural resources, mutual exchange of socialist methods of management and socialist methods of high labor productivity, scientific and technological mutual aid, and mutual aid in the peaceful uses of atomic energy."[14] Trade among the East European and the Asian communist countries grew considerably in the late fifties. The Soviet Union and the East European states extended credits and exchanged specialists and technicians. Armed with "fraternal help," the more backward Asian countries reached a higher growth rate than the more developed East European countries and seemed on their way toward catching up with the economic level of Eastern Europe (Table 12–1).

TABLE 12–1:

ANNUAL GROWTH OF NATIONAL INCOME AND FOREIGN TRADE
(average for 1951–60; 1950 = 100)

Country	National Income	Foreign Trade
Soviet Union	10.3	13.2
European Countries		
Poland	7.5	8.1
Rumania	10.1	11.6
East Germany	9.3	17.4
Czechoslovakia	7.5	10.2
Hungary	6.0	11.1
Bulgaria	9.2	13.9
Albania	10.0	16.2
Asian Countries		
China	14.4	15.2
North Korea	24.9	23.6
North Vietnam	14.5	20.9
Mongolia	14.6	18.8

SOURCE: G. Sorokin, "Nekotorye problemy mezhdunarodnovo sotsialisti-cheskovo razdeleniya truda," *Voprosy Ekonomiki*, July, 1962.

However, a real adjustment of the levels of development was farther away than was suggested by the optimistic evaluation of growth rates provided in communist propaganda. Despite their slower growth rates, the already industrialized East European countries were in fact modernizing their economies faster than the Asian ones, and the economic gap between the European and the Asian parts of the communist camp was not narrowing but widening. The "fraternal help" of the more developed communist countries was not sufficient to push the Asian economies forward, nor did it fulfill the expectations of the Asian communist regimes. The Soviet Union and the East European commu-

TABLE 12–2:

FOREIGN TRADE OF EAST EUROPEAN AND ASIAN COMMUNIST COUNTRIES, 1960

(in percentages)

Foreign Trade	Albania	Bulgaria	Czecho-slovakia	East Germany	Hungary	Poland	Rumania	Soviet Union
With Socialist States.........	95.9	83.5	71.5	73.0	67.0	60.8	72.1	70.6
With Soviet Union.........	35.8	53.1	34.3	43.0	29.7	30.3	40.1	—
With European Communist States.........	35.0	27.2	29.4	24.6	32.8	26.3	26.7	53.2
With Asian Communist States.........	7.1	1.4	6.4	5.3	4.5	3.9	5.4	17.4
China.........	6.9	1.3	5.4	4.5	4.2	3.4	4.2	14.8
North Korea.........	—	0.1	0.4	0.2	0.1	0.1	0.6	1.0
North Vietnam.........	0.2	—	0.3	0.4	0.1	0.4	0.5	0.4
Mongolia.........	—	—	0.3	0.2	0.1	—	0.1	1.2
With Capitalist Countries.....	4.1	16.5	28.5	27.0	33.0	39.2	27.9	29.4
Total............100.0	100.0	100.0	100.0	100.0	100.0	100.0	100.0	100.0

SOURCE: *Sotsialisticheski lager* (Moscow, 1962), pp. 47ff.

nist countries, despite their avowed enthusiasm for extending "fraternal help," were unwilling to let their own economic interests suffer and reluctant to tighten their belts for the sake of their Asian comrades. This was, in fact, to become an issue in the Sino-Soviet split.

Economic relations with the Asian communist countries was of secondary importance for the East European economies even after the initiative taken in 1958. Trade between Eastern Europe and Asia, despite a significant rise between 1956 and 1960, constituted only a fraction of East European trade (Table 12-2). The volume of East European bloc trade with the capitalist countries, meanwhile, was expanding. In 1960, for example, 39.2 per cent of Poland's trade was with free world countries, as against only 3.9 per cent with Asian communist states; 33 per cent of Hungary's trade was with the capitalist world, as against 4.5 per cent with the Asian communist countries; the same pattern obtained as regards trade by the other European satellites—28.5 per cent as against 6.4 per cent in the case of Czechoslovakia, 27.9 per cent as against 5.4 per cent for Rumania, 27 per cent as against 5.3 per cent for East Germany, and 16.5 per cent as against 1.4 per cent for Bulgaria. In the Polish and Hungarian cases, trade with the West was greater even than with the Soviet Union.

THE SINO-SOVIET SPLIT

Countercurrents were already in evidence during the period of "equalizing economies," when the Chinese reportedly declined to join the Warsaw Pact during Khrushchev's visit to Peking in July, 1958, and established the people's communes, with extravagant accompanying claims to have embarked on a short cut to communism. They were further in evidence when Khrushchev abrogated the secret Sino-Soviet nuclear treaty of October, 1957, after Peng Te-huai's fall from grace in June, 1959. With the withdrawal of the Soviet technicians from China in the summer of 1960, Khrushchev dealt the *coup de grâce* to his program of "simultaneous building of communism" through equalization of the economies. The ups and downs of the growing Moscow-Peking conflict put a brake on the co-operation between the East European and Asian communist countries and set centrifugal forces in motion in the communist camp. The world party conference at the end of 1960 produced an eighty-one-party document in which an ostensible compromise was reached on key ideological sore points. But the divisive forces continued to develop momentum. The East European parties supported Moscow's position, with varying degrees of firmness, while the Korean and North Vietnamese parties gravitated toward Peking's line in the ideological dispute, albeit with reservations. Moscow's defense treaty with North Korea of July 6, 1961, followed by a similar Chinese-Korean defense treaty of July 11, 1961, seemed to mark one last attempt to span the dividing line. Mongolia was admitted to full membership in CEMA on June 7, 1962, but North Korea and North Vietnam retained observer status along with the Chinese and hewed to the "self-reliance" line. The Chinese, Korean, and Vietnamese observers attended CEMA commission meetings less regularly. Khrushchev's plans to reorganize CEMA, with Yugoslav participation, into a political and economic core of the communist camp in the summer and fall of 1962 were answered by Chinese hints that a sphere of economic co-operation and state federation in the Far East might be established, including China, North Vietnam, North Korea, Indonesia, Cambodia, and Burma.

The process of polarization set in motion in the communist bloc by the Sino-Soviet conflict cannot be traced simply to traditional animosities or to geopolitical or racial factors. The roots of the schism can be found in the communist regimes themselves. The post-Stalin leaders of the Soviet Union and Eastern Europe wanted to maintain their power and win the competition with the capitalist system by modernizing the totalitarian party rule, by adapting their economies and societies to the conditions of the second industrial revolution, and by protecting this process of change against outside interference with a foreign policy of "peaceful coexistence." In the less developed Asian communist countries, not only were the social and economic conditions for such a modernization from above not ripe, but the party rule itself was still in an unstable condition. The erosion of party rule during a limited attempt at de-Stalinization in China and North Vietnam during 1956 was a warning to Mao Tse-tung and Ho Chi Minh.

The determination of the communist minorities in the Asian bloc countries to remain at the helm of power compelled them to continue Stalinist methods and to shun the example set by the Soviets at the Twentieth CPSU Congress, which became the actual point of departure for the present differences within the communist camp. In order to keep the masses in line, the Chinese, Korean, and Vietnamese party leaders still needed an "objective enemy," with whom peaceful coexistence was out of the question. At the same time, Communist China, North Korea, and North Vietnam still have territorial claims outstanding vis-à-vis Taiwan, South Korea, and South Vietnam. As long as the Soviet leaders were unwilling to give up the line established at the Twentieth Congress and to give tangible backing to the Chinese, North Korean, and North Vietnamese territorial aspirations in Asia, as long as they were unwilling to renounce de-Stalinization and coexistence with the United States, a basis for genuine reconciliation did not exist.

Party and state relations between the East European and Asian communist countries accordingly deteriorated during 1963 and 1964. The governments in Peking, Pyongyang, and Hanoi refused to sign the partial nuclear test-ban treaty concluded in Moscow in August, 1963. The Korean and Vietnamese parties followed the Chinese party's lead and came out against the CPSU proposals for a new world communist conference. Economic relations, affected by the ideological dispute and the decline of party and state relations, dropped to the freezing point. Soviet trade with the Asian communist countries decreased by some 40 per cent from 1959 to 1962 and concurrently increased by about 20 per cent with the East European bloc countries.[15] Between 1959 and 1962, Communist Chinese trade with Rumania dropped 75 per cent, with Czechoslovakia, 62 per cent, with East Germany, 60 per cent, and with Poland, 55 per cent; the decline of trade relations had a negative effect on Eastern Europe, on East Germany especially.[16]

A significant downward trend was observed in the trade between the East European bloc countries and North Korea. Only Polish and Hungarian trade with North Vietnam showed some increase (Table 12–3). The decline of trade between East European and Asian communist countries, which even at its height before 1960 was only a fraction of East European foreign trade, was balanced by a significant growth of trade relations with capitalist countries (Table 12–4). Eastern Europe's trade, even

Table 12–3:

East European Trade with Asian Communist Countries

(volume and trade balance)

Soviet Union (Million Rubles)	1956	1960	1963	1964
China	1,347.5	1,498.7	540.2	404.5
	(−28.1)	(−27.9)	(−203.2)	(−161.1)
North Korea	94.5	102.7	153.2	147.2
	(+2.3)	(−31.7)	(−5.5)	(+2.0)
North Vietnam	6.4	42.8	82.8	73.8
	(+4.0)	(+1.2)	(+19.2)	(+11.2)
Mongolia	141.9	125.3	149.1	178.5
	(+44.3)	(+23.9)	(+46.1)	(+75.1)

Albania (Million Lek)	1955	1960	1962	1963
China	63.4	452.7	2,692.3	3,251.8
	(−63.4)	(−244.5)	(−1,522.0)	(−915.2)
North Korea	—	—	22.7	61.0
			(−2.5)	(−7.5)
North Vietnam	—	12.9	27.7	19.1
		(+12.9)	(−11.9)	(−2.9)

Bulgaria (Million Lew)	1956	1960	1962	1963
China	12.0	20.0	7.7	4.2
	(0.0)	(−2.4)	(+0.1)	(−1.2)
North Korea	0.5	2.0	2.0	2.8
	(+0.5)	(−2.0)	(−0.8)	(+1.8)

Czechoslovakia (Million Korunas)	1956	1960	1963	1964
China	944.0	1,459.0	276.0	215.0
	(−12.0)	(+115.0)	(−142.0)	(−81.0)
North Korea	96.0	110.0	61.0	84.0
	(+84.0)	(+58.0)	(−17.0)	(−22.0)
North Vietnam	77.0	70.0	76.0	68.0
	(+13.0)	(+10.0)	(+6.0)	(−4.0)
Mongolia	1.0	87.0	91.0	110.0
	(+1.0)	(+7.0)	(+13.0)	(+20.0)

East Germany (Million Valuta-Mark)	1956	1960	1963	1964
China	723.2[a]	828.7	147.6	147.6
	(+36.0)	(−12.7)	(−60.2)	(−17.5)
North Korea	39.9[a]	39.1	27.0	19.7
	(+26.5)	(+0.5)	(+3.6)	(+1.9)
North Vietnam	20.3[a]	75.8	26.7	23.3
	(+17.3)	(+18.4)	(+3.5)	(+0.7)
Mongolia	—	28.4	22.9	30.3
		(+11.4)	(−0.3)	(+13.9)

[a] Million Rubles.

Hungary (Million Deviza-Forint)	1956	1960	1963	1964
China	698.9	898.0	—	226.0
	(+30.0)	(+46.0)		(−124.0)
North Korea	48.0	92.4	50.1	43.0
	(+43.0)	(+15.0)	(+13.7)	(−1.0)
North Vietnam	15.0	59.6	54.8	89.0
	(+13.6)	(+8.8)	(+0.1)	(−27.0)
Mongolia	—	37.2	48.6	—
		(0.0)	(+0.1)	

Poland (Million Zloty)	1956	1960	1963	1964
China	280.2	385.3	143.8	159.8
	(−1.2)	(+14.3)	(−54.2)	(−40.0)
North Korea	31.0	12.9	33.0	31.4
	(+31.0)	(−2.1)	(+2.2)	(+1.4)
North Vietnam	0.9	48.3	17.0	29.4
	(−0.9)	(+3.5)	(−6.4)	(−12.4)
Mongolia	—	20.1	31.7	29.9
		(+4.5)	(+8.7)	(+11.1)

TABLE 12–3 (*Continued*)

Rumania

(Million Lei)	1958	1960	1963	1964
China	254.7	341.6	167.6	203.4
	(+55.5)	(+58.4)	(−1.8)	(−12.2)
North Korea	21.3	49.6	63.5	66.1
	(+16.9)	(+14.2)	(−9.7)	(+0.1)
North Vietnam	8.1	39.7	65.7	21.8
	(−0.9)	(+13.9)	(+13.3)	(−4.8)
Mongolia	0.9	2.7	7.7	10.5
	(+0.1)	(−0.1)	(−0.5)	(+2.3)

SOURCES:
Soviet Union: *Vneshnaya Torgovlya Soyuza SSR za 1959–1963 gody* (Moscow, 1965), pp. 15f.; *Vneshnaya Torgovlya Soyuza SSR za 1964 gody* (Moscow, 1965), pp. 12f.

Albania: *Vjetari Statistikor i R. P. Sh. 1964* (Tirana, 1964).

Bulgaria: *Statisticheski Godishnik na Narodna Republika Bolgariya 1964* (Sofia, 1965), p. 305.

Czechoslovakia: *Statistická ročenka Československé Socialistické Republiky 1964* (Prague, 1965), p. 387.

East Germany: *Statistisches Jahrbuch der Deutschen Demokratischen Republik 1965* (Berlin, 1965), p. 390.

Hungary: *Statisztikai Evkönyv 1963* (Budapest, 1964); *Aussenhandel*, April, 1965.

Poland: *Rocznik statystyczny 1964* (Warsaw, 1964); *Maly rocznik statystyczny 1965* (Warsaw, 1965), p. 160.

Rumania: *Anuarul Statistic al R. P. R. 1964* (Bucharest, 1964), pp. 435f.

with Yugoslavia and with such underdeveloped countries as India—and in some instances the United Arab Republic and Indonesia—surpassed its economic exchanges with the "fraternal" Asian countries. This economic reorientation toward the West served to accentuate a shift of the political climate in Eastern Europe, marked by tendencies toward greater assertion of independence and the spread of polycentrism. The Asian communist countries, too, especially China and North Korea, built up their economic relations with the capitalist countries. No official figures are available, but there are indications that their trade with non-communist countries began to surpass their trade relations with East European communist countries in 1964.

Khrushchev failed in his attempt to bring Peking and its Asian satellites into line through economic pressures. He was even less successful in his efforts in the fall of 1963 and the spring of 1964 to convene a new world communist conference for the purpose of excommunicating or at least isolating the Chinese heretics.[17] The apparent power decline of the Moscow center encouraged the

TABLE 12–4:

TRADE RELATIONS WITH ASIAN COMMUNIST AND CAPITALIST COUNTRIES

Poland (Million Zloty)	1963		1964	
Total Foreign Trade	14,996.2	100.0%	16,674.2	100.0%
Communist countries	9,796.3	65.3	10,627.1	63.7
China	143.8	0.9	159.8	0.9
North Korea	33.0	0.2	31.4	0.2
North Vietnam	17.0	0.1	29.4	0.2
United States	512.1	3.3	673.7	4.1
France	265.2	1.8	324.7	1.9
West Germany	597.7	4.0	685.6	4.1
Great Britain	869.2	5.8	843.0	5.1
India	161.8	1.1	213.8	1.3

Rumania (Million Lei)	1963		1964	
Total Foreign Trade	11,622.2	100.0%	13,009.2	100.0%
Communist countries	8,002.6	68.8	8,894.3	68.4
China	167.6	1.4	203.4	1.6
North Korea	63.5	0.5	66.1	0.5
North Vietnam	65.7	0.6	21.8	0.2
United States	10.7	0.09	42.3	0.3
France	335.6	3.0	429.8	3.3
West Germany	780.6	6.7	848.5	6.5
Great Britain	444.8	3.8	439.9	3.4
Italy	577.5	5.0	584.9	4.5
United Arab Republic	112.6	1.0	150.7	1.2
India	64.3	0.5	76.4	0.6

East Germany (Million Valuta Mark)	1963		1964	
Total Foreign Trade	20,965.5	100.0%	23,203.6	100.0%
Communist countries	16,472.3	78.6	17,745.4	76.4
China	147.6	0.7	147.6	0.6
North Korea	27.0	0.1	19.7	0.08
North Vietnam	22.9	0.1	30.3	0.1
West Germany	1,824.8	8.7	2,167.4	9.3
Great Britain	267.9	1.3	241.1	1.0
Netherlands	172.0	0.8	245.3	1.0
India	208.0	1.0	190.1	0.9
United States	15.8	0.07	19.2	0.08

SOURCES:

Poland: *Rocznik statystyczny 1964* (Warsaw, 1964); *Maly rocznik statystyczny 1965* (Warsaw, 1965), p. 160.

Rumania: *Anuarul Statistic al R.P.R. 1964* (Bucharest, 1964), pp. 435f.

East Germany: *Statistisches Jahrbuch der Deutschen Demokratischen Republik 1965* (Berlin, 1965), p. 390.

East European parties to strive for greater individual latitude. The Rumanians in particular adopted an independent stance, refused to subordinate their national interests to a supranational CEMA, and underscored their new posture with Maurer's trip to Peking and Pyongyang in March, 1964. The Chinese leaders, out to split the pro-Moscow parties and to exploit the centrifugal forces at work in Eastern Europe, introduced the question of "unresolved territorial claims" into the ideological dispute. In a meeting with Japanese socialists on July 10, 1964, Mao Tse-tung attacked the Soviet territorial acquisitions after 1945 not only in Asia but in Eastern Europe as well: "There are too many places occupied by the Soviet Union. . . . They appropriated a part of Rumania. Having separated a portion of East Germany they chased away the local inhabitants to West Germany. They divided a part of Poland and annexed it to the Soviet Union and gave a part of East Germany to Poland as compensation. The same thing took place in Finland. They took everything they could."[18]

In a long article on September 2, *Pravda* violently rebutted Mao's provocative statement, and in Prague Khrushchev accused the Chinese leaders of "proposing the division of the territory of the Soviet Union."[19] The vehement rebuttals attested to the uneasiness created by Mao's accusations against Soviet "great power chauvinism" in Eastern Europe and to growing fears—with racial overtones—of a threat from Asia. Bulgaria's *Rabotnichesko Delo* on September 6, 1964, in a comment reprinted in *Pravda* the next day, expressed these fears openly: "Isn't this a call to Japan, to the Chinese people, the yellow race to rise in a campaign to win an 'area of vital importance' in the Soviet Union? . . . The actual intentions of the Chinese leaders now appear clear and unretouched: limitless nationalism and chauvinism, unbridled great-national and racial expansion, unprecedented encroachment over territories and interests of both neighboring and more distant nations."

Khrushchev's Downfall and the Crisis in Vietnam

Khrushchev's overthrow on October 14, 1964, and the first Chinese nuclear test on October 16 accentuated the division within the communist bloc. The East European parties and leaders did not hide their concern over Khrushchev's downfall and their uneasiness about the Chinese atomic ventures. Peking's followers, on the other hand, reacted enthusiastically to the elimination of the "arch-revisionist" and praised the success of the first Asian nuclear explosion. But there was new hope, as expressed by Indonesian CP leader Aidit and others, that Khrushchev's fall would open the doors to a Sino-Soviet *rapprochement*. Chou En-lai's presence with other East European and Asian party leaders in Moscow for the October Revolution anniversary celebration on November 7—a trip later acknowledged by the Chinese to have been a failure—seemed to have thawed the ice. The new Soviet leaders turned away from Khrushchev's collision course vis-à-vis Peking and stressed as priority goals of Soviet foreign policy the re-establishment of unity between the communist parties and countries and all-out aid for national liberation movements. The East European countries followed suit, and the stagnant relations were refurbished through a new wave of exchanges of friendly greetings, cultural delegations, and economic missions between the East European and Asian communist countries. The 1965 trade agreements between these countries were signed more speedily than in the preceding years and provided for an increase in the volume of trade over 1964. Observers from China, North Korea, and North Vietnam began to participate more regularly in the meetings of CEMA commissions. Premier Kosygin on December 28, 1964, endorsed Chou En-lai's proposal for an international conference of heads of state to discuss the prohibition of nuclear weapons and declared the Soviet Government's "complete agreement with and support for" the proposal. Some of the East European governments followed suit: the Chairman of the G.D.R. Council of Ministers, Willi Stoph, on January 4, 1965; Czechoslovak Premier Josef Lenart, on January 7; Bulgarian Premier Todor Zhivkov, on January 9; and Hungary's János Kádár, on January 15, supported Chou's proposals and announced their willingness to take part in such a conference. The members of the Warsaw Treaty Organization, meeting in the Polish capital on January 20, also came out in favor of the Chinese proposal. The new atmosphere of hopefulness was pointed up in the *Pravda* editorial of January 2: "New steps forward will be taken for the development of co-operation among the socialist countries."

On February 5, 1965, a Soviet delegation led by Kosygin went to Hanoi via Peking, with the stated purpose of "contributing actively to the consolidation and promotion of the solidarity and friendship among the socialist countries."[20] Kosygin's mission undoubtedly represented an attempt to re-establish Soviet influence in Southeast Asia by providing North Vietnam with additional Soviet military assistance. The American bombing of North Vietnamese targets, in response to Viet Cong attacks on U.S. military installations in South Vietnam, began on February 7 while Kosygin was in Hanoi. Moscow, of course, gave prompt verbal support to Hanoi's angry outburst, with a Soviet government statement on February 8 declaring that in the face of these "serious provocations of the American armed forces" against North Vietnam, "the Soviet Union will be forced, together with its allies and friends, to take further measures to safeguard the security and strengthen the defense capability of the D.R.V."[21] Yet compared with the fierce language used in the statement of the Peking government on February 9, the Soviet reaction was guarded and reluctant. Kosygin, in the center of the new crisis, pointed out in Hanoi that "the present situation is full of grave complications." He declared: "The people need peace, and not war. They want to build and not to destroy. The D.R.V., the Soviet Union, People's China, all the socialist countries do not want war."[22]

Kosygin's talks with Ho Chi Minh and Pham Van Dong produced agreement "on the steps which shall be undertaken with a view to strengthening the defensive capacity of the D.R.V."[23] But Kosygin's discussions in Hanoi, in Peking with Mao Tse-tung on February 10, and in Pyongyang from February 11 to 14 failed to overcome the divergencies within the communist camp, and he had to concede after his return to Moscow that "the difficulties and differences which have developed in the international communist movement cannot be resolved right away."[24] The East European governments published routine statements denouncing American "escalation" of the war in Vietnam but did not commit themselves to action.[25] All the outcries, protests, and demonstrations in the East European capitals against American "aggression" in Vietnam could not conceal the fact that these countries were far more concerned with their own economic reforms and with the development of their political and economic ties with the West than with the distant plight of "fraternal" North Vietnam.[26]

During 1965 a host of party leaders and premiers from Eastern Europe visited India, Egypt, Ethiopia, Yugoslavia, and France, not to mention the frequent top-level meetings and exchanges among East European and Soviet leaders. But no major delegation from an East European communist country went to Peking, Hanoi, or Pyongyang. The seeming indifference to the fate of Vietnam on the part of the broad masses and party leaders alike stood in contrast to a growing uneasiness within the lower party echelons, especially in East Germany, about Soviet caution in the Vietnam crisis and the possible implications of this behavior for Soviet protection of the East European communist regimes.

The "consultative meeting" of nineteen communist parties "to exchange opinions on the ways and means of surmounting differences and strengthening the unity of the world communist movement" took place from March 1 to 5 in Moscow, boycotted by the Asian parties and by the Rumanians. In their statement on Vietnam the participants of the March meeting expressed their "internationalist solidarity with the fraternal people of the D.R.V., the heroic Vietnam Workers Party and the National Front for the Liberation of South Vietnam (NFLSV)." They urged all communist parties and socialist states "to strengthen unity of action and solidarity in the active struggle against imperialist aggression."[27] The East European CP's which had participated in the meeting duly ratified its decisions. But the appeal for "united action" and the proposals for preparation of a new world party conference, rebuffed by the Chinese, found no response in North Korea or North Vietnam.

The warnings against the United States and the verbal declarations of support for the Vietnamese "comrades" came to a crucial test with the landing of U.S. Marines in Danang on March 6, 1965. The East European capitals, following Moscow's lead, hardened their attitude toward the United States. The East European governments and parliaments supported the NFLSV's March 22 demands for a total U.S. withdrawal from South Vietnam and the inclusion of NFLSV representatives in a neutralist government in Saigon; they also backed the peace conditions put forward by D.R.V. Premier Pham Van Dong on April 10. The East European party press also duly denounced President Johnson's April 7 proposals in Baltimore for "unconditional discussions." Yet the appeal by the NFLSV leaders on March 22 for "volunteers" for Vietnam[28] found only a lukewarm response in the East European countries. The loud proclamations of sympathy for the Vietnamese peoples needed, of course, to be supported at least by political and economic actions. In addition to the already existing representations in Prague, Sofia, and East Berlin, new permanent missions of the NFLSV with a pseudo-diplomatic status were established during 1965 in Warsaw, Budapest, and Bucharest, as well as in Moscow. On July 12 the Soviet Union (and on July 13 Communist China) signed agreements with North Vietnam for new aid programs, and similar aid agreements were concluded with the D.R.V. by Poland, East Germany, Bulgaria, Hungary, Czechoslovakia, and Mongolia, as well as by North Korea.[29] On a second trip westward in December, 1965, a North Vietnamese delegation concluded additional aid agreements with the Soviet Union, Hungary, East Germany, and Poland.[30]

The Soviet Union's effort to re-establish its influence in Asia and to entice the Korean and Vietnamese comrades to loosen their ties with Peking appeared to be enjoying a measure of success. Shelepin's visit to North Korea in June, 1965, was followed by a slight movement of the Korean leaders away from Peking and toward a "Rumanian" position. Brezhnev, in his speech at the September CPSU Central Committee plenum, claimed a "strengthening of interstate and interparty contacts and relations" with North Korea and North Vietnam.[31] But an October visit by a Hungarian delegation led by Jenö Fock to Hanoi and Pyongyang demonstrated that the long interruption of relations had proved a handicap to a new understanding. Fock's public remarks on his talks in North Korea attested to the frustrations in the relationships between the East European and Asian communist countries. In his radio and television report in Budapest on November 5, he declared:

> In Korea, at the beginning of the talks, it was very strongly felt that for years we had had no intensive relations between our parties. I should say that the talks had a difficult start. We warmed to them slowly, and only gradually did they become truly frank, comradely,

and fraternal. We disagreed on a great many questions, namely the well-known contentious issues of the international communist movement. On several questions our stands are different. . . . We told Kim Il-song frankly that we were dissatisfied with the outcome of the talks and that we had failed to receive concrete and satisfying replies to specific questions and suggestions.

And in Hanoi, according to Fock's report, "we discussed not only matters on which we agree but also questions on which the views of the two parties are not identical."[32]

Soviet and East European appeals for "joint action" were repeated at meetings in Moscow and Prague in October commemorating the thirtieth anniversary of the Seventh Comintern Congress. CPSU Secretary Boris Ponomarev declared at the Comintern memorial meeting in Prague:

Under current conditions we see a path toward rallying the international communist movement primarily through insuring unity of all communist actions in coordinating an international policy concerning the struggle against imperialism. . . . The unwavering struggle of the communist movement against manifestations of a nationalist character is a most important condition for the strengthening of a united world-wide anti-imperialist front. The primary criterion of internationalism in our time is the attitude toward the entire system of socialism.[33]

The Soviet standpoint was supported at the meeting by Czechoslovak delegate Koucky, Bulgarian Politburo member Staikow, and Polish delegate Jarosinski, who advocated a "unified foreign policy of socialist states."

The growing tension between Moscow and Peking, exacerbated since the March consultative meeting, came to a new climax on November 11 with the publication of the *Red Flag—People's Daily* joint editorial board article, "Refutation of the New Leaders of the CPSU on 'United Action.'" In stating that "antagonistic contradictions" exist between the Marxist-Leninist-Maoist order in China and a "restoration of capitalism" in Soviet society, Peking underscored the ideological break. It accused Moscow of giving insufficient aid to Vietnam and of using the call for "united action" as a smoke screen to cover Soviet-American collusion. There existed now in the international communist movement, the article said, "only separating and no unifying elements, only contradictions and nothing in common." The Chinese proclaimed their intention to draw a "clear line of demarcation both politically and organizationally between themselves and the modern revisionists."[34]

The Soviet reaction to this Chinese blast was cautious at first, as in the *Pravda* editorial of November 16. In a programatic statement set forth in the article, "The International Duty of the Communists of All Countries," in *Pravda* on November 28, the Soviet leaders served notice of their line of defense. Rather than repaying Peking's attacks in kind, Moscow stressed the necessity of rallying all the parties under the banner of united action. The East European parties, up to now more or less reserved in the Sino-Soviet dispute, for the first time went all out in support of Moscow's position.[35] Only the Rumanians sustained their independent stance.[36] The Korean communists, as in former phases of the dispute, gave ideological support to Peking and attacked "modern revisionism," but did not back up the specific Chinese charges against the Soviet leaders.[37] Hanoi did not participate in this ideological head counting but sought to maintain its precarious balance, praising both Soviet and Chinese aid.[38]

The cleavage between Moscow and Peking, exacerbated by the escalation of the Vietnam crisis, has changed the relationship between the East European and the Asian communist countries. As long as the finality of the Sino-Soviet split remained in question, the East European parties were able to exploit the situation effectively to wrest greater independence from Moscow and to accelerate the spread of polycentrism. As the break has become more clearly irreversible, however, new opportunities have arisen for Moscow to press for a realignment of its adherents around the Soviet center. The visible Chinese setbacks, at the Algiers conference, in Africa, in Indonesia, on the Indian subcontinent, and in Cuba, have shifted the power balance in favor of Moscow and have increasingly isolated Peking.

The division within the communist camp into an East European sector under Moscow's tutelage and an Asian section under Peking's hegemony, with Mongolia as Moscow's Asian outpost and Albania as Peking's, has become deeper than ever. The

Moscow-Peking split, the emergence of open nationalist tendencies in the Soviet Union and Eastern Europe and of racist prejudices in Peking, stand as testimony to the inability of the communist system to superimpose a new kind of relationship between states and peoples, to overcome historical, social, and political differences, and to solve the basic conflict between developed and underdeveloped communist societies.

NOTES

1. "Declaration Concerning the Formation of the Union of Soviet Socialist Republics, December 30, 1922," in: X. J. Eudin and H. H. Fisher, *Soviet Russia and the West 1920–1927* (Stanford, Calif., 1957), p. 155.

2. Lenin, *Collected Works* (5th ed.; Moscow), XLI, 164.

3. *Pravda*, March 27, 1959, speech at the Second All-German Workers Conference in Leipzig, March 7, 1959.

4. Cf. Zbigniew K. Brzezinski, *The Soviet Bloc, Unity and Conflict* (Cambridge, Mass., 1960), p. 109, and Boris Meissner, *Das Ostpaktsystem* (Cologne, 1955).

5. Ernst Kux and J. C. Kun, *Die Satelliten Pekings* (Stuttgart, 1964), pp. 103ff. and 214ff.

6. Nikita S. Khrushchev, *K pobede v mirnom sovernovanni s kapitalismom* (Moscow, 1959), p. 408.

7. *Kommunist*, No. 14 (1955), p. 127; see Kurt London, "The Socialist Commonwealth of Nations," *Orbis*, III (Winter, 1960).

8. Ts. A. Stepanyan, "Oktyabrskaya revolutsiya i stanovlenie kommunisticheskoi formatsii," *Voprosy Filosofii*, No. 10 (1958).

9. P. Figurnov, "Evening out the Economic Levels of the Socialist Countries," *International Affairs*, No. 7 (1960), p. 70.

10. Boris Meissner, *Der Warschauer Pakt* (Cologne, 1962).

11. Richard Lowenthal, *Chruschtschow und der Weltkommunismus* (Stuttgart, 1964).

12. *Pravada*, May 25, 1958.

13. *Mezhdunarodnye ekonomicheskie organisatsii* (Moscow, 1962), pp. 926f.

14. E. A. Korovin, "Proletarski internationalizm i mezhdunarodnoe pravo," *Sovetskii ezhegodnik mezhdunarodnogo prava 1958* (Moscow, 1959), pp. 50ff.

15. *Sovremenye mezhdunarodnye ekonomicheskie otnosheniya* (Moscow, 1964), p. 78.

16. V. I. Zolotarev, *Vneshnaya torgovlya sotsialisticheskikh stran* (Moscow, 1964), p. 238.

17. William E. Griffith, *Sino-Soviet Relations 1964–1965* (M.I.T. C/65–19) (Cambridge, Mass., 1965).

18. Mao's attack was not published in China. It was reported in the Japanese journal *Sekai Shuho*, on August 11, 1964, and long excerpts appeared in *Pravda*, on September 2, 1964. These reports were never refuted by Peking. According to a report of the Japanese news agency *Kyodo* on August 1, 1964, Chou En-lai, in talks with a visiting Japanese Socialist Party delegation in Peking in July, 1964, made sweeping charges about Soviet "gobbling up" of territory. *Kyodo* quotes Haruo Okada, the chairman of the Japanese delegation, as reporting that Chou declared: "When I visited Moscow in 1957, I

pointed out to Premier Khrushchev that the Soviet Union had taken too much territory, ranging from Japanese territory in the east to Communist China, the Middle East, Eastern Europe and Finland." Okada quoted Chou as saying that the Soviet Union had gobbled up "too much territory" and that it was only reasonable to demand its return. He said Chou's statement followed an earlier statement made by Mao Tse-tung to the effect that Communist China supported Japan's demand for the return of the Kuriles.

19. *Pravda,* September 5, 1964.

20. *Nhan Dan,* January 31, 1965, commenting on the announcement of Kosygin's visit to Hanoi.

21. TASS, February 8, 1965.

22. Vietnam News Agency (VNA), February 8, 1965.

23. *Izvestiya,* February 16, 1965. Kosygin and Pham Van Dong signed agreements for the extension of loans and for new credits to continue Soviet technical assistance programs in the D.R.V.; as a gift, Kosygin promised the delivery of Soviet fishing boats.

24. *Pravda,* February 27, 1965.

25. The reactions of the East European governments were remarkably different in emphasis and in degrees of anti-American propaganda invective, bearing out William Griffith's description of attitudes of East European regimes (see William E. Griffith [ed.], *Communism in Europe* [Cambridge, Mass., 1964], I, 3). At first, only Bulgaria and the G.D.R. hinted at a willingness to provide some kind of material assistance for the D.R.V. The Bulgarian government declaration of February 9, 1965, expressed solidarity with the D.R.V. and "readiness, together with the Soviet Union and the other socialist countries, to support all measures aimed at the preservation of the independence of the DRV and peace" (*Rabotnichesko Delo,* February 10, 1965). The G.D.R. government statement, dated February 12, proclaimed "brotherly solidarity with the Vietnamese people in their just struggle" and assured the D.R.V. of "every possible assistance in safeguarding its security (ADN, February 13, 1965). The Czechoslovak government declared on February 10 only that it stands "firmly at the side of the fraternal socialist country, which has become the victim of imperialist aggression" and "considers it indispensable that the U.S. government strictly observe the 1954 and 1962 Geneva agreements" (CTK, February 10). According to the Polish government statement, February 12, "Poland is in solidarity with the just struggle of the Vietnamese people; the Polish government is convinced that the only road leading to the restoration of peace in Southeast Asia is the observance of the Geneva agreements" (PAP, February 12). A Hungarian National Assembly resolution on February 12 pledged "complete solidarity with the long-suffering Vietnamese people" and supported "proposals for convening a new Geneva conference in order to restore peace and security in Southeast Asia" (MTI, February 12, 1965). The Rumanian government statement of February 12 pledged "full solidarity, sympathy and fraternal support" (*Agerpress,* February 12, 1965). The Rumanian reaction to the escalation in Vietnam was more reserved than that of the other East European countries: the Rumanian press carried only brief reports on Vietnam, and student demonstrations against the U.S. Embassy were not allowed in Bucharest.

26. While some of the East European bloc countries were later to avow readiness to let "volunteers" go to Vietnam, a general caution and reluctance was evident. Bulgaria's Zhivkov did declare militantly on April 18 that "we are ready to send volunteers to North Vietnam for the complete defeat of the invaders." And the Hungarian *Népszabadság* on April 26 said editorially that

"a great number of [Hungarian] workers, students, and soldiers are requesting permission to go as volunteers to Vietnam if the need arises"—the cautious "if the need arises" phrase harmonizing with Moscow's own careful approach. In the same period, the *Junge Welt* of April 23 quoted G.D.R. army chief Hoffmann as expressing a notably cautious attitude toward involvement in Vietnam: "To the question of volunteers—also from the GDR—to Vietnam, Army General Hoffmann stated: 'Despite all passion and rage, one must coolly weigh what one undertakes. We do not want escalation of the war, but we do want to do everything to hinder it and force the United States to leave the Vietnamese people in peace. The sending of volunteers, whether Chinese, Soviet, or German, is not decisive aid. The Vietnamese people have the will to fight to the last drop of their blood for their freedom, and they are themselves absolutely in a position to deal with the aggressors if they have the proper modern weapons and qualified cadres at their disposal. Such modern weapons, particularly for air defense, the DRV did not have, but it will now get them. This aid, however, cannot become fully effective in only four or six weeks. The delivery of modern weapons, the training of the cadres—that is not so simple." More than a half-year later, on the East German radio, party propagandist Gerhard Eisler answered a listener's question about sending trained people to help D.R.V. industry, so that the Vietnamese could be freed for the defense of their country: "The DRV has enough people to manage its industry. There is no point in our sending people to the DRV who probably would not be able to work successfully under the climatic conditions there. We are sending people there who can be useful, and if the DRV deemed it expedient that we send more people, we would do so." (*East Berlin Domestic Service*, November 28, 1965.)

27. TASS, March 3, 1965.

28. The statement of the Central Committee of the National Liberation Front of South Vietnam, dated March 22, declared: "The NFLSV is ready to accept any moral and material aid, including aid in weapons and military materials from socialist and other countries. . . . If the American aggressors continue to increase their armed force in South Vietnam, the NFLSV will appeal to the peoples of various countries to send volunteers to South Vietnam, so that they can struggle against the common enemy shoulder to shoulder with the South Vietnamese people."

29. VNA, July 28, 1965.

30. There are indications that the deliveries from East European countries to the D.R.V. ran into the same transport difficulties through China as did the Soviet aid (revealed in the Moscow-Peking polemics in December, 1965).

31. *Pravda*, September 30, 1965.

32. MTI, November 5, 1965.

33. *Pravda*, October 23, 1965.

34. *Peking Review*, No. 46 (November 12, 1965).

35. *Neues Deutschland* on November 28, 1965, printed excerpts from the Soviet article and supported it strongly in an editorial. *Rude Pravo* on December 2 attacked the "fantastic assertions" of the Chinese "that an 'irreconcilable antagonism' exists between some communist parties and the leaders of the CPSU" and applauded *Pravda's* editorial for "clearly and calmly answering this slanderous campaign." The Czechoslovak party paper added: "The Military aid supplied by the Soviet Union to the DRV in the form of modern antiaircraft weapons can hardly be called 'mere verbal attacks on American imperialism'; rather it is very effective aid." *Trybuna Ludu* on December 3 pointed out editorially that "the DRV receives considerable

military and economic assistance from brotherly socialist countries, first of all
from the Soviet Union, as well from our country"; on the other hand, "the
Chinese People's Republic, without whose cooperation no real help can be
given to Vietnam, refuses any cooperation with the Soviet Union on a
common course on the problem of Vietnam." In the strongest rebuttal of
Peking yet to come from Warsaw, the paper denounced the "openly disruptive
attitude" of the Chinese article of November 11 as "undermining from the
very foundations the unity of the communist movement and the socialist
camp." Hungary's *Nepszabadsag* on December 4 defended Soviet policy as
"true to socialist principles" and forecast ultimate isolation of the Chinese. But the Hungarian party paper stressed that "it will take a long time
to overcome the differences and to unify the anti-imperialist forces. It
concluded that "the most effective way to successfully struggle for unity is to
strengthen our solidarity with the Soviet Union." The Hungarian party organ
continued: "Today we regard the strengthening of ties of friendship with the
Soviet Union more than ever as the touchstone of proletarian internationalism. Our vital interests have proven that our place is at the side of the
Soviet Union." *Rabotnichesko Delo* on December 5 expressed "deep anxiety"
over the Chinese policy of "political and organizational demarcation." The
Bulgarian party paper also invoked the Dimitrov formula of three decades
ago: that "friendship and unity with the Soviet Union and the CPSU are the
touchstone of the internationalism of every communist party." The Bulgarian
party organ applauded the "vanguard role of the Soviet Union and the CPSU
in the communist movement and the world revolutionary process." The
Mongolian party paper *Unen* also supported the Soviet position in an
editorial on December 2, 1965.

36. *Scinteia* on December 18, in an article entitled "The People's Interests
Demand the Strengthening of Unity of the International Communist Movement," abstained from criticism of the latest Chinese attacks, but deplored the
polemic, declaring that without the differences within the communist camp
"the aggressor would not have dared to amplify the war it is waging against
the Vietnamese people." The Rumanian party organ lectured: "What unites
the communist parties is essential and prevails over any differences of views."

37. *Nodong Sinmun,* December 6, 1965.

38. The D.R.V. party organ *Nhan Dan* on December 11, 1965, for example,
carried an editorial entitled "The 200 Million Soviet People Warmly Approve
and Support the Vietnamese People's Struggle Against U.S. Imperialist Aggression," thanking the Soviets for their aid and support. In the same period,
the North Vietnamese paper carried an editorial entitled "The Chinese
People Will Spare No Effort to Support the Vietnamese People in Defeating
the U.S. Aggressors."

Eastern Europe and the West

Chapter VII.

13. Westerly Winds over Eastern Europe

Klaus Mehnert

Prior to the establishment of communist regimes, the peoples of Eastern Europe considered themselves, in varying degrees, as members—even as outposts—of the West. Unlike the Russians, they did not experience anti-Western currents. For centuries their cultural orientation was toward Vienna, Munich, and Paris, not toward Moscow. This attitude did not disappear with the communist takeover. But the Iron Curtain which cut them off from the larger part of Europe allowed neither the theoretical expression nor the actual practice of pro-Western sentiments. The distance from Europe grew. Personal contacts with the West were reduced to a trickle. The orientation shifted from the traditional European centers to Moscow.

A new development is taking place in the sixties. Moscow's hold has been weakened, and the attraction of the West is reasserting itself. The eastward trend is no longer as clear and triumphant as it was in the first decade after Stalin's victory. We will examine first the remarkable increase in both physical and intellectual contacts between Eastern Europe and the West, and then the manifestations of Western influence in Eastern Europe.

CHANNELS OF COMMUNICATION WITH THE WEST

Travel. To the first category belongs the remarkable growth of travel across the Iron Curtain. Border crossings between East and West had long been rare occurrences. But the past five years have seen an increase of travel from West to East in the form of family visits, business trips, and the first hesitant tourist excursions, and as these contacts grew, an emergent westward traffic also began to expand. The available statistics are not very reliable in that they do not always clearly distinguish between the various forms of border crossings nor between travel contacts

with non-communist and with communist countries. Still, the
increase is obvious.

In 1956 and 1958 Czechoslovakia was entered by 35,000 and
82,000 foreigners, respectively, about a third of whom came from
non-communist countries; entries for the years 1962, 1963, and
1964 totaled 697,000, 907,000 and 3,715,000. The 1964 visitors
included 744,000 visitors from the West, the largest group being
West Germans, followed by Austrians and French. The travels of
Czechoslovaks abroad, while negligible in the fifties, rose to 1,-
313,000 in 1964, although only 143,000 of these went to Western
countries.[1]

The number of Western visitors to Hungary rose from 50,000
in 1960 to 170,000 in 1964; and the number of Hungarians
traveling to Western countries rose from 32,000 in 1961 to 83,000
in 1963.[2]

In Rumania the number of tourists from abroad rose from
5,000 in 1956 to 162,000 in 1963, the latter total including 36,000
from non-communist countries; and the number of Rumanians
who traveled abroad—the great majority to communist countries
—showed an equally dramatic rise from 2,000 to 30,000.[3] In 1964,
foreign tourists in Rumania totaled some 200,000.[4]

Officials of Bulgaria's state travel agency told me proudly in
September, 1965, that they hoped to have one million foreign
travelers by the end of the year and that more than half would
come from Western countries, the largest group from West Germany. On the other hand, only 30,000 Bulgarians had been
allowed to leave the country for trips abroad in 1964, a very small
percentage of them going westward.

Both Bulgaria and Rumania are rapidly developing their
Black Sea resorts. In Varna, Bulgaria, there is one hotel next to
another. Mamaia, Rumania, offers 13,000 hotel beds. The Rumanians have also started to build hotels in the Carpathian
Mountains for winter tourists from the West.

So far, Poland has been least ready to exert herself to increase
tourist trade. In 1963 and 1964 the number of tourists from the
West was 68,000 and 90,000, respectively.[5]

By far the largest tourist business is that of Yugoslavia. Among
its 1,700,000 foreign tourists in 1963, the overwhelming majority
came from the non-communist world. The government is also
relatively generous in granting exit visas. In West Germany alone

there are some 60,000 Yugoslavs involved in temporary labor.

One should not, of course, overestimate the impact of the vast armies of foreigners who travel each year into Eastern Europe, since most of them have little contact with the local population and do not know the languages. The governments of the host countries make appreciable efforts to keep these tourists segregated from the local populace. From the official point of view, the ideal tourist comes in a group by airplane, is taken by bus to his resort, stays in a hotel for Western nationals, swims at the adjacent beach, spends his evenings in a segregated bar, and then flies home—without ever having talked to anybody except the maid and the driver. There is no doubt that far too many Western tourists fall into this category.

But there are others, too. Many travel in their own cars, some as campers. Their automobiles and tents, their clothing and camping utensils—all serve to expose the local populace to the hallmarks of the vastly superior standard of living on the other side of the border.

Academic Co-operation. Countless conferences offer valuable meeting grounds for intellectuals from both sides of the divide. Figures are not available, nor are they necessary; such conclaves have proliferated to the point that they are beginning to become routine, everyday affairs. It is, for obvious reasons, still much easier to draw people from the East to conferences on natural or technical sciences than to symposia in the fields of the social sciences or philosophy, but the number of meetings in the latter categories is on the rise.

Only the naïve will overlook the limitations involved in the conferences and in academic exchanges generally. The scientist from the East, no matter how prominent, feels the invisible—and sometimes not so invisible—cord which holds him to the surveillance organs at home. From the point of view of their governments, these people are sent abroad to promote the image of the regime and to absorb Western research and know-how. But the fringe benefits can be incalculable.

Fairs. Industrial and other fairs which attract large numbers of of Western guests and exhibits also offer important opportunities for personal contacts. The fairs such as those in Poznań, Brno,

Bucharest, and Plovdiv are "windows to the West" for millions who have no chance of traveling abroad. German business has begun to appreciate the value of such fairs. Almost half a million Rumanians thronged the twelve-day German fair in Bucharest in the spring of 1965. The Poznań fair in June, 1965, was attended by three of West Germany's top industrialists—Beitz (Krupp), Nordhoff (Volkswagen), and Grundig. Although a formidable barrier of red tape must be overcome before the Western exhibits are ready for their Eastern visitors, the firms go and their governments support them in these endeavors with increasing enthusiasm.[6]

Visits of Western orchestras, jazz bands, theatrical troups and circuses furnish additional occasions for personal contacts, and the trips of the corresponding Eastern organizations to the West afford their members an opportunity to gather impressions about life abroad.

Radio, Television, and Films. It is hard to say which of the impersonal contacts with the West are the most important ones. This writer would be inclined to put radio in first place. Radio Free Europe, Österreichischer Rundfunk (Vienna), the B.B.C., Deutsche Welle, Voice of America, and other Western stations enjoy wide audiences in these countries. Jamming has been reduced during the last years, though in varying degrees from country to country and station to station. With regard to Czechoslovakia, for example, Radio Free Europe reported in its March, 1965, publication *The Audience of Western Broadcasters in Czechoslovakia II:* "Neither the Voice of America nor the BBC is at present subjected to jamming by the Communist regime. In contrast to these favorable reception conditions, Radio Free Europe broadcasts have been recently subjected to intensified regime jamming. Moreover, a strong station overlap on the RFE frequencies adds to reception difficulties."

The effect of television is still unlimited in areas close to Western transmitters, such as western Czechoslovakia and parts of Hungary and Yugoslavia. Some television networks co-operate occasionally with Eurovision, but only in non-political programs.

Films. In countries where television is not yet widely used, the movies remain an important mass medium, and the percentage of

Western films shown is relatively high. According to Czechoslovakia's statistical yearbook for 1964, for example, ninety-six full-length films were imported from the communist world, including Yugoslavia, and forty-one from the other—principally Western—countries. It is true that films from the West which show its seamier side, picturing depravity, social tension, and perversion, have the best chance of obtaining import licenses, but this is not the aspect which gets them a full house. The audience swarms to the Western films because it wants to see something different, something of the life and fashions and habits of the West.

Books. It is difficult to measure the impact of Western literature. The books most readily passed by the censors are those in the fields of science and technology. Scholarly writings on other subjects are less easily admitted and, once admitted, tend to be confined to a limited circle of readers. As for belles-lettres, Western books directly or implicitly critical of social conditions in the West have predictable priority, but others manage on occasion to get past the censorship.

There are no import figures available about book titles—only information as to the numbers and titles translated into the language of the importing country. Thus we have statistics indicating that in 1963, 92 English, 72 German, 55 French, and 18 Italian books were translated into Czech (excluding Slovak). By way of comparison, 28 were translated into Czech from Polish in the same period.[7] Books of the belles-lettres type translated into Hungarian in 1963 included 37 from English, 58 from French, 31 from German, and 11 from Italian. Again by way of comparison, 71 were translated from Russian. But the total printing of the 71 translations from Russian amounted to only 1,030,111 copies, as against 1,132,100 copies of the 37 translations from English.[8] The Western authors whose works have been translated into Czech and Slovak include Agatha Christie, William Faulkner, Graham Greene, Ernest Hemingway, Jack Kerouac, Arthur Miller, Eugene O'Neill, and John Steinbeck. Also to be mentioned is Franz Kafka who had been taboo until a year or two ago. Western playwrights, too, have been admitted to the stages of Eastern Europe. Rumania, for example, has recently produced plays by Jean Cocteau, Friedrich Durrenmatt, Eugene Ionescu, F. Garcia Lorca, Arthur Miller, and Tennessee Williams.[9]

The number of titles known to the Eastern reader is, of course, much larger than that of titles translated. The pages of the Eastern European press have carried increasingly lively discussions of Western literature, and some literary magazines have published excerpts from Western novels or plays—for example, Rumania's *Sacolul 20* (*The Twentieth Century*) and Czechoslovakia's *Mezinarodni Literatura*, which introduced Salinger's *Catcher in the Rye* to Czechoslovak readers. Moscow's *Inostrannaya Literatura* is widely read in Bulgaria.

Periodicals. Lest there be exaggerated hopes as to the extent of liberalization, the extreme reluctance of the communist powers to admit Western newspapers and periodicals must be noted. Generally speaking, people who are interested in such publications must be content with the communist press of the West—the *Öesterreichische Volksstimme* (Vienna), *L'Humanité* (Paris), *L'Unità* (Rome), and the *Daily Worker* (London). Some countries, to "prove" their broad-mindedness, do admit a few copies of non-communist Western papers, but far too few to satisfy the demand, and principally for foreign visitors.

Mlada Fronta, the Czechoslovak youth organ, on January 26, 1964, offered this rationalization of the failure of the supply to meet the demand. "It is indeed difficult to persuade a person that certain experiences, knowledge, and information are not beneficial but are harmful for him. . . . We would be guilty . . . if on the one hand we explained world events to the best of our knowledge and conscience, and on the other hand permitted and helped the dissemination of conflicting capitalist interpretations, which are often arbitrary and malicious."[10]

Nor are professional periodicals easily obtainable, and here again there is an increasingly vocal demand. Typical of appeals to the authorities are these words in *Kulturni Tvorba* by the Czechoslovak economist Radoslav Selucky, who explains that "the capitalist employs the lessons of the economic-technical revolution much more quickly and consistently than we do. . . . We must learn from whoever knows how to produce better goods."[11]

Languages. The prerequisite, of course, for the use of foreign publications is knowledge of the language in which they are written. Undeniable progress has been made in this respect. Even in Bulgaria every pupil must study a Western language from the seventh grade on. At the moment French is the language most widely studied, followed by German and English. There are, in addition, language courses for adults. The study of Russian has declined in relative importance throughout Eastern Europe, partly in reaction to the overemphasis given to it in the initial period after the victory of the communists. Interest in Western languages will inevitably continue to grow as travel and tourism to and from the West increases.

Manifestations of Western Influence

Comparison and criticism go hand in hand. Hence the roughly one-to-one relationship between exposure to the West and awakening to deficiences at home. It is this writer's experience that the most vocal complaints about conditions at home can be heard from people in Yugoslavia, the country which is the most generous in its handling of exit and entry visas. From these people, former laborers in the West, primarily in West Germany, there are also some complaints about the way they were treated abroad —but these complaints are directed against individuals, while the praise is directed at conditions in general and at specific aspects of the system.

The relatively low standard of living throughout Eastern Europe impels the tourist-eager governments to create special conditions for Western tourists—hotels, shops, waiting rooms, etc. But the sword is double-edged. By surrounding the guest with a relative abundance of Western comforts, they inevitably stimulate among their own people an awareness of such comforts and foster discontent and resentment of conditions at home—a resentment which tends to be directed less against the foreigner than against the regime.

To cite one of the many examples, the Czechoslovak author Vladimir Blazek, after a visit to the Brno fair, wrote in *Literarni Noviny* of February 1, 1964, that the people look "wide-eyed at the Chevrolets, Mercedes, Opels, and Taunusses. . . . People seem to lose their dignity before cars. One wonders how this is possible in our country, a country which is industrial and has a cultural tradition." Blazek complained of the *ersatz* character of many establishments which existed only for the duration of the fair and only for the foreigner: "The special dining room is closed as soon as the fair is over, and the sign EATING PLACE FOR FOREIGNERS is put away in the cellar. . . ." He writes that during the fair

> Brno ceases to be a city and becomes one gigantic stage-set for foreigners. People cease to be people and turn into bit players and extras in a bad propaganda film— bad not only because it disappears after the fair, but because reality, the ordinary life of the city, is concealed beneath the masquerade. The drama of ordinary life [in Brno] is a different thing, corroded with everyday uncertainties; having clothes cleaned, getting hold of some coal, or buying paprika can be major world problems. In this ordinary life the smooth operation of the Hotel International is tied by invisible but very real threads to the dirt and rotten service at the Brno railroad station, to the chronic breakdowns of the municipal transportation system, to the ignorance and incompetence of sales personnel, cashiers, and conductors.[12]

In the years after 1945 the Germans were in a similar position with regard to their Western occupiers, particularly the rich and well-fed Americans. But at that time not much resentment was produced because every German knew that Germany had been defeated—and, before long, prosperity returned anyway. It was with humor that one sang the carnival song composed for 1948: "We are the natives of Trizonesia." But it is with bitterness that the citizens of East European countries call themselves "natives" in comparison with the well-to-do foreign tourists. Prague's *Kulturni Tvorba* wrote on April 2, 1964, that during the tourist season "natives" are only "second-class visitors" to Czechoslovak restaurants, "suffered only as a necessary evil": "The native guest is only allowed to look at what is being served at the foreign table and is not allowed to order the same. . . . Even ordinary rolls are reserved for the foreigners, unless some are left over."[13]

Everything that is Western is superior, at least as far as consumer goods are concerned. This is the general understanding in Eastern Europe: Western airlines treat you better in the air;[14]

Western factories turn out better contraceptives;[15] Eurovision, the West European television network, is better than Intervision, its communist counterpart;[16] Henry Ford II is a shining example of effective management.[17]

Popular warmth toward the West has been expressed in a variety of ways—in the spontaneous welcome accorded Robert Kennedy, in the enthusiasm shown in June, 1965, to the visiting Archbishop of Canterbury in, of all places, orthodox Rumania. This writer is inclined to believe that even the Soviet poet Yevgeni Yevtushenko owed his impressive welcome to a feeling that he was an *ersatz* Westerner, a man acclaimed in the West and attacked by his own government.

The changes which have drawn Eastern Europe closer to the West during the past several years included some which might have grown spontaneously from within, without stimulation from the West. Perhaps the consumer and the market economy and sociology would have been "discovered" even if the Iron Curtain had remained what it was in Stalin's days. But it is undeniable that the influence of the West has at the very least speeded if not engendered these momentous changes. And once "discovered," they developed, because the people concerned had at their disposal the huge body of Western experience and literature on these subjects.

Much has been written in the West about the trends toward consumer and market orientation, toward new methods in the fields of economics and management.[18] We also know that the conclusions drawn by the East European economists from their studies are rather far-reaching. Professor Benedikt Korda has even demanded in *Planovane Hospodarstvi*[19] the rethinking of the Marxist dogma according to which "socialism is irreconcilable with any form of private ownership of means of production."[20] We are particularly well informed about the growth of sociology in Eastern Europe—in the bloc as a whole by Ralph K. White,[21] in Poland by Wladyslaw Markiewicz[22] and Emilia Wilder,[23] and in Czechoslovakia by Edward Taborsky.[24]

The implications of these "discoveries" will not be dealt with here. The important thing is that such concepts are now being recognized in the communist world for their merits, not purely as instruments of the party. Of course the party tries to harness them and to turn them into tools; of course it applies to them in effect—as to everything else that it had to accept—the well-worn cliché: "Under socialism, sociology (or profit or interest or whatever it may be) is good, under capitalism it is bad." Nor would anyone doubt that sociology and the other social sciences do change at the hands of communists, if only to a limited extent. The "discovery" of what might be described as autonomous moral values by the Polish philosopher Leszek Kolakowski[25] is an example of the kind of development that must inevitably erode the monolithic power of the party.

Literature in particular can have such a corrosive effect. It was not only their lack of education that made Stalin and Khrushchev detest Kafka. Communism and Kafka just do not go together. The reintroduction of Kafka, hesitant and incomplete as it is, cannot but affect communism. This writer was impressed with the reactions of the Czechs at the opening of the small Kafka exhibition in Prague in the autumn of 1964: They clearly viewed it as a historic occasion.

Sooner or later, "socialist realism" was bound to be diluted. But its decline was hastened by the impact of Western literature. The communist leaders of Eastern Europe know this—as Khrushchev did and as Brezhnev does. Concern has been expressed in countless speeches and articles decrying the new literary trends, in the closing of *Przeglad Kulturalny* and *Nowa Kultura* in Poland, in the complaints against *Kulturny Zivot, Literarni Noviny,* and *Plamen* in Czechoslovakia.[26] There can be no doubt as to the intrinsic dangers from the communist point of view, in the pessimism of much of Western literature, its "alienation," its detachment from—if not hostility toward—the affairs of the state, its uncompromising quest for truth, its disruptive experimentation with new forms, its addiction to the analysis of fear and solitude.

We may consider alienation as an example. Marx regarded alienation as the lot of the laborer who had been deprived of his tools and of his normal relationship to society by the capitalist. Now it turns out that alienation is the sad lot of the citizen of the "socialist" countries and particularly of their intellectual elites. In his study on alienation Peter Christian Ludz wrote in the chapter, "Alienation as Expression of an Ideological Crisis": "Die geistige Krise im Ostblock hat ihre vielleicht tiefste Wurzel in dem Verfall des naiven anthropologischen Optimismus und der unkritischen Fortschrittsgläubigkeit, die für den sowjetrussischen Marxismus-Leninismus jahrzehntelang typisch waren. . . . Die neue Intelligenz fuhlt sich in ihrer Existenz entfremdet."[27]

Closely linked with alienation is withdrawal and solitude. In countries whose ideology demands the incessant, whole-hearted, enthusiastic participation of everybody in everything that pertains to the collective, such attitudes are far less palatable than in the West. What becomes of socialism, after all, if poets like Hungary's János Pilinszky and László sing:

> We must live and die, fighting each other,
> choking amidst sharp stones and pebbles

and

> Woe to me, woe to us.
> We must die, because we don't love.
> All dreams shall die,
> and your great solitude and
> my sinister orphanhood haunt us forever.[28]

Small wonder that a state of tension exists between the communist rulers and the intellectual elite, the poets in particular, and that from time to time open battles are fought such as the one between Gomulka and "the thirty-four" in the spring of 1964.[29]

Why Was It Allowed?

Why, then, did the communist leaders permit the Iron Curtain to dissolve into an Iron Sieve? They could have prevented it, or at least postponed it considerably. But they did not want to pay the price. Khrushchev understood that the upkeep of the Iron Curtain was extremely costly and that the price was loss of momentum in the process of modernization. The Soviet Union's isolation from the West put a brake on its development; therefore the Iron Curtain had to be made more penetrable. Khrushchev's lieutenants in Eastern Europe went still further, not without logic, most noticeably in the case of Rumania. National considerations prompted a Rumanian desire for greater independence of the Moscow-controlled CEMA, and in loosening her ties with the U.S.S.R. and the other CEMA countries Rumania had to develop her trade relations with the West. In so doing, she came up against the problem of offering sufficient goods to bring in Western currencies. She was forced to tap all possible currency reserves, and in the process she found that one such reserve was untouched: hence the effort to promote the tourist trade.

The Iron Curtain was allowed to become more penetrable because of two main considerations: to improve the quantity and quality of the technological elite and to procure more foreign currency. It was hoped, of course, that this might be done with a minimum of disturbances. To be sure, distinctions were made between the technological elite, which was badly needed, and the more vulnerable artistic elite. But it proved virtually impossible to stimulate intellectual intercourse with the West in the field of science and technology without also permitting it in other areas; and, conversely, the artistic elite—afflicted by alienation and withdrawal—could not be crushed without adverse effect on the scientific-technological intelligentsia. Recognition of the integrity of the intellectual world by the communist leaders has been one of the most encouraging developments in Eastern Europe from the viewpoint of the West.

Re-Stalinization?   The question of the reversibility of the thaw has preoccupied students of Soviet and East European affairs since 1956. A parallel arises with regard to the relative penetrability of the Iron Curtain. In the crude sense of the word, of course, everything is reversible. There is no law which insures the world against the rule of a new Stalin in Russia, of a new Bierut in Poland, a new Rákosi in Hungary. One of the old Stalinists, after all, is still on the scene in East Germany. The re-establishment of regimes of terror, of nightly arrests, the prohibiton of travel abroad and of Western books, periodicals, films, the brutal persecution of poets and philosophers—all this, unfortunately, is not impossible.

Not impossible, but not likely. It could only be brought about at the price of new isolation and all that this would mean for the progress of the communist world. In the unlikely eventuality of a tightening of the Iron Curtain and a regression to Stalinism, we may be certain that it will be neo-Stalinism, not a carbon copy of the Stalinism that expired with its creator twelve years ago. Far more likely than re-Stalinization, in this writer's view, is a recurrence of efforts by the Soviet and East European leaders to reap the benefits of contacts with the West while seeking to mitigate and offset the obvious liabilites for their regimes that are inherent in such contacts. There will be attempts to stem the attraction of the Western way of life, of Western freedom; there will be prohibitions of Western films, discouragement of personal relations with Westerners; there may well be periods marked by a general pulling in of the reins, followed by periods of new relaxation—the pattern we have been witnessing during the last several years.

The Keyhole Effect. One might ask: How was it possible that the relatively few and narrow openings in the Iron Curtain could have such powerful effects on the nations of East Europe? The answer lies in what could be called the keyhole effect. If one looks through a keyhole into a room which is closed, and about whose contents one is insatiably curious, one will observe the few things in one's line of vision with much greater attention than if the door were open and one could simply walk in.

Therefore it would be wrong to conclude that the more numerous and the wider the contacts between countries, the more they will want to know of each other. Nor would it be correct to conclude, conversely: the fewer contacts the better. The optimum lies somewhere in between the two extremes—probably not far from where relations between the East European countries and the West are today.

One could argue, from this vantage point, that a total disappearance of the Iron Curtain would be to the detriment rather than to the advantage of the West's image in the East. As matters stand now, there is a certain exciting mystery about the West; many people in the East are tired of the drabness of their everyday lives; anything that is different seems full of color and attraction. As they get to know us better, there will be inevitable disappointments and some disenchantment. Before the still relatively ingenuous curiosity of our neighbors in the East is replaced by a more mature and analytical perspicacity, we would do well to take a long look at ourselves and consider what we might do to enhance our fitness for the intellectual and material competition between the West and the East which moves closer to the forefront as the Iron Curtain dissolves.

NOTES

1. These figures are taken mainly from the Czechoslovak Statistical Yearbook for 1964, p. 377, and from *Rude Pravo*, June 19, 1965.
2. *Problems of Communism*, January, 1965, p. 35; *East Europe*, October, 1964, p. 18; *Hinter Dem Eisernen Vorhang*, February, 1965, p. 33.
3. According to an interview by the director of the Rumanian travel agency Carpati, G. Teodorescu, *Lumea*, September 3, 1964, p. 18.
4. "40 times the number of 1956," according to *Agerpress*, December 20, 1964.
5. *East Europe*, November, 1964, p. 25.
6. Some of the difficulties encountered by the Germans in connection with the Bucharest Fair are enumerated in *Münchner Merkur*, May 26, 1965.
7. *Bibliograficky katalog CSSR. Ceske Knihy*, 1963.
8. *Magyarorszag*, September 9, 1964, quoted in *East Europe*, November, 1964, p. 42.
9. *Agerpress*, September 19, 1964, p. 14.
10. Quoted from *East Europe*, March, 1964, p. 14.
11. Quoted from *Die Politische Meinung*, January, 1965, p. 82.
12. Partly translated in *East Europe*, April, 1964, p. 82.
13. Quoted from *East Europe*, July, 1964, p. 33.
14. *Kulturni Tvorba*, November 11, 1963.
15. *Literarni noviny*, November 9, 1963.
16. *Pravda* (Bratislava), March 14, 1965.
17. *Kulturni Zivot*, January 16, 1965.
18. See, for example, the articles by Heinz Machowski on Poland, *Osteuropa-Wirtschaft*, January, 1964, pp. 18–37, by Vaclav Holesovsky on Czechoslovakia, *East Europe*, November–December, 1964, by Wolfgang Eggers on Yugoslavia, *Osteuropa-Wirtschaft*, January, 1964, pp. 37–46, and by Michael Garmanikow, *East Europe*, May and July, 1964, and Alan A. Brown and Richard Yui, *Communist Affairs*, January, 1965, pp. 3–9, on East Europe in general. For a Czechoslovak view see Rudolph Kozanda in the Moscow *Kommunist*, September, 1965, pp. 84–93.
19. Prague, January, 1965.
20. Quoted from *Hinter dem Eisernen Vorhang*, March, 1965, p. 27.
21. *Public Opinion Quarterly*, January, 1964, pp. 20–26.
22. *Österreichische Osthefte*, January, 1965, pp. 22–32.
23. *Problems of Communism*, January, 1965, pp. 58–62.
24. *Problems of Communism*, January, 1965, pp. 62–66. *Osteuropa* has printed a bibliography of bloc publications on sociology by Dr. Gábor Kiss in the November–December, 1965, issues.
25. In *Der Mensch ohne Alternative* (Munich, 1960), *passim*, esp. p. 242.
26. *Rude Pravo*, April 3, 1964.
27. "The spiritual crisis in the Eastern bloc is perhaps most deeply rooted in the decline of the naïve, anthropological optimism and the uncritical belief in progress which were typical of Soviet Russian Marxism-Leninism for decades. . . . The new intelligentsia feels alienated from its existence." (Editor's translation.) *Osteuropäische Rundschau*, May, 1965, pp. 6f. An interesting disclosure of the internal discussion about alienation (and Kafka) can be found in Roman Karst's article "Horyzonty realizmu," in *Polityka* (Warsaw), January, 1964.

28. William Juhász, "The Literature of Solitude," *East Europe*, December, 1963, pp. 18–22.

29. For an excellent review of recent developments on Czechoslovakia's literary scene see Rudolf Urban's "Die 'verlorene' Zeit," *Osteuropa*, November–December, 1963, pp. 772–84.

14. Polycentrism, West and East: East European Implications of the Western Debates*

Pierre Hassner

Converging Western Reactions to the Evolution of Eastern European Polycentrism

This essay seeks to approach East European polycentrism from the outside, considering it less in itself than as a subject of Western speculation and debate. By raising questions about the general nature of polycentrism and about the mutual influence of the Western and Eastern aspects of the phenomenon, these discussions in the West, while concerned with the effects of such Western institutions or policies as NATO, the Common Market, or Gaullism, seem to this writer to be directly relevant to an understanding of Eastern Europe; for it is difficult to understand the recent developments and likely prospects of East European polycentrism without relating them to Western policy toward Eastern Europe and, more generally, to the evolution of East-West relations and of the West itself.

Two features seem to characterize the present stage; taken together they point to a paradox which constitutes our subject. First, the Western debates have entered a stage where the Atlantic Alliance and the European Community seem to be considered at least as much from the point of view of their geographical boundaries and of their relationship to the external environment —particularly in Eastern Europe—as from the point of view of their defense and internal stability.[1] At the same time, the debate about policies toward Eastern Europe tends to place in opposi-

---

*This title does not assume any identity of nature between the divisive tendencies in the West and the East. It is the author's view that both their origins (from success in the West, from failure in the East) and their context (a pluralistic alliance or a universalistic movement) are fundamentally different. The purpose of this essay is precisely to question to what extent the widely held impression about the symmetry and interaction between the developments in the West and the East, in the EEC and CEMA, in NATO and the Warsaw Pact, in France and Rumania, have any validity. The title indicates the problem, not any particular answer.

tion not so much these policies themselves, as it does the diverging views of the effects which the various forms of organization or
disorganization of the West can have upon them. On the one
hand, the Atlantic and European debate points to the long-range
problem of German and European reunification and to the short-
range problem of relations with Eastern Europe; on the other
hand, the discussion of both these problems leads us back to the
debate on the present and future nature of Europe and on its
present and future relationship with the United States.

This need not constitute a vicious circle. Whether one starts
from the West or the East, the question to which the discussion
leads is: What is the relationship, if any, between, on the one
hand, the evolution (economic, institutional, political) of Western Europe and its links with the United States and, on the
other, the evolution of Eastern Europe and its links with the
Soviet Union?

The ambiguous and reciprocal character of this question shows
how Europe today is both still divided and already united—how
the destinies of its two halves are both solidary and distinct. As a
consequence of the evolution of Eastern Europe, Western Europe
can no longer define and organize itself without asking itself
what immediate and long-range effects its choices will have on
the evolution of Eastern Europe and on the prospects for reunification; at the same time these indirect consequences of its own
evolution seem both more important and more debatable than
those of its direct action.

This in a sense has been the situation ever since the partition
of Europe. Every step in the organization of the West has been
haunted by the ever recurring debate over whether the integration of Western Europe in NATO and of Western Germany in
Western Europe is a prerequisite or a substitute for the reunification of each with its Eastern half, or an obstacle to reunification.
The simultaneous emergence of very different forms of polycentrism in both halves has given this debate a new urgency and a
new dimension.

The emergence of new perspectives in the East (Soviet *détente*
and East European differentiation, both pointing to the historical defeat of the Soviet empire in Eastern Europe) [2] was bound to
add fuel to the new debates of the West. It occurs precisely at a
time when both NATO and the Common Market, having ful-

filled their most immediate military and economic tasks, are faced on the one hand with fundamental political choices concerning further steps toward unity and, on the other, with the emergence of new factors of disunity within the West—the result of a certain shift in American orientation and, above all, of the existence and designs of General de Gaulle. Hence there is a certain readiness to see Eastern Europe in a new light, as an opportunity either for raising new alternatives or for scoring new points in an old debate.

Precisely because of intra-Western competition, the responses of Western states to the new situation in Eastern Europe are very similar in content while very dissimilar in ultimate motives and objectives. Western governments disagree, less because they believe in different policies toward the East than because they believe in the same one but disagree over who should implement it or whose "grand design" it should serve.

Every Western government favors a "policy of movement" in Eastern Europe, a policy which implies the encouragement of East European polycentrism and hence of further independence of the one-time satellites from the Soviet Union, and at the same time the encouragement of *détente* and hence of a dialogue with the Soviet Union itself. Of course, Western governments have at various times stressed different aspects of this policy. Some governments have at times seemed on the verge of rejecting some of its aspects. At one time, Germany and France seemed committed to a rigid cold war approach which would mean de-emphasizing both the realities of change in Eastern Europe and the necessity of East-West contacts. At times the United States has seemed tempted to accept the status quo in Europe, including Soviet hegemony in the East, for the sake of a bilateral understanding with the Soviet Union. However, Germany is becoming increasingly impatient with her division; France has entered a phase in which the Gaullist concept of "Europe from the Atlantic to the Urals" has become the policy goal of an "opening to the East"; and the United States has chosen to encourage the differentiation of the East. Washington knows that progress on arms control cannot be made without an understanding with the Soviet Union, but that this understanding is impossible without the participation of the Western Allies and that acceptance of the division of Europe and of Germany would mean buying Soviet good will at the price of instability, dissatisfaction, and division in the West, especially in the German Federal Republic. Hence it would be self-defeating for any of the three countries, and particularly for the United States or France, as long as they value their relationship with Germany, to declare itself in favor of the status quo.

But by the same token, nobody pretends any longer to believe in the possibility of a sudden or spectacular reversal of the present state of affairs. While every Western government professes to favor the reunification of Europe, and to link the latter in turn with the encouragement of polycentrism and the building of bridges to Eastern Europe, the implication of these very links is that reunification will be a very long and indirect process. If pure containment no longer seems sufficient, both pure disengagement and military rollback have lost whatever plausibility they may once have seemed to possess. The debate in the various Western countries no longer turns around the simple alternatives of the fifties. In the United States, while some quarters still favor an essentially defensive Atlantic orientation[3] and others an acceptance of Germany's and Europe's division in the name of polycentrism and liberalization,[4] Dean Acheson[5] has urged a more active concern with German reunification. Zbigniew Brzezinski[6] and Henry Kissinger[7] have, in various ways, attempted to indicate a path toward a more active and complex policy dedicated to preparing an "alternative to partition" in a wider European framework. In Great Britain, the traditional sympathy for disengagement and nuclear-free zones does not inspire any current debate on policy, while on the other hand links with Eastern Europe are actively encouraged. France is the country where these links receive the highest priority: they seem to meet with practically no opposition. Other policies such as disengagement have never been taken very seriously except by some individual statesmen—Pierre Mendès-France or Jules Moch. Germany is the only country where the new policies are really controversial. But even there, both the old CDU policy of containment in the hope of a rollback in the distant future and the old SPD policy of negotiation for disengagement seem, as Theo Sommer has remarked, to have died with the erection of the Wall.[8] For want of any alternative, the debate turns more on the scope and nature of the "little steps" in contacts with the East than on the policy itself. No wonder, then, that at the governmental level the policy of "peaceful engagement in Eastern Europe"[9] seems to have been adopted by President Johnson[10] and President de Gaulle,[11] by the West German government and the SPD,[12] including even, for the time being, the most controversial feature of this strategy: the isolation of East Germany within a framework of contacts with the other East European communist countries. It constitutes the ideal answer to the necessity of taking active steps toward reunification combined with the inability to fundamentally challenge the status quo.

However, every lucid advocate of peaceful engagement will admit that "bridge-building," if it is not to be simply a substitute for a policy, can only be an element or an instrument of one.[13] It addresses itself to the most accessible or vulnerable parts of the Soviet European empire: the rapidly differentiating regimes of Eastern Europe. The two more intractable elements, Soviet military power and the German problem, remain; while it is true that the "return to Europe" of the East European states may, indirectly and in the long run, strongly contribute to bringing about a reconsideration by the Soviets of their presence in East Germany, for the time being it is this very presence which makes East European polycentrism possible, by enabling the Soviet Union to tolerate it precisely because she has a reasonable chance of maintaining it within certain bounds.[14] Hence, the two problems to which containment and disengagement had addressed themselves—the building and keeping of a stable military balance and the devising of a negotiating formula (in terms of *quid pro quo,* guarantees, and a general European framework) which would make a free and united Germany acceptable to the Soviet Union—are still the beginning and the end of a meaningful *"Osteuropa politik."*

They are also its most controversial parts. While almost everyone favors contacts with Eastern Europe, there is no agreement on the question of *who* should have contacts with *whom,* nor on the distant goals to whose realization these contacts are supposed to contribute. For the questions of one common or several competitive approaches to the East today, of the participants in an eventual European settlement tomorrow, and of the structure, limits, and external relationships of the reunited Europe of the day after tomorrow all involve a choice—or at least a distribution of roles—among the alternatives of an Atlantic, a European, or a national framework. These, much more than the alternatives of containment, rollback, disengagement, and peaceful engagement, are the real issues in the debates of the various countries.

In the United States, the decisive problem for the fate of the "bridge-building" and "peaceful engagement" policies is the future relationship of America to Europe on the one hand and to Asia on the other. The feeling is spreading in England that Britain's entry or non-entry into Western Europe is bound to have more important consequences for her relations with Eastern Europe than any of her diplomatic initiatives. In France, while there never was a real debate focused specifically either on disengagement or on policies toward Eastern Europe, the old debates on Germany, on Europe, and on neutralism are obviously decisive for Eastern Europe. Even in Germany, for whom the freedom to choose her own orientation and framework is so vital a matter, the immediate debate between the government and the "German Gaullists" concerns Germany's orientation within the West much more than her policies toward the East. The deepest question seems to be whether the twin and sometimes conflicting goals of security and reunification are to be pursued within the framework of integration in the West or of a new European or old German nationalism. To a very significant extent, then, the battle for the future of Eastern Europe is fought within the West's debate about its own identity and future.

CONFLICTING WESTERN PERSPECTIVES ON THE
FUTURE OF EASTERN EUROPE

The debate on the actual and the desirable relationship between Western and Eastern polycentrisms is taking place on several levels. One can distinguish first between the Atlantic debate, which is focused on the proper relationship between America and Europe, and the European debate, which centers on the nature of the proper relationship between European states. Secondly, in a Europe based on the competing and mutually balancing policies of several nation-states, the initiative in policies toward the East should either belong to Germany or to France, or may be contested between the two.

The various debates all seem to imply certain conflicting postulates or theoretical choices. In each of them one side tends to take for granted what we could call the *contrast postulate* and the other what one could call the *symmetry postulate*. According to the first, the stronger, more stable, and more united we are, the more the other side will be weak, unstable, and divided. Our disunity helps their unity, by enabling them to exploit our divisions; our unity fosters their disunity by producing frustration, and our stability and prosperity foster it by acting as a magnet on their more accessible or detachable members. According to the opposing postulate, the more united we are, the more we solidify the unity of our opponents; our military alliances and economic communities induce them to imitate us by integrating militarily and economically themselves. Thus, let the United States withdraw and the Soviet Union will do the same; let the West Europeans be polycentric and non-aligned, and polycentrism and non-alignment will flourish in the East; the two blocs will only be loosened or dissolved together, by mutual example.[15]

It is enough to enunciate these postulates to see that they can have no complete or universal validity one way or the other. However, one cannot simply close the debate by an appeal for empiricism and for judgment of each case on its merits. Throughout the Atlantic and European debate, a genuinely universal contest is indeed being waged. It opposes the two fundamental conceptions of international politics and of international order in our time: Should a solution to the European problem be based on the growing interdependence of societies or on the restored independence of states? Should it be based on the steady growing together of peoples and regimes through functional relationships and through the progress of such enterprises as European integration and arms control, based on new common interests transcending old conflicts, or on the eternal ends and means of foreign politics, national ambition, and the art of diplomatic strategy? Here again, some middle ground or combination should be found. But it could not obscure the fundamental opposition between the two perspectives symbolized by Jean Monnet and Charles de Gaulle—between the expansion, from a central core, of a zone of stability and co-operation which would devaluate national borders, limit the freedom of action of states through sub- and supranational ties, and reach finally from San Francisco to Vladivostok, or a dialectical strategy according to which the two Europes should first liberate themselves from their embrace of the two hegemonies before meeting again from the Atlantic to the Urals in a restored concert based on a new balance among Gauls, Germans, and Slavs. The opposition between the two methods—the primacy of domestic construction versus the primacy of external strategy—is maintained in the eventual results: The reunification of Europe would be both a means and a result either of getting away from, or of getting back to, the freedom of action of the nation-state.

The Atlantic Debate.   Being a defensive military alliance, NATO can be said to have a built-in bias in favor of the status quo, or at least in favor of the policies which would modify it without challenging the existing military system. It is sometimes described as the instrument of American hegemony, resulting from a tacit or explicit understanding with the Soviet Union on the partition of Europe.[16] Secondly, NATO has been said to represent a reaction to, rather than an instrument of, the division of Europe, but to have deepened that division by reacting to the Soviet threat in an excessively rigid and military way. Thirdly, NATO has been said to have been justified in the past, but to have outlived its usefulness. Precisely because it *has* succeeded and because the Soviet threat is declining, according to this third view, it can now have a negative effect by perpetuating the situation it was established to counteract and by becoming an obstacle to the very evolution it has provoked. The postwar world is past, and the United States, as a non-European power, should retire in order to encourage a similarly natural withdrawal of Russia and to let the European family get together without the presence of strangers.[17]

Finally, the criticisms of NATO can be focused on the problem of Germany. The defensive character of the alliance and the unsatisfied aspirations of a divided Germany are held to be incompatible, giving rise to the twin dangers of contributing to the division of Germany and to the unity of the East by tying Germany to an alliance of satisfied powers while creating the fear that it might be Germany which would draw the alliance into support of its revisionist drives. German participation in NATO —with eventual participation in the collective control of nuclear weapons—is blamed for preventing German and European reunification by promoting the military integration of the two camps and raising in Poland and Czechoslovakia the specter of German access to nuclear weapons.

The positive counterpart of these criticisms can be summed up in the two famous and ambiguous slogans: "European Europe" and "Europe from the Atlantic to the Urals."[18] In order to be Europe again, Europe must be purely European; in order to reach to the Urals it should stop at the Atlantic Ocean. The basic idea is that geographical Europe has a historical existence which is more natural and, in the long run, more real than any ideological or strategic cleavage. This historical geography involves an interpretation of Europe's recent past and distant future. For General de Gaulle, the two antinatural phenomena of 1944–45 — Europe's division and its subordination to the two great powers —are two faces of the same reality: its partition among its conquerors. The objective is to obtain their departure, which will mean the restoration of Europe—that is, the restoration both of its external role and of an intra-European concert based on an equilibrium which would encompass the whole of Europe precisely because it would encompass only Europe. This permanent reality and this long-range perspective produce certain immediate possibilities. Between the two halves of Europe there are greater affinities, memories, and mutual understandings than with their "daughter America." Not only are Eastern Europe's economic, touristic, and cultural relations more important with Western Europe because of geographical proximity, but they are also politically less compromising. Indeed, according to the anti-Atlantic thesis, the more detached Western Europe is from the United States, the less dangerous it is for Eastern Europe to have contacts with her.

But what about the passage from this immediate geographic and sentimental proximity to the distant prospect of historical reunification? As regards the goal to be sought, General de Gaulle's ideas are best expressed in his February 4, 1965, press conference. It appears there that the true and only originality of his solution to the problem of German and European unification consists precisely in the choice of the partners in a settlement and of the participants in the resulting equilibrium. In both cases they are the same. The goal and the road have the same characteristic: Europeanization and exclusion of the United States. It is the six states of the European Economic Community which will have to organize their defense in order to permit a new European balance. It is Germany's neighbors, East and West, which will have to agree on its borders and armaments and guarantee the settlement. The solution is to take place outside and beyond the confrontation of the present two camps and within the new "Europe between the Atlantic and the Urals" made possible by the abandonment of Soviet ambition and the transformation of the satellites.

As for the strategy which should lead Europe toward this goal, it seems to be limited to variations of a threefold basic idea. Thanks to Chinese and East European polycentric nationalism, the Soviet Union wants, or can be persuaded, to abandon its exclusive domination of Central and Eastern Europe; but for her to leave, the United States has to leave Europe too. To obtain this double result, an active role on the part of Western Europe is both possible and necessary. According to the Gaullist interpretation, the Soviet threat to Western Europe is becoming less and less real, Eastern Europe is becoming more and more independent, American protection of Western Europe is both less and less reliable and less and less necessary, and Western Europe is more and more able to stand on its own feet and to balance by its own means a less hostile and less powerful East.

Obviously, it is this assessment of the present situation which is the most vulnerable to pro-Atlantic counterattack. That the Cold War should wither away through the recession of the Soviet threat, that Western Europe should be sufficiently strong to balance it alone—these are two possibilities which, in the abstract and in the long run, are conceivable although debatable, but are absurd today. There is no reason to believe that in the present world system, military and political balances necessarily could or should be established within the old geographical limits of continents. On the contrary, as Raymond Aron[19] and Dean Acheson[20] have pointed out, there is every reason to believe that the United States is needed to balance the power of the Soviet Union as long as the military sovereignty of the latter stretches to the middle of the continent, and that all the unsolved problems of Germany, Central Europe, arms control, etc., can only be solved through joint European and American participation.

But along what lines can they be solved? While the Atlantic

side obviously has the best of the debate in terms of security and stability, it is incumbent upon it either to admit that these have to be brought about at the expense of accepting the status quo, or to show concretely to what extent Europe's transatlantic ties offer the best chances not only to maintain the status quo but also to modify it in the right direction[21]—that is, toward the reunification of Germany and Europe. It would seem to us that the best chances lie in the direction of concerted action and mutual influence (however narrow and difficult this well-meaning path may be) between Europe and the United States, who would protect each other against the temptations of defensive status quo and isolated adventure. On the economic level, the Eastern European countries seem equally interested in receiving aid from or concluding commercial agreements with both the United States and Western Europe if they are profitable. Politically, just as a bilateral Soviet-American *détente* raises fears of an agreement on the division of Europe, so a polycentric *détente* with neutralist overtones creates the risk of instability resulting from Soviet exploitation of the divisions of the West.[22]

This brings us to the problem of the way toward a negotiated settlement in Europe. It is here—in the distinction between the *negotiation*, the *content*, and the *guarantees* of the agreement— that the cleavages between the narrow Atlantic, the narrow European, and the broad Western or co-operative attitude are most important. The first of these attitudes holds that all three stages must be Atlantic, for an opposition of interests or a separation between the United States and Europe is unthinkable. The second holds that all three stages must be "Europeanized"; only Germany's neighbors can "examine together, then settle in common and finally guarantee jointly the solution of a problem which is the problem of their continent."[23] But for the third school, the three stages must be distinguished: The *means* of reaching an agreement necessarily imply the presence and participation of the United States. Moreover, this agreement should necessarily be approved and *guaranteed* by them and be part of a system in which they participate. But its *content* may, and perhaps should, include a withdrawal of American troops and a status for a reunified Germany and a reunified Europe which would imply a fundamental differentiation within the Western whole. The interest of the United States in Europe and the presence of its troops is the major card of any negotiation; the permanence of this interest would be the main guarantee of an eventual settlement; but it is precisely the presence of these troops that would be one of the subjects of negotiation, and their withdrawal might be one of the elements of the agreement.[24] On the other hand, if the agreement were imposed unilaterally and prematurely through a kind of West European revolt, it would lead to disorder and insecurity. Only the United States, through its active participation in the agreement, could both obtain a fair price and provide a safe cover for its own retreat. To that extent, one could say that the three concepts of containment, peaceful engagement, and disengagement all have a useful role to play— but only in that order. To start with disengagement before Europe is sufficiently transformed to make containment certain or superfluous would be disastrous, and this applies both to the well-meaning but premature disengagement plans of the fifties and to De Gaulle's grand disengagement on a continental scale. Seen from the point of view of the United States, there is a dialectical relationship between peaceful engagement and disengagement: It is only by more engagement today that the conditions can be created for a possible disengagement tomorrow. As asked rhetorically in the common declaration of the Action Committee for the United States of Europe on May 4, 1965, in obvious answer to the February 4 press conference: "How would it be possible to arrive at an arrangement of peaceful coexistence between the Soviet Union and the West if Europe and the United States did not seek it together? How would it be possible that a settlement providing for the reunion of Germans from East and West should intervene if the Soviet Union, Europe and the United States did not find in it the indispensable elements of security?"

This last and central problem, how to reconcile Germany's rebirth and consequently inevitable power with the security of its partners, constitutes the link between the problem of yesterday and today—Germany's rearmament and participation in Western nuclear strategy—and the problem of tomorrow and the day after tomorrow—Germany's reunification and role in a united Europe. If the United States is indispensable to protect and guarantee Europe, including Germany, against a real danger from Russia, is it not needed almost as much to protect and guarantee Europe, including the Eastern countries, against a possible danger from Germany? Within a purely European concert of powers Germany's weight may become so preponderant that some of its neighbors would quite happily settle for a divided Germany within a reunited Europe. Conversely, in the case of a reunited Germany within a reunited Europe, just as that of a divided Germany within a divided Europe, the moderating influence of American presence and power can become a reassuring element to the Eastern countries just as to the Germans themselves. For the smaller countries of Europe the only acceptable prospects are either an equilibrium which, in order to avoid dominance by either Germany or Russia, or both, or a confrontation between them, would include the United States, or a long-range transformation of the situation which would be so radical that the problem of establishing an equilibrium between the presently existing states would be left behind, together with these states themselves. The goal of Western policy since the war has been to combine these two prospects by passing progressively from an emphasis on the first one to an emphasis on the second. The widening to include Eastern Europe—which was encouraged from the beginning but has been more or less lost sight of in practice—calls for important modifications; but it does *not* modify the fundamental perspective in either respect.

The European Debate. Like NATO, the European Community faces the twin problems of inner diversity and outer boundaries, and the twin criticisms of threatening the independence of its member nations and of separating them from those left outside. The proposed alternative is based in both cases on both criticisms. Just as Western Europe is supposed to be able to restore its ties with Eastern Europe only by becoming independent from NATO, so the nations of Western Europe itself are said to be able to restore their traditional ties with the nations of Eastern Europe only if they do not allow community institutions to threaten their national independence and identity.

Like the Marshall Plan, but unlike NATO, the European integration movement was not originally based on the division of the continent. Its permanent goals were and are valid for the whole of Europe. But once the process is under way, by force of circumstances in one half of Europe it may, by transforming the economies, the societies and the political regimes, and ultimately the very existence of the member-states, create a more fundamental and more permanent differentiation from the other half than is represented by a military alliance. The same is true in the case of Germany, whose integration in the Europe of the Six can create a deeper if less explosive problem than its rearmament. Both a divided and a reunified Germany may be taken to point toward a wider Europe as a way of satisfying the one or of balancing the other.

It is essentially through this paradox of Germany that a uniting Western Europe has been kept aware of the problem of "the other Europe." The reunification of Europe cannot be said to have been a direct goal of the integration of the Six. But it would be even less valid to infer that this integration, having been started within the framework of the division of Europe, was based on a belief in the permanence of this division or was driven to consider the division as final or even as desirable. President Hallstein has applied specifically to relations with Eastern Europe what seems to have been the consistent—Monnet-inspired— philosophy of European integration: doing what was immediately possible with those willing to embark on the enterprise, while hoping that others would join later on when they got rid of their prejudices.[25] It remains true, however, that the arrival of newcomers does pose important and reciprocal problems of adaptation. Direct contacts with the erstwhile satellites on particular questions, as well as the devising of flexible forms of association which can be reconciled with political neutrality, as in the case of Austria,[26] are interesting if difficult first steps. Even more important to Eastern Europe's development have been the indirect effects of Western Europe's own movement up the community path.

A first aspect of the reactions of the communist states to Western unification and the Common Market was an acute worry about the effects of the new tariff union on the "economy." To that extent, the conventional criticisms against a protectionist and inward-looking Common Market can be applied to commercial relations between the two Europes and can find in this way a political, *détente*-oriented justification. The critique has a certain validity, although it can be exaggerated: The trade of East Europe with Western Europe is expanding, adjustments have been made, and it can be argued that precisely the difficulties and problems created by the Common Market for the countries of Eastern Europe, far from frightening them away, have had the effect of drawing those countries closer to the West by forcing them into contacts with it and into adaptations under its impact.[27]

Probably deeper and more permanent is the intellectual disarray caused by the vitality of Western capitalist economy and its ability to co-operate and even invent new forms of integration.[28] Khrushchev's attempt to revitalize CEMA obviously was an answer to the challenge of the Common Market; it was meant, on the one hand, to prevent satellite states from being attracted into the orbit of the Common Market and, on the other hand, to imitate the Common Market through a parallel organization and eventually to bring about co-operation between the two organizations. Here our theory of symmetry seems to register the clearest of its triumphs. Professor Marshall Shulman, while recommending the pursuit of unification, wrote in his article on "The Communist States and Western Integration"[29] that Western European integration was producing an "integration through induction" in Eastern Europe, and that the "ambiguous degree of autonomy" enjoyed by the East European states tended to decrease through the Soviet reaction to the Common Market. The sequence of the story, however, seems decisive both for the reality and for the theory. Surely the significant point is that these efforts to imitate the Common Market and thus promote the economic and perhaps the political unity of the bloc have failed. One bloc's or one community's unity may produce a corresponding desire for unity on the other side; but for this desire to be fulfilled, for symmetric initiatives to produce symmetric results, the two sides must have a strong element of symmetry to begin with, and this is no more the case between the two Europes than between the two social systems. The theory of symmetry can underline some real and sometimes important mechanisms. It is not by itself sufficient to predict the effects of a policy.

Nor, of course, is the opposite theory sufficient. The failure of the Khrushchevian formula for co-operation with the West has acted as a spur to alternative forms.[30] It is striking that it should be the Rumanians, the staunchest opponents of CEMA integration, who are also the most eager of all East Europeans for economic relations with the West.[31] The Rumanian practice would seem to reproduce exactly the Gaullist doctrine of universal co-operation coupled with absolute sovereignty.

More generally and empirically, it seems fair to say that economic relations between the two Europes, an essential factor in polycentrism, are likely to take on a predominantly bilateral character. However, some kind of region-to-region approach would still be useful to encourage co-operation and to prevent a return to the economic and political nationalisms which have plagued the area in the past. Somewhere between the two unacceptable extremes of solidarity among falsely similar regional organizations or partly similar nationalisms, it should be possible to arrive at a general empirical agreement on the inevitability and desirability of a mixture of bilateralism and multilateralism in economic relations.

If, however, doctrinal quarrels are unavoidable, it is because everyone agrees that the real European debate is not about economics but about politics. It is the ideas of political unification of Europe and of supranational institutions which are the real targets of the opponents of European integration. Here again, especially during the present Common Market crisis, the problem of Eastern Europe has played a significant role in the argument. According to critics ranging from François Mauriac to Walter Lippmann, the European federalists are coldly sacrificing Eastern Europe. "A federal government in Western Europe with a supranational parliament and a supranational cabinet and a supranational bureaucracy would close the door for a long time to the inclusion of Eastern Europe in the European community. In fact, the underlying issue between General de Gaulle and the federalists is between a tight little Europe of the Six and a looser, greater Europe which would include the whole continent."[32]

This helps us to distinguish between two problems concerning the links between Europe's institutions and its geographical dimensions: The first is about the chronological and political priority to be given to institutional integration or geographical widening; the other is about the very nature of the enterprise— its goals as well as its means.

The first question seems to call for a necessarily imperfect and qualified answer. Certainly the structure of a political organism does change with its dimensions, and newcomers will be more attracted if they are called upon to participate in a living creation rather than to fit into the Procrustean bed of a solidified institutional framework. There is no less certainty that if one had waited for all potential members before starting the enterprise, it would never have gotten off the ground and would never have offered the present perspectives of extension. Hence, the solution seems to be that the problem of the relationship between the unification of Western Europe and the reintegration of Eastern Europe can be approached not as a choice between two incompatible goals, but as a judgment of expedience—varying according to circumstances—as to the respective rhythms of two interdependent and equally desirable evolutions. Advocates of the "federalizing process" should be able to accept George Liska's plea for a temporarily relatively loose union in Western Europe: "The great unknown which militates against a premature definition of the institutional structure of Europe is the evolution of relations between the Soviet Union and China and among members of the European Soviet bloc. . . . Western European structure must be sufficiently independent and flexible to facilitate the rearrangements that would be necessary to fit Soviet Russia and the Central-Eastern European states into a single European system."[33] Incompatibility would only exist if the advocates of supranationality proposed the immediate adoption of a political federation complete with definitive institutions.

In fact, the real issue between the two sides is the second one, concerning the general conception of relations between nations and Europe; it is not the choice between a smaller and a wider Europe, but one's idea of both, and of the ways to reach them. De Gaulle can at times be seen to be favoring a smaller Europe than Jean Monnet (when he opposes the British candidacy) and at times a wider one. But whether for today's Western Europe or tomorrow's geographic Europe favored by both sides, the essence of the Gaullist notion is the creation of "another order, another equilibrium" based on the exclusive responsibility of the states and the absolute independence of nations, and on the idea that it is France, once again a "nation with free hands," which constitutes the instrument and the chance of the new order and the new equilibrium.

In the case of the two Europes, however, many think that the concept which takes the nation as a base, the French diplomacy

and nuclear force as means, and the restored concert of equilibrium as a goal can only succeed by leaning on and tending
toward the concept based on integration. They point out that the
concepts of "European Europe" and "Europe from the Atlantic
to the Urals" owe much of their success to the fact that while
being geographically very—perhaps excessively—precise, they are
very vague on the link constituting Europe. Hence, these ideas
seem to lose much of their power of seduction when it seems to
turn out that nothing more than classical relations of alliance
and co-operation between independent and rival nations is intended. If the Six must organize for their defense in order to
permit a new equilibrium for the continent (De Gaulle's press
conference of February 5, 1965), can this defense be purely
national? Leaving aside the strategic arguments, a nationally
based European defense can neither solve nor ignore the problem
of German participation. For the political organization of the
European states, the same problem arises. Would not Western
Europe have to be integrated if it is to speak with one voice in
negotiations with Soviet Russia, and does the same not apply to
continental Europe if it is to provide a stabilizing framework for
a reunited Germany?

It is true that in the absence of political integration the diplomatic possibilities are much greater for every state than the
military ones. Germany and France both carry on highly successful bilateral relations with Eastern Europe. West Germany seems
to succeed in driving a wedge between the Ulbricht regime and
the other people's democracies; French policy probably serves in
Bucharest both as model and as an alibi. Cross-cutting bilateral
relations between European national states certainly have a positive balance to show.

Is this still the case when it comes to relations with Soviet
Russia and to perspectives for negotiating a European settlement? Is it not obvious, on the contrary, that as long as France
and Germany act separately nothing is easier for Moscow than to
play off one against the other and, far from modifying the status
quo by withdrawing, to modify the status quo by destabilizing
the West and thus stabilizing the East? Without excessive sub-
tlety, Soviet Russia has declared many times either to France or
to Germany that she is the other great power of the continent
and that if they could agree, all European problems would be

solved. Even more important, perhaps, it does seem that when she talks to Germany there are more chances for Russia to go beyond a simple, immediate tactic of dividing her opponents through flattery than when she talks to France. After all, Germany has been her great preoccupation for the last fifty years. Nor is there any lack of precedents for a bilateral understanding with her. If one is to negotiate seriously, will one not rather do it with those from whom one has something to fear and to whom one has something to offer? The two factors are certainly present in relations with the United States and perhaps one day will be with Germany; they are hardly present in the case of France. Nevertheless, according to advocates of the Gaullist grand design such as George Liska, France would play the leading role in any European settlement. For that she needs the support of Germany. The whole strategy is based on Germany's quest for reunification, which her alliance with the Anglo-Saxons cannot provide. But Germany, in turn, needs France; for "only France can legitimize the German interest in reunification and in politically and otherwise unprovocative military rehabilitation in the eyes of the less forgiving smaller nations of Western and Eastern Central Europe."[34]

Liska does note the existence of a third possibility for Germany, that of an independent negotiating adventure with Russia, but he simply dismisses it as dangerous and unpopular. Certainly, there is no doubt that the Poles and the Czechoslovaks fear Germany more than they do France, nor is there any doubt that the Rumanians are more attracted by France than by Germany; but however much one may understand this factor, one is surprised to see it considered as absolutely crucial for the settlement. After all, the two main interested powers *are* Soviet Russia and Germany, and they certainly must consider that, to quote a French saying, one is never better served than by oneself. France, after having made the introductions, may well find out that she has worked, as in another French saying, for the King of Prussia. If the Soviet Union were determined to run the risks of German reunification in a framework other than through an agreement with the United States, her interest would certainly be to do it in the framework of a direct dialogue with Germany, thereby hoping to gain influence on Germany's political evolution. Even supposing she had abandoned every temptation of a political offensive, one does not see very well how, from the point of view of her security, she wouldn't count on herself rather than on French, Polish, or Czechoslovak guarantees to balance and control a reunified Germany.

When all is said, if Germany is reunited in a geographically European and politically national framework, one does not see how the first political reality in Europe can help being that of an equilibrium between Germany and Russia. France and East Central Europe can place their hopes of security in this equilibrium, and participate in it, but only in a secondary role, unless they hope to hold the balance of power by playing the two stronger forces against each other. But that would be highly dangerous and destabilizing, if only because the Soviet-German equilibrium has had ways in the past of changing into an agreement with unpleasant consequences for others; again, France, Poland, or Rumania would remember then that the last European Concert ended in 1939–40.

One may, on the other hand, look toward a solution which would stop short of complete German and European reunification and would settle for a kind of generalized ambiguity: The states of Eastern Europe would be neither truly communist nor truly liberal, neither true satellites nor quite independent. As for Eastern Europe, this is more or less what Liska means. As for Germany and Europe, it is quite likely that, according to General de Gaulle, it should be by throwing as thick a cloud of dust as possible over the clear-cut divisions between Western and Eastern Europe and over the distinction between a divided, a confederal, and a federal Germany, etc., that one should create the conditions for *rapprochements* to take place within a large and loose whole, and for ideological and institutional barriers to be crossed without being completely suppressed.

This indeed is probably the only realistic perspective for short-run contacts. But it is by no means certain that a settlement could—as George Liska would like and as Churchill seemed to seek—regulate the proportion of Eastern or Western influences over a country's regime, even though the realities of national and of liberalized communism do lend themselves to numerous *de facto* nuances. Above all, the German obstacle would remain, since it is doubtful whether the nature of the East German regime is not such as not to allow for a middle ground between tyranny and freedom or between separation and reunification, the lack of national basis and of popular half-acceptance making both de-satellization and de-Stalinization impossible.[35] Once more, Germany would constitute the insoluble factor which would cause the failure of the other solutions as well. Just as the nuclear defense of a Western "European Europe" can neither include the participation of Germany nor do without it, it would appear that the equilibrium of a "Wider Europe" would be made impossible or unstable both by the active presence of Germany and by its absence, both by its reunification and by its division. This is why the objectives of the *Europe des patries* would seem to be attainable only through the opposite road—by building a European federation whose dimensions would enable both the containment of Russia and the control of Germany, while including them both in a system based on stability and mutual ties. For the advocates of European integration, an impatient and ambitious strategy which starts by being negative not only is less likely to really favor European reunification than the slower and more indirect road of community-building, but it may destroy what had already been achieved in the latter direction. As the *Economist* put it on July 10, 1965: "It creates chaos now, and you cannot build on chaos."

Once more we seem confronted with the same problem as in the Atlantic debate. The advocates of European integration seem, just as those of the Atlantic Alliance, to be right as far as prudence and Western stability are concerned. But it seems less obvious that they have a positive perspective to offer on policies toward the East which would justify the claim made by the declaration of the Action Committee for the United States of Europe (May 9, 1965) that "the European Community, as it progresses and organizes its partnership with the United States, . . . opens the way to a basic improvement of relationships between Eastern Europe and Western Europe."

However, in the July, 1965, issue of the *Journal of Common Market Studies,* Mr. Christopher Layton, who addresses himself directly to the theme of a settlement in Central Europe, points out that "even if the European Community remained confined to Western Europe, the Franco-German reconciliation will inevitably make it easier, not harder, to reunite the rest of Germany." It is only if they participate in the same federation that France can play, at the side of Germany, the reassuring role toward the East which was assigned to it by George Liska. But ultimately, it would be only through its extension eastward, to include Poland and Czechoslovakia, that "a United Europe, burying national conceptions for good, can both make German unity possible and provide security for Germany's neighbors at the same time." As for the timetable for reconciliation with Eastern Europe, he distinguishes three phases, probably spread over decades, going from co-operation through association to full membership for Poland, Czechoslovakia, and possibly the Balkan countries. This would accompany the reunification of Germany. For this third step, Liska suggests the possibility of great common enterprises, such as common planning and development of the coal and steel industries of Silesia, common oil enterprises, the rejoining of transport roads, etc. Russia probably would have to be a partner, but not a member.

Just as important, perhaps, is the warning following these long-term perspectives, which imply, as Christopher Layton rightly acknowledges, a transformation of world politics: "The wide roof of the house of Europe cannot be built before the foundations are laid in the West. Any attempt to rush into intimate links with Eastern Europe before the community is consolidated in the West will be self-defeating. . . . The order of priorities remains unchanged: first, build up the European Community and bring Britain into it; then develop an Atlantic partnership between a strong Europe and America; then open the door to the communist world. But these processes are overlapping and depend partly on each other. Just as the attempt to bring in Britain implies a whole new system of partnership with the United States, so . . . if a political union in Western Europe is to make sense, it must turn its eyes from the start towards Europe's other half."[36]

Raymond Aron expresses the same cautious optimism in an article on "The Reunification of Europe."[37] Pointing out that "after 20 years the reconstruction of Europe, the weakening of the communist empire and ideas, enable us to look forward, to go beyond the defensive strategy based on the status quo," he warns that the lesson of the last twenty years should not be forgotten: "The Europeans have influenced the Soviet bloc less by their diplomacy than by their prosperity and cooperation. The circumstances have changed but the lesson has not yet lost its value."

While this is perfectly sound advice as far as it goes, it should not be construed as a prescription for minding our own prosperous business and waiting for the walls between the two Europes to crumble as a result of some kind of historical or economic determinism. Recent crises are certainly sufficient to shake our confidence in irresistible tides even concerning the unity of Western Europe itself. But whatever their outcome, certainly no amount of "spill-over" is going to make diplomacy unnecessary for solving the German question; nor, more generally, is it going to produce a viable European and international order without a conscious effort for organizing it. But then, this is precisely the strength of the internationalist case as opposed to the belief in the ultimately beneficient and sufficient effects of the not-so-obsolete balance of power and the not-so-delicate balance of terror.

Here the tables are turned in a most interesting way if we follow the presentation of the European case by the *Economist's* editorialist, M. François Duchene, in the *Journal of Common Market Studies* symposium. For him, as for Liska, the message of recent events and tendencies seems to be "that the Cold War is slowly settling down into a new concert of powers,"[38] the "post-war cult of internationalism" being replaced by "a switch in world politics from grand designs and sweeping historical tides to professional political maneuvers." The crucial difference is that while Liska praises Gaullist-like strategy against Monnet-like design and sees in the victorious return of classical diplomacy and power politics a call to action as opposed to determinism, Duchene sees in it a coming down from the hopes of actively transforming the international environment and hence, behind all the multipolar—or polycentric—maneuvers, a fundamental relapse into passivity and optimistic illusion. Hence the key diplomatic question, encompassing all others, may well be "how far the movement in international affairs is likely to go from the post-war aspiration to apply conscious controls to the acceptance of a new kind of political *laissez-faire.*"[39]

Producers of grand designs do, of course, have to reckon with the reactions of self-interested consumers, and they ignore them at their own peril. There is also a danger in seeing too perfect a continuity between the quest for Western stability and the quest for the solution of East-West problems. After all, it should be surprising if it took quite the same method to build upon a status quo as to challenge one. Looking for partners for co-operative institutional enterprises, just as looking for partners for competitive diplomatic realignments, may lead one into the pitfalls of the non-ideological interstate approach—that is, into consolidating in Eastern Europe the very status quo one wants to modify. But it is precisely these two qualifications which point to the essence of the task ahead, in a direction which remains that indicated by François Duchene. To apply "conscious controls," one needs a minimum of common purpose. Are not, however, some nations more interested in stabilizing the status quo and some in challenging it, some in arms control and some in reunification? This only makes adjustments of partially conflicting objectives doubly necessary, none of the allies being strong enough either to impose her own objective on the others or to pursue it in isolation.

Polycentrism, West and East, calls for more diplomacy within the West, for more diplomacy with the East, and above all for more diplomacy within the West about diplomacy with the East; and this increased activity and flexibility calls for more, not less, co-operation. This is precisely what the celebrated and decried "community method" is about.[40] Here again, one sees the relevance of European integration to East-West relations: not through any automatic extension of existing institutions, but through new methods and instruments for finding the right measure of unity and diversity among Western countries in their policies toward the East. This would go a long way toward solving the essential problem created by Western diversification—a problem made the more acute by the opportunities and dangers involved in dealing with a polycentric East: how to maintain a common Western framework by adapting to a situation which makes such a framework both more difficult and more necessary than ever.

POLYCENTRISM, ALLIANCES, AND NON-ALIGNMENT

The most important feature of this adaptation may well be a more flexible redistribution of roles among the three tiers or levels of the West—the national, the European, and the Atlantic.

The significant change in the nature of alliances and alignments which is loosely designated by the term "polycentrism," by increasing the freedom of action of the various members, increases the value of bilateral ties not only within the two basic groupings but across their boundaries. Certainly, within the framework provided by alliances and communities, the day-to-day relations, initiatives, and exchanges must proceed on a bilateral basis. The less monolithic the groupings are, the more hope there is for their eventual coming together. Here we see the complex reality behind the simple postulates. Just as there can be harm in too much unity, which would preclude initiatives and cross-cutting links, so there can be equal harm in too much diversity, which would endanger the indispensable collectively organized ground from which these initiatives are taken and the desirable co-ordination without which economic aid and trade can hardly be made to serve a long-range purpose.

Each of the three levels—national, European, and Atlantic— would have its specific part to play in a broadly conceived Western view. In a sense, of course, a distribution of roles already exists on a geographical basis: West Germany has a preponderant voice in the matter of relations with East Germany; Western Europe seems to be able to take advantage of traditional links and sympathies as well as of geographic proximity in relations with Eastern Europe, where, according to Viktor Meier, "the concept of 'Europe' has set many things into motion which the concept of 'the West' had been unable to do previously";[41] the United States maintains, by necessity, a permanent dialogue with the Soviet Union. And it is just as well that these concentric zones overlap, for all of them play fundamental roles: the *Atlantic* framework by providing the military conditions of security and the economic conditions of peaceful engagement today and, hopefully, one day those of a negotiated settlement; the *European* community by offering a solid basis of stability, a center of attraction, and the long-range prospect of transforming the political problem by devaluating the nation-state; the various *nations* by constructing through their daily contacts the ties which should prepare the collective initiatives and long-range transformations.

Today, each of the three is relatively inhibited in playing these positive and harmonious roles. The United States, through its deepening military engagement in Asia, is in an unfavorable position—both in terms of its own freedom of action and of the reactions it encounters—for any active peaceful engagement in Europe.[42] The Common Market is in crisis and at any rate has only the timid beginnings of a foreign policy. The West European states, especially France and Germany, are too far from any agreement on foreign policy to accept a common political framework for their individual contacts. However, a basis should exist in converging estimates of the desirable short-run evolution of Eastern Europe for traveling together at least part of the way along the narrow path which combines independence with solidarity and avoids fission as well as fusion, thus preserving the chances of alternative future developments.

This indeed is the challenge of polycentrism and diversification to statesmen and theorists alike. Never have the basic problems of foreign policy—striking the right balance between competition and co-operation and hence constructing the right hierarchy between conflicting and common interests, finding the right margin of initiative between varying and contradictory aspirations and commitments, interests and dangers—assumed a more complex and delicate shape. The word "polycentrism" could be very misleading if it drew one to turn away from this complexity and to imagine constellations made of separate and more or less equal, more or less interchangeable bodies, perhaps grouped together in front of other constellations but each following its own independent course. The striking element is the multiplicity of dimensions, of levels of power, of cleavages, of solidarities, and of conflicts within and between states and alliances. No abstract formula about poles or centers can be really very helpful to describe the situation of either West or East Germany, or even, at the opposite extreme in terms of assumed freedom of action, of France or Rumania. "Polymorphism," as suggested by Professor Ferenc Váli,[43] would be a much more accurate term. Not only does it correspond more closely to the political preferences and realities of East European communist regimes, such as that of Hungary, which do not claim the status of independent centers and value both their identity and their ties with the Soviet Union; it also has a more general and theoretical superiority in an international system which is characterized precisely by the multiplicity and variety of special and conflicting relationships and entanglements.

Just as the Cold War has not been suppressed but replaced by several cold wars which relativize the original one to a certain extent, so monolithic blocs have been replaced not by non-alignment, but by a multiplicity of alignments which do not suppress but relativize the original ones. A country like Rumania is still aligned with the communist states against the non-communist ones, but it is also aligned with France against bipolarity or with the underdeveloped countries against the rich ones, and so forth. Alliances and states are all sovereign from one point of view and prisoners from another, aligned in some respects with their enemies against their friends, caught in a network of cross-cutting special relations of alignment and conflict which permits them an infinite number of moves and shifts, but restricts the amplitude and scope of each of them.

Some links, some conflicts, and some interests will always be more vital than others, and therefore alliances are not obsolete. But the way is open, from within them, to a full range of differentiated special situations between full-fledged participation and neutralization, between the presence of foreign troops and demilitarization, between a maximum freedom of action and a practical renunciation of foreign policy, as in the case of Finland. Neutrality and alliances become more the two extremes of a continuum than the two sides of an antinomy. Rather than in the breakup of alliances, it is in their inner differentiation and their interpenetration that the hopeful and challenging significance of the meeting of the two polycentrisms is to be found.

This again, however, should not be taken to imply a fundamental symmetry between the two Europes and the two alliances. To say that alliances are not obsolete does not mean that the Soviet empire in Eastern Europe is tied by natural or everlasting bonds, or that it should be left to die a natural death. It does mean that one should distinguish between different types of ties, of presences, of influence, of security guarantees, some more negotiable, more vulnerable, or more tolerable than others. It does mean that one should distinguish between short-run and long-run, direct and indirect, policies.

It would be self-defeating to take a rash approach which either would start by dismantling the West or, at the other extreme, would claim every differentiation in the East and every contact with the outside world as a victory for the Free World in the Cold War. Just as self-defeating would be, more generally, any overly simple Western policy taking no account of the East's evolution or, at the other extreme, any over-subtle policy designed to direct the East's evolution through complicated tactical calculations.

To promote the long-range evolution of the East, perhaps our most powerful weapon is what we in the West do with ourselves and to each other, provided we do it while keeping constantly in mind its effects on the other side, and provided we show our readiness to acknowledge and take into account what the other side is doing. Bridge-building and peaceful engagement—which are, for the time being, the only realistic and positive policies open to the West—can be endangered from two seemingly opposite directions: by being oversold, through too much publicity and too spectacular schemes, to a point at which they might become embarrassing to their potential targets and provoke a counterreaction; and by receiving too low a priority in Western policy and being made fruitless by other aspects of East-West relations or by intra-Western strife. Both dangers could come from insufficient awareness of the indirect effects of our general policies and attitudes and from insufficient attention to the various realities and reactions of the other side. Relations with Eastern Europe probably mean more than anything else, for the time being, a lesson in "creative listening." Even more than to bilateral communications between the United States and Soviet Russia, Thomas Schelling's advice seems to apply to the preconditions of any fruitful way for a diversified West to encourage polycentrism in the East: "First, don't speak directly to them, but speak seriously to some serious audience and let them overhear. Second, to get their ear, listen."[44]

NOTES

1. Alastair Buchan, "The Changed Setting of the Atlantic Debate," *Foreign Affairs*, July, 1965.

2. For a general account see Ghita Ionescu, *The Break-up of the Soviet Empire in Eastern Europe* (Baltimore, 1965).

3. See, for instance, Robert R. Bowie, *Shaping the Future* (New York and London, 1964).

4. See George F. Kennan, *On Dealing with the Communist World* (New York, 1964).

5. Dean Acheson, "Withdrawal from Europe: an Illusion," *New York Times* (international edition), December 21, 1963, and address to the Fifth Annual Conference of the Institute for Strategic Studies, *Adelphi Paper No. 5*, October, 1963.

6. Zbigniew K. Brzezinski, *Alternative to Partition* (New York, 1965).

7. Henry A. Kissinger, *The Troubled Partnership* (New York, 1965), Chapter 7: "East-West relations and the future of Germany."

8. Theo Sommer, "Initiativen in Deutschland," of "Die Wiedervereinigung Politik der Parteien," *Die Zeit,* July 9, 1965.

9. Zbigniew K. Brzezinski and William E. Griffith, "Peaceful Engagement in Eastern Europe," *Foreign Affairs,* July, 1961.

10. The basic formulations of American policy are President Johnson's speech at the University of Virginia, May, 1964, and Secretary of State Dean Rusk's on February 25, 1964. "Why We Treat Different Communist Countries Differently." For a comprehensive treatment of official policy and possible alternatives see John C. Campbell, *American Policy Toward Communist Eastern Europe—the Choices Ahead* (Minneapolis, 1965), and Robert Bass, "Die Vereinigten Staaten und Osteuropa," *Europa Archiv,* May 25, 1965.

11. A particularly lucid exposition of French policy toward Eastern Europe is to be found in W. Schütze, "Die Ostpolitik Frankreichs," *Europa Archiv,* March 10, 1965.

12. See Sommer, "Initiativen in Deutschland," and "Kleine Schritte—Wie Gross?" of "Die Wiedervereinigungspolitik der Parteien," II, *Die Zeit,* July 18, 1965; H. Gressmann, "Politik mit dem Osten," *Die Zeit,* July 2, 1965. The most comprehensive formulation of the German Foreign Secretary's position is: Gerhard Schröder, "Germany Looks at Eastern Europe," *Foreign Affairs,* October, 1965.

13. Brzezinski, *Alternative to Partition,* pp. 127–28.

14. Philip Windsor, "Berlin," in *The Cold War,* ed. Evan Luard (London, 1964), pp. 138–39.

15. Prof. Adam Bromke has pointed to the same paradox independently; see his "The Communist States and the West" in *The Communist States at the Crossroads,* ed. Adam Bromke (New York, 1965), p. 236.

16. This first view appears implicitly in many speeches by President de Gaulle against "the double hegemony." It is explicitly formulated in books such as A. Conte, *Yalta ou le Partage du Monde* (Paris, 1964), and articles such as A. Kawalkovski, "Pour une Europe independante et réunifée," *Politique Étrangère,* No. 3, 1963, pp. 196–97, and "Vers la fin d'une double hégémonie," *ibid.,* No. 3, 1964, pp. 260–83.

17. The views of several American authors seem to oscillate between the second and the third view. See Kennan, *On Dealing with the Communist World,* Walter Lippmann, "The Post-postwar Era," *New York Herald Tribune,* July 12, 1963, "The Two Europes," *New York Herald Tribune,* Nov. 19, 20, 21, 1963, and "Our Foreign Policy," *New York Herald Tribune,* February 5, 1965; Ronald Steel, *The End of Alliance: America and the Future of Europe* (New York, 1964).

18. The best source for the relevant texts on "Europe from the Atlantic to the Urals" until 1963 is the book by René Courtin, *L'Europe de l'Atlantique à l'Oural* (Paris, 1963).

19. Raymond Aron, *Le Figaro*, March 12, 1963, and "Note Finale," in "Le Grand Debat Nucleaire," *Bulletin SEDEIS*, February 10, 1965.

20. Dean Acheson, "Isolationists are Stupid," *The Saturday Evening Post*, July 31, 1965.

21. Theo Sommer, "For an Atlantic Future," *Foreign Affairs*, October, 1964.

22. Alastair Buchan and Philip Windsor, *Arms and Stability in Europe* (London, 1963), p. 61.

23. De Gaulle, press conference of February 5, 1965.

24. See, among others, Raymond Aron's interview with *Entreprise*, June 12, 1965.

25. Hallstein's speech in Paris on June 22, 1962, and the comments of Gerda Zelletin in *Die Kommunisten und die Einigung Europas* (Frankfurt, 1964), p. 116.

26. M. Fitz, "Österreich und die EWG," *Europa Archiv*, October 10, 1965, and the account of Maurer's visit to Austria in *Neue Zürcher Zeitung*, November 24, 1965.

27. See John P. de Gara, *Trade Relations between the Common Market and the Eastern Bloc* (Bruges, 1964); R. Sannwald, "Die Europäische Wirtschaftsgemeinschaft und der Osthandel," *Europa Archiv*, February 25, 1965, and H. Gross, "Trading with the East," *East Europe*, June, 1965.

28. See Zbigniew K. Brzezinski, "Russia and Europe," *Foreign Affairs*, April, 1964, p. 428; Zellentin, *Die Kommunisten*, pp. 71–123, and A. Domes (ed.), *West Integration und Osteuropa* (Cologne, 1965), especially the article by Wenzel Jaksch, pp. 75–97.

29. *Problems of Communism*, September/October, 1963.

30. Michael Kaser, *COMECON—Integration Problems of the Planned Economies* (London, 1965).

31. Viktor Meier, *Neue Zürcher Zeitung*, August 6, 1965.

32. *New York Herald Tribune*, July 14, 1965.

33. George Liska, *Europe Ascendant* (Baltimore, 1964), p. 80.

34. *Ibid.*

35. See, among many others, J. Brown, "East Germany," in "International Communism Today," *Survey*, January, 1965, p. 81, and M. Croan, "East Germany," in *The Communist States at the Crossroads*, p. 126.

36. Christopher Layton, "Europe, Road to Coexistence," *Journal of Common Market Studies*, July, 1965, p. 283.

37. *Le Figaro*, May 22–23, 1965.

38. M. François Duchene, "Britain in a Harder World," *Journal of Common Market Studies*, July, 1965, p. 317.

39. *Ibid.*, p. 322.

40. See Ernst B. Haas, "International Integration—the European and the Universal Process," in D. J. Hekhuis, J. McClintock, and A. L. Burns, *International Stability* (New York, 1964), p. 229.

41. V. Meier, "On the Idea of 'Europe,'" *East Europe*, June, 1965, p. 5.

42. See Richard Lowenthal, "America's Asian Commitment," *Encounter*, October, 1965, and "Should We Make Common Cause with Russia?" *New York Times Magazine*, November 21, 1965; see also Duchene, "Britain in a Harder World," pp. 319–20.

43. Ferenc A. Váli, "Hungary," in *The Communist States at the Crossroads*, p. 78.

44. Thomas C. Schelling, "Signals and Feedback in the Arms Dialogue," *Bulletin of the Atomic Scientists*, January, 1965, p. 10.

Index

EASTERN EUROPE IN TRANSITION

EDITED BY
KURT LONDON

designer: Edward King
typesetter: Kingsport Press, Inc.
typefaces: Baskerville text, Granjon display
printer: Kingsport Press, Inc.
paper: Paperback Eggshell
binder: Kingsport Press, Inc.